after identity

after identity

A READER IN LAW AND CULTURE

Edited by

Dan Danielsen and **Karen Engle**

Routledge   New York   London

Published in 1995 by
Routledge
29 West 35th Street
New York, NY 10001

Published in Great Britain by
Routledge
11 New Fetter Lane
London EC4P 4EE

Library of Congress Cataloging-in-Publication Data
After identity : a reader in law and culture / edited by Dan Danielsen
    and Karen Engle.
        p.   cm.
    Includes bibliographical references and index.
    ISBN 0-415-90996-1 (cloth)   0-415-90997-X (pb)
    1. Sociological jurisprudence.   2. Group identity—United States.
    3. Sex and law—United States.   I. Danielsen, Dan.   II. Engle, Karen.
    K376.A37   1994
    340'.115—dc20   94-3734
                                                                        CIP

CONTENTS

v

for my grandmother,
    Amy Gaines Fabra
        K.E.

for my parents,
    Roy Danielsen and Sylvia Danielsen
        D.D.

in memory of Mary Joe Frug
        K.E. & D.D.

ACKNOWLEDGMENTS

MANY PEOPLE HAVE ASSISTED in the production of this collection, from early discussions about the project to indexing the book.

The book, of course, could not have happened without all of the contributing authors, whom we thank for their terrific work, and for their indulgence of our sometimes ruthless editing.

We are grateful to Nathaniel Berman, Heidi Buchi, Fred Burmester, Michele Cipriani, Dan Cooper, Jodi Dean, Martha Minow, Michele Mladejovsky and Paul Van Dyk for their invaluable assistance at various stages of the book's production.

We are especially grateful to Matthew Diamond, David Kennedy, Duncan Kennedy, Barbara McFarlane, Ileana M. Porras, Lee Teitelbaum, and Gerald Torres for their heroic efforts in helping us move the book from idea to reality.

The University of Utah College of Law and Foley, Hoag & Eliot contributed greatly appreciated institutional support. Part of the funding for the project was provided by a grant from the University of Utah Research Committee.

Finally, we would like to thank Stewart Cauley, William Germano, and Eric Zinner at Routledge for all of their help and support.

INTRODUCTION

IDENTITY POLITICS AFTER IDENTITY: this is both the challenge and the aspiration for this collection of essays. In this volume we have brought together a body of recent legal scholarship that has emerged as an extension, but also as a critique, of traditional identity politics. In one sense, this work, which we term post-identity scholarship, would be unimaginable without the diversity of discourses enabled by identity politics—voices of women, gay men and lesbians, blacks, and others. At the same time, the scholarship represented in these essays critiques the tendency of these discourses to obscure the differences among women, among gays, among blacks, and others, and to ignore the significance of multiple allegiances, communities and experiences to the construction of these identities. Broadly stated, the authors assert that, in order to generate more effective legal strategies, legal consciousness should take account of the role of law in the constitution of identities and of the simultaneity of multiple identities and perspectives. The new ways of thinking about identity developed in this scholarship also have general implications for progressive thinking about theory, culture and political strategy. We brought these essays together to suggest the contours of a post-identity politics of law.

The essays collected here represent a variety of contemporary writings about law and legal culture. Influenced both by recent trends in cultural studies and recent developments in critical legal studies, feminist legal studies, critical race theory and queer legal theory, the authors are all participants in debates about multiculturalism and political correctness, and all cross and confound disciplinary boundaries. At the same time, all are engaged with the articulation of progressive strategies for addressing pressing legal and social problems.

Post-identity Scholarship in Context

For some forty years, progressive lawyers, scholars and activists have been engaged in the elaboration of what we now might term identity politics. In what could be considered the first stage of identity politics, individuals identified with general characteristics such as race, gender, or national origin to contend that discriminatory distinctions should not be made on the basis of those categories. The early civil rights and women's movements, for example, argued that African-Americans and women were entitled to the same rights as white men. Asserting that there was no significant difference between blacks and whites or between women and men, these movements aimed to achieve a system by which skin color or sex did not determine one's place in society.

Subsequent movements rejected this paradigm of liberal pluralism on the ground that its colorblind and sexblind mentality obscured real cultural and political (and some even argued biological) differences between the groups. Some individuals and groups in a proliferating list of movements based on identity began proudly to (re)assert, or perhaps reclaim, their identities—as African-American, Asian-American, Latino or Native American, as female, as gay or lesbian, as disabled, as working class and so forth. Eventually, identity politics called upon dominant groups to acknowledge their positionality as well, so that some began classifying others or themselves as white, as male, as straight, as able-bodied, as upper middle class.

Lawyers have played an important role in this development by attempting to provide legal protection for identities through anti-discrimination statutes, sexual harassment policies, constitutional rights, hate crime statutes and affirmative action policies. Taken as a whole, these legal strategies have pursued a complex agenda. They have sought both to recognize identity groups and to make them irrelevant as they have aimed to correct for the irrationalities and distortions of discrimination, to enable individuals to flourish in a society freed of group prejudice, to enshrine a notion of equality of sameness underneath the (dis)regard of our differences. Yet these two tendencies within identity politics seem contradictory. On one hand, lawyers and activists have sought to design legal remedies for broad classes of disadvantaged groups, focusing on generally drawn status categories to define these groups. On the other hand, these same group remedies have often sought to transcend these categories by making it unlawful to take them into account. Perhaps the paradigmatic example of this conflict is expressed in the apparent incommensurability of colorblindness and affirmative action. Other examples of these conflicting tendencies include debates over whether strategies should focus on equality or difference, and disputes between liberals and radicals, or assimilationists and nationalists.

The scholarship in this collection emerges from a growing dissatisfaction with these efforts to theorize and strategize identity and a desire to develop methodologies for thinking affirmatively about cultural identity without freezing differences among social groups. In response to the "choice" between treating identity as a manifestation of essential difference or as an effect of social prejudice to be transcended, post-identity scholars articulate a set of strategies that acknowledge our simultaneous and ambivalent desire both to affirm our identities and to transcend them. They do so through the combination of a consciousness of the power and importance of identity in contemporary culture and a refusal to treat any particular identity category as determinate, or fixed. This focus on the multiple and complex meanings of identity in legal culture challenges the aspiration of transcendence of difference. At the same time, it resists the essentializing tendency toward the organizing of politics around single and presumably stable identity categories.

Doing Post-identity Politics

The works included in this book elaborate these themes through a number of different methodologies and critical perspectives. For example, Kimberlé Crenshaw's work on violence against women of color and Karen Engle's work on multicultural feminism in the context of clitoridectomy explore some of the ways that racial, cultural and religious differences among women are often missed or suppressed in traditional analyses that focus exclusively on gender identity. The works of Mary Joe Frug on prostitution, Janet Halley on the construction of gay and lesbian identities, and Dan Danielsen on the relationship between gender and sexual identities explore how gender and sexual identities seem too rigid to transcend, but at the same time are subject to multiple cultural representations and consequences. Post-identity historians such as Nathaniel Berman on nationalism in Europe and Gary Peller on race consciousness in America consider the institutional and cultural construction of group identities.

Beyond these substantive analyses, many of the essays develop surprising and novel styles of cultural interpretation. For example, David Kennedy and Patricia Williams use first person narrative to demonstrate the fluid construction and ambivalence of one's identity and the identity of others. Other scholars like Rosemary Coombe and Gerald Torres and Kathryn Milun explore some of the ways that Western legal conceptions of identity and community frustrate the articulation of identities of persons with non-Western cultural traditions.

Many of the essays juxtapose topics and social groups with seemingly quite different identities, exploiting the synergies of disparate topics and ideas. Sometimes this method parallels quite closely the author's approach to identity issues. For example, Dan Danielsen's discussion of the legal treatment of pregnancy and of homosexuality examines two common social practices one might assume would be treated quite differently under the law. What he finds instead are a number of common strategies for representing these traits and identities, even across categories of difference. For other authors, jarring juxtapositions help destabilize distinctions between disparate, even seemingly opposite, groups and thereby increase our understanding of both the groups and the constructed nature of the categories that define them. Ileana Porras, for example, uses the distinction between the extra-normal violence of terrorists and the normalized violence of criminals and state actors to show the function terrorism plays in defining that very boundary. Regina Austin calls for a breakdown of the accepted division in the black community between criminals and role models. Jerry Frug examines the apparent divide between the city and the suburb, Mary Joe Frug the madonna and the whore, and Elizabeth Spelman and Martha Minow the perpetrator and the victim (in the context of women outlaws). Many of these articles suggest that these apparent cultural oppositions often arise only in relation to one another. The suburb only exists, for example, in relation to the city, and straights (law-abiders) create their meaning largely in opposition to criminals and outlaws. The opposite scenarios would also be true.

Although this book is about law, the arguments and issues it confronts are not unique to legal discourse. As several of the essays included in the book attest, law is just one of many social discourses, and legal culture is a less distinctive or autonomous part of our culture than is often imagined. This idea is perhaps most explicit in Nathaniel Berman's work on the relationship between cultural modernism in art and music and the structure of international legal responses to minorities and national group identity between the World Wars. It also appears in the work of Rosemary Coombe about how European notions of art and culture developed during the nineteenth century still affect the ability of Native Peoples to articulate the injury of cultural appropriation today. Indeed, many of the authors who dip into the neighboring disciplines of literature, sociology, anthropology or psychoanalysis do so less to import ideas and methods to legal study than to unravel the imagined line that often separates law from other fields of thought. In this way, the essays are less interdisciplinary than counterdisciplinary.

Other essays focus on the power of legal discourse itself. Law involves the state, and the state has power—to protect, to punish, and seemingly to leave alone. This perspective is perhaps most recognizable in Kendall Thomas's study of "private" violence against gay men and lesbians, in which he argues that the state implicitly condones such violence through its outlawing of sodomy. Janet Halley's essay on the closet and Mary Joe Frug's discussion of prostitution also focus on the ways that legal rules discipline those who appear to be gay or prostitutes, thereby regulating everyone's behavior. Kimberlé Crenshaw emphasizes law's power by demonstrating that the failure of legal reformers to address the intersectional position of women of color facing domestic violence can prove deadly.

This book, then, brings together essays that focus on the disciplining power of legal rules with those that primarily view discourse about law as a manifestation of societal beliefs and norms. The difference between these two approaches, we believe, is largely one of emphasis. Those who take the latter approach do not deny that law is powerful, just as those who take the former approach do not privilege legal rules over discourse. Most of the articles do not even explain or justify their emphasis. They all act on the assumption, however, that legal discourse is an important site for struggle about the meanings of identities.

Following this assumption, discussions in the book range from Duncan Kennedy's proposals for radical affirmative action in law school faculty hiring, to explorations of international legal discourse, to the analysis of Supreme Court opinions. In other books on law, it might be unusual to find such a range of topics. The examples above are listed in ascending order as you would find them on a traditional scale of enforceability. That is, rules of faculty hiring would be seen as less enforceable than international law, which in turn is generally considered to have less force than domestic law (particularly as found in Supreme Court opinions). This book rejects such a hierarchy. Rather, the articles all take seriously the force, consequences and possibilities of rules and discourse in whichever legal or cultural arena such rules and discourse emerge.

With this book, then, we have sought to suggest the possibility of a post-identity politics of law and culture and simultaneously to engage in its practice. Rather than dividing the book by reference to traditional, if quite complex, identity categories, we have organized it around broadly conceived social issues: Sexuality, Affirmative Action, Community, Postcolonialism and Violence. This focus enables us to explore some of the complex ways that identity functions in the constitution of these social issues, rather than the other way around. In Violence, for example, the articles explore both those who seem to be victims of violence (gay men, lesbians, women of color) and those who seem to be perpetrators of violence (terrorists and outlaws), as well as the ways some groups come to seem like victims or outlaws depending upon the group's relationship to law.

Our intention is that each Part will exploit the interaction of disparate methodological approaches and perspectives to transform traditional understandings of the topic. Our sense, however, is that the articles have more in common than these rather artificial divisions might suggest. For example, both Kendall Thomas and Janet Halley explore the impact on gay and lesbian identity of a Supreme Court case refusing to recognize a right to practice homosexual sodomy. While Thomas focuses on how criminal sodomy statutes legitimize acts of violence against gay men and lesbians, Halley focuses on how criminalizing sodomy encourages and reinforces the closet. We hope that placing these two articles about the same context in different Parts will enable their separate insights to shed light on questions beyond identity: Thomas on violence and Halley on sexuality generally. At the same time, the articles serve to remind us that sexuality and violence are often interrelated.

A Post-identity Policy Proposal

In sum, although neither this book nor the essays we have included are organized around the usual categories of identity, all acknowledge the vital importance of identity in people's lived experience. At the same time, they recognize the inadequacy of traditional notions of identity to explain or describe our complex experiences of law or culture. In fact, it might not be too much to see this collection as a foundation for a new approach to the cultural study of law and identity. All the authors are committed to the political practice of engaging in critical struggle over the meaning and representation of identities in law, culture and politics. All are skeptical about the significance of perceived differences between law, culture and politics, while all are convinced that, notwithstanding its frustrations, contradictions and indeterminacy, law matters. In the same way, all believe that notwithstanding the instability and frustrations of identity politics, identity matters for those of us committed to social struggle. This collection is dedicated to furthering our ability to embrace differences within ourselves, and within and between groups, while disrupting the ways we normally think about, understand and engage in identity politics. In putting it together, we hope to suggest and perhaps enable a new provisional politics after identity.

PART ONE

Sexuality

Introduction to
SEXUALITY

WE BEGIN OUR PRESENTATION of post-identity scholarship with essays on sexuality. Sexuality seems a good place to start, in part because of the curious and often contradictory images of sexual identity that pervade contemporary culture. On one hand, sexuality seems biologically determined and beyond our control, while on the other it is championed as a realm of private freedom and choice where our most secret desires might find expression. At once public identity and private practice, compulsive and consensual, natural and nurtured, sexuality, like gender, both tracks and violates legal categories. The articles in this Part explore these conflicting faces of sexuality and gender while seeking a progressive agenda for law.

Liberal legal rules often negotiate these different images of sexuality through the assertion of an unduly formal distinction between status and conduct. In some ways, such a distinction seems to make sense. Although we are generally unable to choose (at least initially) whether to be biologically male or female, it seems most of us can decide whether to engage in prostitution or to have a child. Or while we might feel that we have little choice about whether to be homosexual or heterosexual, we can probably opt to participate in or abstain from certain types of sexual activity. In other words, our status often seems fixed, while our conduct usually seems controllable. Not surprisingly, then, liberal legal rules generally tolerate a greater diversity in the status category than in the conduct area. The Clinton Administration's "Don't Ask, Don't Tell" military policy provides a good example of such rules, as does the criminalization of homosexual sodomy and prostitution.

4   The essays in this Part explore and explode this distinction between conduct and status. They do so by challenging both the asserted stability of status and the consensual nature of conduct, while maintaining that status and conduct can only be understood in relation to each other. For example, legal rules both construct and represent images of gender and sexuality by encouraging or proscribing certain types of behavior.

Mary Joe Frug investigates this relationship between status and conduct by looking at the criminalization of prostitution. She argues that rules about prostitution effectively divide all women into good girls and prostitutes. Potential ambiguity about one's good girl or bad girl status disciplines all women by encouraging certain forms of acceptable behavior. This criminalization of an apparently marginal activity has further meaning for all women as part of a complex of legal rules and cultural meanings. For example, when considered with such rules as restrictions on abortion that encourage reproduction and motherhood (thereby maternalizing the female body), and rules about rape and sexual harassment that fail to provide adequate protection against physical abuse to women (thereby terrorizing the female body), the prohibition against prostitution sends a message to all women that if their safety lies anywhere, it is in a monogamous heterosexual reproductive relationship. The more women deviate from this framework of acceptable gendered behavior, the more they risk being disciplined, either directly by the rules criminalizing prostitution, or indirectly, through the law's failure to protect them from abuse.

Similarly, Janet Halley argues that legal rules reinforce "the closet" by directly disciplining or failing to protect individuals who claim a homosexual identity. Once a soldier steps out of the closet, she or he can be discharged; the rule works to keep homosexuality covered. But just as rules that proscribe prostitution influence all women's conduct, those that proscribe sodomy or permit discrimination against homosexuals operate against everyone. The fear of being mistaken for gay encourages "straight" appearance and behavior in all types of people. This fear also discourages gay/straight alliances, since support for homosexual rights might be mistaken for homosexual conduct.

For both Frug and Halley, then, the law creates and defines "woman" or "homosexual" or "heterosexual" even as it restricts and punishes particular conduct. While Frug is interested in the plight of the prostitute and Halley is concerned with the homosexual, their analysis reaches much further. For both of them, legal rules and doctrine "matter," in that they have serious consequences for all of us. By policing the margins, the rules reinforce a normative core.

Dan Danielsen's exploration and comparison of cases about pregnancy and homosexuality takes a slightly different route. He uses the courts' conflicting and contradictory images of gender and sexual orientation—and their relationship to pregnancy and sodomy—to demonstrate the indeterminacy of these categories. But rather than concentrating on the disciplining effect of legal definitions of identity, Danielsen focuses on the ways that images of gender or sexuality generated by the courts mirror those produced in the rest of society, even by people who happily or unhappily find themselves pregnant or gay. Pointing out that women and homosexuals differ among themselves in their perceptions of their own identities, he concludes that we should not expect to find one doctrinal solution or strategy that will guarantee positive political outcomes for women and homosexuals (assuming that we could even agree on what such an outcome might be).

Danielsen does not end on a pessimistic note. Rather, he argues that there is more room in law for multiple and complex images of sexual identity than appears on first reading of the cases he discusses. Consequently, the law is an important site for cultural struggles over the meanings of identities. Danielsen ends his article with a quotation from Mary Joe Frug, bringing the chapter (perhaps a little too neatly) full circle. He cites Frug for her focus on the semiotic nature of sex differences and for her assertion that exposing those differences can affect legal power. Halley would probably agree. Were we better to understand the semiotic nature of the heterosexual/homosexual divide, we would probably be more open to different possibilities for defining/expressing our sexualities.

Frug, Halley and Danielsen all see legal rules and discourse as crucial sites for grappling with identity. They do not contend, however, that law should (or even could) help us find our "true selves." Rather, they suggest it is through interpretive struggles over the meaning of sexuality in law that we participate in the production of our selves in culture.

CHAPTER ONE

⊱─◈──○──◈─⊰

A POSTMODERN FEMINIST
LEGAL MANIFESTO

(AN UNFINISHED DRAFT)

Mary Joe Frug

Preliminaries

I AM WORRIED about the title of this article.

Postmodernism may already be passé, for some readers. Like a shoot-ing star or last night's popovers, its genius was the surprise of its appear-ance. Once that initial moment has passed, there's not much value in what's left over.

For other readers, postmodernism may refer to such an elaborate and demanding genre—within linguistics, psychoanalysis, literary theory, and philosophy—that claiming an affinity to "it" will quite properly invoke a flood of criticism regarding the omissions, misrepresentations, and mistakes that one paper will inevitably make.

The manifesto part may also be troublesome. The dictionary describes a manifesto as a statement of principles or intentions, while I have in mind a rather informal presentation; more of a discussion, say, in which

8   the "principles" are somewhat contradictory and the "intentions" are loosely formulated goals that are qualified by an admission that they might not work. MacKinnon, of course, launched feminism into social theory orbit by drawing on Marxism to present her biting analysis.[1] Referring to one word in a Karl Marx title may represent an acknowledgement of her work, an unconscious, copyKat gesture; but I don't want to get carried away. I am in favor of localized disruptions. I am against totalizing theory.

Sometimes the "PM"s that label my notes remind me of female troubles—of premenstrual and postmenopausal blues. Maybe I am destined to do exactly what my title prescribes; just note the discomfort and keep going.

One "Principle"

The liberal equality doctrine is often understood as an engine of liberation with respect to sex-specific rules. This imagery suggests the repressive function of law, a function that feminists have inventively sought to appropriate and exploit through critical scholarship, litigation, and legislative campaigns. Examples of these efforts include work seeking to strengthen domestic violence statutes, to enact a model anti-pornography ordinance, and to expand sexual harassment doctrine.

The postmodern position locating human experience as inescapably within language suggests that feminists should not overlook the constructive function of legal language as a critical frontier for feminist reforms. To put this "principle" more bluntly, legal discourse should be recognized as a site of political struggle over sex differences.

This is not a proposal that we try to promote a benevolent and fixed meaning for sex differences. (See the "principle" below.) Rather, the argument is that continuous interpretive struggles over the meaning of sex differences can have an impact on patriarchal legal power.

Another "Principle"

In their most vulgar, bootlegged versions, both radical and cultural legal feminisms depict male and female sexual identities as anatomically determined and psychologically predictable. This is inconsistent with the semiotic character of sex differences and the impact that historical specificity has on any individual identity. In postmodern jargon, this treatment of sexual identity is inconsistent with a decentered, polymorphous, contingent understanding of the subject.

Because sex differences are semiotic—that is, constituted by a system of signs that we produce and interpret—each of us inescapably produces herself within the gender meaning system, although the meaning of gender is indeterminate or undecidable. The dilemma of difference, which the liberal equality guarantee seeks to avoid through neutrality, is unavoidable.

On Style

Style is important in postmodern work. The medium is the message, in some cases—although by no means all. When style is salient, it is characterized by irony and by wordplay that is often dazzlingly funny, smart, and irreverent. Things aren't just what they seem.

By arguing that legal rhetoric should not be dominated by masculine pronouns or by stereotypically masculine imagery, legal feminists have conceded the significance of style. But the postmodern tone sharply contrasts with the earnestness that almost universally characterizes feminist scholarship. "[T]he circumstances of women's lives [are] unbearable," Andrea Dworkin writes.[2] Legal feminists tend to agree. Hardly appropriate material for irony and play.

I do not underestimate the oppression of women as Andrea Dworkin describes it. I also appreciate what a hard time women have had communicating our situation. Reports from numerous state commissions on gender bias in the courts have concluded that one of the most significant problems of women in law is their lack of credibility. Dworkin puts this point more movingly:

> The accounts of rape, wife beating, forced childbearing, medical butchering, sex-motivated murder, forced prostitution, physical mutilation, sadistic psychological abuse, and other commonplaces of female experience that are excavated from the past or given by contemporary survivors should leave the heart seared, the mind in anguish, the conscience in upheaval. But they do not. No matter how often these stories are told, with whatever clarity or eloquence, bitterness or sorrow, they might as well have been whispered in wind or written in sand: they disappear, as if they were nothing. The tellers and the stories are ignored or ridiculed, threatened back into silence

or destroyed, and the experience of female suffering is buried in cultural invisibility and contempt.[3]

Although the flip, condescending, and mocking tones that often characterize postmodernism may not capture the intensity and urgency that frequently motivate feminist legal scholarship, the postmodern style does not strike me as "politically incorrect." Indeed, the oppositional character of the style arguably coincides with the oppositional spirit of feminism. Irony, for example, is a stylistic method of acknowledging and challenging a dominant meaning, of saying something and simultaneously denying it. Figures of speech invite ideas to break out of the linear argument of a text; they challenge singular, dominant interpretations.

I confess to having considerable performance anxiety about the postmodern style myself. It may require more art, more creativity and inspiration, than I can manage. But I don't think feminist legal activists need to adopt the postmodern medium in order to exploit the postmodern message; my point about the style is simply that it doesn't require us, strategically, to dismiss postmodernism as an influence on our work.

Applying Postmodern "Principles": Law and the Female Body

Most feminists are committed to the position that however "natural" and common sex differences may seem, the differences between women and men are not biologically compelled; they are, rather, "socially constructed." Over the past two decades this conviction has fueled many efforts to change the ways in which law produces—or socially constructs—the differences and the hierarchies between the sexes. Feminists have reasoned, for example, that when women are uneducated for "men's work," or when they are sexually harassed in the men's work they do, they are not "naturally" more suited for "women's work"; they have been constructed to be that way. Although law is by no means the only factor that influences which jobs men and women prefer, how well they perform at work, or the intensity of their wage market commitment, outlawing employment discrimination can affect to some degree what women and men are "like" as workers. What law (at least in part) constructs, law reform projects can reconstruct or alter.

Regardless of how commonplace the constructed character of sex differences may be, particular differences can seem quite deeply embedded within the sexes—so much so, in fact, that the social construction thesis is undermined. When applied to differences that seem especially entrenched—differences such as masculine aggression or feminine compassion, or differences related to the erotic and reproductive aspects of women's lives—social construction seems like a clichéd, improbable, and unconvincing account of experience, an explanation for sex differences that undervalues "reality." This reaction does not necessarily provoke a return to a "natural" explanation for sex differences; but it does radically stunt the liberatory potential of the social construction thesis. One's expectations for law reform projects are reduced; law might be able to mitigate the harsh impact of these embedded traits on women's lives, but law does not seem responsible for *constructing* them.

The subject of this part is the role of law in the production of sex differences that seem "natural." One of my objectives is to explain and challenge the essentializing impulse that places particular sex differences outside the borders of legal responsibility. Another objective is to provide an analysis of the legal role in the production of gendered identity that will invigorate the liberatory potential of the social construction thesis.

I have chosen the relationship of law to the female body as my principal focus. I am convinced that law is more cunningly disguised but just as implicated in the production of apparently intractable sex-related traits as in those that seem more legally malleable. Since the anatomical distinctions between the sexes seem not only "natural" but fundamental to identity, proposing and describing the role of law in the production of the meaning of the female body seems like the most convincing subject with which to defend my case. In the following sections, I will argue that legal rules—like other cultural mechanisms—encode the female body with meanings. Legal discourse then explains and rationalizes these meanings by an appeal to the "natural" differences between the sexes, differences that the rules themselves help to produce. The formal norm of legal neutrality conceals the way in which legal rules participate in the construction of those meanings.

The proliferation of women's legal rights during the past two decades has liberated women from some of the restraining meanings of femininity. This liberation has been enhanced by the emergence of different feminisms over the past decade. These feminisms have made possible a stance of opposition toward a singular feminine identity; they have demonstrated that women stand in a multitude of places, depending on time and geographical location, on race, age, sexual preference, health, class status, religion, and other factors. Despite these significant changes, there remains a common residue of meaning that seems affixed, as if by nature, to the female body. Law participates in creating that meaning.

I will argue that there are at least three general claims that can be made about the relationship between legal rules and legal discourse and the meaning of the female body:

1. Legal rules permit and sometimes mandate the terrorization of the female body. This occurs by a combination of provisions that inadequately protect women against physical abuse and that encourage women to seek refuge against insecurity. One meaning of "female body," then, is a body that is "in terror," a body that has learned to scurry, to cringe, and to submit. Legal discourse supports that meaning.

2. Legal rules permit and sometimes mandate the *maternalization* of the female body. This occurs with the use of provisions that reward women for singularly assuming responsibilities after childbirth and with those that penalize conduct—such as sexuality or labor market work—that conflicts with mothering. Maternalization also occurs through rules such as abortion restrictions that compel women to become mothers and by domestic relations rules that favor mothers over fathers as parents. Another meaning of "female body," then, is a body that is "for" maternity. Legal discourse supports that meaning.

3. Legal rules permit and sometimes mandate the *sexualization* of the female body. This occurs through provisions that criminalize individual sexual conduct, such as rules against commercial sex (prostitution) or same sex practices (homosexuality) and also through rules that legitimate and support institutions such as the pornography, advertising, and entertainment industries that eroticize the female body. Sexualization also occurs, paradoxically, in the application of rules such as rape and sexual harassment laws that are designed to protect women against sex-related injuries. These rules grant or deny women protection by interrogating their sexual promiscuity. The more sexually available or desiring a woman looks, the less protection these rules are likely to give her. Another meaning of "female body," then, is a body that is "for" sex with men, a body that is "desirable" and also rapable, that wants sex and wants raping. Legal discourse supports that meaning.

These groups of legal rules and discourse constitute a system that "constructs" or engenders the female body. The feminine figures the rules pose are naturalized within legal discourse by declaration—"women *are* (choose one) weak, nurturing, sexy"—and by a host of linguistic strategies that link women to particular images of the female body. By deploying these images, legal discourse rationalizes, explains, and renders authoritative the female-body rule network. The impact of the rule network on women's reality in turn reacts back on the discourse, reinforcing the "truth" of these images.

Contractions of confidence in the thesis that sex differences are socially constructed have had a significant impact on women in law. Liberal jurists, for example, have been unwilling to extend the protection of the gender equality guarantee to anatomical distinctions between female and male bodies; these differences seem so basic to individual identity that law need not—or should not—be responsible for them. Feminist legal scholars have been unable to overcome this intransigence, partly because we ourselves sometimes find particular sex-related traits quite intransigent. Indeed, one way to understand the fracturing of law-related feminism into separate schools of thought over the past decade is by the sexual traits that are considered unsusceptible to legal transformation[4] and by the criticisms these analyses have provoked within our own ranks.[5]

The fracturing of feminist criticism has occurred partly because particular sex differences seem so powerfully fixed that feminists are as unable to resist their "naturalization" as liberal jurists. But feminists also cling to particular sex-related differences because of a strategic desire to protect the feminist legal agenda from sabotage. Many feminist critics have argued that the condition of "real" women makes it too early to be postfeminist. The social construction thesis is useful to feminists insofar as it informs and supports our efforts to improve the condition of women in law. If, or when, the social construction thesis seems about to deconstruct the basic category of woman, its usefulness to feminism is problematized. How can we build a political coalition to advance the position of women in law if the subject that drives our efforts is "indeterminate," "incoherent," or "contingent?"

I think this concern is based upon a misperception of where we are in the legal struggle against sexism. I think we are in danger of being politically immobilized by a system for the production of what sex means that makes particular sex differences seem "natural." If my assessment is right, then describing the mechanics of this system is potentially enabling rather than disempowering; it may reveal opportunities for resisting the legal role in producing the radical asymmetry between the sexes.

14   I also think this concern is based on a misperception about the impact of deconstruction. Skeptics tend to think, I believe, that the legal deconstruction of "woman"—in one paper or in many papers, say, written over the next decade—will entail the immediate destruction of "women" as identifiable subjects who are affected by law reform projects. Despite the healthy, self-serving respect I have for the influence of legal scholarship and for the role of law as a significant cultural factor (among many) that contributes to the production of femininity, I think "women" cannot be eliminated from our lexicon very quickly. The question this paper addresses is not whether sex differences exist—they do—or how to transcend them—we can't—but the character of their treatment in law.

Sexualization, Terrorization and Maternalization: The Case of Prostitution

Since most anti-prostitution rules are gender neutral, let me explain, before going any further, how I can argue that they have a particular impact on the meaning of the female body. Like other rules regulating sexual conduct, anti-prostitution rules sexualize male as well as female bodies; they indicate that sex—unlike, say, laughing, sneezing, or making eye contact—is legally regulated. Regardless of whether one is male or female, the pleasures and the virtue of sex are produced, at least in part, by legal rules.[6] The gendered lopsidedness of this meaning system—which I describe below—occurs, quite simply, because most sex workers are women. Thus, even though anti-prostitution rules could, in theory, generate parallel meanings for male and female bodies, in practice they just don't. At least they don't right now.

The legal definition of prostitution as the unlawful sale of sex occurs in statutes that criminalize specific commercial sex practices and in decisional law, such as contract cases that hold that agreements for the sale of sexual services are legally unenforceable. By characterizing certain sexual practices as illegal, these rules sexualize the female body. They invite a sexual interrogation of every female body: is it for or against prostitution?

This sexualization of the female body explains an experience many women have: an insistent concern that this outfit, this pose, this gesture may send the wrong signal—a fear of looking like a whore. Sexy talking, sexy walking, sexy dressing seem sexy, at least in part, because they are the telltale signs of a sex worker plying her trade. This sexualization also explains the shadow many women feel when having sex for unromantic reasons—to comfort themselves, to avoid a confrontation over some domestic issue, or to secure a favor—a fear of acting like a whore.[7]

This reading of the relationship between prostitution rules and the female body is aligned with but somewhat different from the radical feminist description of the relationship between prostitution and female subjectivity. Catharine MacKinnon's 1982 *Signs* piece describes the relationship this way:

> [Feminist] investigations reveal . . . [that] prostitution [is] not primarily [an] abuse[ ] of physical force, violence, authority, or economics. [It is an] abuse[ ] of sex. [It] need not and do[es] not rely for [its] coerciveness upon forms of enforcement other than the sexual. . . .
>
> If women are socially defined such that female sexuality cannot be lived or spoken or felt or even somatically sensed apart from its enforced definition, so that it *is* its own lack, then there is no such thing as a woman as such, there are only walking embodiments of men's projected needs.[8]

MacKinnon's description of the impact of prostitution on women suggests that the sexual experience of all women may be, like sex work, the experience of having sex solely at the command of and for the pleasure of an other. This is a more extreme interpretation of the sexualized female body than mine and not one all women share.

> The feminists' point of view? Well, I would like to point out that they're missing a couple of things, because, you know, I may be dressing like the typical bimbo, whatever, but I'm in charge. You know. I'm in charge of my fantasies. I put myself in these situations with men, you know. . . . [A]ren't I in charge of my life?[9]

Although I believe Madonna's claim about herself, there are probably a number of people who don't. Anyone who looks as much like a sex worker as she does couldn't possibly be in charge of herself, they are likely to say; she is an example of exactly what MacKinnon means by a "walking embodiment[ ] of men's projected needs."[10] Without going further into the cottage industry of Madonna interpretation, it seems indisputable that Madonna's version of the female sexualized body is radically more autonomous and self-serving than MacKinnon's interpretation, and significantly less troubled and doubled than mine.

16   Because sex differences are semiotic—because the female body is produced and interpreted through a system of signs—all three of these interpretations of the sexualized female body may be accurate. The truth of any particular meaning would depend on the circumstances in which it was asserted. Thus, the sexualized female body that is produced and sustained by the legal regulation of prostitution may have multiple meanings. Moreover, the meaning of the sexualized female body for an individual woman is also affected by other feminine images that the legal regulation of prostitution produces.

Anti-prostitution rules terrorize the female body. The regulation of prostitution is accomplished not only by rules that expressly repress or prohibit commercialized sex. Prostitution regulation also occurs through a network of cultural practices that endanger sex workers' lives and make their work terrifying. These practices include the random, demeaning, and sometimes brutal character of anti-prostitution law enforcement. They also include the symbiotic relationship between the illegal drug industry and sex work, the use of prostitutes in the production of certain forms of pornography, hotel compliance with sex work, inadequate police protection for crimes against sex workers, and unregulated bias against prostitutes and their children in housing, education, the health care system, and in domestic relations law. Legal rules support and facilitate these practices.

The legal terrorization of prostitutes forces many sex workers to rely on pimps for protection and security, an arrangement which in most cases is also terrorizing. Pimps control when sex workers work, what kind of sex they do for money, and how much they make for doing it; they often use sexual seduction and physical abuse to "manage" the women who work for them. The terrorization of sex workers affects women who are not sex workers by encouraging them to do whatever they can to avoid being asked if they are "for" illegal sex. Indeed, marriage can function as one of these avoidance mechanisms, in that, conventionally, marriage signals that a woman has chosen legal sex over illegal sex.

One might argue that the terrorized female body is not that much different from the sexualized female body. Both experiences of femininity often—some might say always—entail being dominated by a man. Regardless of whether a woman is terrorized or sexualized, there are social incentives to reduce the hardships of her position, either by marrying or by aligning herself with a pimp. In both cases she typically becomes emotionally, financially, physically, and sexually dependent on and subordinate to a man.

If the terrorized and sexualized female bodies can be conflated and reduced to a dominated female body, then Madonna's claim that she's in charge, like the claims other women make that they experience sexual pleasure or autonomy in their relations with men, is suspect—perhaps, even, the product of false consciousness. But I argue that the dominated female body does not fully capture the impact of anti-prostitution rules on women. This is because anti-prostitution rules also maternalize the female body, by virtue of the interrelationship between anti-prostitution rules and legal rules that encourage women to bear and rear children. The maternalized female body triangulates the relationship between law and the meanings of the female body. It proposes a choice of roles for women.

The maternalization of the female body can be explained through the operation of the first and second postmodern "principles." That is, because we construct our identities in language and because the meaning of language is contextual and contingent, the relationship between anti-prostitution rules and the meaning of the female body is also affected by other legal rules and their relationship to the female body. The legal rules that criminalize prostitution are located in a legal system in which other legal rules legalize sex—rules, for example, that establish marriage as the legal site of sex and that link marital sex to reproduction by, for example, legitimating children born in marriage. As a result of this conjuncture, anti-prostitution rules maternalize the female body. They not only interrogate women with the question of whether they are for or against prostitution, they also raise the question of whether a woman is for illegal sex or whether she is for legal, maternalized sex.

The legal system maintains a shaky line between sex workers and other women. Anti-prostitution laws are erratically enforced; eager customers and obliging hotel services collaborate in the "crimes" prostitutes commit with relative impunity, and the legal, systemic devaluation of "women's work" sometimes makes prostitution more lucrative for women than legitimate wage labor. Anti-prostitution rules formally preserve the distinction between legal and illegal sexual activity. By preventing the line between sex workers and "mothers" from disappearing altogether, anti-prostitution rules reinforce the maternalized female body that other legal rules more directly support.

The legal discourse of anti-prostitution law explicitly deploys the image of maternalized femininity in order to contrast sex workers with

18   women who are not sex workers. This can be observed in defamation cases involving women who are incorrectly identified or depicted as whores. In authorizing compensation for such women, courts typically appeal to maternal imagery to describe the woman who has been wrongly described; they justify their decisions by contrasting the images of two female bodies against each other, the virgin and the whore—madonna and bimbo. The discourse of these decisions maternalizes the female body.[11] The maternalized female body is responsible for her children. Madonna's bambino puts her in charge.

The conjunction and displacement of these alternative meanings of the female body are rationalized in legal discourse, where they are presented as both "natural" but also necessary, for reasons associated with liberalism. A Massachusetts case involving a rape prosecution[12] and feminist controversy regarding the decriminalization of prostitution provide two examples.

Sometime after three o'clock in the morning on a December night in Malden Square, a police cruiser entered a parking lot where police officers had heard screams. "Seeing the headlights of an approaching car," Judge Liacos wrote for the Supreme Judicial Court, a woman "naked and bleeding around the mouth, jumped from the defendant's car and ran toward [the police cruiser] screaming and waving her arms."[13] She claimed that she had been raped, that the defendant had forced her to perform oral sex and to engage in intercourse twice. After the defendant was convicted on charges of rape and commission of an unnatural and lascivious act, he appealed. He claimed that he had wrongfully been denied the opportunity to inform the jury that the complainant had twice been charged with prostitution. He argued that the complainant's allegation of rape, which he denied, "may have been motivated by her desire to avoid further prosecution."[14]

The trial court had prohibited the defendant from mentioning the complainant's arrests to the jury because of the Massachusetts rape-shield statute,[15] a rule that prohibits the admission of reputation evidence or of specific instances of a victim's sexual conduct in a rape trial. The purpose of the rule is to encourage victims to report rapes, to eliminate victim harassment at trial, and to support the assumption that reputation evidence is "only marginally, if at all, probative of consent."[16] Reasoning that a defendant's right to argue bias "may be the last refuge of an innocent defendant," the Supreme Judicial Court lifted the shield.[17]

> We emphasize that we do not depart from the long held view that prostitution is not relevant to credibility.... Nor do we depart from the policy of the statute in viewing prostitution or the lack of chastity as inadmissible on the issue of consent. Where, however, such facts are relevant to a showing of bias or motive to lie, the general evidentiary rule of exclusion must give way to the constitutionally based right of effective cross-examination.[18]

This interpretation of the rape-shield statute, broadly applied, denies sex workers who dare to complain of sexual violence the presumption of innocence. Because prostitution is unlawful, this ruling simultaneously terrorizes, sexualizes, and de-maternalizes sex workers. This triple whammy is accomplished by an appeal to fairness:

> [T]he defendant is entitled to present his own theory of the encounter to the jury.... The relevancy of testimony depends on whether it has a "rational tendency to prove an issue in the case." ... Under the defendant's theory he and the complainant, previously strangers to each other, were in a car late at night parked in a vacant parking lot. Having just engaged in sexual acts, they were both naked. A police car was approaching. The defendant intended to show that the complainant, having been found in a similar situation on two prior occasions, had been arrested on each occasion and charged with prostitution. We cannot say that this evidence has no rational tendency to prove that the complainant was motivated falsely to accuse the defendant of rape by a desire to avoid further prosecution.[19]

Seems perfectly reasonable. Fair. If a guy can't explain a gal's reasons for misrepresenting a situation, that bleeding mouth might compromise *his* credibility.

It might seem obvious, at this point, that decriminalization of prostitution would be an appropriate strategy for feminist legal activists concerned about the physical security of sex workers. However, although the feminists I've read all agree that prostitution should be decriminalized, they disagree about *how* decriminalization should occur. The arguments in this dispute are another example of how legal discourse reproduces and is mired in the interpretations of the female body produced by legal rules.

Should the reform of prostitution law be restricted to the repeal of rules penalizing the sale of sex, or should other legally supported structures that create, sustain and degrade sex work also be challenged?

20   Feminists in favor of legalization—this is the postmodern position—
argue that, unlike a narrowly defined decriminalization campaign, legalization might significantly improve the lives of sex workers. Legalization,
for example, might extend unemployment insurance benefits to sex
workers; it might allow sex workers to participate in the social security
system; it might prohibit pimping; it might authorize advertising for
their business.

Feminists who are against legalization—this is the radical position—
envision a decriminalization project that would develop strategies for
preventing women from participating in sex work, rather than strategies
that would make prostitution a more comfortable line of work. Radical
feminists, such as Kathleen Barry, are sympathetic to the plight of sex
workers.[20] But their conviction that women are defined as women by
their sexual subordination to men leads them to argue that sex workers
are particularly victimized by patriarchy and that they should be extri-
cated from their condition rather than supported in their work. These
arguments against legalization are in the language of the terrorized
female body.

Not all legal feminist believe that prostitutes are terrorized full time.
Some feminists—I'll call this group the liberals—believe that at least
some sex workers, occasionally, exercise sexual autonomy. But these
feminists do not favor assimilating sex work into the wage market. They
oppose legalization because they object to the kind of sexual autonomy
legalization would support.[21] That is, although they support the right of
women to do sex work—even at the cost of reinforcing male dominance—they resist the commodification of women's sexuality.

Sex workers themselves—who inspire the postmodern position as I
develop it here—want legal support for sex that is severed from its reproduction function and from romance, affection, and long-term relationships.[22] Because "legal" sexual autonomy is conventionally extended to
women only by rules that locate sexuality in marriage or by rules that
allow women decisional autonomy regarding reproductive issues, arguments in support of law reforms that would legalize sex work conflict
with the language of the maternalized female body. The arguments that
sex workers are making to assimilate their work into the wage market
appeal to a sexualized femininity that is something other than a choice
between criminalized and maternalized sex or a choice between terrorized and maternalized sex. This appeal to a fresh image of the female
body is based on a reorganization of the three images of femininity I

described earlier; it arises within the play of these three images. Its originality suggests, to me, resistance to the dominant images.

It is significant that sex workers have "found" a different voice of feminine sexuality through the process of political organizing, through efforts to speak out against and to change the conditions of their lives. For me, the promise of postmodern legal feminism lies in the juncture of feminist politics and the genealogy of the female body in law. It is in this juncture that we can simultaneously deploy the commonalities among real women, in their historically situated, material circumstances, and at the same time challenge the conventional meanings of "woman" that sustain the subordinating conditions of women's lives.

I do not think that the sex workers' claims for legalization constitute *the* postmodern feminist legal voice. I am also unsure whether I support their position on legalization. But I believe that my analysis of the decriminalization dispute in which they are participating illustrates how postmodern legal feminism can seek and claim different voices, voices which will challenge the power of the congealed meanings of the female body that legal rules and legal discourse permit and sustain.

Notes

1. *See* Catharine A. MacKinnon, *Feminism, Marxism, Method, and the State: An Agenda for Theory*, 7 SIGNS: J. WOMEN CULTURE & SOC'Y 515 (1982) [hereinafter MacKinnon, *Agenda for Theory*]; Catharine A. MacKinnon, *Feminism, Marxism, Method, and the State: Toward Feminist Jurisprudence*, 8 SIGNS: J. WOMEN CULTURE & SOC'Y 635 (1983) [hereinafter MacKinnon, *Toward Feminist Jurisprudence*].

2. ANDREA DWORKIN, LETTERS FROM A WAR ZONE 65 (1989).

3. ANDREA DWORKIN, RIGHT-WING WOMEN 20 (1983).

4. For the radical feminist focus on male domination, see ANDREA DWORKIN, PORNOGRAPHY: MEN POSSESSING WOMEN 14–18, 53–56 (1989); DWORKIN, *supra* note 3, at 78–87; CATHARINE A. MACKINNON, FEMINISM UNMODIFIED 40–45, 171–74 (1987); MacKinnon, *Agenda for Theory*, *supra* note 1, at 530–34; and MacKinnon, *Toward Feminist Jurisprudence*, *supra* note 1, at 643. For the cultural feminist focus on the ethic of care, see CAROL GILLIGAN, IN A DIFFERENT VOICE: PSYCHOLOGICAL THEORY AND WOMEN S DEVELOPMENT 64–105 (1982); and Leslie Bender, *A Lawyer's Primer on Feminist Theory and Tort*, 38 J. LEGAL EDUC. 3, 28–37 (1988) (suggesting the incorporation of Gilligan's ethic into tort law's standard of care).

5. For a race-conscious critique of liberal, radical, and cultural feminism for overlooking minority women concerns, see Kimberlé Crenshaw, *Demarginalizing the Intersection of Race and Sex: A Black Feminist Critique of Antidiscrimination Doctrine, Feminist Theory and Antiracist Politics*, 1989 U. CHI. LEGAL F. 139, 140, 152–60; Angela P. Harris, *Race and Essentialism in Feminist Legal Theory*, 42 STAN. L. REV. 581, 585–86 (1990); and

22

      Marlee Kline, *Race, Racism, and Feminist Legal Theory*, 12 HARV. WOMEN'S L.J. 115, 120–23, 144–50 (1989). For the lesbian feminist critique of heterosexist assumptions in liberal, radical, and cultural feminisms, see AUDRE LORDE, SISTER OUTSIDER 114–23 (1984); Adrienne Rich, *Compulsory Heterosexuality and Lesbian Existence*, in POWERS OF DESIRE: THE POLITICS OF SEXUALITY 177, 178–82 (Ann Snitow, Christine Stansell & Sharon Thompson eds., 1983). For a class-conscious feminist critique of the class bias inherent in liberal, radical, and cultural feminisms, see KRISTIN LUKER, ABORTION AND THE POLITICS OF MOTHERHOOD 192–215 (1984).

6. *Cf.* LOUIS ALTHUSSER, LENIN & PHILOSOPHY & OTHER ESSAYS (Ben Brewster trans., 1971) (demonstrating the role of ideology and social structure in shaping personality); MICHEL FOUCAULT, 1 THE HISTORY OF SEXUALITY 6–7 (Robert Hurley trans., 1978) (discussing the power-sex relationship in terms of affirmation).

7. Even sex workers who are "in the life" feel interrogated by the sexualization question; they too struggle against acting like whores. Consider, for example, one sex worker's description of the discomfort she experienced because she sexually responded to her customer during an act of prostitution. Her orgasm in those circumstances broke down a distinction she sought to maintain between her work and the sexual pleasure obtained from her non-work-related sexual activity. *See* Judy Edelstein, *In the Massage Parlor*, in SEX WORK: WRITINGS BY WOMEN IN THE SEX INDUSTRY 62, 62–63 (Frédérique Delacoste & Priscilla Alexander eds., 1987) [hereinafter SEX WORK]. Consider also the many accounts of sex workers who feel degraded or angry about their work; this is an experience of sexual division, a fear that, in their work as whores, they are acting like whores. *See, e.g.*, Jean Johnston, *Speaking in Tongues*, in SEX WORK, *supra*, at 70, 70; Sharon Kaiser, *Coming Out of Denial*, in SEX WORK, *supra*, at 104, 104–05; Rosie Summers, *Prostitution*, in SEX WORK, *supra*, at 113, 114–15.

8. MacKinnon, *Agenda for Theory, supra* note 1, at 533–34.

9. *Nightline: Interview with Madonna* (ABC television broadcast, Dec. 3, 1990).

10. MacKinnon, *Agenda for Theory, supra* note 1, at 534.

11. *See, e.g.*, Veazy v. Blair, 86 Ga. App. 721, 726 (Ga. Ct. App. 1952) (holding that a cause of action existed when the defendant had stated that "the plaintiff, a pure and chaste lady of unblemished character, was a 'public whore'"); Mullins v. Mutter, 151 S.W.2d 1047–1048, 1051 (Ky. 1941) (upholding a large slander award when the defendant called the plaintiff a "damned whore"). In *Mullins*, the court noted that:

> In this case plaintiff is an orphaned girl, bearing—so far as the record discloses—a good reputation.... Up to the time complained of no breath of suspicion had been leveled against her chastity. But, so emphatically repeated charges by defendant was calculated to leave a scar upon her reputation that might follow her to her grave.

Id. at 1051.

12. *See* Commonwealth v. Joyce, 415 N.E.2d 181 (Mass. 1981).

13. *Id.* at 183.

14. *Id.* at 184.

15. *See* MASS. GEN. L. ch 233, § 21B (1991).

16. *Joyce*, 415 N.E.2d at 186.

17. *Id.* at 186.

18. *Id.* at 187 (citations omitted).

19. *Id.* (citations omitted).

20. *See* KATHLEEN BARRY, FEMALE SEXUAL SLAVERY 226–37 (1979)

21. *See* Margaret J. Radin, *Market-Inalienability*, 100 HARV. L. REV. 1849, 1921–25 (1987)

(favoring limited decriminalization of prostitution, at least for the short term). *But* see   *23*
Jody Freeman, *The Feminist Debate Over Prostitution Reform: Prostitutes' Rights Groups,*
Radical Feminists, and the (Im)possibility of Consent, 5 BERKELEY WOMEN'S L.J. 75,
107–08 (1989–1990) (arguing that "the best short-term approach to reform entails
removing prostitution from the criminal realm ... and, at the same time taking
affirmative steps to destroy the conditions that create consumption and drive women to
the trade").

22. Not all sex workers seek to legalize as well as decriminalize their work, but many do.
    See, e.g., GAIL PHETERSON, A VINDICATION OF THE RIGHTS OF WHORES 33–34 (1989);
    Draft Statements from the 2nd World Whores' Congress (1986), *in* SEX WORK, supra note
    7, at 307; *International Committee for Prostitutes' Rights World Charter, in* SEX WORK,
    supra note 7, at 305.

CHAPTER TWO

> ─ ◆ ─ ○ ─ ◆ ─ ◄

THE POLITICS OF THE CLOSET

LEGAL ARTICULATION
OF SEXUAL ORIENTATION IDENTITY

Janet E. Halley

Interrogatory No. 30: ... In other words, how many members of the Navy, identified as "homosexuals" have been retained in the Navy?

Answer No. 30: The use of the term "identified" makes this question impossible to answer. The term is imprecise. More information is needed.

> —Interrogatory of Plaintiff James Miller and
> Answer of Defendant U.S. Navy, in *Beller v. Middendorf*[1]

TO BORROW THE LANGUAGE of semiology, the public status "heterosexual" is an unmarked signifier, the category to which everyone is assumed to belong. Something has to *happen* to mark an individual with the identity "homosexual." Though this marking is accomplished only in complex social interactions, we can roughly distinguish two basic narratives: (1) an individual, acting in some sense voluntarily, publicly assumes a gay or lesbian identity; and/or (2) some other agent—a friend, parent, employer, prosecutor, judge—ascribes or imposes a gay or lesbian identity on an individual, with or without her consent. In the discussion that follows, I treat these categories as distinct, though it will repeatedly become apparent that, in the interpretive interactions that make up the world, they are inextricably intertwined.[2]

Homosexual Identity Imposed

The legal burdens imposed on homosexuality in our society deter people from *appearing gay*. Of the total number of self-identified gays and lesbians, only a fraction will voluntarily "come out," and of the remaining "closeted" gays, only a fraction will become subject to the public ascription of gay identity. Furthermore, because the assumption of heterosexuality applies in virtually every social interaction—from the encounter of teacher with student, salesperson with shopper, mother with daughter, Supreme Court Justice with clerk—even the most forthright and fearless gay man or lesbian cannot "come out" once and for all in a single public disclosure; as she moves from one social setting to another, she will have to come out afresh or acquiesce in the assignment to her of a nonreferential public identity. The public identity "homosexual" at any one moment, then, is vastly underinclusive of self-identified gay men and lesbians. It is, therefore, an even less accurate indicator of individuals who entertain homoerotic desires or have had homosexual experiences without labelling themselves gay or lesbian.

Simultaneous counterforces are at work to ensure that the public identity "homosexual" is overinclusive, encompassing individuals who do not (or do not very often) feel or act on homoerotic desires and who do not denominate themselves gay or lesbian. Consider, for instance, the process and criteria for assigning homosexual public identity which the Sixth Circuit approved in *Gay Inmates of Shelby County Jail v. Barksdale*.[3] Enforcing a county jail's policy of segregating all homosexual inmates, the intake officer is authorized to "make a purely subjective judgement," and to segregate (among others) inmates who "appear[] weak, small or effeminate."[4] The problem here is not only that the lack of physical strength or monumental build has no reliable correlation to gay male

26   identity. Nor do we exhaust the error by pointing out the fallacy, inscribed into the homosexual role, that men who desire men must be like women. The scene at the Shelby County Jail emphasizes a more profound element of public homosexual identity that is too often forgotten: in order for the sign to "mean" the signified, there must be an *interpreter*, and the interpreter cannot escape the web of signifiers that purport to indicate public sexual identity. If he is small himself, or delicate of build; if he is a behemoth; if he is just an average guy; no matter how many pounds of flesh lie on his bones, he will exercise his power of interpretation to channel interpretations of his own body. As Martha Minow has observed, "[i]n assigning the label of difference, the group confirms not only its identity, but also its superiority, and displaces doubts and anxieties onto the person now called 'different.'"[5]

Two forms of immutability are being created in such interactions: the segregated inmate is marked—irrevocably for many social purposes[6]—as homosexual, and the officer so marking him confirms his own heterosexuality. Neither form of the immutability of public identity, however, is at all stable.

Nowhere is this phenomenon so clear as in the case law attempting to define homosexuality and to justify the current regime of judicial restraint. Courts, legislators, and regulators have encountered intractable difficulties in their efforts to write coherent definitions of the homosexuals upon whom legal burdens may be placed. Consider the morass into which the D.C. Circuit strides when it announces that sodomy provides a definition of the class, homosexuals. In *Padula v. Webster*,[7] the court reasons that *Bowers v. Hardwick*,[8] by refusing to hold that the constitutional right to privacy extends to homosexual sodomy, foreclosed arguments that "practicing homosexuals" constitute a suspect classification. Crucial to this wide leap from due process to equal protection is the assertion that sodomy statutes "criminalize the behavior that defines the class."[9] But do they?

The statute upheld in *Hardwick* defined sodomy as "any sexual act involving the sex organs of one person and the mouth or anus of another."[10] Let us take the act of definition in *Padula* seriously. Lesbians who forego cunnilingus, the many gay men who have abandoned fellatio and anal intercourse to protect themselves and their lovers from AIDS, self-identified gay men and lesbians who remain celibate—the *Padula* court has determined that none of these groups belongs to the class "homosexual." The court fails to observe that it may well have defined

the lesbian plaintiff before it out of the class "homosexual" that it both
creates and condemns. Note, furthermore, that not all states define
sodomy as Georgia does. The definition imposed in *Padula* produces the
amusing result that the contours of the class "homosexuals" vary from
state to state. And some states do not criminalize homosexual sodomy at
all: how, in those states, is the class to be defined?

The *Padula* definition offers an interpretation of homosexual identity:
indeed, the decision as an act of judicial violence[11] makes its interpretation, in an important sense, real. Its almost completely nonreferential
definition of the class "homosexuals" provides an outstanding example of
the imposition of a putatively clear, fixed, and rigid identity on gay men
and lesbians. It also exemplifies the tendency of such rigid classifications
to crumble under even light pressure from empirical fact.

Other courts, legislatures, and regulators have attempted to contain
these deconstructive forces by tempering legal definitions of the homosexual person more carefully, but have wound up with the same contradictions that lie under the surface of *Padula*'s clear equation of status
with act. When the New Hampshire legislature, in an effort to exclude
homosexuals from adoption, foster care, and daycare center employment,
proposed a definition of homosexuals virtually identical to that advanced
in Padula,[12] the New Hampshire Supreme Court determined in an advisory opinion that exceptions had to be made to save the bill's constitutionality. It construed the bill to exclude victims of homosexual rape and
made an exception for acts not "committed or submitted to on a current
basis reasonably close in time to the filing of the application. . . . This
interpretation thus excludes from the definition of homosexual those persons who, for example, had one homosexual experience during adoles-
cence, but who now engage in exclusively heterosexual behavior."[13] The
court maintains a conviction, which we have seen contradicted by the
empirical findings, that homosexual status is occupied exclusively by persons who have engaged in homosexual acts. It reproduces without noting
the underinclusiveness problems so apparent in the *Padula* definition.

Interestingly, the court is worried instead about the overinclusiveness
of a definition that fails to distinguish as heterosexual individuals who,
though they engaged in the physical acts described in the bill, did not
intend them in such a way as to merit the label "homosexual." Those who
gave no consent to an act of homosexual sex (rape victims), and those who
consented *but only once*, stand out in the court's mind as true heterosexuals. The patterns of intention in the latter category are deeply problem-

28 atic. The category includes individuals whose desires may be predominantly homosexual, who have acted on them, but who have determined to mask these facts from themselves by embracing a purely heterosexual subjective identity, and from others by passing as straight. The court's example forgives these lies and builds them into the scheme of state enforcement. Furthermore, the "only once" heterosexual is merely the example forwarded by the court of a much broader category, much more sweepingly permissive of heterosexual self-deception and self-protection: all those whose homosexual acts are not "committed on a current basis reasonably close in time to the filing of the application" shall be deemed to be heterosexual. Even as the New Hampshire Supreme Court, like the D.C. Circuit in *Padula*, attempts to erect a conceptual structure that will render the status "homosexual" rigid and immutable, it recognizes and privileges certain kinds of changes. The mutability of sexual identity is recognized, and its civil advantages are accorded exclusively to currently self-identified heterosexuals.

An attempt to avoid the difficulties that entangle the New Hampshire justices appears in regulations adopted by the Navy in 1978. These regulations further limit the exception for one-time-only sodomites—but in doing so they display a whole new range of contradictions inherent in the project of imposing a public homosexual identity on the complexity of living human beings. Before 1978, the Navy expressly mandated that any member found to have engaged even in a single homosexual act be processed for discharge.[14] Like the New Hampshire Supreme Court, it found this absolute act-based definition of homosexuals too broad, and in 1978 adopted a new regulation providing for discretionary retention of "[a] member who has solicited, attempted or engaged in a homosexual act on a single occasion *and who does not profess or demonstrate proclivity to repeat such an act*."[15] Two new limiting elements are introduced: demonstrated proclivity to homosexual acts and professed proclivity to homosexual acts. The Navy has embroiled itself in another series of epistemological difficulties here, but in order to discern them, it is helpful to understand the problems it was attempting to solve.

Before reformulating its regulations, the Navy defended a series of actions brought to challenge discharges made under the old rules, those equating act with status. In *Beller v. Middendorf*,[16] an appeal consolidating three such cases, one plaintiff posed a particularly sharp challenge to the definitional process. Both the hearing board convened to consider James Miller's discharge and the Senior Medical Officer who examined him balked at applying the strict act/status equation to Miller. The board found that he had committed homosexual acts while in service but recommended that he be retained.

It is not clear from the published opinion whether this vote expressed a view that Miller was an erring heterosexual, a harmless homosexual, or a human being who could not be fit into rigid ideal categories. The appellate opinion's report of the Senior Medical Officer's evaluation suggests the more critical third alternative. According to Judge (now Justice) Kennedy's opinion, the medical expert found that Miller "did not *appear* to be '*a homosexual.*'"[17] The typography here recognizes the social artifice of the category "homosexual." And the careful reference to the problem of appearance points to the problem of interpreting social signals that is occluded—but evidently not eliminated—by the rigid equation of act with status. Judge Kennedy was able to render these highly equivocal reports legally nugatory and to stabilize the legal assignment of homosexual identity to plaintiff Miller only by interpreting the old rules as creating absolutely no discretion in those charged with carrying them out.[18] In contrast to the other plaintiffs, Kennedy concludes, "[t]he case of Miller is closer but no less clear."[19] Clarity here is surely the product of legerdemain, but Judge Kennedy showed rare judicial honesty in including within his opinion the procedural history that belies it.

We may surmise that the 1978 regulations, by recognizing the possibility of exceptions to the strict act/status equation, were intended to mitigate its procrustean crudity. But there need be no doubt that they merely reformulate the same old epistemological crises. The official Navy evaluations of plaintiff Miller's status show how uncharted are the waters opened up for decisionmakers by the 1978 regulations, with their exception for "once-only" heterosexuals who "[do] not demonstrate proclivity to repeat such an act." All the uncertainties of interpretation that pestered the hearing board and Senior Medical Officer in Miller's case are here invited back into the new regulatory scheme.

Moreover, by cognizing the self-descriptions of accused servicepersons in the exception for "once-only" heterosexuals who "[do] not profess . . . proclivity to repeat such an act," the new regulations give new life to a second, perhaps deeper, and certainly more disturbing ambiguity of the Miller case. Plaintiff Miller admitted to committing homosexual acts while on leave in Taiwan and at some unspecified earlier time, yet he also "has at various times denied being homosexual and expressed regret or repugnance at his acts."[20]

30   It is tempting to see Miller's confession as a clear indication of some frame of mind or strategy proper to him. As we have seen, the stigma and deprivations attached to the status of homosexual—a good example being involuntary discharge from the Navy—deter individuals who engage in same-sex behavior from acknowledging to themselves that they have any component of homosexuality in their makeup. But Miller's statements are not fragments of an internal process of self-assessment, however inchoate: he made them to Navy officials under the threat of compulsory punishment. We oversimplify again if we conclude that Miller cynically declared himself a true heterosexual revolted by his inconsistent actions in order to dupe his inquisitors and obtain an undeserved clemency. For by the inquisitorial interaction recorded here, Miller and the Navy create for him a *new public identity*. The possibility of sincerity is simply foregone by such an utterance.

     Instead, the process of social construction, the interaction in which an individual interprets himself to a world interpreting him, has reached a crisis at which, Robert Cover has suggested, both interpretation and language itself break down:

> Taken by itself, the word "interpretation" may be misleading. "Interpretation" suggests a social construction of an interpersonal reality through language. But pain and death have quite other implications. Indeed, pain and death destroy the world that "interpretation" calls up. . . .
> The deliberate infliction of pain in order to destroy the victim's normative world and capacity to create shared realities we call torture. . . . [T]orturers almost always require betrayal—a demonstration that the victim's intangible normative world has been crushed by the material reality of pain and its extension, fear. The torturer and victim do end up creating their own terrible "world," but this world derives its meaning from being imposed upon the ashes of another. The logic of that world is complete domination, though the objective may never be realized.[21]

     As I have argued elsewhere,[22] the relationship Cover calls "complete domination" is not static but continues to unfold over time. As it does so, it manifests patterns of interaction and mutual interpretation, but everyone now understands—or should understand—that the utterances of the confessor and the categories imposed by the inquisitor have lost all referential power. In the case of plaintiff James Miller, the possibility of discovering any "true" sexual orientation, if it ever existed, has now been destroyed.

In this epistemological crisis, the knower of others' sexual identities can be expected to act a little defensive. In particular, he or she will attempt to render invisible the processes by which official knowledge is produced, while refusing to cognize any answering subterfuge in the object of official description. A striking example of these protective strategies is Judge Bork's opinion in *Dronenburg v. Zech*[23]—fittingly, a Navy discharge case that arose under the revised 1978 regulations and that replays the crisis of *Beller v. Middendorf*. Rejecting the argument that the privacy rights established by Supreme Court precedents encompass homosexual acts, Judge Bork declares: "*It needs hardly be said* that none of these [privacy rights established by Supreme Court precedents] *covers* a right to homosexual conduct."[24] Bork here asserts his own right to say nothing, to remain inscrutable and silent, even as he determines that existing privacy doctrine does not hide from official view—does not "cover"—homosexual conduct. Homosexual conduct must be visible to a knower who is not to be known.

The doctrinal result of such a dynamic has been judicial endorsement of definitions of homosexuality that are not definitions at all. It only seems old-fashioned to declare, as a Texas court did in 1909, that a statute prohibiting "the *abominable and detestable crime against nature*" is perfectly sufficient because "the charge was too horrible to contemplate and too revolting to discuss."[25] Much more recently Maryland's prohibition of oral/genital contact and of "any other unnatural or perverted practice"[26] was held not to be unconstitutionally vague because the language employed conveyed "a clear legislative intention to cover the whole field of unnatural and perverted practices"; the state court of appeals "thought it unnecessary to describe in detail practices which are matters of common knowledge."[27] And in 1986, Chief Justice Burger placed his *imprimatur* on such definitions, intoning with approval: "Blackstone described 'the infamous crime against nature' as an offense of 'deeper malignity' than rape, an heinous act 'the very mention of which is a disgrace to human nature' and 'a crime not fit to be named.'"[28] Well within this tradition of reticence, silence, and modest submergence in "common knowledge," Judge Bork's opinion in *Dronenburg v. Zech* repeatedly deploys locutions which both assert that his position is patently obvious and mark his reluctance to expose it. His articulations are either unnecessary ("It need hardly be said that. . . ."; "To ask the

32   question is to answer it."), redundant (evidence may be drawn from "common sense and common experience"), or reluctantly ceded to the exigencies of the moment (".... and, it must be said....").[29]

These gestures create the character of the official knower, a man whose "common sense and common experience" render him unexceptionably a member of a stable, common majority that knows without having to find out. The *Dronenburg* opinion nevertheless admits the epistemological difficulties that its magisterial epistemology pretends to negate. Providing the list of dangers which the Navy policy might rationally be supposed to redress—precisely the list that has been declared needless—Judge Bork supposes the need to obviate encounters that might "make personal dealings uncomfortable where the relationship is sexually ambiguous."[30] Discomfort with such ambiguity could hardly arise if heterosexual identity were as absolute and secure as the unnameability trope suggests. Indeed, Judge Bork deepens his suggestion that antihomosexual discrimination functions not to punish and separate a clear and preexisting class of homosexuals but to secure the confident subjective and public identities of heterosexuals when he concludes his list of dangers thus: "Episodes of this sort are certain ..., it must be said, given the powers of military superiors over their inferiors, to enhance the possibility of homosexual seduction."[31] Judge Bork is not worried about homosexual rape, in which the victim is *ex hypothesi* an unwilling partner. Instead, his anxious concern focuses on the heterosexual sailor *who can be seduced* into a homoerotic encounter. A key rationale for antihomosexual discrimination, then, is anxiety about the ambiguity of heterosexual interactions, about a potential for mutability that undermines heterosexual identity. Lest the change actually take place, "known" homosexuals must be segregated.

Homosexual Identity Assumed

Some individuals are "exposed" as gay or lesbian; others expose themselves. Official discovery of individuals *in flagrante delicto* and the reports of former sex partners will rarely be available to provide evidence of homosexual conduct and give color to the official conclusion that an individual is "homosexual." It is much easier to rely on the professions of homosexuals themselves. Acts of discrimination in this setting seem to avoid the epistemology difficulties that undermine rules founded on homosexual conduct. After all, the open lesbian or gay man has inserted her- or himself into the legally defined class.

Miriam benShalom, for example, while a member of the U.S. Army Reserves, "publicly acknowledged her homosexuality during conversations with fellow reservists, in an interview with a reporter for her division newspaper, and in class, while teaching drill sergeant candidates."[32] In response to this candor the Army moved to discharge her, invoking a regulation providing for the discharge of any soldier who "evidences homosexual tendencies, desire, or interest, but is without overt homosexual acts."[33] This interaction is apparently unequivocal, benShalom and the Army agreeing as to her status and merely disagreeing as to its substantive value and consequences.

In fact, a series of cases involving self-professed homosexuals and bisexuals suggests that, to the contrary, legal strictures on sexual orientation carefully manage passage in and out of the closet, giving new and often unwanted meaning to sojourns on either side of the threshold. *Doe v. Casey*[34] offers a complex example of the legal meaning of secrecy in the context of homosexual stigma. The plaintiff, "out of the closet but under cover," was dismissed from his employment as a CIA agent after he voluntarily presented himself as homosexual to a CIA security officer. As the appellate opinion carefully notes, "John Doe is proceeding under a pseudonym only because his status as a CIA employee cannot be publicly acknowledged, not because of any embarrassment about his homosexuality."[35] The context reminds us that legally enforced secrecy can often be a vigorously pursued government goal.

The court held that if Doe's dismissal arose from a CIA policy of firing all homosexuals, the key to his due process claim was whether that action burdened him with a stigma.[36] In a congested and difficult passage, it denied that Doe, as a self-professed homosexual, could be stigmatized by his dismissal. Because the "real stigma imposed by [the government employer's] action . . . is the charge of homosexuality,"[37] and "[b]ecause Doe himself does not view homosexuality as stigmatizing—and indeed, admits that he is a homosexual," the court ruled that Doe would not be stigmatized by the CIA's disclosure to other government agencies that he was dismissed on the grounds of his homosexuality.[38] The court purports to view the problem of stigma from Doe's point of view: if he disclosed his homosexuality, he clearly sees nothing scandalous in it; and if he sees nothing scandalous in his homosexuality, he has no liberty interest in evading its legal consequences. The apparent respect paid here to Doe's self-conception and self-description is revealed as a sham if we note the implication of the court's reasoning: a self-identified homosexual in gov-

34　ernment employment, in order to retain a liberty interest in his or her job, must (1) subjectively regard his or her homosexuality as degrading and (2) hide it.

This reasoning creates a new form of the public identity "homosexual" for individuals who, like Doe, reject this invitation to self-denigrating secrecy. The court construes men and women who choose not to remain closeted to have made a simultaneous choice to wear whatever badge the majority determines is appropriate for them. Even as the court monopolizes the power to define and control the subjective experience of stigma, it simultaneously establishes the legal fiction that those harmed by government discrimination have chosen their injury.[39] As an alternative to this violent appropriation of the public identity of a self-professed homosexual, the case opens a pocket of legal protection for individuals who obey a prohibition on homosexuality not by eschewing homosexual acts or rejecting a homosexual subjective identity, but by appearing straight. One cost to them of accepting that protection is that they must also accept the public meaning of their equivocal position—the court's equation of their closetedness with the assumption that they have internalized the substantive determination that homosexuality is degrading to them.

Legal deterrence of homosexuality thus anticipates that many self-identified homosexuals, if allowed to pass as heterosexual, would rather switch than fight. It does all it can to motivate people to change their public self-presentations, fostering a pervasive and unquantifiable regime of mutability. Moreover, because control over the meaning of public identity is kept firmly in the hands of the anti-homosexual majority, that majority retains the power to dictate still more changes.

Department of Defense regulations for granting security clearances have recognized how profoundly volatile the closet can be by providing for deeply skeptical review of any applicant who, because she has concealed *anything* about her homosexual conduct or identity, is deemed to be susceptible to blackmail. Regulations in effect in 1987 regard as a disqualifying factor "the fact that an applicant has concealed or attempted to conceal his homosexuality from his employer or from his immediate family members, close associates, supervisors or co-workers."[40] As a federal court observes in upholding a challenge to these regulations, they obligate individuals to reveal not only sodomy, not only the very loosely defined group of acts deemed by the regulations to be "homosexual," but even desires: "because the policy relates to sexual preference itself, a person who is merely attracted to people of his own sex, but engages in no activity with them, must reveal his preference to all immediate family members, close associates, co-workers, or supervisors."[41] It is not even clear that, in the Department of Defense's eyes, full public disclosure of homosexuality protects one from the transformative power of blackmail: in *High Tech Gays*, the Department of Defense offered as evidence of the homosexual's susceptibility to blackmail the fact that plaintiff Timothy Dooling, an openly gay man, was approached for purposes of black-mail—even though Dooling had "unequivocally rejected" the offer.[42]

On the threshold between the closet and public homosexual identity, anything can happen. The beliefs of others can suddenly be transformed into one's public identity. Killian Swift, a White House stenographer, lost his job after his employer asked his immediate supervisor whether he was homosexual. She "confirmed that, to her knowledge, he is,"[43] and he was dismissed. The threshold is broad indeed, appearing under the feet even of the noncommittal and the inquisitive. Mere advocacy of homo-sexual rights and even mere investigation into the issue of sexual orienta-tion can trigger suppositions that one is gay, and suppositions can become public reality. When the Army imposed the regulation contested in *benShalom v. Secretary of the Army*, requiring discharge of any soldier who "evidences homosexual tendencies, desire, or interest," it formalized this interaction. As the District Court recognized in that case, under such a regime of sexual identity

> [n]o soldier would dare be caught reading anything that might be construed as a homosexually-oriented book or magazine. No soldier would want to be observed in the company of any person suspected of being a homosexual. Most importantly, no soldier would even want to make any statements that might be interpreted as supporting homosexuality.[44]

The rapidity with which an individual can lose control of the secret of her sexual orientation and find it transformed into the opprobrium and civil disabilities of imposed public identity is illustrated by the story of Marjorie Rowland. Employed as a nontenured guidance counselor in a public high school, Rowland confidentially disclosed to a coworker that she was bisexual; the coworker reported her disclosure to the school's principal. Some time later, Rowland upset a parent by advising her not to panic at her child's confusion over sexual identity, and, fearing that her job might be threatened, confided the story, and her bisexuality, to

36   the school's vice principal. Soon her sexual identity became a matter of
public knowledge, the object of a local effort to get her fired. Throughout
the growing turmoil, and with increasing publicity, Rowland continued
to make confessions of her sexual identity. Finally she lost her job.[45]

The majority opinion of the Sixth Circuit classified Rowland's first
two disclosures as mere private utterances on matters of personal interest,[46] and denied them the protection granted to public speech. It concluded: "[P]laintiff has attempted to make homosexual rights the issue in
this case. However, her personal sexual orientation is not a matter of
public concern."[47] Having once attempted to keep her bisexuality secret,
Rowland could never join a public discourse about her own dismissal.
This amputation of part of the body politic results from a view of sexual
identity as a *thing*, immutably present prior to discussion of it. But the
chain of events that led to Rowland's dismissal, more clearly than any
other narrative I have found in gay rights case law, demonstrates that the
disclosure of homosexual identity, no matter how secretive, *is always* a
political act.

Notes

1. Beller v. Middendorf, 632 F.2d 788, 804 n.13 (9th Cir. 1980) *cert. denied sub nom.* Beller
   v. Lehman, 452 U.S. 905, and *sub nom.* Miller v. Weinberger, 454 U.S. 855 (1981).

2. For an exposition of the peculiarly unstable dynamics that attend the disclosure or discovery of gay identity, see Eve Kosofsky Sedgwick, Epistemology of the Closet,
   1–90 (1990).

3. Gay Inmates of Shelby County Jail v. Barksdale, No. 84–5666, 1987 WL 37–565 (6th
   Cir. June 1, 1987).

4. *Id.* at 3–4.

5. Martha Minow, *The Supreme Court 1986 Term, Foreword: Justice Engendered*, 101 Harv.
   L. Rev. 10, 51 n.201 (1987).

6. Inmates at the Shelby County Jail may be classified as homosexual if they have been so
   classified in the past. *Gay Inmates*, no. 84–5666, 1987 WL 37–565 at 4. Even without
   this policy, peers of an inmate classified as a homosexual are not likely to forget it.

7. 822 F.2d 97 (D.C. Cir. 1987).

8. 478 U.S. 186 (1986).

9. *Padula*, 822 F.2d at 103.

10. Ga. Code Ann. § 26–2002(a) (Harrison 1983).

11. *See* Robert Cover, *Violence and the Word*, 95 Yale L.J. 1601 (1986).

12. New Hampshire House Bill 70 defined "a homosexual" as "any person who performs or
    submits to any sexual act involving the sex organs of one person and the mouth or anus

of another person of the same gender." *In re* Opinion of the Justices, 129 N.H. 290, 293, 530 A.2d 21, 22 (1987).

13. *Id.*, 129 N.H. at 295, 530 A.2d at 24.

14. The Navy's Personnel Manual, Bupersman § 340220, *quoted in* Beller v. Middendorf, 632 F.2d at 803 n.11.

15. SEC/NAV Instruction 1900.9C P6b (Jan. 20, 1978) (emphasis added), *quoted in* Dronenburg v. Zech, 741 F.2d 1388, 1389 n.1 (D.C. Cir. 1984).

16. 632 F.2d 788.

17. *Id.* at 794 (emphasis added).

18. *Id.* at 801–05.

19. *Id.* at 802 n.9.

20. *Id.*

21. Cover, *supra* note 11, at 1602–03 (footnotes omitted).

22. Janet Halley, *Heresy, Orthodoxy, and the Politics of Religious Discourse: The Case of The English Family of Love,* 15 REPRESENTATIONS 98 (1986) *reprinted in* REPRESENTING THE ENGLISH RENAISSANCE 303 (S. Greenblatt ed. 1988).

23. 741 F.2d 1388 (D.C. Cir. 1984).

24. *Id.* at 1395–96 (emphasis added).

25. Baker v. Wade, 553 F. Supp. 1121, 1148 (1982) (quoting TEX. PENAL CODE, art. 342 (1860); Harvey v. State, 55 TEX. CRIM. 199, 113 S.W. 1193 (1909).

26. MD. CRIM. LAW CODE ANN. § 554 (1987).

27. Hughes v. State, 14 Md. App. 497, 500 n.3, 287 A.2d 299, 302 n.3 (1972) (citing Blake v. State, 210 Md. 459, 124 A.2d 273 (1956)), *cert. denied,* 409 U.S. 1025 (1972).

28. Bowers v. Hardwick, 478 U.S. 186, 197 (1986) (Burger, C.J., concurring) (quoting 4 W. BLACKSTONE, COMMENTARIES ON THE LAWS OF ENGLAND 215 (1769)).

29. 741 F.2d 1388, 1395–96, 1398 (D.C. Cir. 1984).

30. *Id.* at 1398.

31. *Id.*

32. benShalom v. Secretary of the Army, 489 F. Supp. 964, 969 (E.D. Wis. 1980).

33. Army Regulations Ch. 7–5b(6), 135–178, *quoted in benShalom,* 489 F. Supp. at 969.

34. 796 F.2d 1508 (D.C. Cir. 1986), *aff'd in part, rev'd in part on other grounds sub nom.* Webster v. Doe, 108 S. Ct. 2047 (1987).

35. *Id.* at 1512 n.2.

36. Under the rule of Board of Regents v. Roth, 408 U.S. 564 (1972), a government employee adversely affected in her employment can seek due process protection of her liberty interests only if she can show an actual change of status and an accompanying "injury to the employee's good name, reputation, honor or integrity, or the imposition of a similar stigma." Doe v. Casey, 796 F.2d at 1522–23 (citing Board of Regents v. Roth, *supra,* and Doe v. United States Dept. of Justice, 753 F.2d 1092, 1105 (D.C. Cir 1985)).

37. Doe v. Casey, 796 F.2d at 1523 n.66 (quoting Beller v. Middendorf, 632 F.2d at 806).

38. Doe v. Casey, 796 F.2d at 1523.

39. *Cf.* Plessy v. Ferguson, 163 U.S. 537, 551 (1896) (If "the enforced separation of the two races stamps the colored race with a badge of inferiority [,] . . . it is not by reason of anything found in the act, but solely because the colored race chooses to put that construction upon it.").

38   40. Department of Defense Personnel Security Program Regulation, 32 C.F.R. § 154, app. H (1987), *quoted in* High Tech Gays v. Defense Indus. Sec. Clearance Office, 668 F. Supp. 1361, 1365 (N.D. Cal. 1987), *rev'd in part and vacated in part,* 895 F.2d 563 (9th Cir. 1990).

41. *High Tech Gays,* 668 F. Supp. at 1376.

42. *Id.* at 1375.

43. Swift v. United States, 649 F. Supp. 596, 597 (D.D.C. 1986) (emphasis added).

44. *benShalom,* 489 F. Supp. at 974.

45. Rowland v. Mad River Local School Dist., 730 F.2d 444 (6th Cir. 1984), *cert. denied,* 470 U.S. 1009 (1985). The full story has to be gleaned from the Sixth Circuit's majority and dissenting opinions and from Justice Brennan's dissent from the Supreme Court's denial of certiorari.

46. *Id.* at 449. The court here applies the rule set forth in Connick v. Myers, 461 U.S. 138, 147 (1983) ("[w]hen a public employee speaks not as a citizen upon matters of public concern, but instead as an employee upon matters only of personal interest, absent the most unusual circumstances, a federal court is not the appropriate forum in which to review the wisdom of a personnel decision taken by a public agency allegedly in reaction to the employee's behavior").

47. *Rowland,* 730 F.2d at 451.

CHAPTER THREE

⭲⭲⭲-◦-⭰⭰⭰

IDENTITY STRATEGIES
REPRESENTING PREGNANCY AND HOMOSEXUALITY

Dan Danielsen

THIS ESSAY EXPLORES some of the ways that courts treat pregnancy[1] and homosexuality[2] in employment discrimination cases. In examining several leading cases in this area, I map the doctrinal maneuvers and political strategies that courts have employed in representing these traits. At the same time, I explicate some of the images of gender or sexual identity that the judicial opinions contain.[3]

As an initial matter, this essay juxtaposes judicial representations of what might be construed as social opposites: pregnancy (hope of the race, social good, woman as woman, signification of women's power, signification of women oppressed, sexual difference) and homosexuality (abnegation of the race, social decline, man as woman as man, the ultimate victory of will over gender, the end result of gender hierarchy, deviance). Given the considerable differences in social perceptions of homosexuality and pregnancy—pregnancy being perceived generally as a social good and homosexuality as a social evil (or perhaps more benignly as deviance or abnormality)—one might expect that courts would treat these traits

39

quite differently. In fact, the cases dealing with pregnancy and homosexuality use quite similar modes of argument in assigning legal significance to the traits, and quite similar legal consequences flow from these modes of argument for the individuals involved in the disputes.

While a traditional analysis of legal cases dealing with homosexuality and pregnancy would focus on the outcome or holding of each case, my analysis focuses instead on the ways in which women and homosexuals are represented in each case independent of that case's outcome. The goal of this methodology is to describe the ways courts represent these traits and, by so doing, to begin to explain the apparent disjuncture between the wooden, cartoon-like images of the traits in the cases and the complexity and diversity of people's lived experiences. In principle, articulating such a critique of legal representation might assist in the development of an identity politics that would produce more authentic legal representations of women and homosexuals. As we shall see, however, this type of critical approach proves to be problematic because the images of women and homosexuals one finds in the cases turn out to be not so very different from the approaches to these "identities" that we encounter in our daily lives. In other words, if our experiences of these traits and our legal attempts to represent those experiences are in many ways indistinguishable, then the critique of legal representation as unable to capture "authentic" experience must be reexamined. Nevertheless, to the extent this form of analysis helps us to see the ways in which the simplistic, cartoon-like images of pregnancy and homosexuality in legal cases relate to a number of complex approaches to identity seen in everyday life, it enriches our understanding both of legal representation and of the multiplicity of gender and sexual identity.

Legal Treatment of Pregnancy

In several leading cases dealing with pregnancy, courts have manifested ambivalent or contradictory images of women and pregnancy and of the relationship between pregnancy and gender. As a preliminary matter, the courts rely heavily on an asserted distinction between gender and the physical condition of pregnancy. The assertion, manipulation or denial of this distinction takes three forms: sometimes the cases treat pregnancy and gender as separate, portraying pregnancy as chosen and gender as irrelevant; other times the cases portray gender and pregnancy as inseparable and treat all women, for all intents and purposes, as pregnant; and, in one instance, the Supreme Court has treated gender and the capacity for pregnancy as inextricably related, but without expressing a view on the relationship between reproductive capacity and the condition of pregnancy.

In *Geduldig v. Aiello*,[4] the United States Supreme Court held that discrimination in the provision of disability benefits in public employment based upon pregnancy was not gender discrimination.[5] The court reasoned that the State of California's exclusion of disabilities resulting from "normal" pregnancy and childbirth "does not exclude anyone . . . because of gender. . . . The program divides potential recipients into two groups— pregnant women and nonpregnant persons. While the first group is exclusively female, the second includes members of both sexes."[6] The court's distinction between pregnant women and nonpregnant persons implies two divisions: first, the stated division between pregnant women and everyone else; and second, the division between women and pregnant women. This second division is necessary in order to see pregnant women as a subset of and thus not the same as women generally. By implication, the court suggests a distinction between pregnancy as a condition (pregnant women) and gender.

While this division between pregnancy and gender might seem to make intuitive sense at one level, because clearly not all women are pregnant, the distinction incorporates certain assumptions about the nature and meaning of pregnancy. First, the distinction suggests that pregnancy is not necessarily or even intimately connected with biological sex so that pregnancy is not seen as a biological imperative but as a physical condition that some people get and some people don't. More broadly, the court suggests that to be a "woman" is not necessarily to be (or to want to be) pregnant.

By distinguishing between pregnancy and gender, the court assumes that pregnancy is voluntary, not a condition determined by need or desire. Since there are many people (women) in the world and only some of them are pregnant they must want to be that way. Once pregnancy is posited as a voluntary condition, one can easily assert that the State of California should not have to pay for a condition women choose to undertake. Thus, the "voluntariness" of the condition suggests the justification for the discrimination.

By contrast, in a number of "fetal protection" cases, where employers have prohibited or conditioned women's employment in certain toxic environments to protect fetuses or fetuses to be, courts have not asserted any distinction between the condition of pregnancy and the capacity to be pregnant. In these cases, the doctrinal focus is not on the actual condition of pregnancy, but on women as a class of potential childbearers. Far from seeing pregnancy as chosen, these courts imagine pregnancy as beyond the subjective control of women.

For example, in *Oil, Chemical & Atomic Workers International Union v. American Cyanamid Co.*,[7] an employee union challenged the company's policy of giving women the "option" of surgical sterilization or dismissal. Under its fetal protection program, American Cyanamid excluded all women of "childbearing capacity"—deemed by the company to be all women between sixteen and fifty—from the plant's inorganic pigments department, unless they could present medical evidence that they had been sterilized. The justification for this exclusion was the company's inability to keep the levels of lead in its work environment at a safe level for unborn fetuses. What was unique in this case was the company's decision to provide their female employees with the "option" of surgical sterilization as a means of avoiding dismissal from the plant:

> [The company doctors] explained to the women [employees] that such "buttonhole surgery" was simple and that it could be obtained locally at several places. The women were also told that the company's medical insurance would pay for the procedure, and that sick leave would be provided to those undergoing the surgery.[8]

Reviewing the policy under federal legislation regulating health and safety, the court of appeals that considered the case determined that the policy did not violate the legislation by causing a "hazard" for those employees who agree to the sterilization since "it requires some stretching to call the offering of a choice a 'hazard' to the person who is given the choice."[9] For the court, "[t]he decision to be sterilized grows out of economic and social factors which operate primarily outside the workplace, and hence the fetus protection policy 'is not a hazard within the meaning of the [Act].'"[10]

While the court was prepared to see being surgically sterilized to preserve one's job as an "unhappy," albeit voluntary "choice,"[11] it refused to credit women with any amount of control over their own pregnancies. The court stated as pure fact, "[i]t is clear that American Cyanamid *had to prevent exposure to lead of women of childbearing age*, and, furthermore, that the company could have not been charged under the Act if it had accomplished that by discharging the women or by simply closing the

Department."[12] Implicit in this statement is the notion that the women could not have protected themselves or their potential unborn through control over pregnancy—exclusion was a necessity. Pregnancy therefore could not be "voluntary" in the same sense as the court suggested in *Geduldig* since, if pregnancy were voluntary, it could also be controlled. Thus, the court seemed to deem irrelevant any alternatives to the blanket exclusion of fertile women. For example, the court could have required that the policy be tailored to each individual woman's desire or intent to have children, her use of effective birth control, her engagement in nonpregnancy-inducing sex, or abortion. But instead of treating pregnancy in this way—as chosen, as seen by the *Geduldig* court—*American Cyanamid* treats pregnancy as essentially inevitable.

The Supreme Court recently considered the relationship between pregnancy, gender and fetal protection programs in *International Union, UAW v. Johnson Controls, Inc.*[13] In determining that fetal protection programs that excluded only fertile women employees from toxic work environments violated employment discrimination law, the Supreme Court's majority opinion employs reasoning quite different from that used in *American Cyanamid*. Rather than equating the condition of pregnancy with capacity, and thereby treating all women as in effect pregnant, the court held that fetal protection programs illegally exclude women based upon their *capacity* to become pregnant.[14] By treating fetal protection programs as exclusions based upon women's reproductive capacity, the court asserts a "necessary" relation between pregnancy and gender, at least as it is manifested in women's ability and potential to bear children.

While *Johnson Controls* involved a fetal protection program similar in all relevant respects to the program in *American Cyanamid*, the *Johnson Controls* court asserts its different perspective in the opening lines of its opinion: "In this case we are concerned with an employer's gender-based fetal-protection policy. May an employer exclude a fertile female employee from certain jobs because of its concern for the health of the fetus the woman might conceive?"[15] First, the court makes clear that it understands fetal protection programs that exclude fertile women to be "gender-based."[16] While such a conclusion might seem obvious, one cannot presume, given the analysis in *Geduldig*, that discrimination based upon pregnancy is necessarily the same thing as discrimination based upon gender. Second, the court seems to have immediately recognized what the court in *American Cyanamid* rejected: a distinction between the capacity to become pregnant and the condition of pregnancy. In other

44   words, excluding all women who have the potential to become pregnant from toxic work environments based upon the rationale of protecting "the fetus" *which is not yet conceived* in essence treats all women as pregnant because it presumes that women who can be pregnant will be.[17]

By shifting the focus of its analysis from the condition of pregnancy (either actual or imputed) to the capacity for pregnancy, the court asserts a connection between pregnancy and gender. Further, by asserting a distinction between capacity and pregnancy, the court is able to recast the discrimination involved as based upon women's "status" as women (potential child bearers), rather than upon conduct (pregnancy). Thus, the court avoids any imputation of blame, or the justifiability of discrimination based upon the "voluntary" condition of pregnancy, by shifting its discussion from pregnancy as an "objectively identifiable physical condition"[18] to women's capacity to bear children.

The court's focus on status as opposed to conduct in *Johnson Controls* works in very much the same way the court's focus on conduct—the physical condition of pregnancy—did in *Geduldig*. In *Geduldig,* a focus on the physicality of pregnancy as a medical condition with identifiable and generalizable traits enabled the court to deemphasize the women behind the condition. Pregnancy became just another voluntary condition, whose relation to gender must be recognized but not considered. Gender (or status) faded into the background, as the court's gaze rested on pregnancy as a condition or conduct.

The court's approach in *Johnson Controls* works similarly, but in the reverse. By focusing exclusively on the potential for pregnancy rather than its physical manifestation, the court transforms the (potential) fetus from a being with interests independent of and perhaps contrary to the mother, to a potentiality that must be recognized but not taken into account. Women's status as potential childbearers takes center stage, while the condition of pregnancy, as represented by the fetus, fades into the background. The court's exclusive focus on capacity for pregnancy, and its lack of attention to pregnancy itself except by vague references to chance, leaves the court's image of the relationship between pregnancy and capacity quite open. Despite women's sexual difference from men, the condition of pregnancy might be chosen freely or it might be the product of something other than subjective choice. Further, if pregnancy is understood as chosen, then it may still be possible to rationalize differential treatment based upon the condition of pregnancy as willed conduct, even if such discrimination based upon women's reproductive capacity is prohibited. Thus, while *Johnson Controls* and anti-discrimination law might proscribe discrimination based upon women's reproductive capacity as gender discrimination, the case leaves us with an uncertain notion of the court's conception of the relationship between pregnancy as conduct and gender as status.

Legal Treatment of Homosexuality

As with pregnancy, courts have had a difficult time defining and taking account of homosexuality. Indeed, the doctrinal mechanisms and strategies courts use when encountering homosexuality are very similar to those used when considering pregnancy. As in pregnancy cases, the courts' conceptions of homosexuality can be roughly divided into three categories. Some courts deploy a distinction between homosexual status and homosexual acts or conduct that works in ways similar to the distinction between gender and pregnancy. This distinction results in a similar presumption that homosexual conduct is chosen. Other times, courts disregard any distinction between status and conduct, treating homosexual acts and homosexuality as synonymous. Finally, at least in one case, a court focuses exclusively on sexual orientation as status, treating it as stable and virtually unalterable, while leaving open the question of the legal treatment of homosexual conduct.

For example, in *Padula v. Webster*,[19] the D.C. Circuit accepted a distinction between homosexual status and conduct, creating a conception of homosexuality as chosen. In *Padula*, a female applicant challenged the constitutionality of the FBI policy of excluding homosexuals from employment. In describing its hiring policies to recruitment coordinators at various law schools, the FBI claimed that its "focus in personnel matters has been and continues to be on *conduct rather than status or preference* and [that it] carefully consider[s] the facts in each case to determine whether the conduct may affect the employment."[20] Recognizing this statement as an expression of the FBI's hiring practice, the court found:

> [T]he FBI conducted a routine background check. In addition to revealing favorable information about the applicant's abilities and character, the background investigation disclosed that appellant is a *practicing homosexual*. At a follow-up interview, Padula confirmed that she is a homosexual—explaining that although she does not

flaunt her sexual orientation, she is unembarrassed and open about it
and it is a fact well known to her family, friends and co-workers.[21]

While this passage might be read as denying any distinction between
status and conduct (the phrase "she is a homosexual" might incorporate
both), such a reading would make the court's use of the phrase "practicing homosexual" quite strange. The qualifier "practicing" suggests its
opposite—that some homosexuals are not "practicing" and do not engage
in such "conduct." The court recognizes this at several points in the
opinion, stating, "[s]exual preference per se is not a basis for hiring decisions, but sexual conduct is relevant"[22] and noting, "[a]rguably, the FBI
has committed itself not to consider the sexual orientation of an applicant
who can show he does not engage in sex, but it clearly has done no
more."[23] The court leaves aside the question whether homosexual status
"attaches to someone who does not engage in homosexual conduct,"
claiming that the issue in the case "is only whether homosexuals, when
defined as persons who engage in homosexual conduct, constitute a suspect class."[24] The court then upholds the FBI's practice of excluding
homosexuals from employment. Citing *Bowers v. Hardwick*,[25] where the
Supreme Court upheld a state statute proscribing sodomy, the court
asserts that "[i]t would be anomalous, on its face, to declare *status defined
by conduct* that many states may constitutionally criminalize as deserving
of strict scrutiny under the Equal Protection Clause."[26]

The court's use of the status and conduct distinction, and its discourse
on "status defined by conduct," function in similar ways to the gender
and pregnancy distinction implicit in *Geduldig*. For example, the invocation of homosexuals who might not engage in "homosexual conduct"
evokes inferences similar to the *Geduldig* court's distinction between
pregnant women and non-pregnant persons. For example, the *Padula*
court's suggestion of a homosexual status independent of conduct subdi-
vides the world in two distinct ways. First, it divides homosexuals into
homosexuals and practicing homosexuals. Second, it implies a distinction
between practicing homosexuals and everyone else (straight people and
non-practicing homosexuals).

Suggesting that there might be some homosexuals who do not engage
in "conduct" imputes to those who do a degree of volition. Just as with
pregnancy, the distinction between homosexual status and homosexual
conduct seems to be one of choice by the individual actors rather than a
distinction imputed by the law. Moreover, the presumed voluntariness of

the "conduct" allows the courts to further subdivide "practicing homosexuals" from non-practicing homosexuals and heterosexuals. Thus, the difference in legal treatment is not about sexuality (like gender in the pregnancy cases), but about certain specific physical activities (like the objective physical condition of pregnancy).

As with the court's treatment of pregnancy and capacity, distinguishing orientation from conduct allows the courts to generalize and aggregate homosexual experience, yet enables them to individualize each instance of homosexual conduct as an act of will. Thus, the genius of the structure in both contexts is that it locates responsibility for the separation from the "status" groups (homosexuals and women) in the individual actor, rather than in the relationship between the actor and the law, while simultaneously justifying differential legal treatment based on the voluntary nature of the conduct (homosexual acts and pregnancy).

A similar conception of homosexuality as choice informs at least part of the judicial opinion in *Rich v. Secretary of the Army.*[27] The court characterizes this case as a challenge by Rich to his discharge from the Army for fraudulent enlistment. Specifically, Rich was discharged for falsely claiming not to be a homosexual.[28] In responding to Rich's claim that the Army's policy of excluding homosexuals violated his constitutional rights, the court baldly responded: "We cannot agree. A classification based on one's choice of sexual partners is not suspect."[29] Packed into this statement are a number of comparisons and assumptions. First, and most overtly, it implies that homosexuality is chosen and not the product of some more essential difference between heterosexuals and homosexuals. In other words, the court's statement asserts some notion that unlike race or gender, homosexuality is independent of one's being because it involves choice.[30] Second, the court's use of the word "choice" suggests a simple option—one chooses the gender of one's sexual partners as one chooses the style of one's shoes. Last, the statement suggests that homosexuals must suffer the consequences of their "choice," at least for the purposes of the Constitution. The message is that Rich has his preferences and the Army has its.

Yet the same case displays the seemingly contradictory notion that homosexuality is so much at the core of Rich's being that no amount of will on his part could overcome it. Indeed, this notion lies at the very heart of the case in the claim that Rich is a homosexual and falsely denied it. The idea of fraud or falsehood suggests an idea of homosexuality that is more than mere will—if it were simply chosen one could also choose otherwise. The court therefore suggests, in some very essential sense, that Rich *is* a homosexual.

This idea is strengthened by the court's handling of evidentiary issues in the case. The only evidence the Army had of Rich's homosexuality was his own statements. As the court acknowledges:

> Despite plaintiff's numerous admissions of homosexuality [six months after enlistment], he contends that dismissal for fraudulent entry was inappropriate. He argues that his denials of homosexuality were truthful because he did not know that he was a homosexual at the time he enlisted. Not until after his enlistment did his sexual identity crystalize so that he knew he was a homosexual.[31]

Nonetheless, the court determines:

> In concluding that plaintiff's denials of homosexuality in the enlist-ment process were not truthful, General Dirks [the commanding officer] relied on plaintiff's admissions of homosexuality. While on active duty, plaintiff admitted that he was "gay" or a homosexual on at least six occasions. On one such occasion, he did so in the presence of patients and staff. Like the trial court, we believe that this was sufficient for General Dirks to conclude that plaintiff was homosex-ual before enlisting.[32]

The implication is that "homosexuality" could not involve subjective confusion because it is at some objective level fixed. Perhaps the court concluded that Rich was lying about his sexual confusion, but even this notion presupposes some background "truth" against which it can be measured.

Finally, despite Rich's statement that "the 'gay' side of his life was totally separate from his military life,"[33] the court concludes "that even if privacy interests were implicated in this case, they are outweighed by the Government's interest in preventing armed service members from engaging in homosexual conduct."[34] Despite its alternative notion that homosexual conduct is chosen, in the end the court sees homosexual con-duct as necessarily following from "homosexuality." Hence, it concludes that Rich could be excluded from the Army although there was no evi-dence of any homosexual conduct by Rich in the Army, and Rich claimed that his sexuality was separate from his military duty.

From this perspective, orientation and conduct are collapsed. As with pregnancy in *American Cyanamid,* any control Rich might have over his sexuality is treated as either ineffective or irrelevant. This "control problem" justifies the Army's preemptive intervention to protect individuals from themselves or from others—or perhaps to protect others from homosexuals.

In *Jantz v. Muci,*[35] the court takes quite a different approach to homosexuality than the courts in *Padula* and *Rich.* Jantz alleged that he was denied a teaching position based upon the school principal's perception that he had "homosexual tendencies." In determining that the complaint could not be dismissed on summary judgement, the court held that homosexual status was a suspect classification under the Equal Protection Clause. The court reasoned that if the factual allegations in Jantz's complaint were true, the school's refusal to hire him based on the suspicion that he was homosexual would violate his constitutional rights. In reaching that conclusion, the court focused exclusively on the issue of discrimination based upon Jantz's suspected homosexual orientation. Careful to make clear that Jantz was a married man with children and had coached several sports, the court never implied that homosexual conduct was at issue. By focusing on the fact that the alleged discrimination was based upon Jantz's (perceived) homosexual tendencies, the court sought to distinguish this case from cases involving homosexual acts— this man was discriminated against because of who he was (or wasn't), not what he did.

The court's exclusive focus on Jantz's status—rather than his conduct—leads the court to assert an almost irreducible and stable difference between heterosexuals and homosexuals. However, the court's avoidance of any discussion of homosexual conduct provides no stable theory of the relationship between the protected status and conduct. As in the *Johnson Controls* decision, which was compatible with either a voluntary or involuntary vision of the condition of pregnancy, the *Jantz* decision is compatible with either a voluntary or an involuntary theory of homosexual acts.

In outlining the facts of the case, the court goes to great lengths to present Jantz as a "normal," red-blooded, white American straight male. For example, the court emphasizes that Jantz is from Kansas, is degreed, is a veteran, is a secondary school teacher, is married and has played sports. One can imagine these traits being asserted by a good-hearted and disbelieving friend in response to an allegation that Jantz had "homosexual tendencies." Thus, the court from the outset attempts to cast Jantz as a fine, upstanding, regular, "straight" guy. The foil to this picture can only be the deviant/homosexual person he is accused of being.

The court's pains to present Jantz as heterosexual allows it to treat this case as one involving what might be understood as pure status. Since Jantz is "straight" and straight people don't engage in homosexual conduct (because sexuality is fixed), one might conclude the discrimination against Jantz was purely based upon his suspected homosexual status. Thus, the court simply eliminates homosexual conduct from the picture and with it the attendant need to attribute will or blame to such conduct.

Distinguishing this case from decisions by other courts, the Jantz court asserts, "[d]ecisions which have refused to impose a heightened scrutiny analysis have done so with an emphasis that persons engaging in homosexual *conduct* do not constitute a suspect class."[36] One might understand the court's forceful assertion of the status/conduct divide as a good lawyer's attempt to get around difficult precedent. However, the purpose of the court's focus here seems to be more than that. By isolating the cases dealing with homosexual conduct, the court asserts a sort of moral and/or philosophical divide between being and acting. Unlike homosexual conduct, homosexual orientation as being remains pure—a potentiality untainted by action whether chosen or compelled.

Having isolated the variable at issue—homosexual orientation—the court reasons that sexual orientation should be treated no differently from other classifications, such as race or gender. This conclusion was based largely on the court's assertion that sexual orientation is an "immutable characteristic."[37]

The *Jantz* court does a heroic job of negotiating a sea of difficult precedent. One can't help but admire the judge for attempting to take on really tough questions about homosexuality and its "origins." However, in reading the opinion, it is difficult to say what vision of homosexuality the court has in mind. Since the court focuses exclusively on homosexual status and excludes homosexual conduct from its analysis and consideration, an obvious question arises as to whom, besides Jantz and other apparent heterosexuals who are "mistaken" for homosexuals, the court believes it is describing and protecting? Further, what relationship does the court imagine to exist between a person's sexual orientation and his or her sexual conduct? One might presume that the court's notion of the inextricable relationship between a person's sexual orientation and a person's "personhood" would lead to a conclusion that sexual orientation and sex have everything to do with one another. Yet the court's analysis provides no mechanism for discerning the moral implications of homosexual conduct.

Strategies of Representation

The dominant pattern in all of the cases discussed is the assertion, manipulation and/or denial of a distinction between gender and pregnancy or homosexual status and conduct. In *Geduldig* and *Padula*, the courts focus upon the physical condition of pregnancy or homosexual conduct without investigating or describing the relationship of this conduct to gender or sexual orientation as status. The courts thus treat pregnancy and homosexual conduct as chosen and therefore culpable conduct. In *American Cyanamid* and *Rich*, the courts treat status and conduct as synonymous in the sense that all fertile women can be excluded from toxic work environments, and all homosexuals can be excluded from the Army, because one's status as a woman or a homosexual necessarily leads to pregnancy or homosexual conduct. Finally, in *Johnson Controls* and *Jantz*, the courts again assert a distinction between status and conduct. But in these cases, the courts focus exclusively on homosexual status or the ability to become pregnant, and do not address conduct. These cases treat the relationship between the potential for pregnancy and gender or between sexual orientation and identity as necessary and irreducible, but do not articulate a theory of the relationship between the fixed statuses the courts identify and pregnancy or homosexual conduct. In sum, *Johnson Controls* and *Jantz* treat pregnancy and homosexuality as fixed in certain circumstances (i.e. status), and uncertain in others (i.e. conduct).

All the cases together might be described as evidencing three strategies for understanding the relationship between traits and persons. In the first strategy, courts assert a distinction between status and conduct, and focus only on conduct. In the second strategy, courts deny any distinction between status and conduct. In the third strategy, courts treat status and conduct as separate, but focus only on status. Despite the apparently contradictory images of the traits the strategies produce, a close look reveals a commonality: each strategy seems to incorporate a different method of conceptualizing either the trait or the person or both as *object*.

Strategy 1:

In the pregnancy context, the assertion of a distinction between the condition of pregnancy and gender, with the subsequent focus on pregnancy as
conduct, serves a number of functions. The distinction divides pregnant
women from everyone else. It divides pregnant women from non-pregnant women and each individual woman from her reproductive capacity.
It works to raise a presumption that pregnancy is chosen, while severing it
from biological, social or individual need, desire or compulsion.

In the homosexuality context, the assertion of a distinction between
status and conduct, with an exclusive focus on conduct, works in similar
ways. It divides practicing homosexuals from everyone else. It also
divides practicing from non-practicing homosexuals and suggests that
each homosexual act is an individual act of will, mere conduct, profligate
deviance.

As we saw in *Geduldig* and *Padula*, an important element of this strategy was to separate the self (as women, as homosexual, as potentiality)
and the trait (as pregnancy, as homosexuality, as actuality). In positing
such a divide, the doctrine raised the presumption of will as the media-
tor between self and conduct. The focus of the inquiry then became the
nature of the conduct, its manifestations and how it could be known. For
example, in *Geduldig* the court focused on the physical characteristics of
pregnancy: its temporal nature, its biological effects, its disabling potential. In *Padula*, the court focused on an unspoken list of specific behaviors: certain kinds of sexual acts, certain specific manifestations of desire.
To the extent that these traits could be physicalized, generalized, and
categorized as conduct, the court was willing to attribute to the self subjective control over them. Another way of saying this would be that to
the extent that courts were able to objectify traits, they could imagine a
willing self acting upon those traits as objects.

Aligning this strategy with the outcomes of the cases reveals certain
consistent results. First, since the strategy posits no relation between the
objectified trait as conduct and the person as subject, except through the
act of choice, the discrimination involved in the case is treated as not
based upon status. Since pregnancy is not gender, pregnancy discrimination is not gender discrimination. Similarly, since homosexual conduct is
not the same as homosexual status, discrimination based upon conduct is
not status discrimination. Further, since the person as subject can control
the trait as object, discrimination based upon the trait can be justified.
Since the trait represents a voluntary condition, the actor can be pre-

sumed to have chosen the consequences along with the conduct. In other words, there is no reason employers or other actors can't take account of a voluntary condition.

In sum, under this strategy the trait is conceptualized as separate from any individual subject—all subjects may make all choices. Further, to the extent the trait can be isolated, physicalized or categorized, it is objectified as a finite set of identifiable conduct elements. Thus, by engaging in some or all of these conduct elements, the subject chooses the trait. Finally, the subject may be identified as a subject by recognizing its capacity to choose the trait as object.

Strategy 2:

In *American Cyanamid* and *Rich*, in contrast, the key doctrinal maneuver was to deny any distinction between the self and its conduct and to treat the self and the trait as coextensive. This strategy was managed by rejecting any distinction between status and conduct. Thus, in the pregnancy context, the potential to become pregnant was treated as equivalent to the condition of pregnancy, at least for the purposes of a prophylactic rule of exclusion from toxic work environments. The court's focus turned away from any physical manifestations of pregnancy or even pregnancy as desired conduct. Rather, its concern was with the need to exclude women (those that could get pregnant) because their relation to pregnancy was in some sense outside their control. To the extent that the doctrine recognized any subjectivity in women, it was only in the denial of women's ability to distinguish themselves from the trait through an act of will.

Similarly, in *Rich*, despite the fact that the Army had no evidence of homosexual conduct in the service, that Rich claimed that his sexuality and his Army life were totally separate, and that the court claimed to consider homosexuality as choice, Rich was still excluded from the Army. The implicit rationale of the court was that Rich was incapable of exercising any meaningful control over his sexuality—that he was in some sense his sexuality.

Thus, in these cases the doctrine objectifies the trait by objectifying the self. To the extent that the self is inseparable from the trait, the self cannot act in relation to the trait. To say it another way, the trait is somehow too essential, too central, too dangerous to leave to the control of mere will. The courts intervene as subject, treating women and homosexuals as objects.

Strategy 3:

The third strategy observed in the cases again involved the assertion of a distinction between status and conduct. In this strategy, however, courts focused on status and ignored or disparaged conduct, as seen in *Johnson Controls* and *Jantz*. In both of these cases, as in *American Cyanamid* and *Rich*, the courts sought to assert an inseparable connection between the person and the trait. However, in *Johnson Controls* and *Jantz*, the courts achieved this goal by treating the discrimination involved as based upon the person's potential for conduct rather than upon conduct itself.

For example, the *Johnson Controls* court asserted the inseparable connection between pregnancy and gender by focusing on the way the company's fetal protection program excluded fertile women based upon their potential for pregnancy. Since women's potential for pregnancy (unlike the condition of pregnancy itself?) necessarily implicates women as women, discrimination based upon women's potential for pregnancy was discrimination based upon status. Similarly, the *Jantz* court asserted, through its analysis of immutability, that sexual orientation is inextricably bound to one's being. Reasoning from its premise that one's sexual orientation is, for all meaningful purposes, fixed, the court concluded that discrimination based upon one's sexual orientation alone is discrimination based upon one's being itself, and therefore based upon status.

This strategy works, then, by isolating status as the absence of conduct. In other words, while the capacity for pregnancy may be inextricably linked to a women's gender, the condition of pregnancy may not. Pregnancy may be chosen, thereby giving rise to exclusion based upon a chosen condition, as in *Geduldig*. Alternatively, pregnancy may be compelled, giving rise to exclusion because pregnancy can be presumed from female gender, as suggested in *American Cyanamid*. Similarly, while sexual orientation may be inextricably linked to one's personhood, sexual conduct might not. For example, homosexual conduct may be chosen, thereby giving rise to exclusion as a willful deviance, as in *Padula* and certain parts of *Rich*. Alternatively, homosexual conduct may be compelled because homosexual conduct can be presumed from homosexual orientation, as in other parts of *Rich*.

This strategy, then, seems to incorporate a theory of the coextensiveness of traits and beings but only as those traits/beings are expressed as potentiality. Pregnancy is seen as indistinguishable from gender only to the extent that pregnancy is conceived of as the potential for pregnancy.

Similarly, homosexuality is treated as indistinguishable from personhood only to the extent that homosexuality is conceived of as unexpressed desire. In other words, the trait/being is objectified as existing in potentiality but never acting as subject.

The use of this strategy reveals certain common legal outcomes. For example, the focus on status results in the courts' treating the persons and traits involved as expressive of some essential difference: women are essentially different from men when that difference is expressed in the capacity to bear a child; homosexuals are essentially different from heterosexuals in the fixed nature of their object choice. Since the differences asserted are essential in nature, and not meaningfully subject to change, discrimination based upon these status differences is inappropriate. Thus, as a formal matter, women are treated the same as men to the extent that their special reproductive capacity must be acknowledged and then ignored when distributing certain employment opportunities. Similarly, homosexuals must be treated the same as heterosexuals to the extent that their difference in sexual proclivities must be recognized and then ignored when deciding whether they are suitable for certain jobs.

Yet the moment the objectified potential for pregnancy or homosexual sex is expressed or transformed into acts, the status of these traits/beings becomes unclear. To the extent the acts are treated as chosen, they might then be reobjectified as wholly external to the person, as in the cases that focused upon conduct. To the extent the acts are treated as compelled, they might be reobjectified as inseparable from the person, as in the cases which denied a distinction between status and conduct. In sum, this strategy seems to work by objectifying the person and trait as inseparably linked in eternal potentiality for action. To the extent such a strategy implies a theory of action, the objectification mechanisms in the other two strategies might apply—traits may be objectified as external to the subjects who act upon them or they might be treated as coextensive with the person, and thus the person is objectified as the trait.

Comparing the Strategies:

The courts, then, recognize traits through objectification, either by positing the traits as external to the self or as inseparable from it. Those courts that treat the traits as chosen avoid grappling with the meaning(s) of homosexuality or pregnancy as otherness. For example, by treating homosexuality as chosen conduct, a court need never explore the nature

56   of homosexual status, whether it be the product of difference or desire
or both. Similarly, by treating pregnancy as a chosen physical condition,
courts need never explore the relationship between pregnancy and being
a woman, whether in social, biological or personal terms. Thus, Strategy
One enables courts to treat all selves as the same except to the extent
that a self chooses to be other. Even then the self is not truly other
because it is only other through its conduct. Thus, all such conduct can
be understood as deviance, and deviance can be deterred, controlled,
shamed, and punished.

When courts do examine what they conceive as the inescapable otherness of women and homosexuals, they seem to do so by objectifying
women and homosexuals as coextensive with the traits. For example,
employing Strategy Two, the courts in *American Cyanamid* and *Rich*
focused on what they understood to be "real difference" between fertile
women and men or homosexuals and heterosexuals by treating women
and homosexuals as embodiments of their traits. In this conception,
women and homosexuals are so other that they have to be controlled, by
external means, through law. Thus, Strategy Two seems to represent the
otherness of pregnant women and homosexuals, but only by denying
persons any distance from or subjective control over their traits. Similarly, the *Johnson Controls* and *Jantz* courts, employing Strategy Three,
identified what they understood to be the irreducible otherness of fertile
women or homosexuals, but only by objectifying the person as the trait
forever frozen in the status of potential for conduct. Thus, otherness is
represented in the abstract, but denied any subjective reality, as women
or homosexuals only "are" but never "act."

In sum, regardless of how we might feel about the particular outcomes
of these cases, the images of pregnancy and homosexuality the cases
employ, and the relationships between these traits and identities they
suggest, remain unsatisfying. Each strategy seems to offer a different
dehumanized caricature of traits and identities in which persons can only
"act" as alienated subjects in relation to their traits, or "be" as objectified
embodiments of their traits.

Much of the power of this critique comes from the seeming alienated
insufficiency of legal representation when compared with the rich complexity and diversity of human experience. However, when we actually
compare the images in the cases with people we know, the force of the
critique becomes less clear.

For example, Strategy One, which focuses on conduct and ignores status, could be described as expressing an image of persons who experience themselves as independent of their traits. In the pregnancy context, this strategy might include women who experience pregnancy as choice and understand decisions about childbearing, sex and reproduction to be within their control. Similarly, in the homosexuality context, this strategy might be characterized as describing persons who treat sexuality as open and chosen. Included in this conception of homosexuality or pregnancy might be a number of persons we might recognize from experience: the woman who chooses to forego children to pursue her career; the woman with two boys who tries again to have a girl; the new age man who believes bisexuality to be the norm and all sex to be beautiful; or the lesbian separatist who sees her decision to live with and love women as both a political and a sexual choice.

Strategy Two, which treats conduct and status as synonymous, might be understood as invoking the experience of persons who understand themselves as their traits. This image might include the ACT-UP activist who understands his or her life as constituted around sexuality, the compulsive cruiser who knows sex is a habit but can't quite manage to give it up, the earth mother who understands herself through her womb, and the PTA parent who *is* his or her children.

Strategy Three, which recognizes status only as the potential for conduct, might capture the experience of persons who understand their relationship to their traits as potentiality. This would include, for example, women who experience pregnancy as tied to their self understanding as women and feel the ticking of a biological clock or people who experience the longing or desire for sex of one kind or another as stable or fixed, and yet never act on those desires. Several possible persons come to mind here. For example, this strategy might include the married person who desires same sex partners, but chooses to stay with his or her spouse, or the closet homosexual who prefers just to imagine what gay sex might be like, the forty year-old woman who really wants children but hasn't found the right man, or the priest who has desires but never acts on them out of religious conviction.

Thus, a critique of the cases as flawed due to their objectified images of traits and identities seems inadequate. Since the "objectified" images of women and homosexuals that inhabit the cases are also recognizable as identity strategies used by persons we know from experience, we might conclude that legal representation is no less capable than other forms of discourse to capture or miss our identities and experiences. In fact, to the

58   extent that life and identity are themselves ongoing practices of interpretation and strategy, it is difficult to distinguish, in any meaningful way,
lived experience from the legal representations of identity and experience
found in the cases.

Further, it seems problematic to critique legal representation for being
unable to express the diversity of experiences of homosexuality and pregnancy when each objectified image, whether created by treating the trait
and the self as separate or as unified, could meaningfully describe a
diverse and complex set of personalities and identities. Each image could
be understood to describe a broad spectrum of approaches to the traits
adopted by people who we would not otherwise think of as having anything at all in common, for example, the earth mother and the compulsive cruiser, or the married homosexual and the local priest. It would
seem, then, that a critique of legal representation as being in some sense
incapable of capturing experience, or less authentic than experience,
must be rethought.

Conclusion

The diverse images of identities found in the cases and in everyday life
suggest to me that there is no single doctrinal combination or political
strategy or identity politics or mode of representation that captures the
"reality" of our identities or that necessarily leads to social acceptance or
fair legal treatment. Rather, we might take our cue from the apparently
irreducible diversity, complexity and banality of the life strategies we see
around us. Perhaps we must recognize that legal discourse is itself a site
for ongoing interpretive struggle over the meaning of identity, rather
than an independent system of fixed images and rhetorical tropes which
merely describes and distorts our experience. To do so might involve a
legal practice that seeks to understand and strategize about the ways in
which legal discourse, through its very indeterminacy, might be able to
provide the space for our complexity and differentness to be represented
but not determined.

While more work must be done on how and in what ways a strategy of
legal openness might be pursued, Mary Joe Frug, speaking in the context
of gender identity and sex differences, suggests where such a practice
might lead us:

> In their most vulgar, bootlegged versions, both radical and cultural
> legal feminisms [read also the courts] depict male and female sexual

identities as anatomically determined and psychologically predictable. This is inconsistent with the semiotic character of sex differences and the impact that historical specificity has on any
individual identity. In postmodern jargon, this treatment of sexual
identity is inconsistent with a decentered, polymorphous, contingent
understanding of the subject.

Because sex differences are semiotic—that is, constituted by a system
of signs that we produce and interpret—each of us inescapably produces herself within the gender[/sexuality] meaning system,
although the meaning of gender[/sexuality] is indeterminate or
undecidable. The dilemma of difference, which the liberal equality
guarantee seeks to avoid though neutrality, is unavoidable.[38]

[However, t]his is not a proposal that we try to promote a [more]
benevolent and fixed meaning for sex differences. . . . Rather, the
argument is that continuous interpretive struggles over the meaning
of sex differences can have an impact on . . . legal power.[39]

Notes

1. Throughout this paper, I will use the term pregnancy as a metaphor for the locus of
   social, personal and legal relations of and to women's biological sex, gender, reproductive desires, capacities, or conditions.

2. As with pregnancy, I will use the terms homosexual and homosexuality as shorthand for
   representing a complex set of desires, self-understandings, social and legal relations,
   and sexualities.

3. A good deal of recent legal scholarship has focused on the social construction of "identity" and the relationship between legal practices and the way we conceive of ourselves
   and our potentialities. *See, e.g.*, ROBERTO M. UNGER, THE CRITICAL LEGAL STUDIES
   MOVEMENT (1983); Sylvia A. Law, *Homosexuality and the Social Meaning of Gender*,
   1988 WIS. L. REV. 187; Frances Olsen, *Statutory Rape: A Feminist Critique of Rights
   Analysis*, 63 TEX. L. REV. 387 (1984); Margaret J. Radin, *Market-Inalienability*, 100
   HARV. L. REV. 1849 (1987). *Cf.* ROBERTO M. UNGER, PASSION: AN ESSAY ON PERSONALITY
   (1984). Yet little work has addressed the mechanisms by which courts represent those
   aspects of ourselves that seem in part to make up our identities.

4. 417 U.S. 484 (1974). This case has been effectively overruled in the employment context by Congress through the Pregnancy Discrimination Act of 1978, 42 U.S.C.
   §2000e(k) (1992). There, Congress decided that discrimination must be treated as gender discrimination as a matter of federal statutory law. However, *Geduldig* remains the
   law of the land in terms of women's protection from pregnancy discrimination under
   the United States Constitution.

5. *Geduldig*, 417 U.S. at 494.

6. *Id.* at 496 n.20.

7. 741 F.2d 444 (D.C. Cir. 1984).

8. *Id.* at 466 (citations omitted).

9. *Id.* at 447–48.

10. *Id.* at 449 (citations omitted).

11. *Id.* at 450.

12. *Id.* (emphasis added).

13. 111 S. Ct. 1196 (1991).

14. *Id.* at 1203.

15. *Id.* at 1199.

16. *Id.* at 1202.

17. *Id.* at 1203.

18. General Elec. Co. v. Gilbert, 429 U.S. 125, 134 (1976) (quoting Geduldig v. Aiello, 417 U.S. 484, 496–97 n.20 (1981)).

19. 822 F.2d 97 (D.C. Cir. 1987).

20. *Id.* at 98–99 (quoting a letter from FBI legal council) (emphasis added).

21. *Id.* at 99 (emphasis added).

22. *Id.* at 101 n.4.

23. *Id.* at 101.

24. *Id.*

25. 478 U.S. 186 (1986) (holding that state statutes that criminalize homosexual conduct do not violate the Constitution).

26. *Padula*, 822 F.2d at 103 (emphasis added).

27. 735 F.2d 1220 (10th Cir. 1984).

28. *Id.* at 1222.

29. *Id.* at 1229 (citations omitted).

30. *See also* Watkins v. United States Army, 847 F.2d 1329, 1356–57 (9th Cir. 1988) (Reinhardt, J., dissenting). In arguing that Bowers v. Hardwick, 478 U.S. 186 (1986), bars the conclusion that homosexuals are a suspect class for the purposes of the Equal Protection Clause, Reinhardt asserted that homosexuals are different from other protected groups because their group membership is defined by conduct. *Watkins*, 847 F.2d at 1356–57 (Reinhardt, J., dissenting). Presumably the distinction asserted is that blacks and women are defined by certain immutable traits and that homosexuals are not.

31. *Rich*, 735 F.2d at 1225.

32. *Id.* (citations omitted).

33. *Id.* at 1223.

34. *Id.* at 1228.

35. 759 F. Supp. 1543 (D. Kan. 1991).

36. *Id.* at 1546–47 (citing Padula v. Webster, 822 F.2d 97 (D.C. Cir. 1987)) (other citations omitted).

37. See *id.* at 1547–48.

38. Mary Joe Frug, (1992), reprinted in this volume at 7.

39. *Id.* at 7.

PART TWO

Affirmative Action

Introduction to

AFFIRMATIVE ACTION

FEW LEGAL TOPICS in America have inspired more debate, more controversy, more vitriol from conservatives or more dissension among liberals than race-based affirmative action. While liberals have supported temporary "remedial" affirmative action in some circumstances and conservatives have largely opposed it as race-based special treatment, the debates over affirmative action have most frequently taken place in the context of a more or less shared vision of the goal for social engineering through law: the dream of a colorblind society where equality of opportunity makes race irrelevant and where "merit" and "achievement" determine one's place in the social hierarchy.

The essays in this part challenge both the liberal and the conservative positions on affirmative action by explaining and critiquing the supremacy of colorblindness as the dominant goal of American racial politics. The authors enact this challenge, in part, by adopting radical race consciousness as a methodology. Through their conscious refusal to deny racial difference, even as they explore its multiple, complex and shifting meanings, the authors engage and expose the ideology of colorblindness. In doing so, they undermine traditional conceptions of merit, equality and entitlement. Newly conceived, affirmative action becomes a practice, a politics and a commitment to race consciousness, rather than an embarrassing if necessary reminder that race (still) matters notwithstanding four decades of civil rights struggle in law.

Gary Peller demonstrates that the unstated hegemony of colorblind meritocracy emerged as the dominant ideology out of the civil rights struggles of the 1960s and 70s. The dominance of this conception of racial politics was not inevitable; indeed, it prevailed over an alternative conception articulated primarily by black nationalists. While the nationalists sought to assert racial identity as a basis for solidarity, power and community, the integrationists (as Peller calls them) aimed to transcend racial categories through reason and neutrality. As integrationist discourse gained prominence, any assertion of the importance of racial categories came to seem problematic. In this context, nationalist discourse, with its focus on the importance of race, came to seem racist and even indistinguishable from white supremacy. Peller shows the contingency of integrationism by demonstrating how the conceptions of racial justice and legal equality that have come to dominate traditional modern American discourse about race are themselves the articulation of a particular ideology, one for which racial identity seems racist and race consciousness a failure of transcendent reason.

From an integrationist perspective, race-based legal regimes like affirmative action must always seem at best problematic and at worst counterproductive. Through his historical analysis, Peller attempts to uncover and reclaim race consciousness from its roots in black nationalist discourse. Duncan Kennedy and Patricia Williams suggest how such race consciousness might operate.

Kennedy puts forward two different frameworks of justification for a radical and continuous program of affirmative action in the allocation of jobs in legal academia, both based on an explicit consciousness of race. First, he argues that legal academic jobs are essentially positions of political power and that no one group should control access to or the message of academic institutions. The value at stake is political participation, and the distribution of participatory rights of citizenship—like the right to vote—does not raise a question of merit. Thus, he argues that legal academic jobs should be distributed to insure the participation of minority groups in the political power of legal academic institutions as well as in the production of the ideologies legal academic institutions disseminate.

In his second argument for affirmative action, Kennedy builds on black nationalist insights regarding group identity, integrationist images of the cultural value of group interaction and postmodern notions of subjectivity. Kennedy argues that individual identities are constituted in the context of participation in and definition by groups. While conceding that individual experiences, interactions and cultural understandings within groups may differ, Kennedy maintains that certain groups as a whole are consistently subordinated to others in the struggle for power and economic well-being. These patterns of dominance and subordination influence experiences, outlooks and consciousness, even if they do not determine individual identity. Accordingly, Kennedy argues that members of subordinated groups are likely to have perspectives, experiences and knowledge that are unlikely to be found among members of a dominant group. Kennedy asserts that these perspectives are valuable and important and that large scale affirmative action will likely increase their representation in academic institutions. Further, even if the value of these alternative perspectives is contested, affirmative action can still be justified on the grounds that members of the dominant group who control the academic institutions should not hold exclusive power to determine the value of such discourse through the distribution of academic jobs.

Patricia Williams asserts race consciousness by exploring the irrepressible presence of race even in the colorless promise of colorblind formal equality. For Williams, colorblindness is not neutrality. Rather it is the omission of race, the refusal to see the multiple layers of racial meaning in culture. "It is thus that omission becomes a form of expression, as oxymoronic as that sounds," writes Williams. From this perspective, racial policies of so-called colorblindness both deny the continued experience of racial subordination in modern American society and render invisible the presence, participation and importance of people of color in Western culture.

In contrast to this racial blindness, William's affirmative action becomes not a remedial act for past wrongs, but a prerequisite to equality.

> It is thus that affirmative action is an affirmation; the affirmative act of hiring—or hearing—blacks is a recognition of individuality that includes blacks as a social presence, ... [it] is to require, to seek, and to value a multiplicity of knowledge systems, in pursuit of a more complete sense of the world in which we live. Affirmative action in this sense is as mystical and beyond-the-self as an initiation ceremony. It is an act of verification and vision, an act of social as well as professional responsibility.

In rejecting the aspiration for the colorblind utopia of the integrationists, Peller, Kennedy and Williams assert a race consciousness in law and culture that is neither an apologist deviation from otherwise "race-neutral" norms nor the claim of any essential racial difference. Rather it is

66   an affirmative recognition of the multiple political, social and cultural meanings of race in American society; an affirmation of the presence, value and participation of race and people of color in the production of culture; and a commitment to challenge the stability of systems of dominance and subordination through the continuous affirmative assertion of "the difference that difference makes" even as the meanings of difference are ever changing. Affirmative action becomes, then, not a remedy for past acts, but a methodology of struggle, engagement and perhaps connection.

CHAPTER FOUR

><->-O-<>-><

RACE CONSCIOUSNESS
Gary Peller

Nationalism and Integration

IN THIS ESSAY, I want to explore the ideological roots of a particular political moment—in which the repudiation of race consciousness defines
conventional civil rights thinking—by contrasting integrationist and
black nationalist images of racial justice, and by comparing the ways that
white and black communities have understood race. My argument, in
summary form, is that the boundaries of today's dominant rhetoric about
race were set in the late 1960s and early 1970s, in the context of an
intense cultural clash between black nationalists on one side, and integrationists (white and black) on the other. Current mainstream race reform
discourse reflects the resolution of that conflict through a tacit, enlightened consensus that integrationism—understood as the replacement of
prejudice and discrimination with reason and neutrality—is the proper
way to conceive of racial justice, and that the price of the national commitment to suppress white supremacists would be the rejection of race
consciousness among African-Americans.

To understand the dynamics that produced this particular cultural
bargain, it is important to comprehend the different meaning that race

68   consciousness historically represents for whites and blacks in America. Within the white community, the conflict over race traditionally has been structured around an opposition between white supremacists who supported segregation, and white liberals and progressives committed to integration and civil rights reform. To white liberals and progressives, looking through the prism of integrationist ideology, a nationalist conception of racial identity was understood to distinguish backward, ignorant whites from cosmopolitan, educated whites. Whites who took race as central to their self-identity thereby expressed a commitment to racial supremacy, whereas whites who opposed racism understood that opposition to require the transcendence of racial identity in favor of integration and color-blindness. In other words, most white liberals and progressives, projecting themselves as the enlightened avant garde of the white community, automatically associated race nationalism with the repressive history of white supremacy, and never developed either a consciousness or a political practice that comprehended racial identity and power as centrally formative factors in American social relations.

In contrast, within at least a faction of the African-American community, advocates of black nationalism consistently opposed an integrationist understanding of racial progress. Instead, black nationalists asserted a positive and liberating role for race consciousness, as a source of community, culture, and solidarity to build upon rather than transcend. They developed a thoroughgoing critique of integrationism as either inevitably, or at the very least historically, linked to assimilation. Within the white community, the issue of race consciousness symbolically divided whites committed to racial justice from whites committed to racial domination. But within the black community, the issue of race consciousness historically divided those committed to norms of racial solidarity from two groups: first, from assimilationists who found white culture more attractive; and second from those who concluded that if the price of black racial identity was the continuation of white racial identity in its traditional, repressive form, then integration was preferable.

The conflict between nationalists and integrationists in the late 1960s and early 1970s represented a critical juncture in American race relations. At that time, black nationalism arguably had overtaken integrationism as the dominant ideology of racial liberation among African-Americans, while virtually all liberal and progressive whites embraced a theory of integration as the ultimate definition of racial justice. Although there has been some refinement since this historical moment—particularly with the development of a national commitment to a limited form of "cultural pluralism"—the basic boundaries of contemporary mainstream thinking about race were set in the early 1970s when a loose coalition of "moderate" African-Americans joined with liberal and progressive whites to resist—and equate—black nationalists and white supremacists.

The reemergence of race consciousness among scholars of color should be an occasion for liberal and progressive whites to reevaluate our position concerning the racial compromise that mainstream visions of racial justice embody. I believe that the failure of the progressive and liberal white community to comprehend the possibility of a liberating rather than repressive meaning of race consciousness has distorted our understanding of the politics of race in the past and obscures the ways that we might contribute to a meaningful transformation of race relations in the future. Specifically, deep-rooted assumptions of cultural universality and neutrality have removed from critical view the ways that American institutions reflect dominant racial and ethnic characteristics, with the consequence that race reform has proceeded on the basis of integration into "white" cultural practices—practices that many whites mistake as racially neutral. And even when a commitment to consider the possible ethnocentrism of institutional practices exists, the attempt to construct a racially neutral culture has commonly produced only bland institutional forms whose antiseptic attempts at universalism have ensured the alienation of anyone with any cultural identity at all.

The Analytics and Assumptions of Integrationism

[A] segregated school system isn't necessarily the same situation that exists in an all-white neighborhood. A school system in an all-white neighborhood is not a segregated school system. The only time it's segregated is when it is in a community other than white, but at the same time is controlled by the whites. So my understanding of a segregated school system, or a segregated community, or a segregated school, is a school that's controlled by people other than those that go there. . . . On the other hand, if we can get an all-black school, that we can control, staff it ourselves with the type of teachers that have our good at heart, with the type of books that have in them many of the missing ingredients that have produced this inferiority complex in our people, then we don't feel that an all-black school is necessarily a segregated school. It's only segregated when it's controlled by someone from outside. I hope I'm making my point. I just can't see where if

white people can go to a white classroom and there are no Negroes
present and it doesn't affect the academic diet they're receiving, then
I don't see where an all-black classroom can be affected by the absence
of white children.... So, what the integrationists, in my opinion, are
saying, when they say that whites and blacks must go to school
together, is that the whites are so much superior that just their presence in a black classroom balances it out. I can't go along with that.[1]
    —Malcolm X, April 8, 1964
        Answers to Questions at the Militant Labor Forum (New York)

Today the story of the civil rights struggle commonly is told in linear
fashion, as if progress in race relations followed a teleological evolution—
from an ignorant time when racial status was taken to signify real and
meaningful differences between people, to the present, enlightened time,
when race properly is understood in mainstream culture not to make a
difference except as vestiges of unfortunate historical oppression or in
terms of a vague and largely privatized "ethnic heritage." This sense of
linear evolution has lent an aura of inevitability to the story, as if
progression from the racial caste system of American slavery to the wide-
spread acceptance of integration and the transcendence of race consciousness as the unquestioned goals of social progress was historically
determined. But the process has been neither linear nor inevitable. The
institution of racial integration as a social norm results from a cultural
struggle—played out in various theaters of social power—over the meaning of racial domination and racial justice in America. The sense of integrationism as the inevitable means to achieve racial enlightenment
reflects both the institutionalization of a particular understanding of what
racism means and the marginalization, not only of white supremacists,
but also of the opposing analysis represented in the 1960s by Malcolm X
and other black nationalists.

    It is no longer controversial within mainstream American culture that
the goal of racial justice consists of something called "integration." The
disagreements today revolve around how to achieve integration and identify its violation, or, more generally, over how widely to enforce integrationist norms. Conservatives and liberals distinguish themselves according
to their positions on affirmative action; on whether intent must exist for a
determination of discrimination; on whether rights against discrimination
should be understood on a de jure or de facto basis; and whether there is
merely a negative right against segregation, rather than an affirmative
right to attend integrated institutions. To be sure, these are important
issues, and often the choice between a narrow or a wide interpretation of

the integrationist vision makes a real, material difference. But the constant and repetitive struggle over the proper way to implement integrationist norms suppresses from consideration the fact that the disagreements occur only within the confines of a shared set of beliefs that comprehend racism as a form of "discrimination."

I want to discuss here how integrationism has come to define official racial enlightenment less than thirty years after the goal of racial integration symbolized demands for radical reform of American society. I argue that integrationism has achieved mainstream, institutionalized status in part because it has been domesticated. Rather than constituting a broad-ranging indictment of the reigning social structure, as it once did, the goal of civil rights itself has been "integrated" into the dominant cultural rhetoric. Seen through the universalizing lenses of the liberal American ideology of progress and enlightenment, racial integration appears as part of a general societal discourse that comprehends legitimacy in terms of policing borders between rationality and objectivity on the one hand and prejudice and bias on the other.

The point of discussing integrationism in this way is to show that the currently dominant vision of racial justice is not inevitable or self-evident, but rather is situated within the confines of a particular set of social, cultural, and philosophical assumptions about the world. Its dominance presupposes a set of political and social choices that could have been—and can be—made differently.

The Analytic Components of Integrationism

The goal of racial integration has taken many forms and has been supported by various worldviews. At one time, the idea of racial integration represented a powerful, spiritually-rooted social resistance movement that threatened to destabilize the status quo of American institutional life in profound ways. Under the banner of integrationism, hundreds of thousands of people mobilized to challenge the political, economic, and cultural power relations in cities and towns across the country, employing tactics that included mass protest, economic boycotts, civil disobedience, sit-ins, and strikes.[2] There is therefore nothing intrinsic to the concept of racial integration that demands that it be understood in the way I am about to describe it. What I want to capture here is the general cultural sense that became dominant in the 1960s and 1970s of what racism consists of and how to overcome it.

From this perspective, integrationism should be understood to comprise a set of attitudes and beliefs for perceiving the meaning of racist domination and for identifying the goals of racial justice. The concepts of prejudice, discrimination, and segregation are the key structural elements of this ideology. Each idea embodies a different manifestation of what is seen as the central aspect of racism—the distortion of reason through the prism of myth and ignorance.

In the integrationist perspective, racism is rooted in consciousness, in the cognitive process that attributes social significance to the arbitrary fact of skin color. The mental side of racism is accordingly represented as either "prejudice"—the prejudging of a person according to mythological stereotypes—or "bias"—the process of being influenced by subjective factors. The key image here is of irrationalism—the problem with prejudice is that it obscures the work of reason by clouding perception with beliefs rooted in superstition.[3] The paradigmatic manifestation is the white supremacist myth structure that asserts natural, biological differences between blacks and whites—the familiar identification of whites with the qualities of intelligence, industriousness, and piousness, and the corresponding association of blacks with the qualities of dullness, laziness and lustfulness.[4] The opposite of the ignorance that appears as racism is knowledge—knowledge gleaned from actual interracial experience rather than mythologies of stereotype.

In the integrationist ideology, racism achieves social form when the distortion of prejudice in consciousness subsequently translates into practice. Here racism manifests itself in the practice of "discrimination," in the disparate treatment of whites and blacks that the irrational attribution of difference is supposed to justify. The paradigm practice of racism in its systematic, social form was the Jim Crow system of de jure segregation, which institutionalized racial apartheid on the basis of an ideology of white supremacy.[5] And just as "prejudice" is implicitly contrasted with knowledge, discrimination is contrasted with neutrality—the social practice of equal treatment.

The solution to segregation, then, is integration, understood as a social vision opposed to racism, in each realm in which racism manifests itself. Within consciousness, integration means overcoming prejudice based on skin color. Therefore, reflecting one dimension of integrationist ideology, people began to understand themselves as possible racists to the extent they believed in irrational images of people based on skin-color stereotypes. The ideal was to transcend stereotypes in favor of treating people as individuals, free from racial group identification.[6]

At the level of practice, the integrationist cure for discrimination is equal treatment according to neutral norms. And at the institutional level, integrationism obviously means an end to the social system of racial segregation. In sum, the cure for racism would be equal treatment on an individual level and integration on an institutional level. In any event, integrationists believed the two would go hand in hand. Once neutrality replaced discrimination, equal opportunity would lead to integrated institutions;[7] experience in integrated institutions would, in turn, replace the ignorance of racism with the knowledge that actual contact provides. This deep link between racism and ignorance on the one hand, and integration and knowledge on the other, helps explain the initial focus of integrationists on public education: Children who attended integrated schools would learn the truth about each others' unique individuality before they came to believe stereotypes rooted in ignorance. By attending the same schools, children would in turn have equal opportunity at the various roles in American social life.[8]

The integrationists' diagnosis of the distortions of the white supremacy ideology focuses on the failure of white supremacists to recognize the universal characteristics shared by whites and blacks. According to the integrationists, white racists perceive the world through a false structure of "same" and "other" that utilizes a concept of blacks as "other" and denies that the attributes that characterize whites exist in blacks. Thus the rationality and piousness that supposedly characterize whites are, within racist ideology, denied to blacks. The integrationist proposes to correct this situation by distributing these characteristics across race lines: Blacks can be rational and pious; whites can be emotional and lustful. In other words, according to integrationist ideology, racists make the mistake of "essentializing" racial categories and believing that there is some necessary, intrinsic relationship between race and particular social characteristics. Integrationists are committed to the view that race makes no real difference between people, except as unfortunate historical vestiges of irrational discrimination.[9] In an extreme form of the integrationist picture, the hope is that when contact occurs between different groups in society, not only race, but all "ethnic identity will become a thing of the past."[10]

Race, Universal Reason, and Liberal Progress

Of course, this is a highly abstracted model of what I mean by the "ideology of integrationism"; I assume that these general ideas about race are so familiar that simply evoking them calls to mind the fuller meaning of integrationism in mainstream American culture. But at the same time it is important to grasp the integrationist worldview at this level of generality. Integrationists comprehend racism at a high level of abstraction in part because they wish to transcend the bias of particularity that they see as the root of racist consciousness. Integrationism, in short, links up with a broader set of liberal images—images that connect truth, universalism, and progress.

A commitment to a form of universalism, and an association of universalism with truth and particularism with ignorance, forms the infrastructure of American integrationist consciousness.[11] This universalism is the common theme that connects the integrationist analytic distinctions between reason and prejudice, objectivity and bias, neutrality and discrimination, and integration and segregation. Each dichotomy envisions a realm of impersonality, understood as the transcendence of subjective bias and contrasted with an image of a realm of distortion where particularity and stereotype reign. Integrationist beliefs are organized around the familiar enlightenment story of progress as consisting of the movement from mere belief and superstition to knowledge and reason, from the particular and therefore parochial to the universal and therefore enlightened.[12]

Within this frame for organizing social perception, controversy revolves around how to categorize particular social practices—as either rational and neutral or irrational and biased. Liberals and conservatives can be distinguished by how far they believe the realms of either bias or neutrality extend. But conservatives' and liberals' basic comprehension of racial justice has the same underlying structure—to universalize institutional practices in order to efface the distortions of irrational factors like race, to make social life neutral to racial identity. To both liberals and conservatives, racism consists of a form of distortion that could be superseded by an aracial arena of social understanding. Once we remove prejudice, reason will take its place; once we remove discrimination, neutrality will take its place; and once we remove segregation, integration will take its place.[13]

One way that this universalizing character of integrationism manifests itself in perception is that diverse social phenomena begin to appear the same because they are all viewed through the same analytic lens. From within this structure for cataloguing and organizing thinking about social life, racism becomes equivalent to other forms of prejudice and discrimination based on irrational stereotype. Social domination based on race, gender, sexual preference, religion, age, national origin, language, and physical disability or appearance, can all be categorized as the same phenomena because they all represent bias—understood as a deviation from a neutral, rational standard. Similarly, the fact that relations between Anglos and African-Americans, Asians, and Hispanics are all perceived as presenting the issues of "discrimination against racial minorities" in legal and political discourse reflects the same structure of abstraction. From this structure, it begins to appear that the social subordination of various groups does not have a complex, particular, and historical context, but rather is a formal, numeric problem of the relations of majorities to minorities, unified under the concept "discrimination."

Moreover, given this universalist dimension to integrationist thinking, it is plausible to conceive of a category of "reverse racism," which is really not "reverse" at all. Since racism means a deviation from a universal norm of objectivity, it can be practiced by anyone, and anyone can be its victim, regardless of their particular historical circumstances or power relations. Thus, within the integrationist ideology, a black person who stereotypes whites is racist in the same way as a white person who harbors prejudice against blacks. And blacks who discriminate against whites are guilty of the same kind of racism as whites who discriminate against blacks. Anyone can engage in racism because we can identify racism from a vantage point of race neutrality, of not making someone's race count for anything. In short, the symmetry of the integrationist picture is rooted in the idea that racism consists of possessing a race consciousness about the world, in thinking that race should make a difference in social relations.

Finally, given the idea of immutability common to categories of "discrimination," the story of the struggle against racism can be related in a way that follows the basic script of liberal progress more generally. Race consciousness is associated with status-based social coercion, where individuals are treated in a particular way because of the arbitrary fact of membership in a social group they did not choose. The transcendence of race consciousness represents a social movement toward the freedom of the individual to choose group identification. Like classical images of the common law, the vision underlying integrationist ideology is of American culture working itself pure by overcoming the distortions of various kinds of prejudice in favor of the increasing rationalization of institutional forms, which in turn provides greater individual liberty to choose, free of coercive social power. Freedom from racial discrimination is but one instance of the historical move from status to contract, from caste to individual liberty.[14] Individualism and universalism are thereby linked together.[15]

The aims of racial integration seem self-evident because they are one part of a web of meaning that constitutes the dominant ideology of the nature of social progress itself. The meaning of race has been grafted onto other central cultural images of progress, so that the transition from segregation to integration and from race consciousness to race neutrality mirrors movements from myth to enlightenment, from ignorance to knowledge, from superstition to reason, from the primitive to the civilized, from religion to secularism,[16] and, most importantly, the historical self-understanding of liberal society as representing the movement from status to individual liberty. In other words, integrationist ideology comprehends the issue of racial domination by viewing race relations through stock images about the nature of progress in liberal society and through the prism of a qualitative difference between liberal enlightenment and feudal hierarchy. The struggle against racism thus appears natural and inevitable, as simply another part of the teleological progression toward the liberation of social life.[17]

Integration and Legitimation

This liberal integrationist approach to race has some real attractions. The image of universality, and its correlate aim of transcending racial consciousness, forms a large part of the deep appeal that the integrationism vision has for many of us. This vision seems to reflect, at the ideological level, the occasional glimpses we attain in personal relations of a deep, shared identity as fellow human beings in what are often the very best moments of social life. The aspiration for racial integration confirms our sense of the possibility of true and authentic relations that transcend racial status and other forms of cultural distance and difference. And integrationism appeals to the utopian ideal that these moments could be translated into organized institutional practices because, at the core, we are all the same, "regardless of race."

But this universalism also marks the narrowing limits of integrationist ideology. Understanding this aspect of integrationism helps one to comprehend how well-intentioned people could view the manner in which racial integration has actually proceeded in American life as, without question, a progressive reform of race relations.

As I have described it, integrationism is organized around an image of reason and neutrality that represents the transcendence of bias and prejudice. The liberal discourse of race represented by integrationism actually contains within itself two distinct ways to perceive social practices. On the one hand, the possibility of bias and prejudice constitutes a language of critique and reform that provides a framework to articulate what needs to be changed in society. On the other hand, this liberal discourse also constitutes a narrative of legitimation, a language for concluding that particular social practices are fair because they are objective and unbiased. This second aspect of liberal discourse embodies a conception of a realm of social life outside the influence of racial history and politics.

Take, for example, the debate about affirmative action. In this context, race consciousness is employed by those interested in race reform. The familiar "dilemma" that surrounds affirmative action is that it requires the use of race as a socially significant category, although the deepest aims of integrationist ideology point toward the transcendence of race consciousness.

The dominant discourse about affirmative action reflects the core categories of the liberal theory of race that I described. The issues in the affirmative action debate are organized around the same structural opposition between reason and bias. Here, the category of "merit" represents the universal, impersonal side of integrationist perception. The use of race-conscious means to distribute social goods is problematic because it represents a deviation from the impersonality of merit. Thus, liberal support of affirmative action has always been defensive because its proponents themselves experience it, at least in part, as dissonant with their most fundamental convictions. Affirmative action has been characterized as merely an exceptional remedy for past injustice, rather than an affirmative right rooted in present social circumstances. It has been characterized as temporary and only necessary to achieve integration, at which time equal opportunity can take over. And affirmative action has been defended on the grounds that its beneficiaries have suffered from a "deprived" background, so that putting a thumb on the side of minorities in the scales of social decisionmaking helps even out the otherwise rationalized competition for social goods.[18]

Alternatively, affirmative action has been defended on the grounds of promoting diversity, an approach that challenges the notion of merit as the sole basis on which to distribute social opportunities. According to this justification, merit is only one value to be vindicated in determining admission to various institutions. Alongside merit is the value of having

78   a racially diversified society, a justification that can be used to counter-
balance merit as a criterion.[19]

Whether articulated in terms of remedy or diversity, this discourse
assumes that minority applicants are less qualified on neutral, impersonal, and objective criteria. Thus, to integrate institutions, we must
compromise meritocratic standards either temporarily—in order to break
the cycles of institutional life that racial domination entailed—or perma-
nently, by diffusing merit with other ends such as diversity. Today, conservative integrationists preach a principled commitment to colorblindness in institutional practices, even if it results in segregated institutions, and liberal integrationists advocate limited, effects-oriented race
consciousness in order to ensure that some integration actually takes
place. But from within the discourse through which they perceive the
issues, both commit to the premise that the category of merit itself is
neutral, impersonal, and somehow developed outside the economy of
social power, with its significant currency of race, class, and gender, that
marks American social life.

Given their view of the pervasive nature of American racism, at least
in the recent past, it is conceivable that integrationists might have
demanded a radical transformation of social practices before they assumed the existence of merit-based decisionmaking. But instead, integrationists assumed that fair, impersonal criteria simply would be what
remained once the distortion of race consciousness was removed. One
manifestation of this assumption was that the purportedly broad social
transformation reflected in the national struggle against racism resulted
in hardly any change in administrative personnel. The transformation
from a Jim Crow to an integrationist racial regime was thought to require
only a change in the rules of social decisionmaking. The same whites who
once carried out the formal program of American apartheid actually kept
their jobs as the decisionmakers charged with evaluating merit in the
employment offices of companies and in the admissions offices of schools
in the post-segregation world. In institution after institution, progressive
reformists have found themselves struggling over the implementation of
racial integration with the former administrators of racial segregation,
many of whom soon constituted an old guard "concerned" over the dete-
rioration of "standards."

The point here is not to suggest that racism so permeated those who
managed segregated institutions that the only solution was to purge them
all. There can be no doubt that many people who kept their jobs should

at least have been relieved of institutional authority—but that is not my point. I want to suggest that the continuity of institutional authority symbolizes the limited nature of social reform that most integrationists associated with the achievement of racial justice.

Even more dramatic than the continuity of personnel (since the particular people in power eventually age, retire and die), the same criteria that defined the "standards" during the period of explicit racism continue to be used, as long as they cannot be linked "directly" to racial factors. Within liberal integrationism, racism, seen to consist of a deviation from neutral, impersonal norms, focused on the exclusion of people of color, with the idea that all the rest of the cultural practices of formerly segregated institutions would stay the same. From within the integrationist ideology of neutral standards, no conceptual base existed from which integrationists could question whether "standards," definitions of "merit," and the other myriad features of the day-to-day aspects of institutional life constructed or maintained during segregation might have reflected deeper aspects of a culture within which the explicit exclusion of blacks seemed uncontroversial. And integrationists, organizing their perception of racial justice around images of objectivity, rationality, and neutrality, never considered whether this language for distinguishing the worthy from the unworthy itself might serve to help justify racial domination— if not to its victims, then at least to white beneficiaries who need to believe that their social positions are the result of something more than the brute fact of social power and racial domination.[20]

Liberal integrationist ideology is structured so that some social practices are taken out of the economy of race relations, and understood to be undistorted by racial power. To be sure, no analytically necessary point from within the terms of the integrationist view of race exists at which the line between racial discrimination and neutral meritocracy must be drawn. One can imagine that the very definition of what constitutes qualifications to attend law school, to work as a police officer, to own a home, to live in a particular neighborhood, or to have a particular income could be challenged as either directly rooted in the distortions of race consciousness or more indirectly dependent on a rhetoric through which the powerful generally justify their share of the distribution of social benefits. And, in some contexts, reform within the integrationist tradition followed this path. But integrationism also labels the distribution of social goods as impersonal and neutral once we remove "distortions" like race consciousness. Integrationists tend to understand racism as a partic-

80   ular, identifiable deviation from an otherwise rational decisionmaking process that is not itself based in the history of social struggle between groups and worldviews. This narrow image of the domain of racial power characterizes the tendency of liberal integrationism to become part of a self-justifying ideology of privilege and status. The realm of "neutral" social practices from which to identify bias and deviation constitutes a whole realm of institutional characteristics removed from critical view as themselves historical, contingent and rooted in the particularities of culture—a realm that is itself a manifestation of group power, of politics. This obscures the possibility that the very core values of liberal integrationists—the ideals of objectivity, rationality, and neutrality—were historically constructed out of particular perspectives and as responses to specific historical situations rather than representing the transcendence of perspective itself.

Notes

1. Malcolm X, By Any Means Necessary: Speeches, Interviews And A Letter 16–17 (George Breitman ed., 1970).

2. There is now a substantial body of work describing the early years of the "direct action" civil rights movement. I have found most useful Rhoda Blumberg, Civil Rights: The 1960s Freedom Struggle (1984); Taylor Branch, Parting The Waters: America In The King Years, 1954–1963 (1988) (focusing on King and the Southern Christian Legal Conference (SCLC)); Robert Brisbane, Black Activism: Racial Revolution In The United States, 1954–1970 (1974); Thomas R. Brooks, Walls Come Tumbling Down: A History Of The Civil Rights Movement, 1940–1970 (1974); Claybourne Carson, In Struggle: SNCC And The Black Awakening Of The 1960s (1981); David J. Garrow, Bearing The Cross: Martin Luther King, Jr., And The Southern Christian Leadership Conference (1986); August Meier & Elliot M. Rudwick, C.O.R.E., A Study of the Civil Rights Movement, 1942–1968 (1973); Aldon D. Morris, The Origins of the Civil Rights Movement: Black Communities Organizing For Change (1984); Benjamin Muse, The American Negro Revolution: From Nonviolence To Black Power (1968); Harvard Sitkoff, Struggle For Black Equality, 1954–1980 (1981); Emily Stoper, The Student Non-Violent Coordinating Committee: The Growth of Radicalism in a Civil Rights Organization (1989); Robert Weisbrot, Freedom Bound: A History of America's Civil Rights Movement (1990); Howard Zinn, SNCC: The New Abolitionists (1965); James A. Colaico, *Martin Luther King, Jr., and the Paradox of Nonviolent Direct Action*, 47 Phylon 16 (1986).

3. The classic text embodying this perspective is Gordon W. Allport, The Nature Of Prejudice (1954). The comprehension of racism as embodied in the idea of prejudice has had wide influence in academic study. *See* Robert Blauner, Racial Oppression In America 19 (1972) ("The analysis of race by social scientists has been shaped by an underlying assumption that the concern with color in human society is ultimately irrational or nonrational.").

4. *See* Michael J. Cassity, Legacy Of Fear: American Race Relations To 1900 at 32–63 (1985); St. Clair Drake, Black Folk: Here And There 28–30 (1987) (explaining the origin and perpetuation of the stereotype of "the Negro"); George M. Fredrickson, The

BLACK IMAGE IN THE WHITE MIND: THE DEBATE IN AFRO-AMERICAN CHARACTER AND DESTINY, 1817–1914 53–58, 275–82 (1972); REGINALD HORSMAN, RACE AND MANIFEST DESTINY: THE ORIGINS OF AMERICAN RACIAL ANGLO-SAXONISM 43–61, 116–57 (1981); WINTHROP D. JORDAN, WHITE OVER BLACK: AMERICAN ATTITUDES TOWARD THE NEGRO, 1550–1812 (1968); IDUS A. NEWBY, JIM CROW'S DEFENSE: ANTI-NEGRO THOUGHT IN AMERICA 1900–1930 (1968); COMER VANN WOODWARD, THE STRANGE CAREER OF JIM CROW 56–95 (1958); Kimberlé Crenshaw, *Race, Reform, and Retrenchment: Transformation and Legitimation in Antidiscrimination Law*, 101 HARV. L. REV. 1331, 1373–76 (1988).

5. *See* GEORGE M. FREDRICKSON, WHITE SUPREMACY (1981); COMER VANN WOODWARD, *supra* note 4. The classic study is JOHN DOLLARD, CASTE AND CLASS IN A SOUTHERN TOWN (1949). *See generally* Abdul Alkalimat, *The Ideology of Black Social Science, in* THE DEATH OF WHITE SOCIOLOGY 173, 175 (Joyce A. Ladner ed. 1973) (linking prejudice, discrimination, and segregation as key elements of restrictive "white" ideology about racism).

6. *See* Leonard Fein, *Community Schools and Social Theory: The Limits of Universalism, in* COMMUNITY CONTROL OF SCHOOLS 76, 91 (Henry M. Levin ed., 1970). According to Leonard Fein,

> [T]he central tenet of liberals, when dealing with race, has been to assert its irrelevance. The argument has been that color is an accidental characteristic, which, in the truly rational, liberated, social order, ceases to have any empirical correlates.... The main thrust of the civil rights movement has been, therefore, in the direction of persuading white America to become color-blind. The corollary of the liberal ethic that white people ought not to pay attention to the blackness of Negroes was the proposition that Negroes ought not to pay attention to their own blackness.

James Farmer tells a story indicating the extreme manifestation of the colorblindness affliction, at least among some whites. A 20 year-old white CORE worker was mugged in her apartment. She described the assailant with great detail to the police, including height, weight, eyes, teeth, and clothing, but she didn't mention that fact that he was black "for fear of indicating prejudice." JAMES FARMER, FREEDOM—WHEN? 85 (1965).

As Farmer makes clear, this analysis of racism and prejudice was extremely individualistic; the error of prejudice was taken to be reaching conclusions about people on the basis of any group association at all.

7. The equality of opportunity or formal equality ideology underlying this basic vision of racism is discussed in Crenshaw, *Race, Reform and Retrenchment, supra* note 4, at 1336–49; Richard H. Fallon, *To Each According to His Ability, From None According to His Race: The Concept of Merit in the Law of Antidiscrimination*, 60 B.U.L. REV. 815 (1980); Alan D. Freeman, *Racism, Rights and the Quest for Equality of Opportunity: A Critical Legal Essay*, 23 HARV. C.R.–C.L. L. REV. 295, 354–85 (1988); Patricia J. Williams, *The Obliging Shell: An Informal Essay on Formal Equal Opportunity*, 87 MICH L. REV. 2128 (1989), reprinted in part in this volume at 103. *See also* Malcolm X & James Farmer, *Separation or Integration: A Debate*, DIALOGUE, May 1962, at 14, reprinted in BLACK PROTEST THOUGHT IN THE TWENTIETH CENTURY 387, 404 (August Meier, Elliot M. Rudwick & Francis L. Broderick eds., 1971) (according to Farmer, integration means that "each individual [is] to be accepted on basis of his merit and not on the basis of his color"); Bayard Rustin, *Separate is not Equal, in* BLACK PROTEST THOUGHT IN THE TWENTIETH CENTURY, *supra*, at 622 ("after graduation [black students] will have to engage in free and open competition for jobs in a marketplace where standards are universal"); WEISBROT, *supra* note 2, at xiii ("A basic assumption of liberalism in the 1960s was that equal protection of constitutional rights would afford all Americans, regardless of color, an equal chance to amass wealth, influence, and stature.").

8. *See* THEODORE L. CROSS, THE BLACK POWER IMPERATIVE: RACIAL INEQUALITY AND THE POLITICS OF NONVIOLENCE 609–10 (1984). *See also* Alkalimat, *supra* note 5, at 177

(investing in education is a major integrationist policy because racism is seen to be based in ignorance); Malcolm X & Farmer, *supra* note 7, at 17 (according to Farmer, "[i]t is segregation that produces prejudice, as much as prejudice produces segregation"); Fein, supra note 6, at 90 ("liberals have seen the public schools as society's best hope for achieving comprehensive integration").

9. *See* BLAUNER, *supra* note 3, at 266–68; Alkalimat, *supra* note 5, at 177–82; FARMER, *supra* note 6, at 85–86; Fein, *supra* note 6, at 89–93.

10. TAMOTSU SHIBUTANI & KIAN M. KWAN, ETHNIC STRATIFICATION: A COMPARATIVE APPROACH 589 (1965).

11. *See* Fein, *supra* note 6, at 87–94 (describing the centrality of the idea of universalism to liberal integrationists).

12. *See* BLAUNER, *supra* note 3, at 266–67 ("The liberal wants to judge a man in terms of his individual uniqueness and his universal humanity, not in terms of 'accidental' features like skin color. Universalism thus goes hand in hand with individualism, and in the area of race the two join in the ideal of 'color blindness.'").

13. *See* Fein, *supra* note 6, at 87 ("The liberal commitment, in education as in other spheres, is to universalism. We approach liberal salvation as we move from the sacred to the secular ... from tradition through charisma to rational bureaucracy.").

14. ROBERT NISBET, COMMUNITY AND POWER (1962).

15. *See supra* note 12.

16. *See* BLAUNER, *supra* note 3, at 19–21 (linking repudiation of race consciousness with similar images of religiosity and other forms of "primordial" belief).

17. The link between images of universalism and progress in liberal ideology are well summarized by Robert Nisbet:

> To regard all evil as a persistence or revival of the past has been a favorite conceit of liberals nourished by the idea of Progress. . . . Present evils could safely be regarded as regrettable evidences of incomplete emancipation from the past—from tribalism, from agrarianism, religion, localism, and the like. In one form or another, the theory of cultural lag has been the secular approach to the problem of evil.

NISBET, *supra* note 14, at 214.

18. *See* CHRISTOPHER JENCKS, INEQUALITY: A REASSESSMENT OF THE EFFECT OF FAMILY AND SCHOOLING IN AMERICA 253–65 (1972); Owen J. Fiss, *Groups and the Equal Protection Clause,* 5 PHIL. & PUB. AFF. 107, 154–55 (1976).

19. *See* Regents of the Univ. of Cal. v. Bakke, 438 U.S. 265, 311–15 (1978) (finding the goal of a diverse student body to be a compelling justification for affirmative action admissions); RONALD DWORKIN, A MATTER OF PRINCIPLE 301–03 (1985) ("Places in medical schools are scarce resources and must be used to provide what ... society most needs ... Racial justice is now a special need."); Letter from Robert Lack to the Editors, N.Y. Times, Mar. 9, 1981, at A22 (defending affirmative action plan for *Harvard Law Review* based on "the need for diversity").

20. *See* ROBERT STAPLES, INTRODUCTION TO BLACK SOCIOLOGY 260–61 (1976). Robert Staples linked the origin of the theory that whites and blacks are identical to the ideology of universalism.

CHAPTER FIVE

>─·─·─◦─·─·─<

POLITICAL POWER AND CULTURAL SUBORDINATION

A CASE FOR AFFIRMATIVE ACTION IN LEGAL ACADEMIA

Duncan Kennedy

The Political and Cultural Arguments for Affirmative Action

The Political Case

I FAVOR LARGE SCALE race-based affirmative action, using quotas if they are necessary to produce results. The first basis for this view is that law school teaching positions are a small but significant part of the wealth of the United States. They are also a small but significant part of the political apparatus of the United States, by which I mean that the knowledge law teachers produce is intrinsically political and actually effective in our political system. In short, legal knowledge is ideological.[1]

A second basic idea is that we should be a culturally pluralist society that deliberately structures institutions so that communities and social

84   classes share wealth and power. The sharing of wealth and power that occur automatically, so to speak, through the melting pot, the market and meritocracy are not enough, according to this notion. At a minimum, cultural pluralism means that we should structure the competition of racial and ethnic communities and social classes in markets and bureaucracies, and in the political system, in such a way that no community or class is systematically subordinated.[2]

From these two ideas, I draw the conclusion that, completely independently of "merit" as we currently determine it, there should be a substantial representation of all numerically significant minority communities on American law faculties. The analogy is to the right to vote, which we refuse to distribute on the basis of merit, and to the right of free speech, which we refuse to limit to those who deserve to speak or whose speech has merit. The value at stake is community rather than individual empowerment. In the case of affirmative action, as in those of voting and free speech, the goal is political, and prior to achievement of enlightenment or the reward of "merit" as determined by existing institutions.

Race is, at present, a rough but adequate proxy for connection to a subordinated community, one that avoids institutional judgments about the cultural identity of particular candidates. I would use it for this reason only, not because race is itself an index of merit, and in spite of its culturally constructed character and the arbitrariness involved in using it as a predictor of the traits of any particular individual. My argument is thus addressed to only one of the multiple forms of group subordination, though it could be extended to gender, sexual preference, social class, and ethnicity within the "white community."

The political argument includes the idea that minority communities can't compete effectively for wealth and power without intelligentsias that produce the kinds of knowledge, especially political or ideological knowledge, that will help them get what they want. To do this, they need or at least could use some number of legal academic jobs. It also includes the idea that cultural diversity and cultural development are good in themselves, even when they do not lead to increased power for subordinated communities in markets and political systems.

The political case is complicated by the fact that when law faculties distribute jobs in legal academia, they do more than distribute wealth and the power to participate in politics through the production of ideology. They also distribute power to influence who will participate in the future, because those they choose will vote on those decisions. In deciding who to hire or promote according to colorblind criteria, law faculties make culturally and ideologically contingent judgments about what candidates are most promising or deserving, and about who should make these very judgments in the future. Given the ideological and cultural character of these choices, and their (limited but significant) political impact, white males have no more business monopolizing the process of distributing the benefits than they have monopolizing the benefits themselves.

A serious obstacle to this proposal is the "pool problem."[3] The number of minority teaching candidates is limited, and the prospects for the future are clouded by the decline in the number of black college graduates. (The situation is different for each cultural community.) I would therefore limit affirmative action by imposing a floor or cut-off point in the form of a requirement of minimum actual or anticipated competence in performing the instructional function of a law professor.

It would seem to me a problem (requiring tradeoffs) if the implementation of this view would be unfair to individual whites excluded from teaching jobs, or if it would lead to a decline in the quality of legal scholarship. But I believe that massive affirmative action would not be unfair to excluded whites, and that it would improve the quality of legal scholarship as I assess it. It would also have, I think, a beneficial effect on the quality of life, by undermining the fetishistic, neurotic and just plain irrational attitude toward "standards" and merit-based "entitlement" that prevails in legal academia.

The Cultural Case:
Affirmative Action and the Quality of Work

The standards that law schools apply in deciding who to hire and who to promote function to exclude scholars from cultural communities with a history of subordination. Because we exclude them, we get contributions to legal knowledge from only a small number of people with ties to those communities. I believe that if there were a lot more such people, they would make contributions that, taken as a whole, would have a culturally specific character. Judging by my own culturally and ideologically contingent standards, I think they would produce outstanding work not otherwise available. Law schools would do better to invest resources in evoking this contribution than in the fungible white male candidates at the margin who get jobs under the existing selection systems. (Though quite a few who appear marginal turn out to be terrific.)

I don't mean that there would be a minority "line." But there would be a variety of positions, debates and styles of legal academic writing that everyone would identify as resulting from the rise of minority legal culture. Some of these debates, positions and styles would be produced by whites, but would be no less a product of change in the racial makeup of the academy. Some of the new work would certainly look wrong or mediocre to me. But some would knock our socks off, in unexpected ways and in ways already presaged by Critical Race Theory. I have no doubt that in terms of the social and intellectual value of scholarly output, legal academia would be better off than it is now. We have lost a lot by preventing minorities from making this contribution. We can't get it unless we give them the resources, in the form of legal academic jobs, to make it.

Second, I think some legal scholarship is exciting and enriching and stimulating, but that's not very much. People seem to produce the good stuff through neurotic, often dramatic processes, full of twists and turns and surprises. I think most legal scholarship is pretty much done by the numbers, and it's hard to make any sharp quality differential between articles. This stuff is useful. Writing it is hard work. But it doesn't take deep scholarly quality. There are many, many people who are excluded by the "standards" from teaching law who could do it as well or as mediocrely as those who do it in fact. For this reason, I think we would lose little in the way of quality even if massive affirmative action failed to produce the rich harvest of new ideas and approaches that I anticipate.

The possibility of (dramatically) improving legal scholarship provides a second strong reason for a massive affirmative action program. It is not just that there is no trade-off between quality and affirmative action. The existing system denies us a benefit. Even in the absence of the political justification, I would favor a new system on this ground.[4]

Affirmative Action and White Entitlements

Suppose a law faculty adopts this version of affirmative action because it hopes to improve the quality of legal academic work, as well as because it is politically more just. When the faculty prefers a minority job applicant over a white even though the present system would give the job to the white, it does so, in part, because it thinks that in the long run this approach will improve scholarship and teaching. We are treating race as a credential (as a proxy for culture and community) because we anticipate terrific work from some of these applicants, work that we don't think we can get from the whites they replace. The reason we don't expect it from them is that we believe that work from authors with ties to subordinated communities is likely to have different excellent qualities from work from inside the dominant community.

Are the excluded whites "entitled" to prevent this improvement in scholarship? I would say they are not. Even if all the colorblind criteria of academic promise that we can think of favor a white candidate, he or she lacks something we want in some substantial number of those we will hire. He or she has less promise of doing work with the particular strengths likely to derive from connection to a subordinated cultural community.

The white male law teaching applicant whose resume and interviews would get him the job were it not for affirmative action has indeed accomplished something, and will not be rewarded for it with the job. But if he understands in advance that the terms of the competition are that he is competing against other white males, for the limited number of slots that a politically just system makes available to people who have had his advantages, then I don't think he has any reason to complain when a job he would have gotten under a different (less just) system goes to a minority applicant. But the excluded white candidates do not have as strong a claim as assumed above.

First, those who win out in the existing system have no claim to be "the best," even according to the colorblind criteria, because the underlying systems of race and class and the system of testing excludes so many potential competitors from the very beginning. The competition in which our teaching applicants and tenure candidates win out is restricted, with only a tiny number of notable exceptions, to people born within a certain race-class distance of those positions. At every step, the differences in educational resources and the testing process screen out millions of people who might be able to do the job of law professor better than those who end up getting it. As against those excluded from the competition by race and class and the vagaries of the testing system, those who win out have only a very limited claim of entitlement.

Second, the "standards" that law schools apply in hiring assistant professors and promoting them to tenure are at best very rough proxies for accomplishment as we assess it after the fact. People who get good grades and have prestigious clerkships often turn out to be duds as legal scholars and teachers by the standards of those who appointed them. People with less impressive resumes often turn out to be terrific scholars and teachers. People who get tenure on the basis of an article that looks good to the tenure committee (and those of the faculty who read it) often never produce anything of comparable quality again. "Entitlements" based on these rough proxies are worthy of only limited respect. The white males who would be displaced to make way for large numbers of minority scholars would be hurt, but not in a way that would be unfair, given the importance of the goals to be achieved.

Third, law school faculties apply a pedestrian, often philistine cultural standard in judging white male resumes, interviews and presentations at the entry level, and white male teaching and tenure work at the promotion level. They administer this pedestrian, philistine standard with an unconscious but unmistakable moderate conservative to moderate liberal bias. And they serve it up with a powerful seasoning of old-boyism and arbitrary clique preference as between white males. This doesn't mean a more pluralist academy would necessarily do better or produce more political diversity. It does mean for me that there is an element of laughable exaggeration in the claims often made for the meritocratic purity of existing arrangements. The people who would win out in this system, were it not for affirmative action, have weak claims of unfairness just because they are not so wonderful, even by comparison with other white males, that they can regard themselves as innocent victims.

There is no trade-off between racial justice and legal academic quality. Indeed, both goals point in the same direction. There is no claim of entitlement against these goals even for candidates who are plausibly the best by every colorblind criterion. The actual candidates likely to be rejected have claims weakened by exclusion of competitors, especially competitors from the groups that would gain by affirmative action. Their claims are further weakened by the fact that their accomplishments are mere proxies for legal academic merit, and by the low cultural quality and arbitrary subjectivism of the screening system that would otherwise have delivered them the goods.

A political move to large scale affirmative action would say to minorities, "Here is a part of the resources. Do what you can with it." It would free whites from some of the political obligation that comes from unjust treatment of minorities. It would reduce the nagging sense that our ability to assess merit is consciously or unconsciously corrupted because we now accomplish limited power and wealth sharing through academic decisions on hiring and promotion.

It would reduce the sense that we coerce minorities who want the rewards we have to offer into "being like us." It would also increase integration, the chance for more relations with minorities in our own workplaces. But it would do this without presupposing that our "merit" joins us together in a way that is "more important than" or "independent of" cultural community. In short, it might promote integration while undermining the ideology of colorblindness.

There are obvious dangers. The proposal might increase the stereotyping of minorities as intellectually inferior. It might lead to protracted, destructive racial conflict between majority and minority groups on faculties, and within those groups. It might be impossible to design a scheme of wealth and power sharing that would be easy to administer so as to avoid endless conflict about how to define it in practice. I don't deny these dangers. I just think them worth risking, given the possible benefits.

The proposal obviously contemplates race-conscious decisionmaking as a routine, non-deviant mode, a more or less permanent norm in distributing legal academic jobs. Through the proposal, a "racial distinctiveness" theory (actually cultural distinctiveness) combined with race-conscious decisionmaking is "assimilated into our conception of meritocracy"[5] (which is what Randall Kennedy urges us to avoid at all costs). The position is problematic as well as controversial, because it relies on the idea of cultural subordination, rather than on the more familiar, fundamentalist ideas of prejudice and discrimination.[6]

The Cultural Subordination Thesis

The issue is whether there is enough cultural distinctiveness, and enough subordination and exclusion, so that we must treat representation in academia as a political question, and so that we can expect major intellectual gains from doing so. The argument thus far has been largely hypothetical. Even if one accepted the value of the notions of culture and ideology, one might deny that, in the actual conditions of the United States in 1990, cultural and ideological differences are significant. Or one might merely deny that they are large enough so that we need to structure law schools to take them into account.

The cultural pluralist position to the contrary rests on a whole complex of ideas about American society. I am going to introduce them in highly schematic form. Together they define a variant of the "nationalist" ideology.[7]

Groups exist in a sense that goes beyond individuals having similar traits. People act together, in the strong sense of working out common goals and then engaging in a cooperative process of trying to achieve them. Just as important, they engage in discussion and mutual criticism both about the goals and about what group members are doing (or not doing) to achieve them. This is true of small task-oriented groups (family members getting the car packed for a trip), and also of large, diffuse groups, like "the black community," or a law faculty.

An important human reality is the experience of defining oneself as "a member of a group" in this strong sense of sharing goals and a discursive practice. Another important experience is being treated by others as a group member. One's interlocutor interprets what one says and does as being derived from a shared project. We all constantly identify groups and their members, assuming that we need to in order to understand other people and predict what they will do.[8]

Communities are more than mere statistical groupings of individuals with particular traits, but less than self-organized groups. Membership presupposes interaction, but the interaction may be sporadic, routine, alienated. A community is an historically specific collection of people with a common past, and a future that will take place on the basis of what has gone before. That basis can be reinterpreted but not obliterated. We are stuck, at any given moment, in the communities we started or ended in, and that is never "just anywhere." Wherever it is, it is both more inert than a self-organized group and less demanding. The crucial idea is that communities are made up of living individuals, but they have an element of transindividual stability and particularity; to be a member is to be situated, and you can be situated only in one or two places at a time. Membership is limiting as well as empowering.

Communities have cultures. This means that individuals have traits that are neither genetically determined nor voluntarily chosen, but rather consciously and unconsciously taught through community life. Community life forms customs and habits, capacities to produce linguistic and other performances, and individual understandings of good and bad, true and false, worthy and unworthy. Culture is first of all a product of community. People living in different groups possess different understandings of value and exhibit different capacities and behavior traits (kinship, cooking, dress). But as I am using it, culture is a characteristic of an individual as well. You can break all your ties to a community yet remain a person with that community's cultural identity.[9]

A large part of the population of the United States lives in racial and ethnic communities that have a measure of cultural distinctiveness. The distinctiveness comes in part from the origins in Africa, Asia, Europe and Latin America of the different groups that live here. But the cultures of particular communities have been dramatically transformed by the experience of immigration, forced transportation or annexation, and by the heterogeneous cultural life of this country. Each group has put its culture of origin together with its peculiar circumstances in the United States to produce a distinct set of behaviors, attitudes, beliefs and values.[10]

The racial and ethnic communities of the United States are in constant contact with one another. This contact is asymmetrical. There is a dominant cultural community which is less influenced by and less conscious of the subordinated groups than they are influenced by and conscious of it. As a result, it is hard to identify any aspect of the cultures of subordinated groups that might be relevant to academic production that has not been influenced by contact with the dominant culture.

The boundaries of cultural communities are blurred by the presence of large numbers of people who can trace their family history back into a subordinated community, but who now regard themselves and are regarded by others as situated in a culturally intermediate space, or as assimilated to the dominant culture. There are millions of people for whom the "authenticity" of having always belonged to a relatively homogeneous community with an unselfconsciously shared ethos is simply impossible. Most of those likely to benefit by a program of culturally-conscious distribution of academic power and opportunity come from these intermediate, multi-cultural positions. (The existence of this group may make it more likely that we could actually succeed in implementing cultural diversity.)

Though communities are different in ways that are best understood through the non-hierarchical, neutral idea of culture (some groups do things one way, value one set of things; other groups do it in different ways), some differences are not like that. Americans pursue their collective and individual projects in a situation of group domination and group subordination. By this I mean that we can compare "how well" different groups have done with regard to income, housing, health, education, local and national political power, and access to cultural resources. The groups are not so different that they define these things in radically different ways, or that some groups are just not interested in them. With respect to these common measures of equality and inequality, we all recognize that some groups are enormously better off than others.

The experiences of youth within a particular community, or on the border between communities, equip individuals with resources for competition in markets and bureaucracies. Different communities have different access to wealth and power with which to endow their members. And the rules of competition in markets and bureaucracies are structured in ways (both formal and informal) that advantage people from different communities regardless of the resources they bring as individuals to the competition.

Some of these advantages are overtly or covertly correlated to the community membership of the people competing. Historically, the white community imposed systematic race-based discrimination, outright job and housing segregation, and rules that excluded racial minorities and women from directly exercising political power. In the current situation, particular cultural groups control or dominate some markets and bureaucracies, and these groups exercise their inevitably enormous range of discretion in ways that favor dominant over subordinated communities. Racial and gender discrimination still direct the flow of opportunities and thereby affect the shares groups achieve.

The notion of domination and subordination is meant to indicate that we cannot understand what happens according to a model in which everyone in the society has innate or individual qualities and individual preferences that they bring into a neutrally structured competitive process that correlates their rewards with their social contributions. There are patterns to the characteristics of the individuals society produces—they are identifiably members of the particular communities they grew up in, and their fortunes depend on that fact.

Differences of fortune result from themselves in a circular process. To speak of domination is to say that the group and individual exercise of power given by resources occurs in a competitive struggle in which the better off communities manage over time to reproduce their advantage by winning enough in each game to reconstitute their stakes. Even the rules of the game are produced by the game, in the sense that power to compete is also power to modify the rules. The dominant communities are those that have the most resources and rewards, those that manage to influence the rules that define the game to their advantage, and those that through time manage to reproduce or improve their top-dog position through competitive struggle.[11]

The game is cooperative as well as competitive. In order to be rewarded, the members of the different communities have to cooperate across ethnic lines in producing goods and services. There are all kinds of influences and concrete alliances formed, and there are areas and moments when community identity is actually pretty much submerged in the collective aspects of tasks. Within the communities, there are divisions that are best understood in class terms, and other cross-cutting divisions that represent the community's participation in national life (region, gender, religion, etc.). Power and resistance to power pervade the structure.[12]

Though there is a self-conscious ruling class at the top of this structure, neither the class nor the structure fully controls the outcomes and impacts of the game on the communities whose members play it. All the players are functions of the game, as well as vice versa. There is no "outside position." Communities themselves change internally and through collision with other communities, but the process has as much fate, drift and chance mutation to it as it does mechanical necessity or self-organized group will. Communities can disperse or assimilate and then reform, and they can die out or be killed.[13]

The American racial and ethnic communities have intelligentsias, linked in overlapping patterns to a national intelligentsia and to each other. By an intelligentsia, I mean a "knowledge class" working in education, the arts, social work, the law, religion, the media, therapy, consulting, and myriad spin-offs like charitable foundations, for-profit research ventures, and the like. Intelligentsia members perform multiple functions beyond their formal job descriptions. In self-organizing groups or as individuals, some of them work at defining their community's identity (its cultural distinctiveness) or lack thereof, its interests in competition and cooperation with other communities, and its possible strategies.[14]

The national, racial, and ethnic intelligentsias are internally divided along ideological lines. One national ideological axis is radical-liberal-moderate-conservative-reactionary. Another is traditional-modern-postmodern. Another is science-social science-humanities-arts. There are also a wide range of ideological debates within particular intelligentsias, for example about their relationship to the national community.

An ideology in the sense in which I am using it is a set of contested ideas that provides a "partisan" interpretation (descriptive and normative) of a field of social conflict.[15] The social conflict could be between capital and labor, farmers and banks, men and women, gay and straight, North and South, native born and foreign born, export industries and import industries, or whatever. The concepts that describe and justify the positions of the conflicting groups can be drawn from almost anywhere, from philosophy to economics to religion to biology; within the fields that we use ideologically, complex systems of contested ideas reflect and at the same time influence social conflict.[16]

Ideologists choose their ideas, in the sense that there is no consensus either in their favor or against them. Many people may think a particular system is objectively right and many others that it is objectively wrong, or it may be seen as posing a question you can only resolve by a leap of faith. The most basic critique of the ideologist is that she has chosen her ideas to fit her partisan allegiance, and therefore lacks allegiance to "truth." In the conception of ideology I am using, this must always be recognized as a possibility. People do sometimes distort their intellectual work to serve causes or interests they adhere to. At the same time we have to recognize that where there is social conflict, and contested interpretations of that conflict, there is no intellectual space outside ideology. Intelligentsia virtue consists not in "objectivity" or "neutrality," which are impossible once there is ideological division, but in the attempt to empower an audience to judge for itself.

It follows that being an ideologist doesn't mean being closed-minded, or uninterested in questioning fundamental assumptions, or being blind to evidence that contradicts those assumptions. In this sense of the term, one is in the position of the ideologist just by virtue of having, at any given moment, made choices between contested views that influence (and are influenced by) the intellectual work one does. "Moderates" are ideologists because when they call themselves that they implicitly appeal to a controversial critique of "ideologues." (This is the ideology of moderation.)

Members of minority intelligentsias are linked to their cultural communities in various ways, and divided from them as well, usually by social class, income, intelligentsia interests, and links to the national intelligentsia and culture that are different from those of the "masses." A basic ideological conflict is over how to describe and evaluate the courses of conduct that intelligentsia members adopt in this situation. There are ideologies of assimilation and of authenticity, of group accommodation and of group resistance, of individual self-realization and of collective obligation, and so forth.

The existence of ethnic intelligentsias, their size, and the power they produce for communities, all depend on access to resources, as does their ability to contribute to national intellectual/political life. One index of a community's cultural subordination is its level of dependence on others

to produce knowledge in areas where it would seem, at least superficially,   *95*
that community interests will be affected by what that knowledge is.
Another is the relative ability of its intelligentsia to influence the national
intelligentsia, and indirectly the American mass culture audience, on
issues of importance to the community.[17]

The above definition of cultural subordination is patently ideological.
The conceptual scheme proposed is only one of many available to
describe and judge the status of an intelligentsia, and within each scheme
there is a well-developed critique of its rivals.

What Might Be Gained
Through Large-Scale Affirmative Action

Against this background, I would deny the existence of a "black point of
view" or a "black voice" in any essentialist (or racialist) sense.[18] But that
doesn't answer the particular questions that are relevant to the political
and cultural arguments for large scale affirmative action. The first of
these is whether minority communities would get, from a much larger
minority legal intelligentsia, a scholarly output that would better serve
their diverse political, social and economic interests than what they get
from an overwhelmingly white legal intelligentsia. The second is whether
the legal academic community as a whole would get a more valuable total
corpus of scholarship.

I see two likely changes in this regard. A much larger minority intelligentsia should produce more scholarship about the legal issues that have
impact on minority communities. The subject matter of scholarship is
determined at present by the unregulated "interest" of academics. What
we decide to write about just "flows naturally" from our backgrounds,
education and individual peculiarities. I think it is obvious that some
significant proportion of minority intellectuals would be led in this way
to write about minority legal issues.[19]

The precedent for this is the creation of modern civil rights law by
black lawyers who devised the litigation strategy of the National
Association for the Advancement of Colored People. It would be far-
fetched to argue that the race of these lawyers was irrelevant to their
choice of subject matter, or that the black civil rights cause would have
evolved in the same way had all the lawyers involved been white.[20]

Along with more scholarship on minority issues, there should be more
scholarship on the implications for minorities of any issue currently

under debate. In other words, Hispanic scholars working on the purest of corporate law questions within the most unquestionably Anglo scholarly paradigm are still, I think, more likely than white scholars to devote, over the long run, some time to thinking about the implications of law in their chosen technical area for the Hispanic communities.[21]

The second anticipated change is crucial to my argument. Along with a quantitative change in the focus of scholarship, it seems likely that an increase in minority scholarship would change the framework of ideological conflict within which issues in the race area but also in other areas are discussed. I do not mean by this that there is a black (or other minority) ideology. The point is rather that there are historic, already established debates within the minority intelligentsias that are obviously relevant to law, but that have been largely absent from legal scholarship.

Debates in the black intellectual community that have only begun to get played out and transformed in law include those between nationalists and integrationists,[22] between progressives and conservatives,[23] between those who see current racism as a more or less important determinant of current black social conditions,[24] and between black feminists and traditionalists.[25] The nationalist versus integrationist and gender debates are now for the first time beginning to get a hearing as a result of the presence of more minorities in the legal academy.[26] There are similar debates in the other minority communities.[27]

The Cultural Case in the Context of Cultural Subordination

It comes down to a question of value. I have come (belatedly) to the view that American culture and politics are rendered radically more intelligible when viewed through the lens that intellectuals of color have constructed over the years. There is more in this general literature than any one person can assimilate. But there is nowhere near as much legal scholarship as there ought to be. Scholars with ties to subordinated communities are uniquely situated in respect to these ideological resources, and more likely than white scholars to mobilize them to contribute to our understanding of law-in-society.

They are uniquely situated because, "even taking into account class, gender, and other divisions," there does indeed remain "an irreducible link of commonality in the experience of people of color: rich or poor, male or female, learned or ignorant, all people of color are to some degree 'outsiders' in a society that is intensely color-conscious and in which the hegemony of whites is overwhelming."[28] The ideological literature of subordinated communities comes out of this experience, in all its variants, and is addressed to it. The flowering in legal scholarship of this literature combined with these experiences is just not something we can plausibly expect from white scholars.

Again, the resources are not Truths to which only people of color have access (though, who knows, there may be some of them), but debates involving all the complexity of incompatible conceptual frameworks and flatly contradictory conclusions. They relate the internal dialectics of subordinated communities, and the dialectic of their interaction with the United States at large. They are open to multiple interpretations, including specifically white interpretations. For this reason, a substantial increase in the number of minority scholars should also improve white scholarship.

An increase in scholarship that takes seriously the issues that have been raised by the black intelligentsia would have relevance to the debates in legal scholarship about gender, sexual orientation and class. Indeed, I find it hard to think about, say, the separatist or culturalist strand in modern feminism without relating it to the debate about racial identity with which it is intertwined. The historical influence of black liberation thought on all other forms of late Twentieth Century American theory about subordinated groups has been enormous. But the influence has been indirect in legal thought, in part because of the small size of minority legal intelligentsias. Wherever groups are in question, whether in corporate law or in family law, or in the law of federalism or in local government law, the historic minority debates and their contemporary extensions should have an impact on sophisticated mainstream thinking.

The issue is not whether there should be a cultural bias in judging actual work. When we have the work before us, there is no reason not to consult it and decide for ourselves, individually, who has produced knowledge of value to us. In judging value to us, the cultural status of the producer is irrelevant, and so is the "merit" of the producer. In and of themselves they neither add nor subtract value, though knowing the author's status and accomplishment can change our understanding of a work and allow us to find value in it that we would otherwise have missed. This knowledge can also mislead us. There is no way to eliminate this risk, since we can understand and assess the work only as a text situated in some presupposed cultural and ideological context, and assess it only from our own particular cultural and ideological situation.

There is nothing that precludes white scholars from making the contributions anticipated from scholars of color. An outsider may learn about a culture and its debates and produce work about or even "within"

98   them that is "better" than anything an insider has produced. There are advantages as well as disadvantages to outsider status, and everyone in a multicultural society is simultaneously inside and outside. And there is nothing to guarantee that minority scholars will choose to or be able to make those contributions. They may squander their resources, or decide to do work that is indistinguishable in subject matter and approach from that of white scholars. But their track record, with and without affirmative action, has easily been good enough even as tokens, to sustain a prediction of excellence to come.

The Political Case in the Context of Cultural Subordination

Through scholarship focusing on their own concerns and through ideological debate played out in the legal arena, minority communities (through their intelligentsias) develop themselves internally, assimilate for their own purposes the resources of the culture at large, and build power for the competitive struggle with other groups. The power to create this kind of knowledge is political power. Therefore it should be shared by all groups within the community affected.

This argument has two levels. First, both the choice and the application of academic standards have strikingly contingent cultural and ideological dimensions. Law faculties distribute political resources (jobs) through a process that is political in fact, if not in name. One group (white males of the dominant culture) largely monopolizes this distribution process, and, perhaps not so surprisingly, also largely monopolizes the benefits (jobs). This outcome is politically illegitimate. Second, supposing that you disagree with what I have just said, and believe that standards are and should be apolitical, that position is itself ideological. Law faculties shouldn't make the ideological choice between colorblind meritocracy and some form of race-conscious powersharing without a substantial participation of minorities in making the decision.

Conclusion

If there is a conceptual theme to this article, it is that of "positionality," or "situatedness." The individual in his or her culture, the individual as a practitioner of an ideology, the individual in relation to his or her own neurotic structures, is always somewhere, has always just been somewhere else, and is empowered and limited by being in that spot on the way from some other spot. Communities are like that too, though in a complicated way. One of the things that defines a community's position—its situation, and the specific possibilities that go with it—is its history of collective accomplishment. Another is its history of crimes against humanity. It seems unlikely that there are communities without such histories.

The crime of slavery is deep in the past of white America. But ever since slavery, in each succeeding decade after the Emancipation Proclamation, we have added new crimes until it sometimes seems that the weight of commission and omission lies so heavily on nonwhite America that there just isn't anything that anyone can do about it. All anyone can hope is to be out of the way of the whirlwind, the big one and all the little ones played out in day-to-day life.

The bad history also creates opportunities that other communities don't have, or have in different ways. It would be quite something to build a multicultural society on the basis of what has happened here, where we have neither a consensual foundation in history nor a myth of human benevolence to make it all seem natural. An American multicultural society will arise out of guilt, anger, mistrust, cynicism, bitter conflict, and a great deal of confusion and contradiction, if it arises at all, and would be, to my mind, the more wonderful for it.

Of course, the specific proposal put forth above, for a kind of cultural proportional representation in the exercise of ideological power through legal academia, would be a very small step in the direction of the multicultural society I've described. As is true of any very specific proposal that can be implemented right now by small numbers of people holding local power, it is a drop in the bucket. But the minute we imagine it as a government policy applied in a consistent way across the whole range of situations to which it is arguably applicable, it loses most of its appeal. First, none of us local power-holders could do much to bring it about, and, second, taking the proposal seriously as state policy might lead to all kinds of disastrous, unintended side-effects.

This has been a proposal for drops in the bucket, not for the reorganization of state power. If it made a trivial contribution at vast social cost, we could abandon it as we adopted it, faculty by faculty, decision by decision. If it worked, the "kerplunk" of drops falling in near empty buckets might cause others to prick up their ears. And in any case, legal academics can, and so should, exercise their power to govern themselves in accord with the ideals of democracy and intellectual integrity—ideals that white supremacy compromises all around us.

Notes

1. *See* THE POLITICS OF LAW: A PROGRESSIVE CRITIQUE (David Kairys, ed., 2d ed. 1990); Duncan Kennedy, *Form and Substance in Private Law Adjudication*, 89 HARV. L. REV. 1685 (1976) [hereinafter Duncan Kennedy, *Form and Substance*]; Duncan Kennedy, *The Structure of Blackstone's Commentaries*, 28 BUFF. L. REV. 209 (1979); DUNCAN KENNEDY, LEGAL EDUCATION AND THE REPRODUCTION OF HIERARCHY: A POLEMIC AGAINST THE SYSTEM 14–32 (1983).

2. *See* Alan D. Freeman, *Legitimizing Racial Discrimination through Anti-Discrimination Law*, 62 MINN. L. REV. 1049 (1978); Ruth Colker, *Anti-Subordination Above All: Sex, Race, and Equal Protection*, 61 N.Y.U. L. REV. 1003 (1986); Randall Kennedy, *Persuasion and Distrust: A Comment on the Affirmative Action Debate*, 99 HARV. L. REV. 1327, 1335–36 (1986) [hereinafter Randall Kennedy, *Persuasion and Distrust*]; Randall Kennedy, *McCleskey v. Kemp: Race, Capital Punishment, and the Supreme Court*, 101 HARV. L. REV. 1388, 1424 (1988); CATHARINE A. MACKINNON, FEMINISM UNMODIFIED: DISCOURSES ON LIFE AND LAW 32–45 (1987); Frances Olsen, *Statutory Rape: A Feminist Critique of Rights Analysis*, 63 TEX. L. REV. 387, 390–401, 429–30 (1984); Frances Lee Ansley, *Stirring the Ashes: Race, Class and the Future of Civil Rights Scholarship*, 74 CORNELL L. REV. 993, 1063-64 (1989).

3. *See* Randall Kennedy, *Racial Critiques of Legal Academia*, 102 HARV. L. REV. 1745, 1765–70 (1989).

4. Yet a third important reason for affirmative action is that it will improve the quality of legal pedagogy. The political case anticipates that increasing the number of law teachers of color will influence the experience of law students of color in directions that will empower subordinated communities. This is a part of the general strategy of building minority intelligentsias so that subordinated communities can participate effectively in the political process. The cultural case anticipates that scholars of color will have an impact on the substantive content of what is taught about particular legal issues and on the composition of the curriculum and on the syllabi of particular courses. In all these areas, "white moderate" bias is rampant, by which I mean that white moderate ideological blinders render minority issues invisible. But affirmative action is also important to improve the educational experience and the practical value of legal education for people of color. The availability of "role models" is only a part of what is at issue here. Improvements should derive in part directly from what minority teachers do in and out of the classroom, and in part from their influence on what white teachers do. And the benefits should run to white students as well as to students of color. *See* Kimberlé W. Crenshaw, *Foreword: Toward a Race-Conscious Pedagogy in Legal Education*, 11 NAT'L BLACK L.J. 1 (1989); *cf.* Gerald P. Lopez, *Training Future Lawyers to Work with the Politically and Socially Subordinated: Anti-Generic Legal Education*, 91 W. VA. L. REV. 305 (1989).

5. R. Kennedy, *supra* note 3, at 1807.

6. It is an interesting question, but one I will not deal with in this article, whether the proposed program violates the equal protection clause of the United States Constitution or Title VII of the Civil Rights Act of 1968, as they are currently interpreted by the United States Supreme Court. *See* DERRICK A. BELL, JR., *The Racial Barrier to Reparations*, *in* AND WE ARE NOT SAVED: THE ELUSIVE QUEST FOR RACIAL JUSTICE 123–39 (1987).

7. Gary Peller, *Race Consciousness*, 1990 DUKE L.J. 758 (1990), reprinted in this volume at 67.

8. JEAN-PAUL SARTRE, CRITIQUE OF DIALECTICAL REASON I: THEORY OF PRACTICAL ENSEMBLES (Alan Sheridan-Smith trans., 1976).

9. *See generally* JAMES CLIFFORD, THE PREDICAMENT OF CULTURE: TWENTIETH-CENTURY ETHNOGRAPHY, LITERATURE AND ART (1988).

10. *See* Duncan Kennedy, *Radical Intellectuals in American Culture and Politics, or My Talk at the Gramsci Institute,* in RETHINKING MARXISM, Fall 1988, at 100, 129; ANDREW ROSS, NO RESPECT: INTELLECTUALS AND POPULAR CULTURE (1989).

11. *See* DANIEL R. FUSFELD & TIMOTHY M. BATES, THE POLITICAL ECONOMY OF THE URBAN GHETTO (1984).

12. *See generally* Regina Austin, *Employer Abuse, Worker Resistance, and the Tort of Intentional Infliction of Emotional Distress,* 41 STAN. L. REV. 1 (1988); MICHEL FOUCAULT, *Two Lectures,* in POWER/KNOWLEDGE 78 (1980). On the homologies in the legal treatment of class and race, see Karl E. Klare, *The Quest for Industrial Democracy and the Struggle Against Racism: Perspectives from Labor Law and Civil Rights Law,* 61 OR. L. REV. 157 (1982).

13. *See* Duncan Kennedy, *The Politics of Hierarchy,* in LEGAL EDUCATION AND THE REPRODUCTION OF HIERARCHY, *supra* note 1, at 78–97.

14. *See generally* ANTONIO GRAMSCI, SELECTIONS FROM THE PRISON NOTEBOOKS (Quintin Hoare & Geoffrey Smith eds., 1971).

15. *See generally* KARL MANNHEIM, IDEOLOGY AND UTOPIA: AN INTRODUCTION TO THE SOCIOLOGY OF KNOWLEDGE (1954).

16. *See generally* LOUIS ALTHUSSER, *Ideology and Ideological State Apparatuses (Notes towards an Investigation),* in LENIN AND PHILOSOPHY AND OTHER ESSAYS 127 (Benjamin Brewster trans., 1971).

17. Some important discussions of the role of intellectuals in situations of domination are PAULO FREIRE, PEDAGOGY OF THE OPPRESSED (M. Ramos trans., 1970); FRANZ FANON, THE WRETCHED OF THE EARTH (C. Farrington trans., 1968); EDWARD F. FRAZIER, BLACK BOURGEOISIE (1957); HAROLD CRUSE, THE CRISIS OF THE NEGRO INTELLECTUAL (1967).

18. Angela P. Harris, *Race and Essentialism in Feminist Legal Theory,* 42 STAN. L. REV. 581 (1990).

19. For an example of the kind of work I am talking about see Harold McDougall's articles about the *Mt. Laurel* decision. Harold A. McDougall, *The Judicial Struggle Against Exclusionary Zoning; The New Jersey Paradigm,* 14 HARV. C.R.–C.L. L. REV. 625 (1979); Harold A. McDougall, *Mt. Laurel II and the Revitalizing City,* 15 RUTGERS L.J. 667 (1984); Harold A. McDougall, *From Litigation to Legislation in Exclusionary Zoning Law,* 22 HARV. C.R.–C.L. L. REV. 623 (1987).

20. *See* MARK V. TUSHNET, THE NAACP'S LEGAL STRATEGY AGAINST SEGREGATED EDUCATION 1925-50 (1987).

21. An example of the kind of work I am talking about is Mario L. Baeza, *Telecommunications Reregulation and Deregulation: The Impact on Opportunities for Minorities,* 1985 HARV. BLACKLETTER J. 7.

22. I am referring here to the century-and-a-half long discussion about the character of African-American identity and its implications for strategy. The debate involves famous pairs, among them Martin Delany, *see* THE CONDITION, ELEVATION, EMIGRATION, AND DESTINY OF THE COLORED PEOPLE OF THE UNITED STATES (1852), and Frederick Douglass, *see* MY BONDAGE AND MY FREEDOM (1855); Booker T. Washington, *see* THE FUTURE OF THE AMERICAN NEGRO (1899), and W.E.B. Du Bois, *see* THE SOULS OF BLACK FOLK (1903); Marcus Garvey, *see* E. CRONON, BLACK MOSES: THE STORY OF MARCUS GARVEY AND THE UNIVERSAL NEGRO IMPROVEMENT ASSOCIATION (1957), and the later W.E.B. Du Bois, *see* DUSK OF DAWN: AN ESSAY TOWARD AN AUTOBIOGRAPHY OF A RACE

CONCEPT (1940); E. Franklin Frazier, *see* BLACK BOURGEOISIE (1957), and Harold Cruse, *see* THE CRISIS OF THE NEGRO INTELLECTUAL (1967); Malcolm X, *see* THE AUTOBIOGRAPHY OF MALCOLM X (1965), and Martin Luther King, Jr., *see* A TESTAMENT OF HOPE: THE ESSENTIAL WRITINGS OF MARTIN LUTHER KING, JR. (James M. Washington ed., 1986). This list is just an appetizer.

23. *See* THOMAS SOWELL, MARKETS AND MINORITIES (1981) and THOMAS SOWELL, RACE AND ECONOMICS (1975). For a progressive critique of Sowell, see Kimberlé W. Crenshaw, *Race, Reform and Retrenchment,* 101 HARV. L. REV. 1331, 1339-46 (1988).

24. *See* WILLIAM J. WILSON, THE TRULY DISADVANTAGED: THE INNER CITY, THE UNDERCLASS, AND PUBLIC POLICY (1987); WILLIAM J. WILSON, THE DECLINING SIGNIFICANCE OF RACE?: A DIALOGUE AMONG BLACK AND WHITE SOCIAL SCIENTISTS (1978); *See* R. Kennedy, *supra* note 3, at 1814 n.296.

25. For a classic statement of the conflict, *see* ZORA NEALE HURSTON, THEIR EYES WERE WATCHING GOD (1937). *See generally* PAULA GIDDINGS, WHEN AND WHERE I ENTER: THE IMPACT OF BLACK WOMEN ON RACE AND SEX IN AMERICA (1984); BELL HOOKS, AIN'T I A WOMAN: BLACK WOMEN AND FEMINISM (1981); *see also* LEE RAINWATER & WILLIAM L. YANCEY, THE MOYNIHAN REPORT AND THE POLITICS OF CONTROVERSY (1967); HAROLD E. CHEATHAM & JAMES B. STEWART, BLACK FAMILIES: INTERDISCIPLINARY PERSPECTIVES (1990).

26. Derrick Bell's point of view has always contained elements of nationalism—particularly his writing on school desegregation. Derrick A. Bell, Jr., *Serving Two Masters: Integration Ideals and Client Interests in School Desegregation Litigation,* 85 YALE L.J. 470 (1976) (educational improvement for blacks must take precedence over failed integration policies); Derrick A. Bell, *The Burden of Brown on Blacks: History-Based Observations on a Landmark Decision,* 7 N.C. CENT. L.J. 25, 26 (1975) (recognizing *Brown*'s limitations and arguing that it should be used as "critical leverage for a wide range of [continuing] efforts" by black communities to improve education for blacks). The debate is internal to Bell's book AND WE ARE NOT SAVED, *supra* note 6. With the publication of the articles cited in *supra* notes 4 and 5, and the response in R. Kennedy, *supra* note 3, the issue seems finally to have its own momentum within legal scholarship. On black feminism in law, *see* Kimberlé W. Crenshaw, *Demarginalizing the Intersection of Race and Sex: A Black Feminist Critique of Antidiscrimination Doctrine, Feminist Theory and Antiracist Politics,* 1989 U. CHI. LEGAL F. 139; Harris, *supra* note 18.

27. For example, *compare* RICHARD RODRIGUEZ, HUNGER OF MEMORY: THE EDUCATION OF RICHARD RODRIGUEZ (1982) *with* ALFREDO MIRANDE, GRINGO JUSTICE (1987).

28. R. Kennedy, *supra* note 3, at 1784. Kennedy's article says only that there "might" be a link of commonality among people of color. *Id.*

Chapter Six

THE OBLIGING SHELL

(An Informal Essay on
Formal Equal Opportunity)

Patricia J. Williams

I HAVE DECIDED to attend a Continuing Education of the Bar course on equal-employment opportunity. Bar-style questions are handed out for general discussion. The first question reads:

> Question One: X and Y apply for the same job with firm Z. X and Y are equally qualified. Which one should get the job?

I panic. What exactly is meant by Question One? But apparently this is supposed to be a throwaway question. On the blackboard the instructor writes:

> Right Answer: Whichever one you like better.

As usual I have missed the point and am busy complicating things. In my notebook I write:

Wrong Answer: What a clear, graspable comparison this is; it is like choosing between smooth pebbles. X, the simple crossing of two lines, the intersection of sticks; Y, the cleaned bones of a flesh-and-blood referent. There is something soothing about its static neutrality, its emotionless purity. It is a choice luxuriantly free of consequence.

At any rate, much of this answer probably depends on what is meant by "equal qualifications." Rarely are two people absolutely equally qualified (they both went to Harvard, they graduated in the same class, they tied for number one, they took all the same classes, etc.) so the judgment of equality is usually pretty subjective to begin with (a degree from Yale is as good as one from Harvard, a degree in philosophy is as useful as a degree in political science, and editor of the school paper is as good as the class president) and usually overlooks or fills in a lot of information that may in fact distinguish the candidates significantly (is it the same to be number one in a small class as in a huge class; is the grading done by some absolute standard, or on a strictly enforced bell curve; did X succeed by taking only standardized tests in large lecture courses; does Y owe his success to the individualized attention received in small seminars where he could write papers on subjects no one else knew or cared about?). All such differentiations are matters of subjective preference, since all such "equality" is nothing more than assumption, the subjective willingness not to look past a certain point, or to accept the judgments of others (the admissions director of Harvard, the accuracy of the LSAT computer-grader).

The mind funnels of Harvard and Yale are called standards. Standards are concrete monuments to socially accepted subjective preference. Standards are like paths picked through fields of equanimity, worn into hard wide roads over time, used always because of collective habit, expectation, and convenience. The pleasures and perils of picking one's own path through the field are soon forgotten; the logic or illogic of the course of the road is soon rationalized by the mere fact of the road.

But let's assume that we do find two candidates who are as alike as can be. They are identical twins. They've had exactly the same training from the same teachers in a field that emphasizes mastery of technique or skill in a way that can be more easily calibrated than, say, writing a novel. Let's say it's a hypothetical school of ultraclassical ballet—the rules are clear, the vocabulary is rigid, artistry is judged in probably far too great a measure by mastery of specific placements and technical renderings of kinetic combinations. (The formal requirements of the New York City Rockettes, for example, are that a dancer must be between five feet, five and one-half inches and five feet, eight inches tall precisely and be able to do twenty eye-level kicks with a straight back.) I could probably hire either one, but I am left with the nagging wonder as to my own hypothetical about whether I want either one of these goody-two-shoed automatons. I wonder, indeed, if the fact that the "standard" road is good may obscure the fact that it is not the only good road. I begin to wonder, in other words, not about my two candidates, but about the tortoise-shell nature of a community of employees that has managed to successfully suppress or ignore the distinguishing variegation of being human. (Even if we were talking about an assembly line, where the standard were some monotonous minimal rather than a rarefied maximum, my concern holds that certain human characteristics are being dishonored as irrelevant—such a creativity, humor, and amiability.)

I wonder if this simple but complete suppression of the sterling quirks and idiosyncrasies that make a person an individual is not related to the experience of oppression. I wonder if the failure to be held accountable for the degree to which such so-called neutral choices are decided on highly subjective, articulable, but mostly unarticulated factors (the twin on the left has a higher voice and I like high voices) is not related to the perpetuation of bias.

By the time I finish writing this, the teacher is well along into discussion of the next question, this time a real one:

> Question Two: X and Y apply for the same job with firm Z. X and Y are equally qualified. X is black and Y is white; Z is presently an all-white firm. Which one should get the job?

It feels almost blasphemous to complicate things like this. I feel the anger in the challenge to the calm neatness of the previous comparison; it seems to me that this is a trick question, full of labyrinthian twists and illusion. Will I be strong enough to cut my way through the suggestions and shadows, the mirror tricks of dimensionality? I hold my breath as the teacher writes on the blackboard:

> Right Answer: Whichever one you like better, because race is irrelevant. Our society will impose no rules grounded in preference according to race.

In my notebook I write:

> Left Answer: The black person should get the job. If the modern white man, innocently or not, is the inheritor of another's due, then it must be returned. I read a rule somewhere that said if a thief steals

so that his children may live in luxury and the law returns his ill-gotten gain to its rightful owner, the children cannot complain that they have been deprived of what they did not own. Blacks have earned a place in this society; they have earned a share of its enormous wealth, with physical labor and intellectual sacrifice, as wages and as royalties. Blacks deserve their inheritance as much as family wealth passed from parent to child over the generations is a "deserved" inheritance. It is deserved as child support and alimony. It is ours because our legal system has always idealized structuring present benefit for those who forbore in the past.

But, then, I'm doing what I always seem to do—mistaking the rules of fraud and contract for constitutional principles. How's this: It's important to hire the black person because the presence of blacks within, as opposed to without, the bell jar of a given community changes the dynamic forever.

As I write, a discussion has been raging in the room. One of the course participants growls: "How can you force equality down the throats of people who don't want it? You just end up depriving people of their freedom, and creating new categories of oppressed, such as white men."

I think: the great paradox of democratic freedom is that it involves some measure of enforced equality for all. The worst dictatorships in history have always given some freedom: freedom for a privileged some at the expense of the rest is usually what makes oppression so attractively cost-effective to begin with. Is freedom really such a narrowly pluralistic concept that, so long as we can find some slaves to say they're happy with the status quo, things are fine and free? Are they or the rest of the slaves less enslaved by calling enslavement freedom?

The tension voiced by the growler seems to be between notions of associative autonomy, on the one hand, and socialized valuations of worth—equality and inequality notions—whose foundations are not in view and go unquestioned. Categorizing is not the sin; the problem is the lack of desire to examine the categorizations that are made. The problem is not recognizing the ethical worth in attempting to categorize with not only individual but social goals in mind as well. The problem is in the failure to assume responsibility for examining how or where we set our boundaries.

Privatized terms so dominate the public discourse that it is difficult to see or appreciate social evil, communal wrong, states of affairs that implicate us whether we will it or not. Affirmative action challenges many people who believe in the truism that this is a free country. For people who don't believe that there is such a thing as institutional racism, statements alleging oppression sound like personal attacks, declarations of war. They seem to scrape deep from the cultural unconscious some childish feelings of wanting to belong by forever having others as extensions of oneself, of never being told of difference, of not being rent apart by the singularity of others, of the privilege of having the innocence of one's most whimsical likes respected. It is a feeling that many equate with the quintessence of freedom; this powerful fancy, the unconditionality of self-will alone. It is as if no others exist and no consequences redound; it is as if the world were like a mirror, silent and infinitely flat, rather than finite and rippled like a pool of water.

The "it's a free country" attack on affirmative action is also an argument, however, that is profoundly inconsistent with the supposed rationale for the imposition of "standards," however frequently the arguments are paired. The fundamental isolationism of individual preference as an arbiter is quite different from the "neutrality," the "blindness," and the "impersonality" used to justify the collectivized convenience of standardized preference. I wonder what a world "without preference" would look like anyway. Standards are nothing more than structured preferences. Preferential treatment isn't inherently dirty; seeing its ubiquity, within and without racial politics, is the key to the underground vaults of freedom locked up in the idea of whom one likes. The whole historical object of equal opportunity, formal or informal, is to structure preferences for rather than against—to like rather than dislike—the participation of black people. Thus affirmative action is very different from numerical quotas that actively structure society so that certain classes of people remain unpreferred. "Quotas," "preference," "reverse discrimination," "experienced," and "qualified" are con words, shiny mirror words that work to dazzle the eye with their analogic evocation of other times, other contexts, multiple histories. As a society, we have yet to look carefully beneath them to see where the seeds of prejudice are truly hidden.

If, moreover, racism is artificially relegated to a time when it was written into code, the continuing black experience of prejudice becomes a temporal shell game manipulated by whites. Such a refusal to talk about the past disguises a refusal to talk about the present. If prejudice is what's going on in the present, then aren't we, the makers and interpreters of laws, engaged in the purest form of denial? Or, if prejudice is a word that signified only what existed "back" in the past, don't we need a new word to signify what is going on in the present? Amnesia, perhaps?

We live in an era in which women and people of color compose and literally define both this society's underclass and its most underserved population. A recent study by the Urban League reports:

> The difference in the percentage of blacks and whites holding managerial and professional jobs is unlikely to narrow significantly before the year 2039. Currently, white men are twice as likely as black men to hold sales, managerial or professional positions.
>
> With the wages of white men averaging $450 a week in 1987 as against $326 a week for black men, income parity between the two groups will not be achieved before 2058.
>
> Black children are completing high school at a slower rate than whites. But the paper said that the percentage of blacks finishing high school rose from 55 percent of the white graduation rate in 1967 to 79 percent in 1985, and it estimated that equal percentages of blacks and whites will graduate in 2001.[1]

This last statistic is complicated by the fact that "between 1976 and 1985, the college-going rate of black high school graduates fell from 34 to 26 percent, despite the fact that the percentage of black high school graduates rose from 67 to 75 percent."[2] This decrease was largely due to the Reagan Administration's cuts in federal financial aid to students.[3]

Remedying this, therefore, must be society's most pressing area of representational responsibility; not only in terms of fairly privatized issues such as "more pro bono" or more lawyers taking on more cases of particular sorts, but in closely examining the ways in which the law operates to omit women and people of color at all levels including the most subtle—to omit them from the literature of the law, from the ranks of lawyers, and from the numbers of those served by its interests.

One week after the end of the equal-opportunity course, the Supreme Court came down with its opinion in *City of Richmond v. J.A. Croson Co.* That case presented a challenge, as well as its own model of resistance, to the pursuit of "proper findings ... necessary to define both the scope of the injury [in race and gender cases] and the extent of the remedy."[4]

Croson involved a minority set-aside program in the awarding of municipal contracts. Richmond, Virginia, with a black population of just over 50 percent had set a 30 percent goal in the awarding of city construction contracts, based on its findings that local, state, and national patterns of discrimination had resulted in all but complete lack of access for minority-owned businesses. The Supreme Court stated:

We, therefore, hold that the city has failed to demonstrate a interest in apportioning public contracting opportunities on the basis of race. To accept Richmond's claim that past societal discrimination alone can serve as the basis for rigid racial preferences would be to open the door to competing claims for "remedial relief" for *every* disadvantaged group. The dream of a Nation of equal citizens in a society where race is irrelevant to personal opportunity and achievement would be lost in a mosaic of shifting preferences based on *inherently unmeasurable* claims of past wrongs. [Citing *Bakke*:] Courts would be asked to evaluate the extent of the prejudice and consequent harm suffered by various minority groups. Those whose societal injury *is thought* to exceed some *arbitrary* level of tolerability then would be entitled to preferential classification. We think such a result would be contrary to both the letter and the spirit of a constitutional provision whose central command is equality.[5]

What strikes me most about this holding are the rhetorical devices the court employs to justify its outcome:

(a) It sets up a "slippery slope" at the bottom of which lie hordes-in-waiting of warring barbarians: an "open door" through which would flood the "competing claims" of "every disadvantaged group." It problematizes by conjuring mythic dangers.

(b) It describes situations for which there are clear, hard statistical data as "inherently unmeasurable." It puts in the diminutive that which is not; it makes infinite what in fact is limited.

(c) It puts itself in passive relation to the purported "arbitrariness" of others' perceptions of the intolerability of their circumstances ("those whose societal injury is thought to . . .").

These themes are reiterated throughout the opinion: Societal discrimination is "too amorphous"; racial goals are labeled "unyielding"; goals are labeled "quotas"; statistics are rendered "generalizations"; testimony becomes mere "recitation"; legislative purpose and action become "mere legislative assurances of good intention"; and lower-court opinion is just "blind judicial deference." This adjectival dismissiveness alone is sufficient to hypnotize the reader into believing that the "assumption that white prime contractors simply will not hire minority persons is completely unsupported."[6]

And as I think about the *Croson* opinion, I cannot but marvel at how, against a backdrop of richly textured facts and proof on both local and national scales, in a city where more than half the population is black and in which fewer than one percent of contracts are awarded to minorities or minority-owned businesses, interpretative artifice alone allowed this narrow vision that not just that thirty percent was too great a set-aside, but that there was no proof of discrimination. Moreover, the rhetorical devices that accomplished this astonishing holding are comprehensible less from the perspective of traditionally conceived constitutional standards—whether rational relation or strict scrutiny—than by turning to interpretive standards found in private law. The process by which the court consistently diminished the importance of real facts and figures is paralleled only by the process of rendering "extrinsic" otherwise probative evidence under the parol evidence rule.[7] In particular, I am struck by the court's use of the word "equality" in the last line of its holding. It seems an extraordinarily narrow use of equality, when it excludes from consideration so much clear inequality. Again it resembles the process by which the parol evidence rule limits the meaning of documents or words by placing beyond the bounds of reference anything that is inconsistent with or even supplementary to the written agreement.

A few months after the *Croson* decision, the Supreme Court followed up with a string of famous cases that effectively gutted enforcement of the whole Civil Rights Act, to say nothing of affirmative action. After the first of these, *Martin v. Wilks*,[8] in which consent decrees setting goals for the hiring of black firefighters in Birmingham, Alabama, were permitted to be challenged collaterally by white firefighters, Reagan's Assistant Attorney General, Charles J. Cooper, was reported in the *Washington Post* as having said that the case was "a home run for white men." Two days later the *Post* printed a clarification saying that Cooper's remarks had been "incorrectly characterized": "Cooper felt that the ruling was a 'home run' for the proposition that people injured by affirmative action plans should be allowed to challenge them."[9] In the *New York Times*, David Watkins, a lawyer for the city of Birmingham, hailed reverse discrimination cases as "the wave of the future": "I think whites have correctly perceived the new attitude of the U.S. Supreme Court, which seems to be giving encouragement to white citizens to challenge black gains in virtually every aspect of social and economic life."[10]

A quick review of the parol evidence rule: Before I went into teaching, I practiced consumer protection. I remember one trial in particular, a suit against a sausage manufacturer for selling impure and contaminated products. The manufacturer insisted that the word "sausage" meant "pig meat and lots of impurities." Here is part of my final argument to the jury:

You have this thing called a sausage-making machine. You put pork and spices in at the top and crank it up, and because it is a sausage-making machine, what comes out the other end is a sausage. Over time, everyone knows that anything that comes out of the sausage-making machine is known as a sausage. In fact, there is law passed that says it is indisputably sausage.

One day, we throw in a few small rodents of questionable pedigree and a teddy bear and a chicken. We crank the machine up and wait to see what comes out the other end. (1) Do we prove the validity of the machine if we call the product a sausage? (2) Or do we enlarge and enhance the meaning of "sausage" if we call the product a sausage? (3) Or do we have any success in breaking out of the bind if we call it something different from "sausage?"

In fact, I'm not sure it makes any difference whether we call it sausage or if we scramble the letters of the alphabet over this thing that comes out, full of sawdust and tiny claws. What will make a difference, however, is a recognition of our shifting relation to the word "sausage," by:

(1) enlarging the authority of sausage makers and enhancing the awesome, cruel inevitability of the workings of sausage machines—that is, everything they touch turns to sausage or else it doesn't exist; or by

(2) expanding the definition of sausage itself to encompass a wealth of variation: chicken, rodent, or teddy bear sausage; or, finally, by

(3) challenging our own comprehension of what it is we really mean by sausage—that is, by making clear the consensual limits of sausage and reacquainting ourselves with the sources of its authority and legitimation.

Realizing that there are at least three different ways to relate to the facts of this case, to this product, this thing, is to define and acknowledge your role as jury and as trier of fact; is to acknowledge your own participation in the creation of reality.

At this point there was an objection, overruled, from the sausage maker's lawyer, based on too much critical theory in the courtroom. I continued:

This suit is an attempt to devour the meaning of justice in much the same way that this machine has devoured the last shred of common-sense meaning from sausage itself. But the ultimate interpretive choice is yours: will you allow the machine such great transformative power that everything which goes into it is robbed of its inherency, so that nonconformity ceases to exist? Or will you choose the second alternative, to allow the product to be so powerful that "sausage" becomes all-encompassing, so engorged with alternative meaning as to fill a purposeful machine with ambiguity and undecidability? Or will you wave that so-called sausage, sawdust and tiny claws spilling from both ends, in the face of that machine and shout: this is not Justice! For now is the time to revolt against the tyranny of definition-machines and insist on your right to name what your senses well know, to describe what you perceive to be the limits of sausage-justice, and the beyond of which is this *thing*, this clear injustice.

There was a spattering of applause from the gallery as I thanked the ladies and gentlemen of the jury and returned to my seat at counsel table.

Since that time, I have used sausages to illustrate a whole range of problems: I just substitute "constitution" or "equality" or "black" or "freedom of speech" instead of "sausage." It helps me to think about word entanglements on theoretical as well as prosaic levels. For one thing, the three levels of meaning correspond to

(1) a positivist mode of interpretation, in which the literal meaning of words is given great authority;

(2) a legal-realist, as well as mainstream feminist and civil-rights, mode of interpretation (squeezing room into meaning for "me too"); and

(3) what is often attributed to a "nihilistic" interpretive stance ("I don't know what it is, but I do know what it isn't"). A better way of describing this last category may be as interpretive discourse that explores the limits of meaning, gives meaning by knowing its bounds. (I think, by the way, that an accurate understanding of critical theory requires recognition of the way in which the concept of indeterminacy questions the authority of definitional cages; it is not "nihilism" but a challenge to contextualize, because it empowers community standards and the democratization of interpretation.)

This model also corresponds to the three levels of "integration" of contracts under the parol evidence rule:

(1) Written contracts that are found by a judge to be "totally integrated" are limited to their "plain meaning," just as the dominant social contract as understood by the Reagan court is limited in its meaning and will not suffer any variation of interpretation from evidence of prior or contemporaneous circumstances, events, or sources of meaning.

(2) Contracts that are found to be only "partially integrated" allow for multiplicities of meaning and may have their terms supplemented by additional or "extrinsic" evidence.

(3) And contracts that are found "not integrated" may be altogether undone by a range of possible meaning that includes the wholly inconsistent.[11]

Law and life are all about the constant assessment of where on the scale one's words are meant—and by which level of the scale one evaluates the words of others. But I think the game is more complicated than choosing a single level on which to settle for all time. That truth exists on all three levels is the underlying truth I want to pursue here.

Situational sausage-machine analysis is a way of reexamining what is lost by narrow interpretative ideologies, and of rediscovering those injuries made visible by the bounds of legal discourse. Affirmative-action programs, of which minority set-asides are but one example, were designed to remedy a segregationist view of equality in which positivistic categories of race reigned supreme. "White" had an ironclad definition that was the equivalent of "good" or "deserving." "Black" had an ironclad definition that was the equivalent of "bad" or unworthy of inclusion.

Although the most virulent examples of such narrow human and linguistic interpretations have been removed from the code books, much of this unconsciously filtered vision remains with us in subtler form. An example may be found in the so-called Ujaama House incidents that took place on Stanford University's campus in the fall of 1988. (Ujaama House is one of several "theme" houses set up with the idea of exposing students to a variety of live-in cultural and racial exchanges.) There is a Hispanic theme house, a Japanese theme house; Ujaama is the African-American theme house.)

On the night of September 29, 1988, a white student identified only as "Fred" and a black student called "Q.C." had an argument about whether the composer Beethoven had black blood. Q.C. insisted that he did; Fred thought the very idea "preposterous."

> The following night, the white students said they got drunk and decided to color a poster of Beethoven to represent a black stereotype. They posted it outside the room of Q.C., the black student who had originally made the claim about Beethoven's race.
>
> Later, on October 14, after the defacing but before the culprits had been identified, a black fraternity's poster hanging in the dorm was emblazoned with the words "niggers." No one has admitted to that act, which prompted an emergency house staff meeting that eventually led to the identification [of Fred as one] of the students who had defaced the Beethoven poster.[12]

114   In subsequent months there was an exhaustive study conducted by the university, which issued a report of its findings on January 18, 1989. There were three things about Fred's explanation that I found particularly interesting in the report:

(1) Fred said he was upset by "all this emphasis on race, on blackness. Why can't we just all be human—I think it denies one's humanity to be 'racial.'" I was struck by the word boxes in which "race," "blackness," and "humanity" were structured as inconsistent concepts.

(2) Fred is a descendant of German Jews and was schooled in England. He described incidents that he called "teasing"—I would call them humiliation, even torture—by his schoolmates about his being Jewish. They called him miserly, and his being a Jew was referred to as a weakness. Fred said that he learned not to mind it and indicated that the poster defacement at Ujaama House had been in the spirit of this teaching. He wondered why the black students couldn't respond to it in the spirit in which it was meant: "nothing serious," just "humor as a release." It was a little message, he said, to stop all this divisive black stuff and be human. Fred appeared to me to be someone who was humiliated into conformity and then, in the spirit of the callousness and displaced pain that humiliation ultimately engenders, was passing it on.

(3) Fred found the assertion that Beethoven was black not just annoying but "preposterous." In the wake of the defacement, he was assigned to do some reading on the subject and found that indeed Beethoven was a mulatto. This discovery upset him, so deeply in fact that his entire relation to the music changed: he said he heard it differently.[13]

Ultimately, Stanford's disciplinary board found no injury to Q.C. and recommended no disciplining of Fred because they felt that would victimize him, depriving him of his First Amendment rights. As to this remedy, I was struck by the following issues:

(1) The privatization of remedy to Q.C. alone.

(2) The invisibility of any injury to anyone, whether to Q.C. or to the Stanford community, whether to whites or to blacks.

(3) The paradoxical pitting of the First Amendment against speaking about other forms of injury—so that the specter of legal censorship actually blocks further discussion of moral censure. This is always a hard point to make: I am not arguing against the First Amendment; what I am insisting upon is some appreciation for the power of words—and for the other forms of power abuses that may lurk behind the "defense" of free speech.

As in *Croson*'s definition of equality, I think that the resolution of the Ujaama House incident rested on a definition of harm that was so circumscribed in scope as to conceal from any consideration—legal or otherwise—a range of serious but "extrinsic" harms felt by the decision-makers to be either inconsistent with the First Amendment or beside the point ("additional to," according to the parol evidence rule). In limiting the investigation and remedy to Fred and Q.C. exclusively, the group harm (to the collective of the dorm, to the Stanford community generally, to the group identity of blacks) was avoided. To illustrate this point, I will try to recount my own sense of the Beethoven injury.

Even though the remark was not made to me or even in my presence, I respond to it personally and also as a member of the group derogated; I respond personally but as part of an intergenerational collective. I am the "first black female" in many circumstances. I am a first black pioneer just for speaking my mind. The only problem is that every generation of my family has been a first black something or other, an experimental black, a "different" black—a hope, a candle, a credit to our race. Most of my black friends' families are full of generations of pioneers and exceptions to the rule. (How else would we have grown up to such rarefied heights of professionalism? Nothing is ever really done in one generation, or done alone.) It is not that we are all that rare in time—it is that over time our accomplishments have been coopted and have disappeared; the issue is, when can we stop being perceived as "firsts." I wonder when I and the millions of other people of color who have done great and noble things or small and courageous things or creative and scientific things—when our achievements will become generalizations about our race and seen as contributions to the larger culture, rather than exceptions to the rule, isolated abnormalities. ("If only there were more of you!" I hear a lot. The truth is, there are lots more of me, and better of me, and always have been.)

The most deeply offending part of the Beethoven injury is its message that if I ever manage to create something as monumental as Beethoven's music, or the literature of the mulatto Alexandre Dumas or the mulatto Alexander Pushkin, then the best reward to which I can aspire is that I will be remembered as white. Perhaps my tribe will hold a candle in honor of my black heart over the generations—for blacks have been teaching white people that Beethoven was a mulatto for over a hundred years now—and they will be mocked when they try to make some claim to me. If they do press their point, the best they can hope for is that their tormenters will be absolved because it was a reasonable mistake to assume I was white: they just didn't know. But the issue is precisely the

116   appropriation of knowledge, the authority of creating a canon, revising memory, declaring a boundary beyond which lies the "extrinsic" and beyond which ignorance is reasonably suffered. It is not only the individual and isolating fact of that ignorance; it is the violence of claiming in a way that denies theories of group rights and empowerment, of creating property that fragments collectivity and dehumanizes.[14]

This should not be understood as a claim that Beethoven's music is exclusively black music or that white people have no claim to its history or enjoyment; it is not really about Beethoven at all. It is about the ability of black and brown and red and yellow people to name their rightful contributions to the universe of music or any other field. It is the right to claim that we are, after all, part of western civilization.

The determination that Beethoven was not black is an unspoken determination that he was German and therefore could not be black. To acknowledge the possibility of his mulatto ancestry is to undo the supposed purity of the Germanic empire. It challenges the sanctification of cultural symbols rooted in notions of racial purity. One of the most difficult parts of the idea that Beethoven was not pure white has to do with the implication this has for the purity of all western civilization: if Beethoven, that most western musical warlord, is not really white, if the word "German" also means "mulatto," then some of the most powerfully uplifting, inspiring, and unifying of what we call "western" moments come crashing down to the aesthetic of vaudevillian blackface. The student who defaced the poster said that before he "knew Beethoven was black he had a certain image of Beethoven and hearing he was black changed his perception of Beethoven and made him see Beethoven as the person he drew in the picture."

All of this is precisely the reasoning that leads so many to assume that the introduction of African-American or South American or feminist literature into Stanford's curriculum is a threat to the very concept of "western" or "civilization." It is indeed a threat. The most frightening discovery of all will be the eventual realization of the degree to which people of color have always been part of western civilization.

When Fred's whole relationship to the music changed once he discovered that Beethoven was black, it made me think of how much my students' relationship to me is engineered by my being black; how much I am marginalized based on a hierarchy of perception, by my relation to definitional canons that exercise superhuman power in my life. When Beethoven is no longer ubermensch, but real and really black, he falls to a place beneath contempt, for there is no racial midpoint between the polarities of adoration and aversion. When some first-year law students walk in and see that I am their contracts teacher, I have been told, their whole perception of law school changes. The failure of Stanford to acknowledge this level of harm in the Ujaama House incident allows students to deface me. In the margins of their notebooks, or unconsciously perhaps, they deface me; to them, I "look like a stereotype of a black person" (as Fred described it), not an academic. They see my brown face and they draw lines enlarging the lips and coloring in "black frizzy hair." They add "red eyes, to give ... a demonic look."[15] In the margins of their notebooks, I am obliterated.

The Beethoven controversy is an example of an analytic paradigm in which "white equals good, and black equals bad." Although that paradigm operated for many years as a construct in United States law, it cannot be said to exist as a formal legal matter today. Rather, an interpretive shift has occurred, as if our collective social reference has been enlarged somewhat, by slipping from what I described above as the first level of sausage analysis to the second: by going from a totally segregated system to a partially integrated one. In this brave new world, "white" still retains its ironclad (or paradigmatic) definition of "good," but a bit of word stretching is allowed to include a few additional others: blacks, whom we all now know can be good too, must therefore be "white." Blacks who refuse the protective shell of white goodness and insist that they are black are inconsistent with the paradigm of goodness, and therefore they are bad. As silly as this sounds as a bare-bones schematic, I think it is powerfully hypostatized in our present laws and in Supreme Court holdings: this absurd type of twisted thinking, racism in drag, is propounded not just as a theory of "equality" but as a standard of "neutrality." (This schematic is also why equality and neutrality have become such constant and necessary companions, two sides of the same coin: "equal ..." has as its unspoken referent "... to whites"; "neutral ..." has as its hidden subtext "... to concerns of color.")

Consider, for example, the case of the Rockettes. In October 1987 the Radio City Music Hall Rockettes hired the first black dancer in the history of that troupe. Her position was "to be on call for vacancies." (Who could have thought of a more quintessentially postmodern paradox of omission within the discourse of omission?) As of December 16, 1987, she had not yet performed but, it was hoped, "she may soon do so." Failure to include blacks before this was attributed not to racism but to

118   the desire to maintain an aesthetic of uniformity and precision. As
recently as five years ago, the director of the Rockettes, Violet Holmes,
defended the all-white line on artistic grounds. She said that the dancers
were supposed to be "mirror images" of one another and added: "One or
two black girls in the line would definitely distract. You would lose the
whole look of precision, which is the hallmark of the Rockettes." I read
this and saw allegory—all of society pictured in that one statement.

Mere symmetry, of course, could be achieved by hiring all black
dancers. It could be achieved by hiring light-skinned black dancers, in
the tradition of the Cotton Club's grand heyday of condescension. It
could be achieved by hiring an even number of black dancers and then
placing them like little black anchors at either end or like hubcaps at the
center, or by speckling them throughout the lineup at even intervals, for
a nice checkerboard, melting-pot effect. It could be achieved by letting all
the white dancers brown themselves in the sun a bit, to match the black
dancers—something they were forbidden to do for many years, because
the owner of the Rockettes didn't want them to look "like colored girls."

There are many ways to get a racially mixed lineup to look like a mirror image of itself. Hiring one black, however, is not the way to do it.
Hiring one and placing her third to the left is a sure way to make her stick
out, like a large freckle, and the imprecision of the whole line will devolve
upon her. Hiring one black dancer and pretending that her color is invisible is the physical embodiment of the sort of emptiness and failure of
imagination that more abstract forms of so-called neutral or colorblind
remedies represent. As a spokeswoman for the company said: "[Race] is
not an issue for the Rockettes—we're an equal opportunity employer."[16]

An issue that is far more difficult to deal with than the simple omission
of those words that signify racism in law and society is the underlying yet
dominant emotion of racism—the very perception that introducing blacks
to a lineup will make it ugly ("unaesthetic"), imbalanced ("nonuniform"),
and sloppy ("imprecise"). The ghostly power of this perception will limit
everything the sole black dancer does—it will not matter how precise she
is in feet and fact, since her presence alone will be construed as imprecise;
it is her inherency that is unpleasant, conspicuous, unbalancing.

The example of the Rockettes is a lesson in why the limitation of original intent as a standard of constitutional review is problematic, particularly where the social text is an "aesthetic of uniformity"—as it appears
to be in a formalized, strictly scrutinized but colorblind liberal society.
Uniformity nullifies or at best penalizes the individual. Noninterpretive

devices, extrinsic sources, and intuitive means of reading may be the only ways to include the reality of the unwritten, unnamed, nontext of race.

In *Croson* the Supreme Court responded to a version of this last point by proclaiming that the social text, no matter how uniform and exclusive, could not be called exclusionary in the absence of proof that people of color even *want* to be recipients of municipal contracts, or aspire to be Rockettes, or desire to work in this or that profession. But the nature of desire and aspiration as well as the intent to discriminate are far more complicated than that, regulated as they are by the hidden and perpetuated injuries of racist words. The black-power movement notwithstanding, I think many people of color still find it extremely difficult to admit, much less prove, our desire to be included in alien and hostile organizations and institutions, even where those institutions also represent economic opportunity. I think, moreover, that even where the desire to be included is acknowledged, the schematic leads to a simultaneous act of race abdication and self-denial.

In January 1988, for example, on the day after Martin Luther King's birthday, the *New York Times* featured a story that illustrates as well as anything the paradoxical, self-perpetuating logic of this form of subordination and so-called neutrality. In Hackensack, New Jersey, African-American residents resisted efforts to rename their street after King because it would signal to "anyone who read the phone book" that it was a black neighborhood. It was feared that no white person would ever want to live there and property values would drop: "It stigmatizes an area."[17]

The Hackensack story struck a familiar chord. I grew up amidst a clutter of such opinions, just such uprisings of voices, riotous, enraged, middle-class, picky, testy, and brash. Our house was in Boston on the border of the predominantly black section of Roxbury. For years the people on my street argued about whether they were really in Roxbury or whether they were close enough to be considered part of the (then) predominantly white neighborhood of Jamaica Plain.

An even more complicated example occurred in North Baltimore. Two white men, one of them legally blind, heaved a six-pound brick and a two-pound stone through the front window of a black couple's house. They did so, according to the U.S. attorney, "because they felt blacks should not be living in their neighborhood and wanted to harass the couple because of their race." The two men pleaded guilty to interfering with the couple's housing rights. The couple, on the other hand, criticized the prosecutor's office for bringing the indictment at all. "Describ-

120   ing himself as Moorish-American, [the husband] said he does not consider himself black and does not believe in civil rights. 'I'm tired of civil rights, I hate civil rights,' Mr. Boyce-Bey, a carpenter's apprentice, said. Moorish-Americans associate civil rights with racism and slavery."[18] Subsequently, the couple moved out of the house.

It seems to me that the stigma of "Dr. Martin Luther King Boulevard" or "Roxbury" is reflective of a deep personal discomfort among blacks, a wordless and tabooed sense of self that is identical to the discomfort shared by both blacks and whites in even mentioning words like "black" and "race" in mixed company. Neutrality is from this perspective a suppression, an institutionalization of psychic taboos as much as segregation was the institutionalization of physical boundaries. What the middle-class, propertied, upwardly mobile black striver must do, to accommodate a race-neutral world view, is to become an invisible black, a phantom black, by avoiding the label "black" (it's all right to be black in this reconfigured world if you keep quiet about it). The words of race are like windows into the most private vulnerable parts of the self; the world looks in and the world will know, by the awesome, horrific revelation of a name.

I remember with great clarity the moment I discovered that I was "colored." I was three and already knew that I was a "Negro"; my parents had told me to be proud of that. But "colored" was something else; it was the totemic evil I had heard my little white friends talking about for several weeks before I finally realized that I was one of *them*. I still remember the crash of that devastating moment of union, the union of my joyful body and the terrible power of that devouring symbol of negritude. I have spent the rest of my life recovering from the degradation of being divided against myself; I am still trying to overcome the polarity of my own vulnerability.

Into this breach of the division-within-ourselves falls the helplessness of our fragile humanity. Unfortunately, the degree to which it is easier in the short run to climb out of the pit by denying the mountain labeled "colored" than it is to tackle the sheer cliff that is our scorned mortality is the degree to which blacks internalize the mountain labeled colored. It is the degree to which blacks remain divided along all sorts of categories of blackness, including class, and turn the speech of helplessness upon ourselves like a firehose. We should do something with ourselves, say the mothers to the daughters and the sons to the fathers, we should do something. So we rub ointments on our skin and pull at our hair and wrap our bodies in silk and gold. We remake and redo and we sing and pray that the ugliness will be hidden and our beauty will shine through and be accepted. And we work and we work and we work at ourselves.

We resent those of us who do not do the same. We resent those who are not well-groomed and well-masked and have not reined in the grubbiness of their anger, who have not sought the shelter of the most decorous assimilation possible. So confusing are the "colored" labels, so easily do they masquerade as real people, that we frequently mistake the words for ourselves.

My dispute is perhaps not with formal equal opportunity. So-called formal equal opportunity has done a lot but misses the heart of the problem: it put the vampire back in its coffin, but it was no silver stake. The rules may be colorblind, but people are not. The question remains, therefore, whether the law can truly exist apart from the color-conscious society in which it exists, as a skeleton devoid of flesh; or whether law is the embodiment of society, the reflection of a particular citizenry's arranged complexity of relations.

All this is to say that I strongly believe not just in programs like affirmative action, but in affirmative action as a socially and professionally pervasive concept. This should not be understood as an attempt to replace an ideology controlled by "white men" with one controlled by "black women"—or whomever. The real issue is precisely the canonized status of any one group's control. Black individuality is subsumed in a social circumstance—an idea, a stereotype—that pins us to the underside of this society and keeps us there, out of sight/out of mind, out of the knowledge of mind which is law. Blacks and women are the objects of a constitutional omission that has been incorporated into a theory of neutrality. It is thus that omission becomes a form of expression, as oxymoronic as that sounds: racial omission is a literal part of original intent; it is the fixed, reiterated prophesy of the Founding Fathers. It is thus that affirmative action is an affirmation; the affirmative act of hiring—or hearing—blacks is a recognition of individuality that includes blacks as a social presence, that is profoundly linked to the fate of blacks and whites and women and men either as subgroups or as one group. Justice is a continual balancing of competing visions, plural viewpoints, shifting histories, interests, and allegiances. To acknowledge that level of complexity is to require, to seek, and to value a multiplicity of knowledge systems, in pursuit of a more complete sense of the world in which we all live. Affirmative action in this sense is as mystical and beyond-the-self as an initiation ceremony. It is an act of verification and vision, an act of social as well as professional responsibility.

Notes

1. Julie Johnson, *Prospect of Racial Parity Called Bleak*, N.Y. TIMES, Aug. 8, 1989, at A13.

2. Theresa Miller, *An Anti-Integrationist's Critique of School Desegregation: Making the Case for Black Colleges* (unpublished manuscript on file at University of Wisconsin Law School, Madison) (citing *College Outlook Grim for Blacks 25 Years after Barriers Fell*, CHRON. HIGHER EDUC., Sept. 2, 1987, at A8).

3. *Equity in Higher Education Still Eludes Blacks, Urban League Says*, CHRON. HIGHER EDUC., Jan. 20, 1988, at A31.

4. 109 S. Ct. 706, 730 (1989).

5. *Id.* at 727 (emphasis added, citation omitted) (quoting *Regents of The University of California v. Bakke*, 438 U.S. 296–97 (1978)).

6. *Id.* at 725.

7. RESTATEMENT (SECOND) OF CONTRACTS § 243 (1982); U.C.C. § 2–202, (1989).

8. 109 S. Ct. 2180 (1989).

9. Al Kamen, *Sharply Divided Court Eases Way for Challenges to Affirmative Action Plans*, WASH. POST, June 13, 1989, at A4; *Clarification*, WASH. POST, June 15, 1989, at A3.

10. Peter Applebome, *'65 Rights Act Now a Tool for White*, N.Y. TIMES, Aug. 8, 1989, at A10.

11. RESTATEMENT (SECOND) OF CONTRACTS §§ 215–216 (1982).

12. *Ujaama Incident a 'Gripping Study' in Race Relations*, Stan. U. Campus Rep., Jan. 18, 1989, at 1, 19.

13. Board of Trustees, Stanford University, Final Report on Recent Incidents at Ujaama House (1989), at 2.

14. *See, e.g.*, Regina Austin, *Employer Abuse, Worker Resistance, and the Tort of Intentional Infliction of Emotional Distress*, 41 STAN. L. REV. 1, 41 (1988), exploring the tension between the ideal of free-market worker independence and the reality of workplace harassment based on factors of race, class, and gender. In the examination of informal resistance techniques employed by subordinates against abusive authority, Austin attempts to identify a program that would "universalize the conflict of the workplace, and…shift the focus on the dispute from the narrowly economic to the broadly cultural and political." *Id.* at 49. She provides a nuanced discussion of the mechanics of coercion and control; and illuminates specifics of oppression that are traditionally dismissed or made invisible by assumptions of inevitability or disciplinary necessity. The discussion recaptures, from the discursive inexpressibility of the experience of humiliation, real words of outrage. It models a discourse of moral issue and, literally, of legal claim.

15. Standford Trustees, *Final Report, supra* note 13, at 2.

16. Bruce Lambert, *Rockettes and Race: Barrier Slips*, N.Y. TIMES, Dec. 26, 1987, at 25–27.

17. Michael Winerip, *A City Struggles over an Honor for Dr. King*, N.Y. TIMES, Jan. 19, 1988, at B1.

18. BALTIMORE SUN, Nov. 29, 1988, at D4.

PART THREE

Community

Introduction to
COMMUNITY

CONTEMPORARY LEGAL AND political theorists have discussed at great length issues of community. Their discussions have largely focused on the relationship of the individual to the community, asking whether individuals should be emphasized at the expense of communities, or whether our legal system would not better address human subjectivity if it were centered around communities rather than atomistic individuals. Communitarianism is perhaps the most prominent theory that has emerged from this debate, destabilizing the liberal ideal of individual identity by suggesting that individuals are constituted in relation to the communities in which they are situated. In other words, communities play a large role in the construction of identities. For many communitarians, law should focus on and respect community and group identity, rather than concentrating solely on individual rights.

The essays in this Part agree that communities are important in constituting identities, but they critique particular ways that legal rules operate to situate the self. That is, they each point out in some way how the law's definition of community does not necessarily correspond to the ways that individuals experience their situation. Hence, they challenge any stable notion of community, while recognizing that the self is decentered by, and situated in, multiple, overlapping and often competing connections that we might call community.

This Part covers a wide range of "communities." Gerald Torres and Kathryn Milun discuss the Mashpee Indians in Cape Cod, in the context of a legal dispute over whether the Mashpee constitute a tribe for the purposes of recovering land they claim was alienated from them over the last two centuries. Regina Austin examines the "black community," which she believes "exists out there, somewhere," and explores how a distinction drawn between those blacks who obey the law and those who do not has split this community. Jerry Frug takes us to local government law, where the law is organized around the lines between city and suburb as well as among suburbs, and where people's residences are assumed to constitute the centers of their communal lives.

Just as the essays recognize that each of these communities helps construct the identities of its members, they also examine the roles that law plays in the creation or frustration of communities. For Torres and Milun and Frug, it seems, the law has imagined an idealized community organized around blood lines or zip codes. By requiring or expecting this ideal, the law fails to recognize other important ties that bind particular groups together, thereby stifling the potential for alternative communities.

The judge in the Mashpee trial, for example, decided that the Mashpee Indians did not legally constitute a tribe because they were not pure enough. They had intermarried and their races were mixed (many seemed more black than Indian); their tribal rituals, to the extent they existed, were borrowed from plains Indians; their meetinghouse was built by a white man; they had become Christianized; and their chief did not issue rules and regulations. They were not, as the definition chosen by the court required, "Indians of the same or similar race united in a community under one leadership or government, and inhabiting a particular though sometimes ill-defined territory." By deploying this definition, Torres and Milun argue, the court missed a number of crucial factors about Mashpee tribal identity. Not only did the Mashpee experience themselves as a tribe, they did so in ways that the court's narrow and idealized notion of tribe was unable to assimilate. Torres and Milun maintain, for example, that the Mashpee's relatively open membership policy was a defining characteristic of their community rather than a sign of its fragmentation.

For Jerry Frug, local government law also seems to be based on a fantasy community. Emphasizing the borders among municipalities, local government law assumes an insulated geographic community to which individuals' economic and political interests are tied. For the purposes of local government law, the key to community is formal residency, and one's interests in other localities is of no legal significance. Frug spends much of his essay arguing that people's ties are in fact much more complexly distributed than the law suggests. It turns out, for example, that we generally don't shop, work, or have most of our primary connections in the places we live. The mall we shop at is perhaps more likely to define us than is our zip code.

Legal rules play a different role in community formation for Regina Austin. Rather than seeking to circumscribe the black community, legal rules provide a potential line of division between the black middle class and black lawbreakers. For Austin, black criminal behavior, engendering debate among blacks, poses one of the greatest challenges to an ideal black community. Like Frug, who suggests that our communal ties might not exist where some might expect them, Austin could be understood to suggest that middle class blacks might have more in common with middle class whites than with black city gang members. Yet, in the name of the black community, Austin encourages the embrace of heterogeneity within the community, rather than a "politics of distinction" that might foreclose the possibility of black community. Through what she terms a "politics of identification," she therefore calls for black "role models" to ally themselves with their community's "deviants."

All the essays, then, seek to facilitate individual ties and connections that the law might otherwise obfuscate. Torres and Milun assert that the law should make it more possible for groups to define their own identities, perhaps by broadening the definition of tribe to account for a more heterogeneous community than the law might currently contemplate. Frug proposes that law recognize the postmodern complexity of our communities, acknowledging, for example, that some people in Boston are likely to feel more affinity for mid-town Manhattan than for nearby Medford. Focusing less than Torres and Milun and Frug on how law should change to facilitate various relationships, Austin proposes that blacks respond to and break down the model/deviant divide.

Although Austin asserts connections and longs for community based on a classical identity category—race—she does not advocate suppressing differences within the community. In fact, it seems she speaks for all the essays in this Part (and perhaps in the book) in her description of a politics of identification, which she takes from Stuart Hall. It is, she quotes, a politics that

> works with and through difference, which is able to build those forms of solidarity and identification which make common struggle and resistance possible without suppressing the real heterogeneity of interests and identities, and which can effectively draw the political boundary lines without which political contestation is impossible, without fixing those boundaries for eternity.

128   According to Torres and Milun, the Mashpee should be able to celebrate differences that paradoxically define their group. Frug suggests that Puerto Ricans in New York should be permitted to vote in Puerto Rico and anywhere else they might feel affinity. For Austin, engagement with "bridge people"—those who straddle the model/deviant divide—provides the perfect context for a politics of identification, and maybe even for economic self-sufficiency for black neighborhoods.

For each of the authors in this section, having the law recognize and facilitate multiple opportunities for connection and political action—not community for its own sake—is the goal.

CHAPTER SEVEN

>─┤◆>─●─<◆┤─<

STORIES AND STANDING
THE LEGAL MEANING OF IDENTITY

Gerald Torres & Kathryn Milun

IN *MASHPEE TRIBE V. TOWN OF MASHPEE*,[1] a federal district court decided that an Indian tribe, consisting of people occupying a recognizable territory for well over three hundred years, was not, in legal terms, an Indian "tribe." As a consequence of its finding, the trial court held that the Mashpee had no standing to protect their interest in a land claim and dismissed the case. This essay reveals flaws in the court's judicial reasoning and argues that the *Mashpee Tribe* case provides an illustrative warning of how our legal system can fail to account for compelling cultural particularities in fashioning its decisions.

When Is A Tribe A Tribe?

In 1976, the Indian community at Mashpee on Cape Cod sued to recover tribal lands alienated from them over the last two centuries in violation of the Indian Non-Intercourse Act of 1790.[2] The Non-Intercourse Act prohibits the transfer of Indian tribal land to non–Indians without approval

129

of the federal government. The tribe claimed its land had been taken from it, between 1834 and 1870, without the required federal consent. According to the Mashpee, the Commonwealth of Massachusetts had permitted the land to be sold to non-Indians and had transferred common Indian lands to the Town of Mashpee. The defendant, Town of Mashpee, answered by denying that the plaintiffs, Mashpee, were a tribe. Therefore, they were outside the protection of the Non-Intercourse Act and were without standing to sue.

As a result, the Mashpee first had to prove that they were indeed a "tribe." A forty-day trial then ensued on that threshold issue. The Mashpee were required to demonstrate their tribal existence in accordance with a definition adopted by the United States Supreme Court at the turn of the century in *Montoya v. United States*.[3] In *Montoya*, the court held:

> By a "tribe" we understand a body of Indians of the same or a similar race, united in a community under one leadership or government, and inhabiting a particular though sometimes ill-defined territory.[4]

This is a very narrow and particular definition. Beyond reflecting archaic notions of tribal existence in general, the *Montoya* requirements incorporated specific perceptions regarding race, leadership, community, and territory that were entirely alien to Mashpee culture. The testimony revealed the *Montoya* criteria as generalized ethnological categories that failed to capture the specifics of what it means to belong to the Mashpee people. For example, the Mashpee do not accept the imposition of institutionalized political regulations, which might signify a united government under the *Montoya* standard.[5]

Judge Skinner, who presided over the trial of the Mashpee's claim, explained in his instructions to the jury: "Now, what is the level of the burden of proof? I've said these matters need not be determined in terms of cosmic proof. The plaintiff has the burden of proving . . . if the [Mashpee] were a tribe."[6] To overcome this burden, Judge Skinner agreed to allow expert testimony from various social scientists regarding the definition of "Indian Tribe." By the closing days of the trial, however, the judge had become frustrated with the lack of consensus as to a definition:

> I am seriously considering striking all of the definitions given by all of the experts of a Tribe and all of their opinions as to whether or not

the inhabitants of Mashpee at any time could constitute a Tribe. I let it all in on the theory that there was a professionally accepted definition of Tribe within these various disciplines.

It is becoming more and more apparent that each definition is highly subjective and idiosyncratic and generated for a particular purpose not necessarily having anything to do with the Non-Intercourse Act of 1790.[7]

In the end, Judge Skinner instructed the jury that the Mashpee had to meet the requirements of *Montoya*—rooted in notions of racial purity, authoritarian leadership, and consistent territorial occupancy. Thus, in order to establish their tribal identity,[8] the Mashpee's actual life experiences, and indeed the meaning of their existence, needed to fit, match, fulfill the expectations of *Montoya*'s legal description, despite the fact that *Montoya* itself did not address the Non-Intercourse Act. Because of this disjunction between the ethno-legal categories and the Mashpee's lived experience, the tribe's testimony and evidence never quite "signified" within the idiom established by the precedent.

After forty days of testimony, the jury came up with the following "irrational" decision: The Mashpee were not a tribe in 1790, were a tribe in 1834 and 1842, but again were not a tribe in 1869 and 1870. The jury's finding was "irrational" because the judge had instructed them that if they concluded that the Mashpee had ever relinquished their tribal status they could not regain it. Based on the jury's findings, the trial court dismissed the Mashpee's claim.[9]

Why did the Mashpee fail to meet the *Montoya* standard? A starting point for answering this question is to look back to the Mashpee's particular traditions, history, and cultural development. From this perspective, the Mashpee could not satisfy the court's definition of tribe because 1) the standard's categorization of what constitutes a tribe is inconsistent with the Mashpee experience, and 2) even if the standard was consistent, the rules of evidence preclude the Mashpee's best testimony which could be used to establish such consistency.

"Tribe": White Ethno-Legal Category
V. Mashpee Experience

That the Mashpee existed as a recognized people occupying a recognizable territory for well over three hundred years is a well-documented

132 fact.[10] In order to ascertain the meaning of that existence, however, an observer must ask not only what categories are used to describe it, but also whether the categories adopted by the observer carry the same meaning to the observed.[11]

The Non-Intercourse Act[12]—which prohibits the alienation of Indian lands without consent—applied only if the Mashpee had retained their "tribal identity" from the mid-17th century until they filed their land claim action in 1976. In order to fall within the scope of the Act's protection, the Mashpee had to prove first that they were indeed a "tribe" and that their status as such had not changed throughout this period. If the Mashpee were no longer a "tribe" (or if they never had constituted a "tribe" in the first place), the protection provided by the Non-Intercourse Act evaporated. If, however, the Indians retained their tribal status, then the transactions that resulted in the loss of their village were invalid. At the very heart of the dispute was whether the Mashpee were "legally" a people and thus entitled to legal protection.[13]

One of the several *Montoya* factors to which the court referred in determining the Mashpee's tribal status was the issue whether the Mashpee constituted a "body of Indians of the same or similar race."[14] The trial court's reasoning and decision on this question suggest that the Mashpee were being penalized for maintaining their aboriginal traditions because they did not conform to the prevailing "racial" definition of community and society.

Yet, two hundred years before the 1976 *Mashpee* decision, the Mashpee were on their way toward becoming the melange of "racial types" that ultimately would bring about their legal demise. Colonists had taken Mashpee wives, many of whom were widows whose husbands had died fighting against the British. The Wampanoags, another southern Massachusetts Tribe that suffered terrible defeat in wars with the European colonists, had retreated and had been taken in by the Mashpee. Hessian soldiers had intermarried with the Mashpee. Runaway slaves took refuge with and married Mashpee Indians. The Mashpee became members of a "mixed" race, and the names some of the Mashpee carried reflected this mixture.

What was clear to the Mashpee, if not to outside observers, was that this mixing did not dilute their tribal status because they did not define themselves according to racial type, but rather by membership in their community. In an essay on the Mashpee in *The Predicament of Culture*,[15] Professor Clifford explained that despite the racial mixing that had historically occurred in the Mashpee community, since the Mashpee did not

measure tribal membership according to "blood," Indian identity
remained paramount. In fact, the openness to outsiders who wished to
become part of the tribal community was part of the community values
that contributed to tribal identity.

Other factors the *Montoya* court relied on in determining the
Mashpee's legal status as a tribe were the related issues of whether the
Mashpee were "united in a community under one leadership or government" and whether they inhabited "a particular" territory. These considerations raised the difficult concepts of land "ownership" and
"control"—concepts alien to the Indians yet determinative to the Whites.

One way to understand the Mashpee's regard for political organizing
structures and land ownership is to look at their earliest experiences with
real property. The oldest structure used for communal Mashpee functions—a colonial-style building that came to be known as "the Old
Meetinghouse"—was built in 1684.[16] The meetinghouse was built by a
white man, Shearjashub Bourne, as a place where the Mashpee could
conduct their Christian worship. Shearjashub's father, Richard Bourne,
had preached to the Mashpee and oversaw their conversion to Christianity almost a generation earlier.

The Bourne family's early interest in the Mashpee later proved propi-
tious. The elder Bourne arranged for a deed to be issued to the Mashpee
to "protect" their interest in the land they occupied. Confirmation of this
deed by the General Court of Plymouth Colony in 1671 served as the
foundation for including "Mashpee Plantation" within the protection of
the Massachusetts Bay Colony. As part of the Colony, the Mashpee were
assured that their spiritual interests (as defined by their Christian overseers) as well as their temporal interests would receive official attention.
However, the impact of introducing the symbology of property deeds
into the Mashpee's cultural structure reverberates to this day. Whether
the introduction of European notions of private ownership into Mashpee
society can be separated from either the protection the colonial overseers
claim actually was intended or the Mashpee's ultimate undoing is, of
course, central to the meaning of "ownership."

Colonial oversight quickly became a burden. In 1760, the Mashpee
appealed directly to King George III for relief from their British over-
lords. In 1763, their petition was granted. The "Mashpee Plantation"
received a new legal designation, granting the "proprietors the right to
elect their own overseers."[17] This change in the tribe's relationship with
its newly arrived white neighbors did not last long, however. With the

134   coming of the Colonies' war against England and the founding of the Commonwealth of Massachusetts, all previous protections of Mashpee land predicated on British rule quickly were repealed, and the tribe was subjected to a new set of overseers with even more onerous authority than its colonial lords had held. The new protectors were granted "oppressive powers over the inhabitants, including the right to lease their lands, to sell timber from their forests, and to hire out their children to labor."[18]

In 1833, a series of events began that culminated in the partial restoration of traditional Mashpee "rights." William Apes, an Indian preacher who claimed to be descended from King Philip, a Wampanoag chief, stirred the Mashpee to petition their overseers and the Governor of Massachusetts for relief from the depredation visited upon them. What offended Apes was the appropriation of the Mashpee's worshipping ground by white Christians. In response to the imposition of a white Christian minister on their congregation, they had abandoned the meetinghouse in favor of an outdoor service conducted by a fellow Indian. The petition Apes helped draft began, "we, as a Tribe, will rule ourselves, and have the right to do so, for all men are born free and equal, says the Constitution of the country."[19] What is particularly important about this challenge is that it asserted independence within the context of the laws of the state of Massachusetts. The Massachusetts Governor rejected this appeal and the Mashpee's attempt at unilateral enforcement of their claims resulted in the arrest and conviction of Apes.[20]

The appeal of Apes's conviction, however, produced a partial restoration of the tribe's right of self-governance and full restoration of its right to religious self-determination, for the tribe was returned to its meetinghouse. When the white former minister tried to intervene, he was removed forcibly and a new lock was installed on the meetinghouse doors. By 1840, the Mashpee's right to worship was secured.[21]

Control of the land remained a critical issue for the Mashpee. By late in the 17th century, the area surrounding the homes and land of the Mashpee had been consolidated and organized into a permanent Indian plantation. The Mashpee's relationship to this land, however, remained legally problematic for the Commonwealth. In 1842, Massachusetts determined that the land was to be divided among individual Mashpee Tribe members, but their power over it was closely circumscribed. The Mashpee could sell it only to other members of the tribe. The "plantation" could tax the land, but the land could not be taken for non-payment of those taxes. In 1859, a measure was proposed to permit the

Mashpee to sell land to outsiders and to make the Mashpee "full citizens" of the Commonwealth. This proposal was rejected by the tribe's governing council. In 1870, however, the Mashpee were "granted" rights to alienate their property as "full-fledged citizens" and their land was organized by fiat into the town of Mashpee.[22]

Many of the facts underlying the Mashpee's suit were not disputed. What the parties fought about was the *meaning* of "what happened."[23] Seen from the perspective of the Mashpee, the facts that defined the Indians as a tribe also invalidated the transactions divesting them of their lands. From the perspective of the property owners in the town, however, those same acts proved that the Mashpee no longer existed as a separate people. How, then, is an appropriate perspective to be chosen? As told by the defendants, the Mashpee's story was one about "a small, mixed community fighting for equality and citizenship while abandoning, by choice or coercion, most of its aboriginal heritage."[24]

Using the same evidence, the plaintiffs told a very different story. It was the story of cultural survival: "[T]he residents of Mashpee had managed to keep alive a core of Indian identity over three centuries against enormous odds. They had done so in supple, sometimes surreptitious ways, always attempting to control, not reject, outside influences."[25] Which of the two conflicting perspectives is the "proper" one from which to assess the facts underlying the Mashpee's claim? The answers provided by the courts that considered the Mashpee claims exemplify both the use and abuse of examples in American law.

The Story and the Teller

In response to the Mashpee's claims, attorneys for the Town of Mashpee argued that the tribe lacked racial purity, that it failed to retain a sufficient degree of self-government. It exercised little if any "sovereignty" over specific territory; it maintained no perceivably coherent sense of "community," and therefore was not a tribe as defined by the Supreme Court in *Montoya*.[26] The defense's main witness, Francis Hutchins, a historian, offered five days of exhaustive testimony.[27] Although he and the Mashpee referred to more or less the same documents, his positivistic account of the Mashpee's history left no room to suggest that certain land deeds in fact reflected white, rather than Indian, notions of land ownership. The very acceptance by the court and the witnesses of the symbology of deeds presupposed a certain structure for the Mashpee story. This structure,

136   framed with the European indicia of *ownership*, was asserted by the defense as the only basis for the tribe's claims. In doing so, defendant's counsel translated the tribe's claims into terms foreign to the Mashpee. This rhetorical move stripped the land claim of nuances that deeds could not replace. The deeds not only reconstituted the tribe's basic claim, they also temporalized it; deeds set it apart from the evolving tradition of the Indians' relationship to their physical surroundings, and, at once, both elevated and debased their relationship to the land.[28]

With regard to political leadership, the defendants' historian found scant historical traces of Indian government at Mashpee. The court apparently did not recognize any irony in the defense's attack on the Mashpee's claim of "self-government." According to the defendants, the Mashpee could be "self-governed" only if the tribe adopted political forms susceptible to documentary proof. Unfortunately, the tribe did not see fit to create that kind of proof of its political existence, since the court was asking for evidence of the type of political life that white Europeans, but not the Mashpee, recognized as legitimate. The Mashpee tried to point out that what was "appearing" as a "lack" or "gap" in the defendants' account of their history was something that they simply would not have recorded in written form.[29]

Within the idiom of documentary evidence as written record, their history could only signify silence because the Mashpee Indian culture is rooted in large measure on the passing of an oral record.[30] The commonplace view, replicated in the process of legal proof, is that "facts" only have meaning to the extent that they represent something "real." The stories that members of the Mashpee Tribe told were stories that legal ears could not hear. Thus, the legal requirements of relevance rendered the Indian storytellers mute and the culture they were portraying invisible. The tragedy of power was manifest in the legally mute and invisible culture of those Mashpee Indians who stood before the court trying to prove that they existed.[31]

Exempli Gratia

What were the underlying structures or categories guiding the determination of what evidence in the Mashpee trial was deemed "material"—that is, within the confines of the legally defined dispute? In order to construct an answer, it is necessary to examine two other problems underlying the materiality of the evidence offered by the defense. First, in claiming blood as a measure of identity, the defense argued (to the all-white jury) that "black intermarriage made the Mashpees' proper racial identification black instead of Indian."[32] Because of the racial composition of the community, that the jury would be composed exclusively of white people virtually was guaranteed by the voir dire in which prospective jurors were asked whether they were themselves Indian, had any known Indian relatives, or had ever been identified with organizations involved in "Indian causes."[33] White intermarriage was mentioned only in passing.[34]

Second, "the trial court instructed the jury that the tribe could terminate through social or cultural assimilation of *'English forms'* and *'English labels.'*"[35] The court interpreted Mashpee adaptation to the dominant culture, necessary for their survival as an independent people, as proof the tribe had surrendered its identity. That interpretation incorporates a dominant motif in the theory and practice of modern American pluralism.[36] Ethnic distinctiveness often must be sacrificed in exchange for social and economic security.

In their appeal to the United States Court of Appeals for the First Circuit, the Mashpee argued that "integration and assimilation have expressly been held insufficient to destroy tribal rights."[37] Notions of social and cultural assimilation, such as those upon which the defense relied, impute reified social standards to Indian communities that deny not only their right to historical change, but also the reality of their paradoxical continued existence. If the Mashpee only could be "Indians" by fitting into the definitions relied upon by the court and the defense, then the Mashpee's lived experience was devalued to the extent it did not conform. Moreover, by arguing that the Mashpee had been assimilated into the dominant culture merely because they had adopted some forms of that culture meant that the Mashpee could not change, even if they determined that some cultural adaptation was necessary to their own cultural survival.

Thus, the story of the Mashpee and their "otherness" can be told in several ways. Whether that story could be told in a way that is legally relevant, while still encompassing the multiple paradoxes of the general inquiry, remains the central problem.

At least one version of the Mashpee story begins with the rise of "Indian consciousness" in the late 1960s and 1970s that resulted in compelling political expression, partially through established legal mechanisms and institutions. Among the manifestations of this consciousness

138   were the so-called Indian land claim suits of the 1970s. These legal attacks on what were believed to be secure land titles were devastatingly upsetting to white landowners largely because they had the potential to undercut more than a century of settled expectations and redistribute power in a material way. The suits sought to shift control over the most basic material resource, land. What made the Mashpee's challenge particularly disconcerting to the white landowners was that it was conducted according to rules the now-frightened, non-Indian landowners felt compelled to respect—a lawsuit.

The Mashpee's story might begin another way. From the founding of the plantation for South Sea Indians and the Village of Mashpee until the middle 1960s, the area now known as the Town of Mashpee was controlled by people who identified themselves as Mashpee Wampanoag Indians. The Indian people of Mashpee exercised all the political power normally associated with Massachusetts's municipalities, including control over land use and permits for public activities. How the Mashpee actually described themselves was immaterial to their exercise of power. The normal disputes that arose out of the conduct of municipal affairs were, in effect, family squabbles. Even if some Mashpee did not approve of how others were acting, the integrity of the group remained unchallenged.

Circumstances drastically changed, however, in the mid-1960s. An influx of non-Indians who were not incorporated into the Mashpee people shifted the balance of political power in the town. With a change of political power in the community from Indian to non-Indians came changes in the material conditions of life in Mashpee. Land formerly open to the community was posted by its new private owners. Seaside resort developments were planned where only unspoiled woods and shoreline existed before. These changes were unsettling to the long-term Indian residents of Mashpee, who turned to the Non-Intercourse Act as a means of halting development and restructing political power in their town.

The story might begin yet another way. In 1901 in a case entitled *Montoya v. United States,* the United States Supreme Court declared: "By a 'tribe' we understand a body of Indians of the same or similar race, united in a community under one leadership or government, and inhabiting a particular, though sometimes ill-defined territory ..."[38] The *Montoya* definition of "tribe" was crucial to the Mashpee's claim, since the Non-Intercourse Act—the legal heart of their land claim suit—only protected "tribes" from the depredations of unscrupulous or unwise land deals. Rather than proving tribal identity in their own terms, the Mashpee

were forced to present themselves in terms adopted by *Montoya* and subsequent cases.[39] More importantly, there was little authority on the definition of a tribe. A group of Indians could be described legally as a "tribe"
or a "band," or as a "tribe" for some purposes but not for others.[40] The
structure of the narrative required by the precedent privileged the
definition adopted by *Montoya*.

The privileged *Montoya* narrative rested not merely on the foundation
of rules governing both authoritative and explanatory examples; the legal
narrative was privileged because the rules governing the construction of
the storytelling encompassed a complete perspective. Those rules—rules
of evidence—give preference to documentary evidence over "mere" recollection of the tribe's members. Recorded memory relies less on the
memory of the teller. The elevation of documentary evidence over oral
recollection effectively debased the Mashpee's foundation of self-knowl-
edge—their way of looking at, and knowing, themselves.

More important than just controlling the telling of stories in legal discourse, the rules also project reified social relations. The material social
relations of the Mashpee that cannot be called up through documentary
evidence have to be made to fit the model of Indian society projected by
the rules. The relations must be translated into the form established by the
rules to be comprehended by legal discourse, regardless of whether the
self-constructed reality of the Mashpee corresponds to the legal model.
Worse, these reified social relations are projected upon a background of
settled expectations that run directly counter to the claims the Mashpee
made. In order for the Mashpee's legal claim to make "sense," it must be
phrased within a strictly legal context, and that context must include the
justification for displacing two centuries of "the way things are."

Notes

1.   447 F. Supp. 940 (D. Mass. 1978), *aff'd sub nom.* Mashpee Tribe v. New Seabury
      Corp., 592 F.2d 575 (1st Cir.), *cert. denied,* 444 U.S. 866 (1979).

2.   25 U.S.C. § 177 (1988) (derived from Act of June 30, 1834, ch. 161, § 12, 4 Stat. 730).
      This Act provides: "No purchase, grant, lease, or other conveyance of lands, ... from
      any Indian nation or tribe of Indians, shall be of any validity in law or equity, unless the
      same be made by treaty or convention entered into pursuant to the Constitution." *Id.*
      The original language read: "That no person shall be permitted to carry on any trade or
      intercourse with the Indian tribes, without a license for that purpose under the hand
      and seal of the superintendent of the department...." Act of July 22, 1790, ch. 33, § 1,
      1 Stat. 137.

3. Montoya v. United States, 180 U.S. 261 (1901). *Montoya* involved a company whose livestock had been taken by a group of Indians. The company sued the United States and the tribe to which the group allegedly belonged under the Indian Depredation Act, ch. 538, 26 Stat. 851 (1891). This Act provided compensation to persons whose property was destroyed by Indians belonging to a tribe. The theory underlying tribal liability is that the tribe should be responsible for the actions of its members. The issue in *Montoya* was whether the wrong-doers were still part of the tribe. The court found they were not.

4. 180 U.S. at 266.

5. The questioning of Vernon Pocknett, a Mashpee Tribe member, illustrates the attempt to impose certain preconceived notions of leadership upon the Mashpee Tribe:

> Q: [W]hat was it Mr. Mills did as chief?
> A: What he did?
> Q: Yes. And you said he gives advice.
> A: Very good advice.
> Q: He gives good advice, is that right?
> A: Right.
> Q: He doesn't issue any orders, does he?
> A: No, no way.
> Q: The [Tribe] has no rules or regulations, does it?
> A: Rules or regulations? That would come under way of life. No, we don't have rules or regulations.

Record at 3:191 (Oct. 19, 1977), Mashpee Tribe v. New Seabury Corp., 427 F. Supp. 899 (D. Mass. 1978)(No. Civ. A. No. 76–31, 90–5)[hereinafter Record].

6. Record at 40:7 (Jan. 4, 1978) (instructions to jury on burden of proof); *see also Mashpee Tribe*, 447 F. Supp. at 943.

7. Record, *supra* note 5, at 36:189 (Dec. 28, 1977).

8. *See id.* at 40:36 (Jan. 4, 1978).

9. *Mashpee Tribe*, 447 F. Supp. at 950.

10. Paul Brodeur notes:

> Mashpee was never really settled in any formal sense of the word. It was simply inhabited by the Wampanoags and their Nauset relatives, whose ancestors had been coming there to fish for herring and to gather clams and oysters since the earliest aboriginal times, and whose descendants currently represent, with the exception of the Penobscots and the Passamaquoddies of Maine, the largest body of Indians in New England.

> PAUL BRODEUR, RESTITUTION: THE LAND CLAIMS OF THE MASHPEE, PASSAMAQUODDY, AND PENOBSCOT INDIANS OF NEW ENGLAND 7–9 (1985); *see also* JAMES CLIFFORD, THE PREDICAMENT OF CULTURE: TWENTIETH-CENTURY ETHNOGRAPHY, LITERATURE, AND ART 289 (1988).

11. *See* CLAUDE LEVI-STRAUSS, THE RAW AND THE COOKED at 5–6 (1969).

12. 25 U.S.C. § 177 (1988).

13. *See id.* (referring to "Indian nation" and "tribe of Indians" as those covered by statute).

14. *Montoya*, 180 U.S. at 266.

15. CLIFFORD, *supra* note 10, at 306–07.

16. BRODEUR, *supra* note 10, at 11.

17. *Id.* at 15.

18. *Id.*

19. *Id.* at 17.

20. *Id.*

21. *Id.* at 18.

22. *Id.* at 19–20.

23. "The jury's problem was not so much weighing conflicting evidence as choosing between plaintiff's and defendant's interpretation of the historical data." Mashpee Tribe v. New Seabury Corp., 592 F.2d 575, 589 n.14 (1st Cir.), *cert. denied*, 444 U.S. 866 (1979).

24. CLIFFORD, *supra* note 10, at 302.

25. *Id.*

26. *Montoya*, 180 U.S. at 266.

27. *See* Record, *supra* note 5, at 34 (Dec. 21, 1977), 35 (Dec. 22, 1977), 36 (Dec. 28–29, 1977), 38 (Dec. 30, 1977).

28. In his testimony, Professor Hutchins spoke of the "breakdown" of the Mashpee community, owing to its "choice" to remain on Cape Cod, rather than being relocated to the Western United States when "offered the opportunity" to do so in the 1700s. What Hutchins failed to comprehend, however, is that the command, "If you want a land base, go west," completely misperceives the Mashpee's fundamental sense of place. The irony, of course, is that the tribe's culturally-defined relationship to the land was interpreted in light of Euro-American standards. As Bruce Chatwin writes in another context:

    > White men ... made the common mistake of assuming that, because the Aboriginals were wanderers, they could have no system of land tenure. This was nonsense. Aboriginals, it was true, could not imagine territory as a block of land hemmed in by frontiers: but rather as interlocking network of "lines" or "ways through."

    BRUCE CHATWIN, THE SONGLINES 56 (1987) (exploration of Australian Natives' understanding of time, place, and identity).

29. Vine Deloria, Jr., an attorney, author, and Indian affairs consultant, testified:

    > [Y]ou don't really study tribes. You work with the people to help them prepare the best understanding you can of what the current problems are, how they got into the situation they got into. In the course of that you talk with a great many Indians. A lot of times they remember things that are not in the ordinary train of documents that your standard economic scholar would run across. So in checking the oral testimony, oral tradition of the people, then that gives you additional leads as to where you can find other sources to fill in the history. And there's no really good history on any tribe in the country.

    Record, *supra* note 5, at 16:109 (Nov. 9, 1977).

30. The cultural bias in favor of written, as opposed to oral, history resounded throughout the trial of the Mashpee's land claim suit. Take, for example, the testimony of defense witness Francis Hutchins, a political scientist and historian, regarding his method of researching Indian history: "All the materials which the historian uses when you are dealing with a historical period, you can't pick and choose, you have to use what you can find. And I have tried to look at *every piece of paper* that survives from that period relating to the subject." Record, *supra* note 5, at 34:59–60 (Dec. 21, 1977) (emphasis added).

31. "It is important to remember that the voices to which power responds must be those that it can hear." Gerald Torres & Donald P. Brewster, *Judges and Juries: Separate Moments in the Same Phenomenon,* 4 LAW & INEQ. J. 171, 181 (1986) (discussing the problems feminism has encountered in searching for a voice with which to participate in legal discourse).

32. Petition for Certiorari to the United States Court of Appeals for the First Circuit at 11, Mashpee Tribe v. New Seabury Corp., 592 F.2d 575 (1st Cir.) (No. 79–62), *cert. denied,* 444 U.S. 866 (1979) [hereinafter Petition for Certiorari].

33. *See, e.g.,* Record, *supra* note 5, at 1:21–22.

34. Even the slightest sensitivity to the racial history of the United States makes apparent the racial taxonomy being imposed here. The defense affected a purely external view of the process of intermarriage and assimilation—not just any external view, but a racially *white* external view. The internal perspectives, within the tactical stance adopted by the defense, were irrelevant. See, e.g., Gerald Torres, *Local Knowledge, Local Color: Critical Legal Studies and the Law of Race Relations,* 25 SAN DIEGO L. REV. 1043 (1988); Gary Peller, *Race Consciousness,* 1990 DUKE L.J. 758, reprinted in this volume at 67.

35. Petition for Certiorari, *supra* note 32, at 15–16 (emphasis added); *see also Mashpee Tribe,* 592 F.2d at 586 (addressing trial court's instructions to jury regarding the adoption of English forms and English labels).

36. *See* Torres, *supra* note 34 (arguing, in part, that cultural pluralism as presently defined in American culture reflects systemic inequalities).

37. Petition for Certiorari, *supra* note 32, at 16 (quoting *The Kansas Indians,* 72 U.S. (5 Wall.) 737, 756–57 (1867)).

38. 180 U.S. at 266.

39. At the time the Mashpee's claim was tried, two Supreme Court opinions cited *Montoya* as an appropriate source for the legal definition of "tribe." *See* United States v. Chavez, 290 U.S. 357, 364 (1933); United States v. Candelaria, 271 U.S. 432, 442 (1926).

40. "We are more concerned in this case with the meaning of the words 'tribe' and 'band.' ... [By 'band,' we mean] a company of Indians not necessarily, though often of the same race or tribe, but united under the same leadership in a common design." *Montoya,* 180 U.S. at 266.

CHAPTER EIGHT

—⊷—◦—⊷—

"THE BLACK COMMUNITY," ITS LAWBREAKERS, AND A POLITICS OF IDENTIFICATION

Regina Austin

THERE EXISTS OUT THERE, somewhere, "the black community." It once was a place where people both lived and worked. Now it is more of an idea, or an ideal, than a reality. It is like the mythical maroon colony of the Isle des Chevaliers (for those of you who have read Toni Morrison's *Tar Baby*)[1] or like Brigadoon[2] (for those of you who are culturally deprived). "The black community" of which I write is partly the manifestation of a nostalgic longing for a time when blacks were clearly distinguishable from whites and concern about the welfare of the poor was more natural than our hairdos. Perhaps my vision of the "'quintessential' black community" is ahistorical, transcendent, and picturesque. I will even concede that "the community's" infrastructure is weak, its cultural heritage is lost on too many of its young, and its contemporary politics is in disarray. I nonetheless think of it as "Home" and refer to it whenever I want to convey the illusion that my arguments have the backing of millions.

   "The black community" of which I write is in a constant state of flux because it is buffeted by challenges from without and from within. (The

143

144   same is true for "the dominant society," but that is another story.) There are tensions at the border with the dominant society, at the frontier between liberation and oppression. There is also internal dissension over indigenous threats to security and solidarity. "Difference" is as much a source of contention within "the community" as it is the factor marking the boundary between "the community" and everyone else. "The community's" struggles are made all the more difficult because there is no bright line between its foreign affairs and its domestic relations.

Nothing illustrates the multiple threats to the ideal of "the black community" better than black criminal behavior and the debates it engenders. There is no shortage of controversy about the causes, consequences, and cures of black criminality. To the extent there is consensus, black appraisals of questionable behavior are often in accord with those prevailing in the dominant society, but sometimes they are not. In any event, there is typically no unanimity within "the community" on these issues.

For example, some blacks contend that in general the criminal justice system is working too well (putting too many folks in prison),[3] while others maintain that it is not working well enough (leaving too many dangerous folks out on the streets). Black public officials and others have taken positions on both sides of the drug legalization issue.[4] Black neighbors are split in cities where young black men have been stopped and searched by the police on a wholesale basis because of gang activity or drug trafficking in the area.[5] Those with opposing views are arguing about the fairness of evicting an entire family from public housing on account of the drug-related activities of a single household member,[6] the propriety of boycotting Asian store owners who have used what some consider to be excessive force in dealing with suspected shoplifters and would-be robbers,[7] and the wisdom of prosecuting poor black women for fetal neglect because they consumed drugs during their pregnancies.[8]

Whether "the black community" defends those who break the law or seeks to bring the full force of white justice down upon them depends on considerations not necessarily shared by the rest of the society. "The black community" evaluates behavior in terms of its impact on the overall progress of the race. Black criminals are pitied, praised, protected, emulated, or embraced if their behavior has a positive impact on the social, political, and economic well-being of black communal life. Otherwise, they are criticized, ostracized, scorned, abandoned, and betrayed. The various assessments of the social standing of black criminals within "the community" fall into two predominant political approaches.

At times, "the black community" or an element thereof repudiates those who break the law and proclaims the distinctiveness and the worthiness of those who do not. This "politics of distinction" accounts in part for the contemporary emphasis on black exceptionalism. Role models and black "firsts" abound. Stress is placed on the difference that exists between the "better" elements of "the community" and the stereotypical "lowlifes" who richly merit the bad reputations the dominant society accords them.[9] According to the politics of distinction, little enough attention is being paid to the law-abiding people who are the lawbreakers' victims. Drive-by shootings and random street crime have replaced lynchings as a source of intimidation, and the "culture of terror" practiced by armed crack dealers and warring adolescents has turned them into the urban equivalents of the Ku Klux Klan.[10] Cutting the lawbreakers loose, so to speak, by dismissing them as aberrations and excluding them from the orbit of our concern to concentrate on the innocent is a wise use of political resources.

Moreover, lawless behavior by some blacks stigmatizes all and impedes collective progress. For example, based on the behavior of a few, street crime is wrongly thought to be the near exclusive domain of black males; as a result, black men of all sorts encounter an almost hysterical suspicion as they negotiate public spaces in urban environments[11] and attempt to engage in simple commercial exchanges.[12] Condemnation and expulsion from "the community" are just what the lawbreakers who provoke these reactions deserve.

In certain circumstances the politics of distinction, with its reliance on traditional values of hard work, respectable living, and conformity to law, is a perfectly progressive maneuver for "the community" to make. Deviance confirms stereotypes and plays into the hands of an enemy eager to justify discrimination. The quest for distinction can save lives and preserve communal harmony.

On the downside, however, the politics of distinction intensifies divisions within "the community." It furthers the interests of a middle class uncertain of its material security and social status in white society. The persons who fare best under this approach are those who are the most exceptional (i.e., those most like successful white people). At the same time, concentrating on black exceptionalism does little to improve the material conditions of those who conform to the stereotypes. Unfortunately, there are too many young people caught up in the criminal justice system to write them all off or to provide for their reentry into the mainstream one or two at a time.[13] In addition, the politics of distinction encourages greater surveillance and harassment of those black citizens who are most vulnerable to unjustified interference because they resemble the lawbreakers in age, gender, and class. Finally, the power of the ideology of individual black advancement, of which the emphasis on role models and race pioneers is but a veneer,[14] is unraveling in the face of collective lower-class decline. To be cynical about it, an alternative form of politics may be necessary if the bourgeoisie is to maintain even a semblance of control over the black masses.

Degenerates, drug addicts, ex-cons, and criminals are not always "the community's" "others." Differences that exist between black lawbreakers and the rest of us are sometimes ignored and even denied in the name of racial justice. "The black community" acknowledges the deviants' membership, links their behavior to "the community's" political agenda, and equates it with race resistance. "The community" chooses to identify itself with its lawbreakers and does so as an act of defiance. Such an approach might be termed the "politics of identification."

In fact, there is not one version of the politics of identification but many. They vary with the class of the identifiers, their familiarity with the modes and mores of black lawbreakers, and the impact that black lawbreaking has on the identifiers' economic, social, and political welfare.

The politics of identification envisioned in this essay is

> a politics . . . which works with and through difference, which is able to build those forms of solidarity and identification which make common struggle and resistance possible but without suppressing the real heterogeneity of interests and identities, and which can effectively draw the political boundary lines without which political contestation is impossible, without fixing those boundaries for eternity.[15]

It is a politics that demands recognition of the material importance of lawbreaking to blacks of different socioeconomic strata, however damaging such recognition may be to illusions of black moral superiority. Moreover, the politics of identification described herein would have as an explicit goal the restoration of some (but not all) lawbreakers to good standing in the community by treating them like resources, providing them with opportunities for redemption, and fighting for their entitlement to a fair share of the riches of this society.

There is an enormous comfort that comes from being able to think and talk about "the black community" without doing much more than thinking and talking to insure its continued existence. Many of us treat "the black community" like a capital investment made long ago; we feel entitled to sit back and live off the interest. The only problem is that the criminals are opting out of "the community" faster than we can jettison them. As a skeptical 16-year-old former gang member put it: "Neighbors? Neighbors is for my grandmother. I ain't got the time. Church? People trying to get neat on Sunday and dissing people on Monday. . . . Community? What's that? Only community I know is my boys—when we get together that's my church, home, and community!"[16] There is much evidence that such sentiments are widespread and that the "'quintessential' black community" no longer exists. A new politics of identification, fueled by critically confronting the question of the positive significance of black lawbreaking, might restore some vitality to what has become a mere figure of speech.

There are all kinds of lawbreakers with whom law-abiding blacks might identify, but actual identification with any of them will not come easily. Young, aggressive, even violent, black males may be admired for their defiance of a society that has little use for their productivity. Yet, any regard for them must be tempered because their behavior is so destructive of themselves and others. Middle-class blacks have on occasion adopted the dress, speech, and carriage of male lawbreakers in an effort to project a militant image. This has produced benefits for the middle class, but it has not helped the actual lawbreakers and their kin very much. Finally, women not involved in street life may be sympathetic to the desire for exciting jobs in a public sphere. Unfortunately, however, there is little else about the lives of women in street life that seems worthy of esteem.

"The black community" is not really divided into two distinct segments—one straight, the other street. There are folks in the middle. If blacks who consider themselves totally respectable need role models to help them identify with lawbreakers, the prime candidates are the "bridge people" who straddle both worlds.

Bridge people have a real stake in negotiating the gulf that separates straight and street people and in understanding what constitutes an appropriate balance of the modes and mores of each. Bridge people bear the brunt of the hardship posed by a physical and familial proximity to those heavily engaged in street life. The opportunities of the bridge peo-

148   ple for an improved existence are bound up with the life chances of their deviant kin, all of whom cannot be locked up even if we wanted them to be. Bridge people accordingly maintain a critical yet balanced assessment of the deviance of other community members and of the responsibility that the larger society bears for all their troubles.[17]

Oppressed people need to know when to obey the law and when to ignore it. In the way of promulgating an informal, customary jurisprudence, bridge people are involved in a dialogue with the lawbreakers, their most ardent admirers, and with each other over the line between legality and illegality, between "getting over" and self-delusion, between collaboration and resistance, and between victimizing one's own and extracting justice from the enemy.[18] The discussions occur in homes, day care centers, welfare offices, health clinics, gyms, playgrounds, alternative schools, beauty parlors, and barber shops.

More importantly, the bridge people actualize the distinctions in their own everyday economic activities. Though many of them endure dull and unexciting lives just like straight women and men, bridge people also know how to hustle, in the sense of working aggressively, energetically, and without too much illegality. Hustling is "a way of life" and a "means [of] surviving" for those who must deal with low wages, layoffs, unemployment, and other flaws in the regular job market.[19] It includes "a wide variety of unconventional, sometimes extralegal or illegal activities, often frowned upon by the wider community but widely accepted and practiced in [black urban enclaves]."[20]

Anecdotal evidence suggests that the "hidden," "underground," "irregular," "cash," "off-the-books," or (please excuse the expression) "black market" economy is quite significant in low-income and working-class black neighborhoods.[21] My own observations and a survey of selected informants (who shall remain nameless) reveals that without the benefit of licenses, zoning variances, formal training, or tax reporting, black women are cleaning offices or doing domestic work, catering, providing child care in the home or elder care at the beds of the infirm, styling hair in basements, and conducting home demonstrations of Avon and Amway products. The men are engaged in "jackleg" home maintenance, yard work, back-alley car and appliance repair, gypsy cab driving, moving and hauling, and newspaper delivery. Some of these folks are essentially self-employed, while others merely supplement salaries from full-time jobs or their retirement income with a bit of hustling on the side. Those with extra space in their homes turn it into rental units or take in boarders.

Neighbors sell water ice and sweets from the front porch and conduct flea markets and yard sales from the garage in back. Street vendors are, of course, everywhere. All sorts of folks lined up for surplus butter and cheese when the government held its big giveaway. Clerks in stores cut their friends a break on merchandise, and pilfering employees spread their contraband around the neighborhood. Residential speak-easies have better prices and longer hours than bars and liquor stores. A card party offering good soul food and alcohol for sale may run from Friday night to Sunday morning. Skilled players can pick up more than a few dollars playing cards. Even the kids hustle; they perform in the streets (playing musical instruments or dancing) or sell candy door-to-door. Men on the margins scavenge to fill their shopping carts with recyclable cans and bottles or metal stripped from empty buildings and junk set out on the curb. As for the young men, they do not seem to be doing much of anything but selling drugs.

Further documenting the nature and extent of hustling in black enclaves is difficult. The norms regarding socially acceptable lawbreaking are unwritten, and the activity must be clandestine in order for it to succeed. Scant academic energy has been devoted to investigating how those connected to both the street and straight worlds survive financially. Kathryn Edin's dissertation, *There's a Lot of Month Left at the End of the Money: How Welfare Recipients in Chicago Make Ends Meet*,[22] marks a notable departure from the norm. Edin presents an extended financial profile of a group of twenty-five beneficiaries of Aid to Families with Dependent Children.[23] Included in the sample were not only blacks but also Mexican-Americans, Puerto Ricans and whites. All resided in the Chicago area.[24] "[O]nly seven out of these twenty-five families received enough money [from welfare] to cover their rent, food and utilities."[25] In assessing their overall budgets, Edin concludes that her informants "did not 'waste' much money," although there were a few non-necessities (like cigarettes and soda) and luxury items (like telephones and VCRs) that they might have done without.[26]

Edin catalogues the various ways the women made up the monthly budget deficits that remained after their welfare allotments and food stamps were exhausted.[27] Some of her subjects could rely on help from food pantries and gifts from friends and relatives. All engaged in activities that were illegal because they were not reported to the welfare authorities. This category included doing household chores for neighbors, collecting cans for recycling, mowing lawns, pocketing whatever

150   was left over from an educational grant after books and tuition were paid for, sharing a boyfriend's earnings, and receiving child support directly from the children's fathers. Nearly a third of Edin's informants also did things that were illegal enough to land them in jail (though none apparently did go to jail), and in the case of one informant, illegal enough to get her killed. This category included working at a regular job using a false name and social security number, operating a small-scale lottery or raffle, fencing stolen goods, dealing marijuana, dealing cocaine, occasionally engaging in sexual intercourse for money, and shoplifting. A recipient's opportunity structure (her family, friends, neighborhood milieu, and skill level) determined whether her income-generating activity included the unreportable.[28] Edin concludes that "of the welfare clients observed, most work as hard as their middle class counterparts."[29]

By and large, hustling consists of little more than self-sustaining survival mechanisms. The participants in such economic activity lack the wherewithal to increase its productivity and profitability. This is well illustrated by anthropologist Yvonne Jones's study of black street peddlers in "Riverview," a black enclave of a river-port city of the upper South.[30] Professor Jones concludes that the vendors'

> lack of financial assets *and* access to relevant decision-makers meant that they had to rely upon their ... skills and resources [which were not such as to allow them] to compete with enterprises having expansive resources and range.... [The] Riverview street peddlers ... while exhibiting all the features necessary for successful adaptation to an ethnically segregated urban arena in which there were few retail firms, were largely incapable of transforming their skills into those necessary for the successful operation of a sedentary retail site.[31]

The vendors' strengths were their ability to make flexible marketing decisions that took advantage of changing supply and demand and their capacity to capitalize on their personalities and charisma to foster personal relationships with customers. They were handicapped, however, by being "structurally isolated from professional and service-related firms which functioned to provide a variety of managerial and financial assistance to business enterprises. Thus accountants, tax specialists, bankers, and insurance agents were absent from the marketing arena of Riverview street peddlers."[32] Moreover, they used only cash, and no credit, in transactions with distributors and customers. Finally, Jones maintains, "they lacked control over their marketing niches, as well as those political and economic arenas which were fixed on transforming the economic landscape into an environment conducive to the profitability of the large-scale firms of the formal market sector."[33]

Whatever its limitations, hustling may nonetheless be an important factor in the development of more self-reliant black urban communities. Social scientists would classify much of the hustling described above under the rubric of "the informal economy." There is no single definition of the term. For the purposes of the discussion here, the informal economy encompasses "the range of overlapping subeconomies that are not taken into account by formal measures of economic activity."[34] Moreover, whether the activities are considered illegal or extralegal, the informal economy tends to escape direct regulation by the institutions of society, although other similar activities are not so immune.[35] At the same time, the informal economy is responsive to the regulatory environment whose actual jurisdiction it seeks to avoid or evade. The way harsher penalties for adult drug dealers create "employment opportunities" for juveniles illustrates how the law and the informal economy are dialectically related. Finally, the informal economy is characterized by operations that are "small scale," "labor intensive, requiring little capital," and "locally based," with business transacted "through face-to-face relationships between friends, relatives, or acquaintances in a limited geographical area."[36]

The informal economy has social and entrepreneurial aspects. It may manifest itself largely as a social undertaking, fueled not by money exchanges but by reciprocal gift giving and bartering. Informal activities assure social cohesion and protect folks "from total and abject economic failure" by providing a community with "its own informal safety net."[37] The informal economy also encompasses entrepreneurial market operations whose connection to the dominant economy may be close or distant. In some instances, the informal activity reflects the community's isolation from the formal economy. As such, the informal economy is primarily "a mechanism for maximizing the returns on whatever resources are available . . . by providing jobs, entrepreneurial opportunities, and enough diversity to maximize recirculation of money inside the community where the jobs are located and the goods or services are produced."[38] Alternatively, a community's informal sector may be highly connected to the formal economy in that it produces goods and services for external markets, competes for business with firms in the formal economy, and generates substantial income.[39]

152   Ventures in the informal economy have some of the advantages of legitimate small enterprises, which employment statistics indicate are making
somewhat of a comeback.[40] Economists hypothesize that the reemergence
of small firms is attributable to either a need for flexibility and specialization that mass production cannot satisfy or an effort on the part of large
concerns to reassert managerial control over labor through decentralization.[41] Small enterprises in the informal economy, which escape regulation, can certainly top those in the formal economy, at least in terms of
maximally exploiting workers. Operations in the informal sector are characterized by low wages, few fringe benefits, poor working conditions, no
job security, and work forces composed of women and/or racial and ethnic minorities, categories of employees who have historically been the victims of job discrimination.[42] At the same time, however, the informal
economy blurs the line between employer and employee by turning workers into self-employed artisans, part-time home workers, and small-scale
entrepreneurs.[43] In the informal economy, "workers [may] voluntarily
submit to high levels of exploitation in return for assistance in subsequently establishing and maintaining their own businesses."[44]

In assessing a broad range of informal economic activity in Europe,
Central and South America, and Asia, one group of scholars has concluded that the informal economy has experienced growth under the
following circumstances: (1) the informal sector took advantage of technological advancement and "capture[d] a niche in upscale segments of the
market"; (2) there was a strong "export orientation" that generated goods
and services not exclusively for the local market; and (3) the enterprises
were relatively autonomous and were not vertically connected to other,
larger businesses via multiple layers of subcontracting.[45] Moreover, socio-
cultural factors played a role. In the most successful informal economies,
there existed an "unusual receptivity to technological innovation and
entrepreneurial opportunities,"[46] "a concentration of entrepreneurial abilities in a given location and the consequent emergence of a strong business culture in which later arrivals were socialized," and a common
culture that created "overarching solidarity that facilitate[d] ... cooperation ... rules of conduct, and obligations which can alter ... what would
otherwise be pure market relationships."[47] Finally, the state also made a
contribution. "[E]very successful instance register[ed] evidence of an
official attitude that downplays the lack of observance of certain rules and
actively supports the growth of entrepreneurial ventures through training
programs, credit facilities, marketing assistance, and similar policies."[48]

This list of what are in essence the preconditions for optimal growth of the informal sector strongly suggests that the informal economy is not a "generalizable solution[ ] to [the problems of] economic underdevelopment."[49] Nonetheless, given high levels of poverty and unemployment in poor black urban enclaves, "the possibility of semiformal neighborhood subeconomies should be regarded with interest."[50] Poor black communities will unquestionably have difficulties strengthening and enlarging their informal economies because their inhabitants lack technical skills, business expertise, start-up capital, access to credit, and links to external markets. Yet there may be ways to overcome these obstacles.

Poor and working–class enclaves have an abundance of workers unskilled except in the hard work of hustling. They need on-the-job training. Both the politics of identification and the processes of the informal economy teach the same lesson: Start with people where they are and work with what you get! Grounded in communal kinship and altruism, the informal economy is one in which the son who just got out of jail and the niece who is in a drug rehabilitation program can find employment. It should remain that way. The importance attached to social ties ensures that deviants will have a role in the economic life of the community. We must not forget them. They have something to contribute, and we must bring them along, training them as we go. The social aspects of the informal economy should be infused into as much economic activity as possible.[51] A politics of identification should fight against the extension of market operations into relationships that are now quite adequately governed by social considerations.

The black middle class might provide the expertise that informal entrepreneurs and the poor and poorly trained labor force presently lack. Historically, members of the black middle class were not simply role models for their less-well-off neighbors. They also served as conduits through which family, friends, and young folks from the neighborhood found jobs with mainstream employers. Through employment in the larger society, they generated income that they spent in the community and, as professionals and entrepreneurs, aided in the recycling of income earned by their patients, clients, customers, and parishioners.[52] Members of the black middle class could be substantial generators and recyclers of income, suppliers of technical expertise, and links to the formal economy for individuals and businesses ready to cross over—if the black middle class were willing to accept the entrepreneurial and juridical risks associated with participation in the informal economy.

This call for the bourgeoisie to assist poorer black communities through informal enterprises should not be taken as an invitation to economic abuse. Their incursion should be limited in scope and duration.[53] Members of the middle class who are motivated by racial solidarity and a desire to sustain "the black community" might contribute through non-profit or cooperative ventures. In any event, being a black person employed in an informal, black-owned enterprise located in a black neighborhood is not the ideal situation, but it may be better than the next best alternative. Whatever form the informal economic intercourse between the bourgeoisie and unskilled community folks initially takes, the politics of identification suggests that the latter should become their own bosses and attain incomes that will entitle them to think of themselves as middle-class if that is their desire.

The state might be urged to provide the training programs and credit and marketing assistance other governments have accorded successful informal economies. Social welfare benefits that are not wage-based, such as income guarantees or universal health insurance, would also protect workers from some of the exploitation and abuse that accompany jobs in the informal sector.[54] In addition, the state might support new forms of communal or cooperative ownership that break down the distinction between capital and labor.[55] Unfortunately, the prospects for government assistance do not look particularly bright. Programs that require substantial expenditures have very little chance of being enacted in today's reactionary and recessionary political climate, although efforts to encourage entrepreneurship throughout society may generate some enthusiasm. Furthermore, black capitalism and minority self-help tend to be oversold as panaceas for the structural ills of poverty and limited employment opportunities in regular labor markets.[56] The ideological utility to the government of measures to assist the informal economy in black communities may far exceed their actual monetary payout.

Nonetheless, any liberal politics of economic reform should push for governmental support of black informal entrepreneurship. A politics of identification, however, would take a somewhat different, more deviant tack toward the role of the state. Informal enterprises shrink from the light; their operations are aided by their invisibility and covertness. Legal regulation is what they avoid and undermine, not necessarily what they require in order to prosper. To facilitate the growth of the informal economy, a politics of identification would, upon occasion, work to keep the law at bay. The progressive nature of its support of regulatory avoidance distinguishes it from similar approaches advocated by others. For example, Robert Woodson, a prominent advocate of black capitalism, has also called for curbs on regulations that supposedly interfere with the three *E's*: "[e]mpowerment, economic development or entrepreneurship, and education."[57] He leaves out a fourth *E* implicit in his proposals: exploitation. While a politics of identification might agree with Woodson regarding laws that impede black economic self-sufficiency, it would demand that blacks be the chief beneficiaries of any regulatory-avoidance effort and the owners or controllers of any enterprises thereby promoted. To this end, a politics of identification might support selective enforcement, rather than total elimination of governmental oversight, so as to better protect the interests of the least-well-off blacks working in the informal sector.

There are several areas in which competition from the informal sector has prompted actors in the formal economy to invoke the law to kill off their rivals. The interests of poorer blacks were on the side of informality in each. For example, squatters who move into and fix up abandoned or unoccupied properties with their sweat equity are informal producers of housing stock. Their lawlessness provokes the ire of the private sector, which has no real interest in taking up the slack of unmet demand but which is put out by the squatters' threat to the concept of private property. Local governments, which cannot supply sufficient decent public housing, respond with evictions or concessions in the form of formal homesteading programs that may co-opt the energy of squatting initiatives.[58] Squatting, which is essentially a form of self-help, is not the answer to the housing shortage in poor black neighborhoods, but it is an informal stopgap measure and a starting point for addressing the larger structural problems.[59]

Sidewalk entrepreneurs compete with more formal purveyors of goods and merchandise whose greater political clout not infrequently translates into regulations and ordinances restricting sidewalk vending.[60] Yet the contributions of many of these fixed-location enterprises to the economies of the surrounding neighborhood are limited because their prices are high, their utilization of local suppliers low, and their track record for hiring community residents virtually nonexistent. Furthermore, vendors' stalls once were loaded down with counterfeit high-status, trademark-bearing watches, handbags, and T-shirts. The original makers' efforts to curb the manufacture and sale of such goods seem to be working.[61] The presence of these items on the market had real subversive potential.[62] They made status a commodity within the financial reach of almost everyone. The goods were a tangible critique of the materialism of those who were insecure enough to buy the genuine article. Most purchasers knew from the asking price and the quality that the merchandise was bogus. This should constitute a defense to trademark infringement, but it does not.[63] Here, then, are several instances at the margins between legality and illegality in which a politics of identification could champion the cause of informality. There are surely others.

With regard to credit, a politics of identification might favor more legal formality over less. If really casual mechanisms exist in black communities for pooling cash and lending it to provide capital for informal ventures, they remain hidden (at least to me). Useful devices for laundering money are not likely to be well publicized. Living in an economy fueled by cash, many poor blacks are more familiar with the workings of currency exchanges and check-cashing outlets than with those of banks, savings and loans, and credit unions.[64] Informal credit associations appear to be fairly common among immigrants,[65] but they are not common among indigenous blacks. Pyramid schemes attract large stakes, but because they are not attached to any entrepreneurial activity, they simply redistribute resources in favor of the scams' unscrupulous originators and early "investors."[66] Too many black folks look to state-run lotteries for "dividends," even though lotteries are little more than regressive schemes of taxation that may be less effective at keeping capital within black enclaves than the illegal numbers rackets.[67] Informal arrangements modeled after community loan funds and community-based credit unions[68] would probably help supply investment capital to support entrepreneurial activity. Still, there must be some means to ensure that they are trustworthy and reliable. Whether loan funds and credit unions can exist in a state of purgatory somewhere between the formal and the informal and the legal and the illegal is not clear.[69]

Better than anything, rap music illustrates the possibilities for melding the mores of street and straight cultures with the methods of the informal and formal economies. Rap music is the paradigm for the praxis of a politics of identification. The vocal portion of rap—the message, the poetry—reflects the culture and concerns of poor and working-class urban black youth, particularly the b-boys.[70] It invokes such black modes of discourse as toasting, boasting, and signifying. It aims to alienate and challenge white authority. It is misogynistic, self-congratulatory, and very competitive. Whatever else might be said about it, rap does address subjects like guns, gangs, police brutality, racism, nationalism, money, and sex.[71] And it has also generated its own internal debates, with the strongest opposition to the standard fare coming from some female rappers who are making their presence felt with a strong black brand of feminism.[72]

Rap's material appropriation of sound and speech, however, may be more subversive than its ideological message. The background over which the rap artist orates is a synthesis of modern technology and a flaunting of the laws of private property. Rap is meant to be danced to, yet it requires no musical instruments and no original notes.[73] At its origin, rap (or hip-hop, as it was first known) partook of none of the romanticism and the pseudo-sophistication of disco.[74] It was an outgrowth of the same circumstances that produced the street art forms of breakdancing and graffiti.[75] DJs such as the legendary Kool DJ Herc and Grandmaster Flash worked with the equipment they had. "[R]ecords and tapes were the only source of professional-quality sounds available to people unable to buy anything but prerecorded music and the equipment to listen [to it]."[76] These early hip-hop DJs "turned two turntables into a sound system through the technical addition of a beat box, heavy amplification, headphones, and very, very fast hands."[77] The DJs began to broadcast the scratching that results from cuing a record and further developed the technique of moving a record back and forth over the same chord or beat for as long as the "enraptured" crowd could take it.[78] They also held an audience's attention by playing unfamiliar and obscure selections from their record libraries.[79]

With time and exposure, rap's focus moved from live performance to recordings and the turntable gave way to the digital synthesizer. The background over which the rappers recite their lines can now be produced by borrowing, editing, and combining digital sound bytes.[80] Technology makes for a crazier quilt of snippets and scrapes of this or that bit of sound. The technique of "taking a portion (phrase, riff, percussive vamp, etc.) of a known or unknown record (or a video game squawk, a touchtone telephone medley, a verbal tag from Malcolm X or Martin Luther King) and combining it in the overall mix" is known as "sampling."[81] "[S]ampling, the mother methodology [of rap music], was itself understood in-Scene as an outlaw credential."[82] Rappers didn't pay royalties. Rap was "a domain of the improper, where copyright and 'professional courtesy' are held in contempt. Rappers will take what is 'yours' and turn it into a 'parody' of you—and not even begin to pay you in full."[83]

As rap has crossed the threshold and won a place in the (white, middle-class) mainstream, its production has moved from the subterranean depths of the informal to the limelight of the formal economy. Many of the small independent labels that first produced rap have been bought up by the major recording companies. As a result, rap's message may not be as bold as it once was, and there are concerns that rap will lose its "integrity."[84] More importantly, the samplers are being required to pay royalties.[85] Rap has become a commodity that is sold to the very same community that used to get it for free.[86] Some rappers are getting rich. The question is not how many or by how much, but how deep does it go. One hopes that down on the street, among those left out again, the process of innovation and incubation is continuing and that something else is developing to take rap's place.

Rap music is emblematic, for a number of reasons, of what a politics of identification might accomplish. The rappers capture the drama of street life and serve it up to an audience that is white or middle-class or both, an audience both thrilled and chilled to be reminded of the existence of an angry black mass that might someday rise up and take what it will never be given. Someone should be preparing a list of demands. Rap is a political art form that is strengthened by the clash of viewpoints. It is an arena in which women are coming on strong. Furthermore, the perils of the informal economy—its riskiness, its skirting of the boundaries of legality, its sampling, and its scratching—are explicitly legitimated by rap's appeal and implicitly legitimated by its material success. Rap suggests that for those who want to get ahead and see "the black community" do the same, the bridge, a way station between the street and straight worlds, is an attractive place to be.

A politics of identification requires that its legal adherents work the line between the legal and the illegal, the formal and the informal, the socially (within "the community") acceptable and the socially despised, and the merely different and the truly deviant.

Working the line is one thing. Living on or near the line is another. All blacks do not do that, and some folks who are not black do. Though the ubiquitous experience of racism provides the basis for group solidarity,[87] differences of gender, class, geography, and political affiliations keep blacks apart. These differences may be the best evidence that a single black community no longer exists. Only blacks who are bound by shared economic, social, and political constraints, and who pursue their freedom through affective engagement with each other, live in real black communities. To be a part of a real black community requires that one go Home every once in a while and interact with the folks. To keep up one's membership in such a community requires that one do something on-site. A politics of identification is not a way around this. It just suggests what one might do when one gets there.

Notes

1. TONI MORRISON, TAR BABY (1981).

2. *Brigadoon* is a musical comedy, written by Alan Jay Lerner and Frederick Loewe and produced on Broadway in 1947, about a Scottish town of the same name that materializes once in a century. ABE LAUFFE, BROADWAY'S GREATEST MUSICALS 101–05 (rev. ed. 1977).

3. In the District of Columbia, a black defendant charged with murder was reportedly acquitted because some members of the jury were convinced that there were already enough young black men in prison. Barton Gellman & Sari Horwitz, *Letter Stirs Debate After Acquittal*, WASH. POST, Apr. 22, 1990, at A1.

4. *See* Kurt L. Schmoke, *An Argument in Favor of Decriminalization*, 18 HOFSTRA L. REV. 501 (1990); *Drug Legalization—Catastrophe for Black Americans: Hearing Before the House Select Comm. on Narcotics Abuse and Control*, 100th Cong., 2d Sess. 5–13, 19–21 (1988) (presenting the testimony of the mayor of Hartford in favor of legalization and that of the mayors of Newark and Philadelphia and the president of the National Medical Association against).

5. *See, e.g.*, MIKE DAVIS, CITY OF QUARTZ: EXCAVATING THE FUTURE IN LOS ANGELES 267–322 (1990) (describing various massive gang control crackdowns by the Los Angeles Police Department and the weak responses thereto); MARTIN SANCHEZ JANKOWSKI, ISLANDS IN THE STREET: GANGS AND AMERICAN URBAN SOCIETY 205–06 (1991) (describing community acceptance of the anti-gang sweeps of South-Central Los Angeles); Peter S. Canellos, *Split over Search Policy Widens*, BOSTON GLOBE, Oct. 21, 1989, at A1 (describing how community leaders split over the Boston Police Department's practice of stopping and searching young black males reputed to be gang members).

6. Section 5101 of the Anti-Drug Abuse Act of 1988 requires that public housing authority leases contain a provision that "criminal activity, including drug-related criminal activity, on or near public housing premises" by "a public housing tenant, any member of the tenant's household, or a guest or other person under the tenant's control . . . shall be cause for termination of tenancy." Anti-Drug Abuse Act of 1988, Pub. L. No. 100–690, § 5101, 102 Stat. 4181, 4300 (codified as amended at 42 U.S.C. § 1437d(1)(5) (1988)). Some tenants approve of the provision; *see Drugs and Public Housing: Hearing Before the Permanent Subcomm. on Investigations of the Senate Comm. on Government Affairs*, 101st Cong., 1st Sess. 41 (1989) (statement by a resident of a housing development in the District of Columbia advocating evictions if household heads do not evict the offending children themselves); other tenants do not; *see id.* (statement by a resident of Chicago public housing arguing that evictions are inappropriate because the parents are not the keepers of their children and should not be punished); *id.* at 72 (maintaining that good, long-term tenants are unfairly and summarily being evicted for the conduct of their children, which is only remotely connected with public housing).

7. *See* Seth Mydans, *Two Views of Protest at Korean Shop*, N.Y. TIMES, Dec. 24, 1991, at A10 (concerning boycotts of Korean stores in the Los Angeles area); Lisa W. Foderaro, *One Grocery Boycott Ends, But Earlier Siege Continues*, N.Y. TIMES, Sept. 9, 1990, § 1, at 38; Calvin Sims, *Black Shoppers, Korean Grocers: Need and Mistrust*, N.Y. TIMES, May 17, 1990, at B1.

8. There is evidence that the rate of usage of illicit drugs among pregnant women is fairly uniform across racial and socioeconomic groups. *See* Ira J. Chasnoff et al., *The Prevalence of Illicit-Drug or Alcohol Use During Pregnancy and Discrepancies in Mandatory Reporting in Pinellas County, Florida*, 322 NEW ENG. J. MED. 1202 (1990). Yet the overwhelming majority of the women prosecuted for prenatal drug consumption are black and poor. *See* Gina Kolata, *Bias Seen on Pregnant Addicts*, N.Y. TIMES, July 20, 1990, at A13.

9. *See* ELIJAH ANDERSON, STREETWISE: RACE, CLASS, AND CHANGE IN AN URBAN COMMUNITY 66–69 (1990) (recounting the derision voiced by working and middle-class blacks toward members of the "underclass").

10. *See* Philippe Bourgois, *In Search of Horatio Alger: Culture and Ideology in the Crack Economy*, 16 CONTEMP. DRUG PROBS. 619, 631–37 (1990). Based on his ethnographic research in Spanish Harlem, Bourgois maintains that "upward mobility in the underground economy requires a systematic and effective use of violence against one's colleagues, one's neighbors, and to a certain extent, against oneself." *Id.* at 632. "Individuals involved in street activity cultivate the culture of terror in order to intimidate competitors, maintain credibility, develop new contacts, cement partnerships, and, ultimately, have a good time." *Id.* at 634. *See also* CARL S. TAYLOR, DANGEROUS SOCIETY 66–67 (1990) (noting that gangs use violence to discipline members and earn the respect of others).

11. *See* Elijah Anderson, *Race and Neighborhood Transition, in* THE NEW URBAN REALITY 99, 112–16, 123–24 (Paul E. Peterson ed., 1985); Lawrence Thomas, *Next Life, I'll Be White*, N.Y. TIMES, Aug. 13, 1990, at A15.

12. *See The Jeweler's Dilemma*, THE NEW REPUBLIC, Nov. 10, 1986, at 18; Jane Gross, *When "By Appointment" Means Keep Out*, N.Y. TIMES, Dec. 17, 1986, at B1.

13. It was estimated that on any given day in mid-1989, 23% of black males between the ages of 20 and 29 were in prison, in jail, or on probation or parole, compared with 10.4% of Hispanic males and 6.2% of white males. MARK MAUER, YOUNG BLACK MEN AND THE CRIMINAL JUSTICE SYSTEM: A GROWING NATIONAL PROBLEM 3 (1990).

14. For a critique of the emphasis on role models, see Regina Austin, *Sapphire Bound!*, 1989 WIS. L. REV. 539, 574–76.

15. Stuart Hall, *New Ethnicities, in* BLACK FILM, BRITISH CINEMA 27–28 (Lisa Appignanesi ed., 1988).

16. TAYLOR, *supra* note 10, at 88.

17. *See* James C. McKinley, Jr., *Friendships and Fear Undermine a Will to Fight Drugs in Brooklyn*, N.Y. TIMES, Sept. 18, 1989, § 1, at 1.

18. *See* BETTY LOU VALENTINE, HUSTLING AND OTHER HARD WORK 23, 126–27 (1978).

19. TERRY M. WILLIAMS & WILLIAM KORNBLUM, GROWING UP POOR 12, 55–56 (1985).

20. VALENTINE, *supra* note 18, at 23.

21. WILLIAMS & KORNBLUM, *supra* note 19, at 6–7. *See also* Jagna Sharff, *The Underground Economy of a Poor Neighborhood, in* CITIES OF THE UNITED STATES 19 (Leith Mullings ed., 1987) (describing the activities of the underground economy in a Hispanic community on the Lower East Side of Manhattan).

22. Kathryn J. Edin, There's a Lot of Month Left at the End of the Money: How Welfare Recipients in Chicago Make Ends Meet (1989) (unpublished Ph.D. dissertation, Northwestern University).

23. *Id.* at 1.

24. *Id.* at 9–33.

25. *Id.* at 1.

26. *Id.* at 166–69, 172–73.

27. *Id.* at 9–33, 112–130.

28. *Id.* at 152–53, 204–20.

29. *Id.* at 70.

30. Yvonne V. Jones, *Street Peddlers as Entrepreneurs: Economic Adaptation to an Urban Area,* 17 URB. ANTHROPOLOGY 143 (1988).

31. *Id.* at 166–67.

32. *Id.* at 167.

33. *Id.* at 168.

34. Stuart Henry, *The Political Economy of Informal Economies,* ANNALS, Sept. 1987, at 137, 138–39.

35. *See* Manuel Castells & Alejandro Portes, *World Underneath: The Origins, Dynamics and Effects of the Informal Economy, in* THE INFORMAL ECONOMY: STUDIES IN ADVANCED AND LESS DEVELOPED COUNTRIES 11 (Alejandro Portes et al. eds., 1989) [hereinafter THE INFORMAL ECONOMY].

36. Henry, *supra* note 34, at 140.

37. Joseph P. Gaughan & Louis A. Ferman, *Toward an Understanding of the Informal Economy,* ANNALS, Sept. 1987, at 15, 21.

38. Saskia Sassen-Koob, *New York City's Informal Economy, in* THE INFORMAL ECONOMY, *supra* note 35, at 60, 71.

39. *See* Alex Stepick, *Miami's Two Informal Sectors, in* THE INFORMAL ECONOMY, *supra* note 35, at 111.

40. *See generally* Michael J. Piore, *United States of America, in* THE RE-EMERGENCE OF SMALL ENTERPRISES: INDUSTRIAL RESTRUCTURING IN INDUSTRIALISED COUNTRIES 261 (W. Sengenberger et al. eds., 1990) (laying out statistical evidence to show the increased share of employment held by small businesses) [hereinafter THE RE-EMERGENCE OF SMALL ENTERPRISES].

41. *Id.* at 282–83; Gary Loveman & Werner Sengenberger, *Introduction: Economic and Social Reorganisation in the Small and Medium-Sized Enterprise Sector, in* THE RE-EMERGENCE OF SMALL ENTERPRISES, *supra* note 40, at 1, 46–48.

42. Lourdes Beneria, *Subcontracting and Employment Dynamics in Mexico City, in* THE INFORMAL ECONOMY, *supra* note 35, at 173, 181, 185; Michele Hoyman, *Female Participation in the Informal Economy: A Neglected Issue,* ANNALS, Sept. 1987, at 64.

43. Alejandro Portes et al., *Conclusion: The Policy Implications of Informality, in* THE INFORMAL ECONOMY, *supra* note 35, at 298, 308.

44. Stepick, *supra* note 39, at 125.

45. Portes et al., *supra* note 43, at 302–03.

46. *Id.* at 304.

47. *Id.* at 304–05.

48. *Id.* at 303–04.

49. *Id..* at 302.

50. Sassen-Koob, *supra* note 38, at 74.

51. Louis A. Ferman et al., *Issues and Prospects for the Study of Informal Economies: Concepts, Research Strategies, and Policy,* ANNALS, Sept. 1987, at 154, 171; Henry, *supra* note 34, at 152.

52. *See* WILLIAM JULIUS WILSON, THE TRULY DISADVANTAGED 56, 137–38 (1987) (arguing that the exodus of higher-income families from ghetto areas undermined significant institutions like churches, stores, schools, and recreational centers, and through them the social fabric of the community).

53. *See* Portes et al., *supra* note 43, at 300–02.

54. *Id.* at 309–10.

55. *See* William H. Simon, *Social-Republican Property*, 38 UCLA L. REV. 1335 (1991).

56. Ferman et al., *supra* note 51, at 169.

57. *See* Robert Woodson, *Race and Economic Opportunity*, 42 VAND. L. REV. 1017, 1030, 1041–44 (1989).

58. *See* De Villar v. City of New York, 628 F. Supp. 80 (S.D.N.Y. 1986). *See generally* Seth Borgos, *Low-Income Homeownership and the ACORN Squatters Campaign, in* CRITICAL PERSPECTIVES ON HOUSING 428 (Rachel G. Bratt et al. eds., 1986) (describing the normative values of ACORN squatting movement and accounting for its success). The response to squatting has typically been the creation of homesteading programs that supply monies for rehabilitation and mechanisms for achieving title to properties. *See* Borgos, *supra*; Eric Hirsh & Peter Wood, *Squatting in New York City: Justification and Strategy*, 16 N.Y.U. REV. L. & SOC. CHANGE 605 (1987–88).

59. *See* Tony Schuman, *The Agony and the Equity: A Critique of Self-Help Housing, in* CRITICAL PERSPECTIVES ON HOUSING, *supra* note 58, at 463, 470–71; Leanne G. Rivlin & Josephine E. Imbimbo, *Self-Help Efforts in a Squatter Community: Implications for Addressing Contemporary Homelessness*, 17 AM. J. COMMUNITY PSYCHOL. 705, 725 (1989).

60. *See, e.g.*, Huelsman v. Civic Ctr. Corp., 873 F.2d 1171 (8th Cir. 1989) (holding that an antitrust action brought by self-employed, licensed vendors was barred by an ordinance prohibiting sales in an area bordering a ball park by others than the stadium owner and operator); Brown v. Barry, 710 F. Supp. 352 (D.D.C. 1989) (involving a successful equal protection claim against a 1905 regulation prohibiting the shining of shoes on public streets). The court failed to reach a second claim that the regulation was "a vestige of the Jim Crow era when laws were intentionally designed to thwart the economic self-sufficiency of blacks." *Id.* at 353.

61. *See* United States v. Myong Hwa Song, 934 F.2d 105 (7th Cir. 1991); Ralph Lauren v. Fong Ming Chow, No. 90–0996, 1991 U.S. Dist. LEXIS 6023 (D.D.C. Apr. 30, 1991); Hard Rock Cafe Licensing Corp. v. Parvez, No. 89–C-6966, 1990 U.S. Dist. LEXIS 12146 (N.D. Ill. Sept. 14, 1990), *vacated sub nom.* Hard Rock Cafe Licensing Corp. v. Concession Servs., 1992 U.S. App. LEXIS 1355 (7th Cir. Feb. 4, 1992) (holding that a flea market operator would be liable if it knew of vendor's infringement but was under no duty to seek out or prevent violations).

62. *See generally* Susan Willis, *I Shop Therefore I Am: Is There a Place for Afro-American Culture in Commodity Culture?, in* CHANGING OUR OWN WORDS: ESSAYS ON CRITICISM, THEORY, AND WRITING BY BLACK WOMEN 173 (Cheryl A. Wall ed., 1989) (arguing that male artists like Michael Jackson treat commodities as objects to be played with, enjoyed, or subverted).

63. *See* Gucci Am. v. Action Activewear, 759 F. Supp. 1060 (S.D.N.Y. 1991) (stating that actual confusion, quality of goods, and sophistication of consumers are factors to be considered in assessing liability for infringement and unfair competition).

64. *See Study of Check-Cashing Services*, J. RETAIL BANKING, Spring 1990, at 47 (survey of roughly 500 customers in five cities conducted by the Roper Organization for the Consumer Bankers Association); Robert Reed, *Currency Exchange Shame: City's Poor Pay High Price for Protected, Outdated System*, CRAIN'S CHICAGO BUS., Oct. 30, 1989, at 17; Louise Witt, *City, State Crack Down on Check Cashers*, BOSTON BUS. J., Aug. 6, 1990, at 1.

65. *See* Christine Gorman, *Do-It-Yourself Financing*, TIME, July 25, 1988, at 62 (describing ethnic loan clubs within the Vietnamese, Korean, West Indian, and Mexican communities); Robert Reinhold, *The Koreans' Big Entry into Business*, N.Y. TIMES, Sept. 24, 1989, § 4, at 4; Philip Kasinitz, *From Ghetto Elite to Service Sector: A Comparison of the Role of Two Waves of West Indian Immigrants in New York City*, 7 ETHNIC GROUPS 173,

179–80 (1988); *see also* Sou, *Sou Smart*, Essence, Feb. 1992, at 32 (touting group savings clubs modeled on the Caribbean examples known as "sou sou," "meeting," and "partner").

66. *See* Virgil Burke, *Of Pyramids and Pipe Dreams*, Black Enterprise, Aug. 1988, at 68 (describing an informal scheme styled as "financial networking" that attracted black investors).

67. *See generally* Charles E. Clotfelter & Philip J. Cook, Selling Hope: State Lotteries in America 95–106, 130–33, 222–30 (1989) (describing the demographics of the players, the relationship between lotteries and the illegal numbers racket, and the regressivity of the implicit lottery tax). In what might be seen as a sign of hope, Ebony reports that some blacks are becoming disgruntled with the lotteries because blacks do not appear to be winning big prizes. *Are State Lotteries Stacked Against Blacks?*, Ebony, June 1991, at 126.

68. *See* Michael Swack, *Community Finance Institutions*, *in* Beyond The Market And The State 79 (Severyn T. Bruyn & James Meehan eds., 1987).

69. In Washington, D.C., a concern known as Latin Investment Corporation performed banking functions for a largely Salvadoran immigrant clientele until it went bankrupt. The corporation was never chartered as a bank, its deposits were not insured, and its operations were known to bank regulators, who contended that they were without authority to stop them. *See* Carlos Sanchez & Joel G. Brenner, *Investors in Limbo After D.C. Firm Shuts*, Wash. Post, Dec. 6, 1990, at C1; Joel G. Brenner & Carlos Sanchez, *D.C. Knew Firm Had No Bank Charter*, Wash. Post, Dec. 7, 1990, at A1. *See also* Joel G. Brenner & Carlos Sanchez, *Uninsured Credit Firm Faces Probe*, Wash. Post, Dec. 29, 1990, at B1 (reporting that chain called Community Credit Union Services is not really a credit union; treasurer says firm considers itself "an investment club").

70. Mark Costello & David F. Wallace, Signifying Rappers: Rap and Race in the Urban Present 23 (1990). It is difficult to find a precise definition of the term "b-boys." The "b" could refer to black, bad, block, or breakdancing. Music critic Nelson George says b-boys are "urban males who in style, dress, speech, and attitude exemplified hip-hop culture." Nelson George, The Death of Rhythm & Blues 193 (1988).

71. *See generally* B. Adler & Janette Beckman, Rap: Portraits and Lyrics of a Generation of Black Rockers (1991).

72. *See* Tricia Rose, *Never Trust a Big Butt and a Smile*, Camera Obscura, May 1990, at 109 (profiling Queen Latifah, MC Lyte, and Salt-N-Pepa); Michele Wallace, *When Black Feminism Faces the Music, and the Music Is Rap*, N.Y. Times, July 29, 1990, at H20; Charlotte Greig, Will you still love me tomorrow? Girl Groups from the 50s on ... 204–23 (1989).

73. Costello & Wallace, *supra* note 70, at 85–86.

74. *See* George, *supra* note 70, at 154–55 (contending that disco was romantic music for the upwardly mobile while rap was raw, positive, and imbued with the attitude of self-determination); David Toop, The Rap Attack 78 (1984) (characterizing disco as nostalgic and pseudo-sophisticated).

75. Toop, *supra* note 74, at 12–15.

76. Costello & Wallace, *supra* note 70, at 85.

77. Houston A. Baker, Jr., *Hybridity, the Rap Race, and Pedagogy for the 1990s*, *in* Technoculture 197, 200 (Constance Penley & Andrew Ross eds., 1991).

78. Toop, *supra* note 74, at 26, 65.

79. *Id.* at 65.

80. Costello & Wallace, *supra* note 70, at 85.

81. Baker, *supra* note 77, at 201.

82. Costello & Wallace, *supra* note 70, at 105.

83. Baker, *supra* note 77, at 204.

84. Tony Van Der Meer, *Introduction to* Toop, *supra* note 74, at 5–6. *But see* George, *supra* note 70, at 72 (suggesting that rap's "rebel status and integrity" are not yet lost).

85. Litigation or the threat of it has prompted such rappers as Vanilla Ice, M.C. Hammer, and De La Soul to share credit and royalties with artists whose words were sampled. Guy Garcia, *Play It Again, Sampler,* Time, June 3, 1991, at 69; Betsy Pisik, *Rap: Recycling or Ripoff,* Wash. Times, Aug. 7, 1990, at El. Rapper Biz Markie knowingly released a recording that used, without permission, three words and a bit of the music of Gilbert O'Sullivan's song *Alone Again (Naturally)*. The district court enjoined the usage and referred the matter to the U.S. Attorney for possible criminal prosecution. Grand Upright Ltd. v. Warner Brothers Records, 780 F. Supp. 182 (S.D.N.Y. 1991).

86. To get exposure, DJs would set up in parks or at block parties and perform for free, Toop, *supra* note 74, at 60, 71, and give away tapes of their performances to friends and acquaintances. *Id.* at 78.

87. *See* Diana Fuss, Essentially Speaking: Feminism, Nature and Difference 90–93 (1989) (describing the use of essentialism in the writings of Afro-American literary critics).

>–←⊙–→–⊙–←←

CHAPTER NINE

DECENTERING DECENTRALIZATION

Jerry Frug

The Postmodern Subject as Local Government Law

A POSTMODERN CONCEPTION of local government law must start with a postmodern conception of localities. Instead of envisioning people as located on one side or the other of a city/suburb line, we need to recognize that "[y]oung or old, man or woman, rich or poor, a person is always located at 'nodal points' of specific communication circuits"[1] spread throughout an area.

The city/suburb distinction is often used to contrast two images: a congested, dangerous, deteriorating inner city and a quiet, prosperous residential suburb.[2] Such a picture misrepresents life in contemporary American metropolitan areas. Parts of America's cities are certainly characterized by congestion, poverty and urban decay, but so are many suburbs.[3] Indeed, these suburbs are often worse off than inner cities because their property values are so low that they cannot afford even the limited social services that cities offer their poorest residents. Similarly, if we think of a suburb as a homogeneous residential area dominated by well-

kept single family houses set in yards, "almost all large cities," as Robert
Fishman has noted, "have suburbs ... within their borders."[4] These residential areas within cities (Riverdale in New York, West Roxbury in
Boston, Chestnut Hill in Philadelphia, Chevy Chase D.C. in Washington, Sauganash in Chicago, Palmer Woods in Detroit, River Oaks in
Houston, Sea Cliff in San Francisco) are indistinguishable from neighborhoods on the other side of the city line. Moreover, people of color live
in both kinds of neighborhoods. One-third of African-Americans live in
middle class suburbs;[5] in some suburbs a majority of residents are
African-Americans, Chinese, or Latino. To be sure, lines of race divide
American metropolitan areas as sharply as the Berlin Wall formerly
divided Berlin and the green line divided Beirut. But these racial lines
are more often found within cities and between suburbs than along the
city/suburb boundary (East 96th Street and Howard Beach in New
York, South Side and Bridgeport in Chicago, Roxbury and South Boston
in Boston, Compton/Watts and the Westside in Los Angeles).[6] Finally,
it is not just the middle-class and the underclass who live on both sides
of the border: there are working-class suburbs just as there are working-
class neighborhoods within cities.[7]

The other characteristic that has traditionally been associated with
cities—a central business district with offices and stores—similarly describes suburbs as well as cities.[8] "Most large metropolitan areas have ten
to thirty urban cores, the downtown being just one of them."[9] Two-thirds
of American offices are currently located outside of city downtowns.[10]
Tyson's Corner, Virginia has more office space than downtown Miami;[11]
Southfield, Michigan has more office space than Detroit.[12] "By 1980, 38
percent of the nation's workers commuted to their jobs from suburb-to-
suburb, while only half as many made the stereotypical suburb-to-city
trek."[13] Moreover, shopping malls have not only brought the density and
feel of city commercial life to the suburbs but suburban stores now outsell
their city competitors.[14] Some of these suburban malls are as big as city
downtowns. (On Route 202 in King of Prussia, Pennsylvania, the sign
reads: "MALL NEXT FOUR LEFTS.")[15] The aggregation of restau-
rants, entertainment, shopping, and pedestrian walkways in suburban
shopping malls has, in fact, so captured the image of America's commercial life that cities have begun to restructure their own commercial areas
by copying them (Quincy Market in Boston; the Inner Harbor in
Baltimore; Watertower Place in Chicago; the Skyways in Minneapolis;
Ghirardelli Square in San Francisco; pedestrian zones everywhere).[16]

In sum, in the words of the urban historian James Vance, "[t]oday it is hard to draw a significant concrete distinction between a Clayton and a St. Louis."[17] Except, of course, that most of us have never heard of Clayton. The only difference between St. Louis and Clayton is a legal distinction—local government law treats these two parts of the same region as separate and independent sovereignties.[18] Indeed, during the course of my argument that the city/suburb distinction no longer describes American metropolitan areas, I have repeatedly invoked this legal distinction myself. I have used the words "city" and "suburb" to refer to one side or the other of the invisible line that marks the legally-recognized boundary between them. My use of these terms has masked the plurality and heterogeneity on both sides of the line. The terms thus have had the characteristics of the term *I* in the creation of subjectivity: the unity that "city" and "suburb" has assembled has been a unity of (legal) language. As Foucault suggests, use of this language is the exercise of power: the current identities of cities and suburbs are "an effect of power, and at the same time, or precisely to the extent to which . . . [they are] that effect . . . [they are] the element of its articulation."[19] To promote an alternative to this form of power, we must start by recognizing the arbitrariness of the city/suburb lines that now fracture America's metropolitan areas. We must look at our metropolitan areas anew, without focusing on the legally recognized borders between localities.

Most Americans who live in these areas already disregard jurisdictional boundaries. Instead of sharply dividing city and suburb, residents create their own idea of the region in which they live by organizing it in terms of the places they know.[20] They think nothing of crossing city lines for child care, work, shopping, recreation, entertainment, visiting friends, and the like. Their relevant space is "defined by the locations they can conveniently reach in their cars."[21] They often do not even know the name of the town where the mall they shop in is located; all they need to know is the name of the mall. Areas that do have names are commonly identified in a way that ignores local government boundaries: Route 128 in Massachusetts, Silicon Valley in Northern California, King of Prussia in Eastern Pennsylvania, the Galleria in Houston, Tyson's Corner in Virginia.[22] Other areas both in the city and the suburbs—even some close by—are so unfamiliar that people get lost if they try to go there. The metropolitan area as a whole is a hodgepodge of elements—shopping/office/hotel complexes, strip shopping malls, industrial parks, office buildings, department stores, neighborhoods, subdivisions, condominium communities—that is "impossible to comprehend,"[23] "vertigo-inducing."[24] For many Americans the symbol of this contemporary form of metropolis is Los Angeles. And, as Joel Garreau reports, "[e]very single American city that is growing, is growing in the fashion of Los Angeles, with multiple urban cores."[25]

This reference to Los Angeles suggests more than simply the absence of a metropolitan center. Los Angeles symbolizes another feature of contemporary urban life as well: issues of ethnicity, race, and class cross-cut America's metropolitan areas without stopping at jurisdictional borders. Los Angeles has aptly been labeled the capital of the third world: immigrants from El Salvador, Guatemala, Mexico, the Philippines, Korea, Thailand, Vietnam, Iran, India, Pakistan, Armenia, Russia, and Israel (among other places) have formed communities in both the city and the suburbs.[26] Similar communities are being created across America. This influx of immigrants has not merely changed the character of the neighborhoods where the immigrants reside. As in Los Angeles, many immigrants do business in the region's poorest neighborhoods (Korean and Latino stores in African-American neighborhoods); others work in minimum-wage jobs in the area's shopping/office/hotel complexes; still others spend most of their time in the region's fanciest neighborhoods because they have come to serve as the indispensable maids and babysitters for the upper-middle class.[27] Los Angeles is also famous these days as the site of recent riots and of gang warfare in its South Central neighborhoods. Fears of this kind of urban unrest and gang violence have increased throughout the country,[28] and the proximity between the neighborhoods where the civil unrest and violence have occurred (or threaten to occur) and other neighborhoods has increased with the extent of this fear. Neighborhoods close by were once virtually forgotten ("no one lives in Detroit," someone who lived in a nearby suburb once informed me); now, they seem all too close.

As early as 1923, Frank Lloyd Wright declared that "[t]he big city is no longer modern."[29] He was right: as Garreau points out, "we have not built a single old-style downtown from raw dirt in seventy-five years."[30] It is harder to realize—but it is also true—that the suburban era, the era of lawns and cul-de-sacs, has reached its end as well.[31] Now, as Michael Sorkin argues, people live in "a wholly new kind of city, a city without a place attached to it," one that Sorkin calls the "ageographical city."[32] Sorkin uses the term to describe the pastiche of highways, skyscrapers, malls, housing developments, and chain stores—the endless urban landscape of copies without an original—that constitute the place-bites (the spatial equivalent of sound-bites) of modern America. These place-bites can be combined in an infinite variety of ways, each of which makes equal sense, to represent the metropolitan area. The ageographical city, Sorkin suggests, is the urban form of the 800-number: the area code for no-place-in-particular.[33] To frame local government law in terms of the postmodern subject, we must locate it in this ageographical city.

Local government law, however, now gives priority to a single place-bite within the metropolitan area: the place where people live. Indeed, residency has always been at the center of local government law's conception of people's relationship to the space around them. Perhaps this emphasis on residency was justifiable when, once upon a time, home, work, family, friends, market, past, present, and future were (so we imagine) linked together in one community. But these days some people do not even live at their place of residence: students who spend full-time out-of-state, people who are serving in the military, and business-people who are assigned abroad are all residents of the town they are never in. And those who do live in the area are not found solely at home. Most people spend most of their day in other parts of the region. If the neighborhood where people work deteriorates or their mall closes down, it would affect their lives just as much as an event three blocks away from their residence. In an era when people often do not even know the names of neighbors who live a block away, a person's territorial identity should not be reduced to his or her address.

By locating people in their houses or apartments, local government law romanticizes the home as a haven in a heartless world.[34] But in contemporary America one's place of residence provides "no defense, no retreat. . . . [T]he overexposure and transparence of the world which traverses . . . [people] without obstacle"[35] leaves only a weak sense of "home." The ageographical city is, in other words, the urban form not just of the 800-number but also of the 700-number—the telephone number that is yours regardless of where you live. The average American moves twelve times in a lifetime.[36] I was born and went to school in Berkeley, California; I met and married my wife (who was from St. Joseph, Missouri) in Washington, D.C.; our son was born in New York City; our daughter was born in Philadelphia; most recent family vacations have been taken in the same house in Westport, Massachusetts; I now live in Cambridge, Massachusetts. Where am I from? Where are you from? Most people recognize that the millions of new immigrants in our metropolitan areas

170   are fractured by attachments to their country of origin, their current
neighborhood, the place where they work, and the place where they hope
to move—feeling "at home" in none of these locations. But in the age of
the jet plane, the modem, the fax machine, satellite disks, and USA
Today, it is not just recent immigrants who feel more linked to areas far
away than close to home. Someone in the upper-middle-class in Boston
is likely to be more connected to, and know more about, mid-town
Manhattan than Medford.

Of course, many people still feel an attachment to their neighborhood.
Sometimes this attachment is linked with commonalities of race, ethnicity, or class; sometimes it is attributed to the fact that a family has lived
in the same community for generations; sometimes it is expressed in
terms of maintaining property values; sometimes it is expressed as a negative—residents feel trapped, by poverty and exclusion, in an area from
which they cannot escape. But local government law has never given
legal protection to neighborhoods. On the contrary, recent developments
in local government law have presided over the destruction of many
neighborhoods to which people have felt connected.[37] In the 1960s and
1970s, some reformers sought to recenter local government law's sense of
place from the city or suburb to the neighborhood.[38] They wanted neighborhood to play the role for territorial identity that biology has played for
racial and gender identity—to be the common core that unites the group.
But a postmodern reading suggests that, like the reliance on biology (and
like the mirror image of the self),[39] the concept of neighborhood provides
no stable basis for either personal or group identity.

The image of neighborhood conjures up the ideal of community, but
it is a fantasy community—a (comm)unity that is never achievable. One
can succeed in maintaining an inside/outside distinction that delimits a
neighborhood only by failing to see people who are there but do not fit
in. Property owners who own property in the area but rent it to others,
workers who spend more hours in the area than residents, residents
whose violence or addiction threaten neighborhood stability, the homeless who live on the street, part-time residents who spend much of the
year elsewhere, maids who "live in," undocumented aliens living with
family members—which of these are included in the sense of "neighborhood?" Some local people have always been treated as outside the
definition of the community,[40] while outsiders have often been included
as community members.[41] Even the definition of a neighborhood is contestable: people who have lived in a neighborhood for years often dis-

agree about its borders. Attachment to a neighborhood, like the maintenance of the gender system, is a "ritual social drama[ ] . . . a performance that . . . is at once a reenactment and reexperiencing of a set of meanings already socially established . . . [a performance that] is effected with the strategic aim of maintaining . . . [the neighborhood] within its binary [inside/outside] frame."[42] Such a performance is constantly jeopardized by aspects of the ageographical city that people in the area cannot avoid or even find attractive.

To replace our current legal conception of localities with one that embraces the ageographical city, we have to stop building local government law on residency and on the importance of local jurisdictional boundaries. We must treat people not as located solely in one jurisdiction but as "switching center[s] for all the networks of influence"[43] within the region that affect their lives. Under current law, residency within city limits determines people's legal rights on issues ranging from voting to their entitlement to participate in government programs. And the location of property within city limits determines who pays for these government programs through the property tax, still the predominant source of local government revenue.[44] To illustrate how embracing the postmodern subject would transform local government law, I turn to a discussion of two specific local government doctrines: one dealing with residency (eligibility for government services) and one with the property tax (school financing.)

Many local services are now available only to the people inside specified jurisdictional borders. School attendance requires living within the school district; police and fire protection stop at the city line; city hospitals exclude non-residents.[45] One justification offered for these policies analogizes local government services to property rights: only those who pay for services are entitled to receive them. But those who pay for local services are not the same people as those eligible to receive them. Non-residents who own property in the city pay the property tax, but they cannot send their children to city schools or use city hospitals. On the other hand, residents who own no property and therefore do not pay property taxes (at least directly) can use city services. Moreover, many city services are supported by state and federal as well as locally-generated revenue. Yet residency remains a qualification for services no matter where the funding comes from. The reason that services are allocated only to residents is not the source of financing but the equation of residency and decentralization: local control means control by residents.[46]

A local government law organized in terms of the postmodern subject would recognize that the maids who clean the residents' houses, the grocery store family that provides their milk, and the consumers who drive to the area to shop are also connected to a neighborhood. Even Justice Rehnquist, in *Holt Civic Club v, City of Tuscaloosa*,[47] has acknowledged that decisions made by city residents have an impact on nonresidents whether or not the non-residents enter the city.

> The granting of building permits for high rise apartments, industrial plants, and the like on the city's fringe unavoidably contributes to problems of traffic congestion, school districting, and law enforcement immediately outside the city. A rate change in the city's sales or ad valorem tax could well have a significant impact on retailers and property values in areas bordering the city. The condemnation of real property on the city's edge for construction of a municipal garbage dump or waste treatment plant would have obvious implications for neighboring nonresidents. Indeed, the indirect extraterritorial effects of many purely internal municipal actions could conceivably have a heavier impact on surrounding environs than ... direct regulation. ..."[48]

To be sure, Justice Rehnquist used this analysis to defend a residency requirement, not to attack it. "[N]o one," he concluded, "would suggest that nonresidents likely to be affected by this sort of municipal action have a constitutional right to participate in the political processes bringing it about."[49] Well, I'm suggesting something of this sort, albeit not on constitutional grounds. In the ageographical city, residency within invisible boundary lines should not determine who can use schools, hospitals, addiction treatment centers or the like. Local services should be open to all local people. The problem is to decide who they are and how to do so.

Building local government law on a postmodern subjectivity would similarly transform local government financing. At present, only property located within jurisdictional boundaries is subject to tax, and only people who live within the same boundaries benefit from the tax. School financing provides the best known example of the impact of this inside/outside distinction. The Texas Supreme Court's description of the effect of jurisdictional wealth differences in that state is illustrative:

> Because of the disparities in district property wealth, spending per student varies widely, ranging from $2,112 to $19,333. Under the

existing system, an average of $2,000 more per year is spent on each of the 150,000 students in the wealthiest districts than is spent on the 150,000 students in the poorest districts. The lower expenditures in the property-poor districts are not the result of lack of tax effort. Generally, the property-rich districts can tax low and spend high while the property-poor districts must tax high merely to spend low. In 1985–86, local tax rates ranged from $.09 to $1.55 per $100 valuation. The 100 poorest districts had an average rate of 74.5 cents and spent an average of $2,978 per student. The 100 wealthiest districts had an average tax rate of 47 cents and spent an average of $7,233.[50]

In the celebrated case of *San Antonio Independent School District v. Rodriguez,* the United States Supreme Court rejected an argument that disparities such as these violated the Equal Protection Clause on the grounds that a property-based system enhanced local control, which it defined in classic centered-subject language.[51] State supreme courts, by contrast, have been divided on the question whether property-based school financing systems violated state constitutions.[52] But even those state courts that have held school financing systems unconstitutional have continued to recognize the importance of boundary lines. The Texas Supreme Court, for example, has made clear that its decision to invalidate the state's school financing system does not require localities to educate people who live outside their borders. And, the court indicated, once the state adds enough to money to the system to ensure that there is an efficient system of public schools throughout the state, school districts will be able to supplement the education of their residents through locally raised property taxes.[53] Other state courts have similarly permitted this kind of local supplementation, thereby perpetuating the idea that the property located inside jurisdictional borders exists for the benefit of residents.[54]

By defining the tax base in terms of the property found within a jurisdiction and by defining the beneficiaries of the tax base in terms of residency, local government law creates and intensifies inequality within the metropolitan area.[55] It's no accident that the locations of major sources of tax revenue, such as large suburban malls and office complexes, are often at some distance from the locations where the revenue is most needed. Localities within the region compete for these sources of revenue, just as they compete for the ability to exclude those who need government services.[56] But it is not necessary to organize the imposition and the dispersion of the property tax in terms of jurisdictional lines. Nor is it necessary to treat taxes on sales or income—taxes often paid by people who are not residents—as benefiting only residents. The current mismatch between the ability to raise revenue and the need for the money would be alleviated by a local government law that embraced the postmodern subject. Again, the critical issue (discussed below) is determining how best to do so.

It should be clear by now, I hope, that the transformation of local government law envisioned in this section would be dramatic. Almost no local government law issue would remain unaffected. To date, only a few local government services—such as beaches—have been required to be open to residents and non-residents alike,[57] and property-based tax schemes have been invalidated only in the area of school financing. But it is no more justifiable, in my view, for the quality of police protection, hospitals, or welfare programs to vary with district wealth than it is for the quality of the schools. And the ability to support social programs in innovative ways should, like the power to raise taxes, not depend on where developers choose to put their office complexes. Some localities, for example, now condition zoning approvals for office buildings on the developers' agreement to subsidize low and moderate income housing—a practice known as "exactions."[58] But they can do so only if they can attract the developer, and developers have an incentive to shop around for a jurisdiction not interested in imposing such an exaction. If, however, an exaction could be imposed for the benefit of the region's poor wherever the development is located, more such exactions would be possible and, as a result, more low and moderate income housing could be generated.

In the interest of preserving a national economy, courts have long invoked the dormant Commerce Clause to prevent cities from favoring their own residents over outsiders.[59] But court decisions relying on the Commerce Clause have simply invalidated local ordinances; they have not created a basis for a regional system of revenue-sharing and service-entitlement. A local government law founded on the postmodern subject has a chance of doing so. To be sure, as Justice Brennan suggested in *Holt*, a decision not to build local government law on local boundary lines and residency challenges our basic conception of what it means to be a political community. "At the heart of our basic conception of a 'political community,'" Justice Brennan asserted, "is the notion of a reciprocal relationship between the process of government and those who subject themselves to that process by choosing to live within the area of its authoritative application."[60] Indeed, building local government law in

terms of the ageographical city raises the question of what decentralization means. To whom would power be decentralized if not to people
defined within local boundaries? And where would people participate in
the democratic process if not at their place of residence?

The Institutional Implications
of Postmodern Subjectivity

Many who write in the postmodernist tradition would consider it a very
odd idea to try to build an institutional structure on postmodern subjectivity. After all, the postmodern subject, as described above, resists legal
and institutional forms. S/he seeks to escape established structures
through "subversive repetition," irony and play; not to create them.
Nevertheless, given the account of contemporary American metropolitan
areas just advanced, there are very practical reasons to try to figure out
how localities can best be endowed with this kind of subjectivity. Many
of America's giant shopping malls and office complexes are private businesses located in areas where few people live. What is the role of democracy in places like these? If we can't democratize Tyson's Corner or King
of Prussia—when so many American downtowns have been superseded
by developments of this kind—a vast amount of American life will never
be subject to popular participation and control.[61] And the disjunction
between the locations where America's commercial and business life is
growing and the centers of population is just an example of the urgent
need to reconsider the mix of place-bites that constitute America's urban
areas. In countless ways, the current mix combines, yet separates, areas
of crushing poverty and elaborate wealth. Perhaps postmodern theory is
our most promising source of ideas for changing the present-day allocation of power in metropolitan areas.

One way postmodern subjectivity might be introduced into local government law is through a regional legislature. If, as argued above, people
have multiple attachments to the metropolitan area, including attachments to places where they shop or work (like Tyson's Corner or King of
Prussia), creating a legislature built on a system of representation
reflecting these multiple attachments might be worth trying. Consider a
plan, for example, in which everyone gets five votes that they can cast in
whatever local elections they feel affect their interest ("local" still being
defined by the traditional territorial boundaries of city, suburb, or neighborhood). They can define their interests differently in different elec-

tions, and any form of connection that they think expresses an aspect of themselves at the moment will be treated as adequate. Under such an electoral system, mayors, city council members, and neighborhood representatives in the regional legislature would have a constituency made up not only of residents but of workers, shoppers, property owners in neighboring jurisdictions, the homeless, and so forth. People are unlikely to vote in a jurisdiction they do not care about, but there are a host of possible motives for voting (racial integration, racial solidarity, redistribution of wealth, desire for gentrification, etc.). Indeed, there is no reason to think that the constituency would be limited solely to those who live in the region. These days, as I have already argued, people feel connected to areas far away as well as close to home. Puerto Ricans in New York, therefore, may want to vote not only in New York but in San Juan; of course, if they do, that would leave them one less vote for local elections in the New York region. On the other hand, the voting system might also mimic the idea of proportional representation by allowing someone to cast all five votes in one locality if that is where her/his attachments are felt to be.[62]

What exactly would happen under such a electoral allocation is hard to say: indeed its unpredictability might be felt to reproduce the sense of "vertigo" that life in metropolitan areas is now said to induce. It seems likely, however, that the property tax generated by giant shopping malls and office complexes would be allocated more broadly than simply to those who live within the borders where they are located. Indeed, the rules for the allocation of all property taxes by the regional legislature could easily have a better chance of meeting the needs of people throughout the metropolitan area than rules created through negotiations between the city and the suburbs (defined in terms of residency). The attempt to limit services to those "inside" an area is also likely to be rethought and, perhaps, replaced with another form of allocation. Most importantly, such an electoral scheme would radically change the idea of what a neighborhood or suburb or city is—of who is included in a reference to such a locality. The "self" in the phrase local self-interest would become a gesture toward an unknown and unspecifiable multiplicity.

Still, the change would not be quite as radical as it might at first appear. The idea that Puerto Ricans who live outside of San Juan have an interest in being represented in its governance is not mine. Attempts have already been made to recognize their interests in the organization of San Juan's municipal government.[63] Even the Supreme Court recognized, in *Kramer v. Union Free School District*,[64] that those who vote in school board elections could not be limited to people who own or lease property in the area, their spouses, and the parents or guardians of the children who attend the schools. Many others, the court reasoned, have a direct and distinct interest in school decisions: "senior citizens and others living with children or relatives; clergy, military personnel, and others who live on tax-exempt property; boarders and lodgers; parents who neither own nor lease qualifying property and whose children are too young to attend school; parents who neither own nor lease qualifying property and whose children attend private schools."[65] But why stop there? Many more—including many non-residents the Court did not consider—are just as interested: teachers and staff who work at the school; parents who would like to send their children to the school system if they weren't excluded by residency requirements; parents who are sending their children to schools with fewer resources; citizens who believe in school integration. Of course, adding this group to the list of residents that the Court did include would make the school's constituency very uncertain and unstable. But school constituencies are already uncertain and unstable: residents are constantly moving in and out. In our mobile society, the notion of residency has provided an ever-shifting referent for the population of school districts, neighborhoods, and cities; in fact, reliance on residency has demonstrated that a fixed population is unnecessary to define a political constituency. Constituencies are defined tautologically: a locality includes whoever is defined by its rules of inclusion. And there is no reason to interpret the Constitution as requiring the rule of inclusion to be residency.[66]

A local government law based on a postmodern subjectivity also need not respect the current territorial boundaries of cities and towns, as has so far been assumed. Even now the residents of America's metropolitan areas live in a multitude of legally-defined jurisdictions with different borders: the areas defined by school districts, transportation districts, redevelopment authorities, park districts, and the like often differ not only from city borders but from each other. Currently, however, each of these governmental agencies reproduces the model of the centered subject adopted by cities: special districts and public authorities serve those defined by *their* borders. Thus the experience of the loss of boundaries that might have been produced by the multiple definitions of each citizen's location within the metropolitan area has been eclipsed by the reassuring sense that one's location is defined by the purpose of each territorial definition. (The fact that you're in the same Congressional dis-

178   trict as someone else doesn't mean that your kids can go to her school.)
Endowing localities with a postmodern subjectivity would replace this
comforting feeling with an intensified experience of geographic disso-
nance. Bringing even just the current multiplicity of boundaries to consciousness can help undermine the boundary-fixation that characterizes
so much of present-day local government law.

One form this consciousness-raising could take would be to increase the
level of popular participation in the multitude of territorially-defined governmental bodies that now exist within a metropolitan area. At present
their bureaucratic structure renders the differences among their boundary
definitions virtually invisible; only insiders pay much attention to how the
area is divided up. If, however, members of the public worked together on
education, parks, transportation, and similar issues, they would begin to
recognize the uncertainties of defining who counts as part of their community. Moreover, this experience need not be confined to currently
existing agencies. Often it would be better to set up a series of temporary
task forces—ad-hoc organizations—created to solve specific problems and
disbanded after the task is completed. The temporary character of these
task forces would make it easier for people to participate than would permanent organizations. And the task forces could divide up the region in
new ways to examine aspects of metropolitan life now largely left
untouched: the need for better working conditions in offices (a region of
buildings), the need for health and retirement benefits for people who
work in others' houses (a region of domestic workers), the need for child-
care facilities (a region of kids), the need for consumer protection (a
region of shoppers). I have discussed proposals for participation and
"adhocracy" such as these in greater detail elsewhere.[67] At the moment I
am raising them simply as examples of ways to provoke in the minds of
local residents the kind of questions associated with the postmodern subject ("Which world is this? What is to be done in it? Which of my selves
is to do it? . . . What happens when different kinds of worlds are placed in
confrontation, or when boundaries between worlds are violated?").[68]

Another form that postmodern subjectivity in local government law
might take would question not whom the locality includes but the kinds
of functions it performs. So far, the discussion of localities has referred
only to the traditional tasks of municipal governments, such as zoning,
condominium conversion, school financing, and allocation of public services. But this limited view of the role of local government is by no
means necessary. David Osborne and Ted Gaebler, for example, have

sought to "reinvent government" on a model of entrepreneurial activity.[69] Localities, they argue, should see themselves as profit-oriented
market-innovators and entrepreneurs, not as regulators and law-makers.
They should serve as catalysts for economic development, foster com-
munity-run organizations, and organize their own activities to increase
worker participation. I have made similar proposals for this kind of
change myself.[70] But my ideas, like theirs, treated local territorial boundaries as given. I now think it would be better to combine these ideas with
the other proposals advanced in this section, spreading their risks and
benefits across the region rather than having each locality undertake
entrepreneurial activities as a separate entity (defined in terms of residency). But whether organized locally or interlocally, these proposals
illustrate one more way to destabilize the identity of localities: Osborne
and Gaebler (and I) make the application of the public/private distinction to local governments impossible.

Notes

1. JEAN-FRANCOIS LYOTARD, THE POSTMODERN CONDITION: A REPORT ON KNOWLEDGE 15
    (Geoff Bennington & Brian Massumi trans., 1984).

2. *See, e.g.*, James Q. Wilson, *The Contradictions of an Advanced Capitalist State*, FORBES,
    Sept. 14, 1992, at 110; THOMAS M. STANBACK, JR., THE NEW SUBURBANIZATION:
    CHALLENGE TO THE CENTRAL CITY 1–2 (1991); PAUL E. PETERSON, CITY LIMITS 104
    (1981); HADLEY ARKES, THE PHILOSOPHER IN THE CITY: THE MORAL DIMENSION OF
    URBAN POLITICS 320–26 (1981).

3. Pierre deVise, Shifts in the Geography of Wealth and Poverty in Suburban America:
    1979 to 1989 (1992) (unpublished study, on file with the University of Chicago Law
    Review.). All but one of the ten poorest suburbs is more than 90% black and/or
    Hispanic. Bell Gardens [the other] is 87.5% Hispanic. *Id.* at 21. *See also* John
    McCormick & Peter McKillop, *The Other Suburbia*, NEWSWEEK, June 26, 1989, at 22.

4. ROBERT FISHMAN, BOURGEOIS UTOPIAS: THE RISE AND FALL OF SUBURBIA 6 (1987). *See
    also* JOEL GARREAU, EDGE CITY: LIFE ON THE NEW FRONTIER 149 (1991); DAVID R.
    CONTOSTA, SUBURB IN THE CITY: CHESTNUT HILL, PHILADELPHIA, 1850–1990 (1992).
    Indeed, if we think of suburbanization as "creating the appearance of nonurbanized
    space," cities are becoming suburbanized while suburbs are becoming urbanized.
    Joseph Wood, *Suburbanization of Center City*, 87 GEOGRAPHICAL REC. 325 (1988).

5. GARREAU, *supra* note 4, at 150; David J. Dent, *The New Black Suburbs*, N.Y. TIMES
    MAG., June 14, 1992, at 20.

6. *See* Richard Ford, *Urban Space and the Color Line: The Consequences of Demarcation and
    Disorientation in the Postmodern Metropolis*, 9 HARV. BLACKLETTER J. 117, 139–45 (1992);
    Paul Virilio, *The Overexposed City, in* ZONE 1/2: THE CONTEMPORARY CITY 15 (Jonathan
    Crary et al. eds., 1986).

7. *See, e.g.,* BENNETT M. BERGER, WORKING-CLASS SUBURB: A STUDY OF AUTO WORKERS IN SUBURBIA (1960) (discussing Richmond, California).

8. Joel Garreau has invented a new term, "Edge City," to describe areas, overwhelmingly residential or rural thirty years ago, which now are single-end destinations for jobs, shopping, and entertainment. To qualify as an Edge City, Garreau insists that the area have at least five million square feet of office space, at least six hundred thousand square feet of retail space, and a population that increases during the work day ("more jobs than bedrooms"). *See* GARREAU, *supra* note 4, at 6–7, 425.

9. Christopher Leinberger, *Business Flees to the Urban Fringe*, THE NATION, July 6, 1992, at 10, 11.

10. GARREAU, *supra* note 4, at 5.

11. Robert Fishman, *America's New City: Megalopolis Unbound*, 14 WILSON Q. 25, 28 (1990).

12. JAMES E. VANCE, JR., THE CONTINUING CITY: URBAN MORPHOLOGY IN WESTERN CIVILIZATION 506 (1990).

13. Fishman, *supra* note 11, at 27.

14. U.S. BUREAU OF CENSUS, 1987 CENSUS OF RETAIL TRADE: SPECIAL REPORT SERIES, Tbl. 5 (1991).

15. GARREAU, *supra*, note 4, at 7.

16. *See* Margaret Crawford, *The World in a Shopping Mall*, *in* VARIATIONS ON A THEME PARK: THE NEW AMERICAN CITY AND THE END OF PUBLIC SPACE 22, 22–30 (Michael Sorkin ed., 1992) [hereinafter VARIATIONS ON A THEME PARK]; Trevor Body, *Underground and Overhead: Building the Analogous City*, *in* VARIATIONS ON A THEME PARK, *supra* at 123, 126 (discussing Minneapolis skyways); PETER HALL, CITIES OF TOMORROW: AN INTELLECTUAL HISTORY OF URBAN PLANNING AND DESIGN IN THE TWENTIETH CENTURY 350 (Basil Blackwell ed., 1988) (discussing the influence of James Rouse on American cities).

17. VANCE, *supra*, note 12, at 508. Clayton is the county seat of St. Louis County which surrounds, but does not include, the city. *Id.* at 484.

18. *See* GREGORY R. WEIHER, THE FRACTURED METROPOLIS: POLITICAL FRAGMENTATION AND METROPOLITAN SEGREGATION 47–50 (1991).

19. MICHEL FOUCAULT, POWER/KNOWLEDGE: SELECTED INTERVIEWS AND OTHER WRITINGS, 1972–1977 98 (1980).

20. *See generally*, KEVIN LYNCH, THE IMAGE OF THE CITY (1960).

21. FISHMAN, *supra* note 4, at 185; KENNETH T. JACKSON, CRABGRASS FRONTIER: THE SUBURBANIZATION OF THE UNITED STATES 246–71 (1985) ("The Drive-in Culture of Contemporary America").

22. *See, e.g.,* Langdon Winner, *Silicon Valley Mystery House*, *in* VARIATIONS ON A THEME PARK, *supra* note 16, at 31, 31–60.

23. FISHMAN, *supra* note 4, at 203.

24. GARREAU, *supra* note 4, at 8.

25. *Id.* at 3 (emphasis deleted).

26. DAVID RIEFF, LOS ANGELES: CAPITAL OF THE THIRD WORLD 114-47 (1991). In the Los Angeles school district alone 82 languages are spoken. *Id.* at 105. *See also* Denise Hamilton, *The Changing Face of the San Gabriel Valley*, L.A. TIMES Oct. 25, 1992, at J1; Jack Miles, *Blacks v. Browns; African Americans and Latinos*, THE ATLANTIC, Oct. 1992, at 41; Bill Stall, *Assembly Elections 46th District: Diversity Highlights "The Ellis Island of California,"* L.A. TIMES, May 14, 1991, at B1.

27. *See* RIEFF, *supra* note 26, at 81–93.

28. *See, e.g.,* John Ellement, *More Deadly Violence in Boston,* BOSTON GLOBE, Oct., 8, 1992, at B1 (second gang-related murder in a week in Roxbury).

29. Frank Lloyd Wright, *quoted in* Fishman, *supra* note 11, at 26.

30. GARREAU, *supra* note 4, at 25.

31. *See* FISHMAN *supra* note 4, at 182-207; Jackson, *supra* note 21, at 296–305.

32. SORKIN, *supra* note 16, at xi.

33. *Id.*

34. *See* CHRISTOPHER LASCH, HAVEN IN A HEARTLESS WORLD: THE FAMILY BESIEGED (1977).

35. Jean Baudrillard, *The Ecstasy of Communication, in* THE ANTI-AESTHETIC: ESSAYS ON POSTMODERN CULTURE 133 (Hal Foster ed., 1983).

36. Renee Loth, *Mustering Up to Move,* BOSTON GLOBE, Aug 11, 1991, at 10.

37. *See* Poletown Neighborhood Council v. City of Detroit, 304 N.W.2d 455 (Mich. 1981); ROBERT A. CARO, THE POWER BROKER 850–77 (1975); JANE JACOBS, THE DEATH AND LIFE OF GREAT AMERICAN CITIES (1961).

38. *See, e.g.,* DAVID MORRIS AND KARL HESS, NEIGHBORHOOD POWER: THE NEW LOCALISM (1975); MILTON KOTLER, NEIGHBORHOOD GOVERNMENT: THE LOCAL FOUNDATIONS OF POLITICAL LIFE (1969).

39. For a critique of biological essentialism, see, e.g., KWAME ANTHONY APPIAH, IN MY FATHER'S HOUSE: AFRICA IN THE PHILOSOPHY OF CULTURE 28-46 (1992) (discussing race); JUDITH BUTLER, GENDER TROUBLE: FEMINISM AND THE SUBVERSION OF IDENTITY 1–34 (1990) (discussing gender); Darrell Yates Rist, *Are Homosexuals Born That Way?: Sex on the Brain,* THE NATION, Oct. 19, 1992, at 424 (discussing sexual orientation). For a critique of the mirror image of the self, see RICHARD RORTY, PHILOSOPHY AND THE MIRROR OF NATURE (1979).

40. For a discussion of examples—such as Athenian metics and European guest workers— see MICHAEL WALZER, SPHERES OF JUSTICE: A DEFENSE OF PLURALISM AND EQUALITY 52–61 (1983).

41. *See* Comment, *The Constitutionality of the Exercise of Extraterritorial Powers by Munici-palities,* 45 U. CHI. L. REV. 151 (1977); FRANK SENGSTOCK, EXTRATERRITORIAL POWERS IN THE METROPOLITAN AREA (1962); RUSSELL MADDOX, THE EXTRATERRITORIAL POWERS OF MUNICIPALITIES IN THE UNITED STATES (1955). The practice of regulating outsiders with-out treating them as citizens was held constitutional in Holt Civic Club v. City of Tuscaloosa, 439 U.S. 60, 65–75 (1978). Finally, some residents of ethnic neighborhoods might consider friends and relatives who live elsewhere to be part of their community. For example, Koreans might be included as part of Koreatown simply on the grounds of their ethnicity—despite the fact that a majority of the residents of Koreatown, at least in Los Angeles, are Latino. *See* Miles, *supra* note 26, at 52.

42. BUTLER, *supra,* note 39, at 140.

43. Baudrillard, *supra* note 35, at 133.

44. In *Holt,* the Court, in holding extraterritorial regulation constitutional, emphasized that the city did not seek to impose a property tax on property located outside city lines. 439 U.S. at 72–73 n.8.

45. Martinez v. Bynum, 461 U.S. 321, 325–33 (1983) (schools); Baldwin v. Fish and Game Comm'n, 436 U.S. 371, 378–91 (1978) (hunting); McCarthy v. Philadelphia Civil Serv. Comm'n, 424 U.S. 645 (1976) (public employment); Memorial Hosp. v. Maricopa County, 415 U.S. 250, 255, 267 (1974) (hospitals). *See generally* Gerald L. Neuman, *Territorial Discrimination, Equal Protection, and Self-Determination,* 135 U. PA. L. REV. 261, 267–70, 301–09 (1987). Of course services do not have to be limited to residents; when state law permits, some cities allow non-residents to use their services for a fee.

182   46. *See, e.g., Martinez,* 461 U.S. at 328–30.

47. 439 U.S. 60 (1978).

48. *Id.* at 69. For a reading of Justice Rehnquist's opinion in terms of the perspective of the situated self, see Frank Michelman, *Conceptions of Democracy: The Case of Voting Rights,* 41 FLA. L. REV. 443, 472–80 (1989).

49. *Holt,* 439 U.S. at 69.

50. Edgewood Indep. Sch. Dist. v. Kirby, 777 S.W.2d 391, 392–93 (Tex. 1989).

51.   In part, local control means...the freedom to devote more money to the education of one's children. Equally important, however, is the opportunity it offers for participation in the decisionmaking process that determines how those local tax dollars will be spent. Each locality is free to tailor local programs to local needs.

411 U.S. 1, 49–50 (1973). The school district under attack in *Rodriguez* was the same as the one challenged in *Kirby,* the Edgewood Independent School District.

52. Cases that have declared school financing systems unconstitutional include DuPree v. Alma Sch. Dist. No. 30, 651 S.W.2d 90, 91–92 (Ark. 1983); Serrano v. Priest, 487 P.2d 1241 (Cal. 1971); Horton v. Meskill, 376 A.2d 359, 374–75 (Conn. 1977); Rose v. Council for Better Educ., 790 S.W.2d 186 (Ky. 1989); Helena Elementary Sch. v. State, 769 P.2d 684 (Mont. 1989); Abbott v. Burke, 575 A.2d 359 (N.J. 1990); Carrollton-Farmers Branch Indep. Sch. Dist. v. Edgewood Indep. Sch. Dist., 826 S.W.2d 489, 500–14 (Tex. 1992); Seattle Sch. Dist. No. 1 v. State, 585 P.2d 71, 76–77 (Wash. 1978); Pauley v. Kelly, 255 S.E.2d 859 (W. Va. 1979); Washakie County Sch. Dist. v. Herschler, 606 P.2d 310 (Wyo. 1980). Those that have rejected constitutional challenges include: Shofstall v. Hollins, 515 P.2d 590 (Ariz. 1973); Lujan v. Colorado State Bd. of Educ., 649 P.2d 1005 (Colo. 1982); Thompson v. Engelking, 537 P.2d 635 (Idaho 1975); Hornbeck v. Somerset County Bd. of Educ., 458 A.2d 758 (Md. 1983); Board of Educ., Levittown Union Free Sch. Dist. v. Nyquist, 439 N.E.2d 359 (N.Y. 1982); Board of Educ. v. Walter, 390 N.E.2d 813 (Ohio 1979); Fair Sch. Finance Council v. State, 746 P.2d 1135 (Okla. 1987); Olsen v. State, 554 P.2d 139 (Or. 1976); Danson v. Casey, 399 A.2d 360 (Pa. 1979); Kukor v. Grover, 436 N.W.2d 568 (Wis. 1989). The literature on school financing is enormous. *See, e.g.,* Annotation, *Validity of Basing Public School Financing System on Local Property Taxes,* 41 A.L.R. 3d 1220 (1972); GERALD E. FRUG, LOCAL GOVERNMENT LAW 522–23 (1988).

53. Edgewood Indep. Sch. Dist. v. Kirby, 804 S.W.2d 491, 500 (Tex. 1991).

54. *See, e.g., Rose,* 790 S.W.2d at 211–12; *Abbott,* 575 A.2d at 410; *Helena Elementary Sch. Dist.,* 769 P.2d at 690–91.

55. *See* Christopher Alexander, *A City is Not a Tree, in* ZONE 1/2: THE CONTEMPORARY CITY *supra* note 6, at 129, 144.

56. *See generally* JOHN R. LOGAN AND HARVEY L. MOLOTCH, URBAN FORTUNES: THE POLITICAL ECONOMY OF PLACE (1987).

57. *See* Matthews v. Bay Head Improvement Ass'n, 471 A.2d 355, 360–66 (N.J. 1984).

58. *See, e.g.,* Stewart E. Sterk, *Competition Among Municipalities as a Constraint on Land Use Exactions,* 45 VAND. L. REV. 831 (1992); Vicki Been, *"Exit" as a Constraint on Land Use Exactions: Rethinking the Unconstitutional Conditions Doctrine,* 91 COLUM. L. REV. 473 (1991); DEVELOPMENT EXACTIONS (James E. Frank and Robert M. Rhodes, eds. 1987).

59. *See, e.g.,* Dean Milk Co. v. City of Madison, 340 U.S. 349, 354–56 (1951).

60. *Holt Civic Club,* 439 U.S. at 82 (Brennan, J., dissenting).

61. GARREAU, *supra* note 4, at 200.

62. For an analysis of this form of proportional representation as well as others, see Note, *The Constitutional Imperative of Proportional Representation,* 94 YALE L.J. 163 (1984).

For a discussion of the impact of "proportionate interest representation" on black electoral success, see Lani Guinier, *The Triumph of Tokenism: The Voting Rights Act and the Theory of Black Electoral Success,* 89 MICH. L. REV. 1077 (1991). For an argument that lottery voting would be preferable to proportional representation, see Akhil Reed Amar, Note, *Choosing Representatives by Lottery Voting,* 93 YALE L.J. 1283 (1984).

63. *See* Ortiz v. Hernandez Colon, 385 F. Supp. 111, 113–14 (D.P.R. 1974), *vacating as moot* 429 U.S. 1031 (1977).

64. 395 U.S. 621 (1969).

65. *Id.* at 630.

66. Although a residency requirement is constitutionally permissible, *see* LAURENCE H. TRIBE, AMERICAN CONSTITUTIONAL LAW § 13–12 at 1088–91 (2d ed. 1988), it does not follow that limiting the franchise to residents is constitutionally required.

67. Jerry Frug, *Administrative Democracy,* 40 TORONTO L. J. 559, 577–79 (1990).

68. BRIAN McHALE, POSTMODERNIST FICTION 9–10 (1987).

69. DAVID OSBORNE AND TED GAEBLER, REINVENTING GOVERNMENT: HOW THE ENTREPRENEURIAL SPIRIT IS TRANSFORMING THE PUBLIC SECTOR (1992).

70. *See* Frug, *supra* note 67, at 563–66; Gerald E. Frug, *Property and Power: Hartog on the Legal History of New York City,* 1984 AM. B. FOUND. RES. J. 673, 687–91; Gerald E. Frug, *The City as a Legal Concept,* 93 HARV. L. REV. 1057, 1128, 1150 (1980).

PART FOUR

Postcolonialism

Introduction to
POSTCOLONIALISM

MUCH OF CULTURAL STUDIES ("subaltern studies" in particular) has addressed questions about the meaning and situation of the postcolony. For example, once a colonial power has formally left its former colony to "self-determination," from where is the former colony's "self" to be derived? Can an authentic voice or culture be recovered from the ash heap of colonial rule? Or is postcolonial culture irrevocably a product of the colonial it seeks to transcend?

Essays in this Part explore these issues by examining their ramifications on the deployment of legal rules, both on behalf of the postcolony and in regulating it. Nathaniel Berman situates the issues historically, demonstrating that they are not in fact unique to the postcolony. Exploring the first round of international law's attempt to allow self-determination (between the World Wars), Berman describes how international law attempted both to give voice to nationalist energy and to control it. The other essays explore contemporary contexts. David Kennedy and Karen Engle study the complexities of international human rights law advocacy that aims to represent postcolonial subjects. Kennedy describes his own experiences as a lawyer working on the International Jurists' Platform on behalf of the people of East Timor over Indonesia's treatment of the Timorese. Engle examines the ways that women's human rights advocates have argued for a prohibition against clitoridectomies in Muslim African countries. Rosemary Coombe explores a debate among Canadians over cultural appropriation in the context of who, if anyone, should be able to speak for First Nations peoples.

These essays all examine the often contradictory roles that legal rules have played in the construction of "new identities." Legal rules are used on one hand to facilitate the emergence of "authentic" identities, and on the other to control that emergence. The essays explore how this contradiction unfolds as law encounters raw nationalist energy, the assertion of culture practices that often were outlawed under colonial rule but are now performed in the name of nationalism, and ownership claims to cultural icons. The authors respond by expressing doubts about the progressive role that law—particularly international law—has often claimed for itself as the guarantor of self-determination. At the same time, they reject the position that, by attempting to regulate the exercise of such self-determination, law is merely imposing a neocolonial or Eurocentric perspective. Even as the authors reject both of these positions in their absolute form, they are sympathetic to parts of both claims. Perhaps Rosemary Coombe best displays this ambivalence when she argues that it is "as politically dishonest to deny the objective identity of those making culturally nationalist claims as it is to assert an internationalism that privileges the nation-building imperialist enterprises of the European countries in the name of 'universal human values' or the 'common heritage of mankind.'"

The authors articulate criticisms of legal interventions in colonial and postcolonial conflict that neither rely on the traditional narratives of anti-colonial discourse nor give up the hope of a progressive role for law in the postcolonial era. Kennedy describes both the voyeuristic excitement and the frustrating banality of bringing international law to the service of "the people of East Timor," and Engle examines both the potential utility of and the disappointment in Western feminist legal attempts at addressing clitoridectomy in northern Africa. Coombe explores how Western debates about cultural property both structure our understanding of the injury of cultural appropriation to Native Peoples, and fail to capture the complexities of the postcolonial situation. Berman suggests that interwar innovations in the international law of self-determination and minority protection are just as much about Modernist experimentation as about giving voice to authentic cries for freedom.

These essays strike out in new directions as they explore difficulties posed for the legal reformer by a cultural understanding of law. One difficulty they stress is that of knowing the colonized client on whose behalf law is evoked once law has been situated in the ambivalent narratives of modern legal culture. As Engle suggests, each attempt at law reform seems to bring with it a conception of the "Exotic Other," the imagined subject of law. Should the human rights lawyer treat the woman performing clitoridectomies or the mother or grandmother authorizing the practice on her offspring as a willing subject making (il)legitimate choices, or as a victim of false consciousness and patriarchy who does not know what is good for her? Are the clients we attempt to serve "real," or are they constructions of the legal tools we bring to bear on their behalf? Is legal representation more than the translation of the desires of a client/other into the language of law?

Kennedy describes these issues in the context of the Jurists' Platform for East Timor:

> Characters in a "Jurists' Platform" might stabilize the[ir] internal fantasies by reference to the ground of a "Timor," the client, the base, the terrain of interpretation, application, sanction and struggle, perhaps especially to the touchstone of visible violence.... The activist arranges his polemics and tactics, his righteousness and his realism, to assure the transparent representation of a struggle at another site, the site of the Timorese everyday.... For the lawyer, the mystically receding client operates as a reader of last resort.

These explorations of the meanings of law in postcolonial culture raise new questions about progressive strategy. If law and its clients or subjects are functions of our own colonial imaginations, what assurance have we that we serve the "post" rather than just the colonial? If Berman is right that international law has long defined itself in relation to the foil of an imagined "primitive" other, perhaps postmodernism's fixation on the other is just a rehash of Modernism's invocation of the "primitive." Perhaps in the guise of liberating the authentic speech and participation of the colonized other, we are simply constructing the other anew. Or perhaps the notion of an authentic other, as Coombe puts it, "treated as dead, dying, vanishing or victimized and in need of others to speak on [its] behalf," is itself a colonial image of identity and culture. Maybe we are voyeuristically playing out our own cultural anxieties on the sexy new terrain of the colonial oppressed. Is clitoridectomy one of the predominant problems facing many African women or merely central to our own narratives about native barbarity?

The articles in this Part, then, engage, challenge and provoke the traditional narratives of the postcolonial situation even as they raise profound doubts about the usefulness of the interpretive frames of colonizer/colonized, oppressor/oppressed, normal/exotic, self/other. Per-

190   haps, in this sense, the "post" of postcolonial means not only the imagined end of colonial oppression, but also the exhaustion of the "colonial"
as purveyor of progressive understanding or social transformation. This
is not to say that we can deny history or that the mark of colonialism is
not ever present, but rather to suggest that unreflective homage to the
sacred narratives of colonialism and anti-colonialism may limit our ability
both to grasp the complexities of our late twentieth century world and to
imagine more meaningful engagement with each of our "Exotic Others."

CHAPTER TEN

‣—᛫⟡᛫⟐᛫⟡᛫—‑

AN AUTUMN WEEKEND

AN ESSAY ON LAW AND EVERYDAY LIFE

David Kennedy

Scene One: Setting It Up

THE ESTABLISHMENT CONFERENCE for the International Jurists' Platform on East Timor, a smudged-xerox affair from the start, unfolded as a cantilevered jumble of lawyers, activists, locals and international metropolitans. As I understand it, the project began with Pedro, a Portuguese lawyer working in the Netherlands as an academic of some sort. Pedro had been interested in East Timor since his days at law school in Lisbon, had written about the human-rights violations which had taken place there since the Indonesian occupation and had identified a network of human-rights activists committed to East Timorese self-determination.

East Timor had been a Portuguese colony until the revolution of the mid-seventies and continues to figure in the political imagination of the Portuguese as a non-partisan and rather distant test site for the nation's honor and humanitarian commitment. The struggle for East Timorese liberation from Indonesia might somewhat redeem Portugal's colonial experience, both confirmed (for East Timor is distinguished from the hundreds of other cultures and islands within Indonesia by the boundaries of Dutch and Portuguese administration) and cleansed by righteous defense of self-determination and international human rights.

In an elaborate bank shot, Portugal had recently sued Australia in the World Court over Indonesian treatment of East Timor. The legal issues are probably too procedural to ignite the imagination: does Portugal, as the ex-colonial power, have standing to bring a claim on behalf of the East Timorese; does Australia's entry into a treaty with Indonesia to divide the seabed resources lying between East Timor and Australia give rise to a claim against Australia for recognizing an illegal occupation, and so forth. Nevertheless, it seemed reasonable to establish the Jurists' Platform as a legal person in Portugal, in part to situate international legal work on such issues in a knowledgeable cultural milieu. (I quickly discovered that everyone in Portugal, like longtime activists, knew to drop the "East" when referring to Timor.) In Portugal, moreover, Pedro could implement his plan for an international institution among old friends.

Pedro's idea for a Jurists' Platform borrowed a leaf from the international, nongovernmental human-rights community, an assortment of nonprofit foundations, research centers, advocacy groups and religious organizations. Some of these groups are general, some issue focused, some academic, some litigious, and many are focused in the Netherlands. All circulate around the large intergovernmental organizations of the U.N. system to one degree or another, and all share a number of institutional features: an international membership, an international board, an executive director, a small staff, and so forth. There is a great deal of overlap among the players in this community—the members of one organization may well be the staff of another and so on. The Platform of Jurists for Timor, as Pedro imagined it, would replicate these features to provide a focal point for what would become "our" activity on behalf of Timor.

To inaugurate the effort, Pedro had worked for over a year to identify potential participants and fund an opening conference. I first heard about his efforts from a former doctoral student of mine at Harvard Law School who had returned to Lisbon to teach international law. Paula had called some months before to ask if I and a colleague from Boston would be willing to come to Lisbon to participate in a conference on East Timor. I had said yes in large part out of friendship and respect for Paula, although I suppose also at least partly because I had never been to Portugal.

I had not participated in the more activist side of the international human rights movement for some time. During the international human rights boom of the late seventies and early eighties, I had experienced much of the international conference scene as somewhat tawdry and disappointing, had written up my skepticism about international human rights institutions and advocacy and departed the field. Much of my frustration stemmed from the oscillation between private cynicism and public piety that characterized many of the international lawyers and bureaucrats I had met in the field. My expectation that either the solemn declarations would be fulfilled or the private criticisms be made public was disappointed often enough that I developed a jaded professionalism and lost interest.

I agreed to go to Lisbon partly to see whether things had changed, whether there had come to be others frustrated with the traditional professional posture who might connect with one another at such an event. Substantial criticism of human rights had meanwhile reached the academy from the Left and the Right, and I wondered whether any of this had reached the activist community, whether there was, or might come to be, a different form of activist culture in international law.

Paula had also invited a Boston area specialist in self-determination who was completing a study of cultural modernism in international law. We enjoyed one another's company and often found ourselves reflecting similarly on our profession. It seemed an ideal opportunity to rethink my relationship to international law advocacy. As for Timorese self-determination, there seemed many reasons to favor it and little to be said on the other side.

It is hard to get very far thinking about such an experience in terms as abstract as "law" and "everyday life." From the vantage point of my Cambridge everyday, there is always, of course, an element of fantasy in such events. For activist missions, there is the fantasy that trips to the site of law's deployment will be magic journeys, full of fabulous characters and novel engagements, escapes from the routines of everyday life in the academy. This sort of fantasy distracted my focus from the establishment of a Jurists' Platform and toward the advocacy for which it was the intended vehicle. This is a simple fantasy—law promises to get you there, take you higher, make it real. Be there or be square.

For the earnest advocate, law relates to the "Timor situation" as norms to facts, a simple program for action: international human rights norms are to be translated into everyday practice in Timor. Where everyday life strays from the law, activism will bring them together. Of course, for the cynical advocate pondering the stilted language of "self-determination" or "human rights" and the daily life of Timor, the same normative vision

194 may seem half empty. In either case, the fantasy of law's application frames law as something fabulous, abstract, even magical: words which become deeds. Law as an instrument of social change, a force for freedom, and so on.

This fantasy touches the institutional work of establishment that precedes direct advocacy. The constitutional moment is always a mystical one, lawyers gathered to make law and constitute themselves as activists in its service. Thinking about going to Lisbon, I couldn't help feeling that even if I did not participate in the normative mopping up operation of later advocacy, having been present when lawyers came together as members of a Jurists' Platform, united with a calling, I would have been part of, prior to, whatever activism ensued. At the very least, this sort of thing can sometimes be cashed in for political correctness points with students and colleagues.

Focus on the conference itself brings law's internal mechanisms into the story, contrasting the directly apprehendable language of international norms with the elaborate institutional machinery of international law's interpretation or implementation. The contrast suggests a chronology, progress forward from the everyday clarity of norms to a more speculative institutional site for their interpretation, application and enforcement. An establishment conference straddles these two moments, providing the link between a normative everyday and future institutional pragmatism. Forward ever, backward never.

Focus on the international lawyer himself shifts the image of law and the everyday yet again. I think about myself going to Lisbon—I may become magic, an objective expert, a professional agnostic, a temporary interloper, a generalist, formalist, bringing world public opinion, world public order, the rational and the reasonable into the continuing everyday of Timor activism. As a lawyer, I will be more than my everyday. Of course it is not so simple. I remember past experience. Even with daily discipline the law often disappoints, becomes a messy affair of airports and fax machines, doctrines, and deadlines. Still I can be hopeful.

Lawyers remain divided between the transcendent idealism of their normative vision and the institutional grind of legal practice as well as between the programmatic aspirations of legal institutions and the tedium of doctrinal interpretation or document drafting. And like other professionals, the international lawyer earns his keep as a ventriloquist, throwing his legal idealism forward from the realism of his everyday.

Characters in a Jurists' Platform might stabilize these internal fantasies by reference to the ground of a "Timor," the client, the base, the terrain of interpretation, application, sanction and struggle, perhaps especially to the touchstone of visible violence. This can be prurient, it can be porno-graphic. The activist arranges his polemics and tactics, his righteousness and his realism, to assure the transparent representation of a struggle at another site, the site of the Timorese everyday. For this, St. Timor in agony must be seen. And Timor also sees us, imposes self-discipline. For the lawyer, the mystically receding client operates as a reader of last resort.

As I look back, the Platform seems a kaleidoscope of form and fancy: lawyers and activists, doctrines and institutions, dreamers and tacticians, all refracted against the backdrop of another country and culture, a Timor beyond the exchange of word and deed. Of course, all this was a bit unfocused on Saturday morning when I arrived in Lisbon. Having had tickets for Natalie Cole the preceding Thursday, I left only on Friday and arrived in Lisbon (after a somewhat disorienting stop in the Azores) just as the conference was starting Saturday morning. The meet-ing was held upstairs in a downtown religious cinder block kindergarten from the sixties—ubiquitous Papal insignia, institutional walls and food, dozens of Portuguese children. Inside were perhaps a hundred jurists and activists.

Scene Two: The Entrance

Although Paula reassured me with a wink from the dais, as I entered the conference site to begin my weekend with these people I had the uneasy feeling of arriving in an ongoing conversation among strangers. My cross-cultural anxiety was probably heightened by the fact that they were already there and I was arriving a bit late, and by the unexpected pres-ence of so many Catholic children in what was to have been a project of secular professionalism. As a law professor new to Timor, I imagined the others as committed lawyers and activists, sharing a canon of histories, doctrines and atrocities which I would come at best to recognize, if not learn, by the end of the conference.

As I walked in, it would have been hard for those already in the room reporting their "work" on Timor not to have had a more immediate and ongoing relationship to Timor-the-conference-topic than I. Although I had asked some students to pull together a packet of legal literature on

Timor to read before dozing on the plane, I was still pretty much a blank slate as to Timor. In a way, this relative ignorance came naturally to me as a lawyer. Nothing like ignorance, blind justice, to distinguish the law from everyday plays of power, passion, and prejudice, and I have often been asked to participate in things because I don't know much about them or haven't written about them. Human-rights junkets to places like the Mideast are always looking for someone who is neutral but whose sympathies can be predicted.

In such events, professionals typically start off seriously about roles, loosening ties or removing jackets only later. I entered the room as an attorney, interested to begin a relationship with a group of clients. If there turned out to be any Timorese in the room, I could be their lawyer. For the activists, I might be law to their politics. We might think of the jurists in the crowd as in-house counsel for Timor and I as outside counsel. At the threshold, I constituted the group against my identity as a lawyer, a generalist, an internationalist, above all, someone who legitimately didn't know much about what was to go on. Perhaps this is how it is whenever the lawyer enters the everyday, a man at an airport with a passport.

This messianic or metropolitan posture—a lawyer gone to activism, the general arrived in the specific—brings with it some predictable, even clichéd, resentments. The lawyer not as midwife to justice, but as formalistic distraction from activist passions, agnostic in his commitments, apologetic for imperial power, complicit in things mundane. The first thing we do is kill all the lawyers, etc. At this early stage, the international lawyer has two strong defenses against these entailed resentments. On the one hand, one may simply assert expertise, the power of the objective, the scientific, the broader reality of an international community, of a law which renders any everyday petty. On the other hand, and hopefully simultaneously, one may search for common ground with activists and specialists in an earnestly shared commitment to our clients in Timor.

Harmonizing these defenses may be difficult, a matter of discretion more than valor or expertise. Professional ethics for lawyers is largely a matter of juxtaposing mandated disclosures and confidentialities to reconcile fealty to law and client. Tensions remain, and in my experience it is good to get beyond these early moments of "lawyers" and "activists" as quickly as possible. Well established and mannered participants leave such roles at the door, background to conversation.

The next morning, when I thought we had long since put such things behind us, a peach-skinned activist responded acidly to a lawyer's description of the local disco by mentioning her own evening at a "solidarity meeting." It was a bit rude. But we lawyers could always think of this as naive, and I suppose they could always think of us as cynical or parasitical. At the start, I was reassured that the lawyers were thought needed and had been invited. This was after all to be a Jurists' Platform, constructed as a focal point for legal work on behalf of the Timorese, a site for representation rather than solidarity.

If such differences usually fade only after roles have given way to interpersonal reconciliations that merge private ambitions and public commitments, amused cynicism with shared polemics, sometimes, if only briefly, a more public reconciliation may seem possible. I felt that flicker in the person of Pedro—earnest, activist, lawyer, mobilizer of the metropolis, link to the periphery, Portuguese and Dutch, at once lawyer and client. He was more than just a role, and seemed to yield no purchase for cynical connection. Could we ever be that committed, that certain of our direction? In a way he seemed to have achieved personally what we hoped to achieve as a group over the course of the weekend together—to become one with our mission and with one another. Perhaps, together in a Platform we might find the determination and clarity that eluded us alone.

It seemed right that he should be extremely busy, somehow always just a bit unavailable, attending to some detail that would keep the conference afloat, to some dignitary who would grace our meeting with meaning. It wasn't necessary to speak with him, it was fine that he was kept busy. It was enough that he was there, had brought us there, that we were all his guests, his friends. I knew Pedro only as a name at the end of a fax machine when a good friend of his from the Netherlands picked me up at the airport. He provided a first conversation for any two arrivals, how had we come to know him, what was he really like. If he had conceived the Platform to multiply his advocacy, our goal in joining was also clear; to become more like Pedro.

Scene Three: The Early Work of Establishment

I had come in and sat off to one side just as the first plenary broke into "working groups" to consider litigation, human rights, education, drafting a constitution for the Platform, and some forgotten fifth topic. Having done the constitution drafting at another such conference some years before, I joined the litigation group, thinking, in light of the ongoing case before the International Court of Justice (ICJ), that it might be

198   more interesting. Besides, the constitution–drafting group seemed a dis-
tinctly dull crew of Pedro's more earnest Portuguese acquaintances.

A few minutes after we started, Pedro pulled me out of my working
group for an interview with Portuguese television. Through the authority of expertise, I would establish the Platform in the media somewhat in
advance of our own constitution by reference to two vague alternative
sites: world public opinion and Timor. A charming reporter said she
would have a few questions about the U.S. position on Timor and my
sense for the legal issues underlying Portugal's position in the ICJ. Such
an interview at this stage would have to be a very generic performance. It
would only be later, much later, late the following afternoon at the closing press conference that nuanced expertise, the formal opinions of the
Platform and results of our deliberations, would be available to be voiced.

Her camera man turned on the lights. What was my assessment of the
U.S. position on Timor? Looking back on it, I should admit that I had
no idea what the U.S. position on Timor might be—where were we on
Indonesia these days anyway. I flashed rather unhelpfully on nuclear
ships and New Zealand. But even if a lawyer is supposed to be neutral,
he is not supposed to be totally in the dark.

I said I had, of course, wished for a more forthcoming attitude from
the State Department on Timor (don't they always disappoint), but that
in light of the new found enthusiasm for international law and institutions in Washington (brief invocation of Kuwait, the Berlin Wall, the
New World Order) we might see more. This is what made initiatives like
that of Portugal in the ICJ all the more timely and important. Did I
expect Portugal would win its case? There were certainly a number of
crucial procedural hurdles, and the case would need to be pursued dili-
gently, but the importance of the norms involved could hardly be over-
stated. And so on.

We had to repeat the whole thing with the camera pointing the other
way and without sound, so I asked her a number of questions about life
in the media, in Portugal. And later that evening, there I was, a talking
head—not savvy, it was really too early in my Timorese immersion for
that, but on TV all the same, dubbed into Portuguese and discussing,
somewhat prematurely, the work of the International Jurists Platform
for Timor.

As the conference got going, it would surpass and confirm these media
highlights. At the start, it was quite explicitly the work of the Platform
and of its establishment conference to connect with Timor and the out-

side world precisely by narrowing the gap between the law, with its norms, and the everyday, with its violations. On this, each of the plenary speakers was more earnest and eloquent than the last. We would take law to Timor, make the international law regime practical, demonstrate its relevance, milk it for all it was worth. By about 11:00 AM on Saturday morning, of course, these statements had lost much of their punch, and speakers turned like sunflowers at midday to increasingly practical points. And it was in this spirit that we moved to our working groups.

Nevertheless, a general activism was our shared and public agenda. We had put it on grant applications to fly to Portugal and we would promise at least ourselves to do something about it later. The conference working groups reflected this sentiment: we might choose to assist in litigation, devising tactics of enforced compliance. Perhaps we could get an injunction, or start a shareholders suit involving some oil company. In the education group we could harness the great sanction of public opinion. The human rights group could feed the institutional reporting machinery. And we all thought of Kuwait—why shouldn't the Security Council take this matter in hand and pursue a collective war?

When we were all home writing up our reports, we would try to remember our work in the terms of these opening flourishes, as an instance of law's application to fact. Only in these terms may international lawyers situate such events in the narrative conventions of their discipline, in which international law arose from the chaos of politics in a great social contract three hundred and fifty years before, becoming in this century, after three hundred years of philosophy, a matter of institutional pragmatism, sanctions, obedience, payments, and compliances on a great ledger of legal relevance, responding to international conflicts in conferences such as this, a thousand points of pragmatism, law returned with the power of the norm through our work in the here and now.

By reference to these opening ambitions, it was not surprising that the Platform constitution group, so self-absorbed, should have been the last refuge of the lawyer's lawyer, the nerd's nerd. Pedro's drafters seemed stuck in a moment before the conference, when it was still necessary to bring us together—perhaps Pedro had become himself too occupied with organization to see the importance of getting on with the substantive work at hand. And perhaps we knew, as we fantasized ourselves constituted as collective action, what constitution would in fact entail.

Bringing us together would require more than a simple allocation of tasks among lawyers or activists. As we settled into the petty routines and relations of our conference world, the everyday media world would fade, and so, for that matter, would Timor. Our earnestness would be corroded by the sharing of private doubts. As we came to live ever more in the conference, we would live somewhat less for Timor. By the end, a coincidentally simultaneous massacre in Dili on Timor would barely break into our everyday.

Although we would want to remember the conference as constitution for action, the Platform would need to be established against the background of our experiences in Lisbon as much as against our disciplinary idealism. In the middle of all the working-group rooms stood the plenary session, where we began and where the conference would end. And circulating around it were tables with stray literature—many participants had brought their reprints, notices of other conferences, Cultural Survival T-shirts, human rights studies, bibliographies, recent publications of the professional press, concert announcements, maps of Lisbon, tourist brochures on the southern beaches. Nothing much was for sale, but the milling crowd situated the plenary in a new, petty mercantile atmosphere, smoking, joking, parishioners at a cathedral. The conference plenary had become a shrine, a tourist monument, an Eiffel Tower, with its own bustling everyday.

Scene Four: The Platform Really Takes Off

The bustle in our little Papal kindergarten would be the site for the social relations which would emerge as by-products of our earnest work for Timor. It began in unimportant ways—a sharing of pasts, tiny fragments of a shared present, the ride in, the bad coffee, my ex-student was the former wife of your government's U.N. representative, and so forth. We recognized one another in a mutual remove from the client, situating ourselves in a common tactical terrain. We shared a common project, participants in a broad division of labor, some of us formalists, some administrators, some political tacticians, experts in local or metropolitan knowledges, some doctrinalists, others more practical—all tacticians for the real, together a magnificent pragmatic machine.

And we shared a method, a fantasy of institution building, a process by which to constitute ourselves as a membership with a leadership. Indeed, from our own diverse institutions, nationalities and professions, we shared Pedro's idea: a council, a secretary general, a resolution, a preamble, a resolution, points of order, plenaries, working groups, drafting sessions, all the modern technologies.

Was there any conflict not subject to reconciliation in the metropolis? In plenary, one fashionable Latin American woman from New York stood up, feet together in rather high pumps, held her copy of our draft resolution before her and asked if she might make a few suggestions from her experience in the U.N. Shouldn't our Preamble rather say "taking note that" where we had written "deeply deploring that" and shouldn't the operative paragraphs of our resolution be clearly numbered?

As to the second, she was clearly correct. We all knew we should clearly distinguish the perambulatory recitation of norms and facts from the operational engagement with the everyday. Numbering would do the trick, indentation would help. The differences that had separated us— between law and activism, norms and facts—had migrated to a common text where they might, indeed should, be expressed with increased clarity. As to the preambulatory point, we would need to vote. We quickly agreed, voted, to delegate the "taking note"/"deeply disturbed" issue back to the drafting committee for resolution and, having found consensus, we moved on.

What, in our little metropolitan world, had become of Timor, the collective fantasy with which we had kicked off the exercise? At first we heard the Timorese participants speak with the authority of authenticity. For me the moment of transition occurred early on Saturday when I shared a taxi with one Timorese fellow, a young lawyer from Macau on the make, who announced his hope to meet an American lawyer or law professor who might know how one of his clients could purchase a small U.S. bank. Could I help him in this venture, locate such a bank for him, for Timor, for his client whose identity could not be disclosed? My native had abruptly disappeared into professional courtesies and confidentiality. In our little conference spaceship, Timor became a screen on which we could project our common fantasies and anxieties about the real.

To many in the metropolis, of course, this comes as no surprise. When I shared my taxi-ride encounter with a young Canadian, he smiled and nodded and we began a friendship. Isn't the client, in a way like the earnest activist, the technical lawyer, indeed, the entire public zone, always a disappointment, an immaturity? International sophisticates have come to see the technologies and actors in our public spaces and national realities as more or less shrewd manipulations, constructions. In large part, that is what it means to be cosmopolitan, to have transcended the pull of unreasonable local specificities and passions.

Of course this stance can bring cynicism, a corrosive split between private commitment and public realism, public polemics and private doubts.

Participants in the international activist milieu often bond around this sort of split, as I did with my Canadian friend. As narrator, I am also tempted by such split moments. If I present them correctly, readers will share the alienation of my observation as one might the bemused observation of a newscaster at a political convention ("Well at this point Jed, he needs to make a strong appeal to women between thirty-five and fifty-five, yes and here it is, we go now live to the appeal"). Perhaps we will laugh together about the fragility of institutional forms and the pettiness of activist work.

In the metropolis, although we are moved by invocations of the real and the client, and are careful to orient ourselves towards the practical or the redemptive, as representation displaces the represented, we find ourselves ambivalent—has our everyday displaced their culture or has our law finally achieved its relevance for their project? Sometimes the ambivalence seems more than a routinized cynicism, the bonding more than complicit passivity.

This ambivalence was embodied in Portugal for me by a quite urbane and sexy lawyer from an international nonprofit that had styled itself the "Unrepresented Nations and Peoples Organization." She seemed smart and savvy and a new Australian friend and I determined to recruit her for our evolving affinity group. We asked about her organization. They (a small office in The Hague, a "General Secretary," three lawyers, a membership, a board, a newsletter) were present for the absent. They had correspondents in Tartu and San Francisco. Although they had recently lost three clients (Estonia, Latvia, Lithuania), they hoped for continued Baltic financial support out of solidarity with all the places where boundaries, nations, ethnicities, tribes, or governments had been insufficiently coordinated to perfect the transparency of international representation through statehood.

It was noble work, rendered more palpably significant, if strangely doubled, by their lawyer's assertion that she was herself unrepresented. As I recall her account, she had come from a minority ethnic group in Bangladesh, or perhaps Pakistan, grown up the child of diplomats, become a lawyer, worked for a big Washington law firm, pierced her nose, and moved to Holland, where she had been representing the unrepresented now for almost a year. She told her story with a light ironic touch which made it impossible to respond with either earnest relief that the unrepresented had found their spokeswoman or with any doubts about why this form, why here, why her?

I liked her immediately and when we discussed the work of her education group over lunch, I proposed that her organization sponsor a gigantic blimp, like Goodyear, which would travel around the world labeled with one or another unrepresented people, tethered outside the Olympics or the Clarence Thomas hearings, wherever. Others joined in as we developed a comprehensive blimp-based program for human rights protection. She wrote me some months later to ask whether I had encountered any "blimps hanging outside campus," and reported that "I went off to Estonia for a conference on Population Transfer, which was quite an experience. Very interesting place. There was something surrealistic about Tallinn, reminded me a bit of that weird bar we went to in Lisbon. Which was lots of fun." She was a cosmopolitan all right.

Was this cynicism or irony, destructive or delicious? The routinization of enthusiasm, too many hours together in a small building, we looked to one another for hints of private doubt, small islands of relief from earnestness. A Scotsman who seemed in working group to have memorized the procedural details of every ICJ case for his dissertation turned out to be an extremely ironic devotee of British punk culture. He joined our clique and followed up on our acquaintance in Lisbon with a package of trashy British comics.

At lunch, smoking by the tennis court, drinking with age cohorts, national cohorts, private in-groups, we recognized with a wink or a chortle that our public idealism would not be supported by the realism of our common projects. We entered the zone of flirtation. Of course this brought with it a turn away from the public narrative of law engaging the Timorese everyday, a turn from activism to narcissism. True enough. There emerged the tawdriness of all conferences everywhere. If we could bring law to bear on Timor together, wouldn't we also sleep with one another? Indeed, who would sleep with whom, who befriend whom, who would promote, hire, help whom. Who would reveal their loneliness, exasperation, sexual orientation?

How can laughter in Lisbon be defended when people were being slaughtered in Timor? We could say it's only human, that we should blame the naive idealism of our common project, that laughter is the best medicine. Perhaps it is efficient—it might be these social strands, the tears and fears of the everyday rather than our textual productions, which would hold us together after the conference closed. In this, the promise of the social and the sexual functioned as an idealism, an aspiration, a promise. And I hoped, if only vaguely, that more might come of our affinity cohort than it seemed possible to expect from the official working groups.

This growing private social sensibility offset the sensible, if sterile, formality of our public debates. As the social verged into cliché, the conference plodded along its familiar route: introductory exhortation, working groups, working-group reports to the plenary, working groups, plenary to adopt constitution and resolutions, press conference, social event. Every meeting begins with a recollection of past work and ends with a promise of work to come, two moments that pull us back from the sexual to the social, and render the private cynical. Indeed, this is the very function of the agenda.

At one point my litigation working group flagged, wandered on the patio, suspended in the idea of litigation, having been unable to identify anyone actually working on any actual case. We were left only with duty to the meeting, remoteness from our own individual everydays, and goodwill for the ultimate cause. We traded anecdotes, discussed the weather, and experienced our situation as confusion about the agenda. We asked one another who had brought the agenda. We waited for leadership and were quite good-naturedly ready to follow anyone with a plan.

And along came a young Australian lawyer whom we told about our lack. She sprang into action, jotted a few notes, urged us to return to the meeting room, and simply began the meeting, intoning in the flat locution of all U.N. debate everywhere that it would be good to begin with a restatement of where we had been, and sure enough everything each of us had half-mentioned the day before reappeared as a subject discussed, an observation made, a point taken. In the passive voice of recounting we became active as a collective. What, we wondered, would she have for us for today? And she posed some issues, and we threw them about, and she did it again, and now we were in a hurry, needed to get our report together for the plenary, and off we went to hear from the other working groups.

When we got there, there wasn't time for our report, but it hardly mattered. As a plenary we needed to work on our resolution and our constitution, prepare for the press conference. We didn't want to waste time reporting what had, after all, already been accomplished in the working groups. As it turned out, only the constitutional group really needed to report.

Scene Five: A Constituted Life

When we look back on the Platform's establishment as an institutional narrative, we focus on the final moments, when the constitution drafters returned with their document. But inside the conference, focusing on our substantive accomplishments and objectives, the constitution drafters had come to seem quite beside the point, the terms of our constitution almost trivial, the procedural disputes predictable.

Every platform must apparently have a council, every conference must pass a resolution—regardless of the terrain upon which law acts, these are its points of access. And so we recreated here in the Platform our own model U.N., complete with compulsory geographic distribution—for shouldn't the seats on the Platform's Council be distributed among the continents? As soon as it was proposed, we knew it had to be so. And we had one African, one European, one Latin American, one Asian, and before someone forgot, one Timorese. Even, we were pleased, or surprised, or bemused, someone from the world's largest democracy.

Nevertheless, we focused our determination increasingly on texts, the most practical suggestion often a textual one, as in the case of our dignified Latin American U.N. delegate. We revised resolutions, elected a board, published polemics, commited to doctrinal interpretations, rendering our experience more visible, also to our own memories. The leadership had the constitution read out by a jovial legal activist, bringing our international locutions alive in his somewhat ironic English translation. There were a few open questions. Were corporations to become members, for example, would they receive extra votes in the Council? All this seemed secondary, legal, the usual technical details, and the urge in the plenary to delegate these issues back to the committee or to vote quickly (either would do) was irresistible. By Sunday afternoon there were too many issues to deal with, each crowding for the plenary's attention. We would soon need to face the press again, mobilized into a platform with a resolution. Time in our little world had sped up.

In a way this acceleration was precisely the point—as we moved through stages of mutual recognition and institution building, each hour had seemed suspended, filled with new people, new institutional developments. In such a small space, by the end of the first day the gossip circle could run a full round in well less than an hour. Each hour would find us days, even centuries ahead of the last in the evolution of our common everyday. We had been strangers, now we almost had a constitution, we had been normative, now we were almost pragmatic, we had been generalists, now we were almost specialists. The acceleration of centuries had slowed the conference to a snail's pace.

By the end of the weekend, we each thought increasingly of our return home, to what seemed a jumbled fusion of two scenes—the scene of our origin, the workplace realities from which we had come to the conference, and the scene of Timor, the object of our endeavors. The two had become somehow fused, or confused, in the course of the weekend. Here, we were being productive, enjoying one another, liking our jobs. Somehow, after it was over, we would have been changed, would be Timor activists and members of a Platform. That, after all, is the point of an establishment conference, a great collective narcissism in the name of empathy, a culture of representation which held out Timor as aspiration, a promise of pragmatism, where our work would have bite, effect, relevance. Like successful conferences everywhere, we would end with a call for action. The idea that "we" would be carrying on "work," each in our own way, on behalf of Timor had become a collective fantasy, at once insistent and worrisome. Indeed, I suspect that only those already dedicated, enacting the resolutions of some earlier establishment, could think about their own workplace realities and Timor without anxiety.

Late in the conference, these underlying doubts and shared anxieties came to rest on Pedro and the constitution drafters. Looking back on it late Sunday, it seemed I had felt uneasy about them all along. Five somewhat somber Portuguese men of indeterminate age, suits right out of the Chicago twenties. I wondered what they were putting together for us. Why had Pedro really brought us here? He seemed so earnest about it all, so insistent, more serious across a year's work than we could maintain even for two days. Why didn't he participate in the tiny flirtations of the weekend? Was he really that busy? If it had been somewhat reassuring on arrival to find someone who so clearly knew what we were supposed to do, now it seemed almost ominous. What if we didn't live up to our platform, couldn't bring law to the everyday, if our everyday could never be as unified with Timor as had been his? Would we still get our travel money?

Pedro and his friends had an experience different from the removed disputations of the working groups on education, litigation, or human rights. Their reality was here, with us, however much Pedro sought to project the moment of establishment into the past, onto our agreement to come, or into the future of our rather open-ended commitments to cooperate. He was not promising to be pragmatic, he was being pragmatic. Our narcissism was his empathy.

Our groups had done less well, some had not even found it necessary to report. The human rights group had foundered on what seemed a choice between the self-determination and human rights "approaches" to Timor, the education group boldly decided to establish an as of yet unfunded prize for student writing on Timor. At best we projected future action, contented ourselves that the purpose of our being together was fulfilled by the establishment of the platform—by the work of the constitution group. As everywhere, talk is suspicious of action.

And to some extent, we had become cynical. By the final plenary, I found myself in an ad hoc affinity group with my Boston colleague, our Scottish, Canadian, Australian and unrepresented friends and a few other young law professors. We had become the only mobilized group in the meeting other than the team of would-be founding fathers. Although generally earnest in group, we had become caustic in private and could be off-putting. A young German woman who seemed desperate for an alternative public rhetoric, frustrated by the law's increasing distance from her own fantasy of contact with the Timorese everyday, nonetheless found our alternative corrosive, biting, impolite, unhelpful.

She was right to be worried. To my mind, the most likely direction for our group would be simply to abstain from the main action of the platform and enjoy the hilarity of voting as a bloc on one after another absurd amendment or proposal, modern spectator participants in a social contract repeated now as farce. We would then go home, remembering pleasant private times but without more than the old earnestness to link us professionally to Timor. The question for this group seemed whether any sense of personal commitment to the cause could survive the private cynicism of activism in these tired institutional and doctrinal forms. Pedro was also right to be worried. Pedro balked at the idea that some of us might not wish to "join" the Jurists' Platform. Had we not always already joined, by coming? I began to fear that we were all in Timor for the duration.

I had tried once over lunch to connect with the German woman. Couldn't she see us as a symptom of a frustration she must surely share? I hoped she would teeter between the temptations of the discipline and joining us in recognizing the truth of her own experience. The latter seemed too scary, without direction. What was our little group, where was our commitment, what was our program? As it happened, we seemed in control of the plenary voting, and were careening madly from one position to another—table that, adopt that, reject that, allying now with one, now with another faction, with Paula, still chairing the meeting, with the Director of the Unrepresented, our friend's boss, and so forth. It was fun.

Somewhat offhandedly, as we debated our final resolution, I made a proposal of my own. In part, I thought it might link us back to the group as a whole. And in part it might disrupt the proceedings sufficiently to throw those who would constitute us off their guard. I stood up and made a little speech, proposing that we delete the carefully numbered operative paragraphs in our resolution, following the concerns of our preamble with the statement "1. Express our frustration at the limitations of traditional institutional and doctrinal means of addressing our concerns."

I argued that we might thereby leave a mark in the public space of an experience we had shared, an experience of exhaustion, boredom, frustration. Didn't we all feel worn out by the prospect of yet another resolution from some international institution? Hadn't we all been here before? Rather than allow the parallel narratives of public speech and private pleasure to resume their separate paths after we leave, rather than find our doubts disciplined into fealty to a common program, I propose acknowledging the social experience of our weekend together and learning to live as international legal activists for Timor without the dream (or the excuse) of a law which might be brought to bear for social change.

It was a quixotic moment—I hadn't done the work necessary to mobilize my constituency nor to lay the groundwork for such a suggestion. And I had formulated the proposal so awkwardly that many heard only an exhortation to renewed earnestness—and found it moving. I don't think anyone thought our formal resolution would "have an effect," or that the institution we constituted would be much beyond a shell within which Pedro would raise money to carry on whatever activism he had already begun. Still, unable to think of anything else to do, it seemed absurd to abandon our standard operating procedure. We unanimously adopted the resolution as originally drafted and opened the meeting to a press conference on our conclusions. When the plenary was over, my Boston colleague and I were vaguely down. Perhaps we had been too seduced by cynicism, or immobilized by jet lag to render our faction effective as a cultural alternative to the Platform's closing pieties. We resolved to strategize more self-consciously in the future—perhaps we could build a cosmopolitan culture outside the clichés of private irony and public activism.

The weekend ended that evening with a collective excursion to see native Timorese folk dancing. Gestural primitivism. I passed it up for dinner with friends. The next day I intended to rent a convertible and ride around the Portuguese hills with an old friend and a bottle of wine. The conference would slowly recede into the background. We would come to take it for granted, see its petty social dimensions, its anxieties and erotics as part of our individual private and professional lives, its institutional achievements part of the broader constellation of human-rights machinery grown up around the discipline of international law. This had been one weekend in the metropolis: by turns pragmatic, earnest, and cynical. Whatever possibilities our psychosocial dynamics had opened for a renewal, we had not managed to exploit.

I still get the occasional jaunty card from one or the other Platform friend—they've started calling it IPJET (pronounced ip-jet) and the Council has duly met to review the first year's program of action. I don't suppose I'll hear much more about Timor. Every month or so now I receive notice of some solidarity demonstration, but in my experience those trail off. If I see a news story on Timor I read it with more inter-est—it reminds me of good friends in Lisbon. And I am glad to have been able to help Pedro continue his work, now proceeding on the firm pediment of an International Jurists' Platform.

Chapter Eleven

⊱─◈─◉─◈─⊰

FEMALE SUBJECTS OF PUBLIC INTERNATIONAL LAW

HUMAN RIGHTS AND THE EXOTIC OTHER FEMALE

Karen Engle

FOR CENTURIES, several societies—primarily located in Muslim Africa—have engaged in a practice that is often, perhaps euphemistically, referred to as female circumcision.[1] Some call it genital mutilation. Others use more specific and technical language to describe the particular form the practice takes, such as clitoridectomy or infibulation.[2]

The subjects (some would say objects) of this procedure are young girls ranging in age from several days to just prior to marriage, depending on the particular cultural practices of the region involved. Clitoridectomy serves largely as a prerequisite, if not a direct rite of passage, to a girl's adulthood, or womanhood. A woman who has not participated in the ritual is likely to be denied the possibility of marriage and is thereby foreclosed access to certain privileges of her society. The procedure is almost universally performed by women, either trained or lay. It often proves to be dangerous, sometimes fatal, because it is not always done in hygienic circumstances.

As might be expected, many feminists have attacked this custom, and pointed to it as one more, yet quite extreme, example of misogyny and (male) societal control over female bodies. Many Western feminists have reacted with outrage, calling for an abrupt end to the practice. Their outrage has been fueled, or at least justified, by the condemnation of the practice by some women within societies that engage in it, such as Egyptian Nawal El Saadawi.[3] Some African women who oppose the practice encourage Western women to condemn it, in the belief that Western women have more clout to pressure governments to put an end to it.

For others, including other feminists, clitoridectomy poses a more complex set of issues. The complexity arises in part from the fact that women perform the operation on other females and that girls, if old enough to consider it, often claim to desire the procedure. That the practice is deeply rooted in culture also poses difficulties. One Western feminist has suggested that Western women ought not be so shocked by the practice, given our own forms of bodily self mutilation, through, for example, plastic surgery, incessant dieting, or wearing shoes that are too small.[4] In a similar vein, Gayatri Spivak has discussed what she calls "symbolic clitoridectomy," which "has always been the 'normal' accession to womanhood and the unacknowledged name of motherhood."[5]

As the practice has become more widely known throughout the world, many have begun to talk about it as an international human rights violation. The last decade has paved the way for this kind of analysis, as public international law has expanded—at least formally—to include issues specifically pertaining to women.

With this expansion, a body of literature has developed that advocates women's rights as international human rights.

Three broad approaches have emerged within that literature which I have labeled doctrinalist, institutionalist, and external critique. The three approaches represent different feminist attitudes toward law, ranging from liberal to radical, as well as different approaches to rights discourse in general and to human rights law in particular.[6]

In this essay, I explore some of the ways that these different approaches confront, or would confront, clitoridectomy. I do so with an eye toward the various notions of women's subjectivity the approaches display. Specifically, as Western women's rights advocates attempt to use universal international human rights law, institutions, and discourse as means for eradicating clitoridectomy, I am interested in the ways and extent to which the advocates recognize and respond to differences

212   among women. I focus particularly on their assumptions about and reactions to what I term the Exotic Other Female.

I use Exotic Other Female here to as a signifier, to represent collectively those women who through their action (or inaction) condone the practice of clitoridectomy within their culture. Implicit in this label is the assumption that the Exotic Other Female, or at least her needs and desires, are not totally accessible to someone outside her culture.

I identify and discuss the Exotic Other Female in an attempt to expose her presence in the discourse of women's human rights. Although women's rights advocates rare acknowledge the Exotic Other Female, I argue that their discourse is nevertheless dependent on her. Their projection of the Exotic Other Female (as something "out there") seems to guide much of their advocacy.

In discussing the Exotic Other Female, I do not mean to essentialize her; she is only that when she is merely imagined and not engaged. Once engaged, *she* will become *they*—many and complex—which might be one reason many have for not engaging her (and for not allowing her to engage them.) One of the questions I hope to begin to address in this essay is how it would be possible to move beyond merely imagining this Other.[7]

Exploring the various ways that women's human rights advocates imagine the Exotic Other Female as they approach the issue of clitoridectomy yields some surprising and paradoxical results. It might seem, for example, due to the universalizing nature of international human rights doctrine, that liberal feminists, who are most committed to using legal doctrine to eradicate clitoridectomy, would be least likely to acknowledge differences among women. In fact, doctrinal advocates turn out to be the most overt in taking account of the Exotic Other Female. That they take account of her, however, does not mean that they engage her; rather, they attempt to change her mind about the practice by choosing a doctrinal position with which she might agree.

A similar paradox unfolds through exploration of the radical feminist positions taken by women's human rights advocates. It might seem that those advocates most critical of what they see as the "maleness" of the international human rights framework would be most able to take into account women's differences, since they would not be tied to formal universal norms as embodied in "male" international human rights doctrine. It happens, though, that the radical feminists are much less likely than the liberal feminists to confront the fact that some women defend and practice clitoridectomy. Indeed, the radical feminists do not generally even acknowledge the existence of the Exotic Other Female. The failure to acknowledge her is due largely, I believe, to their radical focus on a male/female dichotomy that they identify in human rights discourse, which they see as the primary obstacle to achieving women's human rights.

The Doctrinalist Approach

Doctrinalists generally approach international human rights law by focussing on one practice that they believe violates a particular right, here the practice of "female circumcision" (as they label it).[8] They then attempt to demonstrate doctrinally how the practice ought to be eradicated on the basis of rights derived from international law. Because no legal provisions specifically mention clitoridectomy or female circumcision, those who advocate its end go through one human rights instrument after another to show that the practice is prohibited by the existence of rights such as "rights of the child,"[9] "the right to sexual and corporal integrity,"[10] and the "right to health."[11]

In attempting to assimilate a particular woman's right to the dominant human rights framework, doctrinalists tend to make liberal feminist assumptions. That is, they do not indicate that bringing women into the human rights structure would radically change or disrupt the structure; indeed, their arguments assume that the positive law already includes women by providing, if indirectly, the right they advocate.

Although doctrinalists basically rely on the assimilation of women's rights to positive human rights law, they recognize that international human rights law is difficult to enforce. Enforcement seems particularly tough in the case of women's human rights, since those claims are plagued by a counter-claim of cultural relativism. So strong is the counter-claim that Alison Slack frames the purpose of her article as determining "at what point the 'tradition' [of] female circumcision becomes a human rights violation justifying pressure from foreign cultures to end this 'tradition.'"[12]

While those who take other approaches to women's human rights do not openly confront this counter-claim of cultural relativism, doctrinalists often do. Although in the end they reject a cultural relativist perspective as they argue for "universal" human rights, they are nevertheless acutely aware that disagreements about the scope and shape of women's rights exist, particularly in the case of clitoridectomy. These disagreements are not just between men and women or between cultures; they actually exist

214   between women. The acknowledgement of disagreements among women is, in my mind, a strength of the doctrinalists' feminist approaches. It allows them to engage women's differences to a greater extent than those who take the other approaches, which tend to assume, albeit to different degrees, a monolithic or essential "woman."

Although doctrinalists acknowledge these differences among women's attitudes, they eventually attempt to work around them. They seem to imagine the existence of the Exotic Other Female, the one who opposes abolition of the practice she might even help perpetuate, as something that must be reckoned with. For the doctrinalists, this imagined Other is a reminder that the right, no matter how enshrined in public international law, is not universally accepted. Rather than denying the existence of the Exotic Other Female, doctrinalists propose strategies for changing her mind and thus for removing an obstacle to universal recognition of the right. In choosing among strategies, they express sensitivity to cultural differences.

At this stage, doctrinalists engage in what I call strategic positivism. Although a number of rights exist in positive law that would seemingly prohibit clitoridectomy (right to corporal and sexual integrity, rights of children, right to health), those who oppose the practice do not stress them all. Instead, they make a strategic decision about which right to pursue, depending on which rights rubric governments and the Exotic Other Female (as victim, and often as victimizer) are most likely to accept. Alison Slack and Kay Boulware-Miller agree that governments are most likely to accept a right to health argument, since, as Boulware-Miller puts it, they "are more concerned with basic health and economic problems than with the arguably more elitist rights they associate with Western countries, such as political rights and fundamental freedoms."[13] Boulware-Miller believes women, too, will be most likely to accept an end to the practice based on a health argument, because, unlike the other potential rights arguments, it avoids an "imposing and judgmental approach."[14]

Doctrinalists, therefore, deal with the tension between cultures by acknowledging the tension and then working around it. While a strength of their approach is that they recognize and even take account of differences among women, they neither engage those women that practice clitoridectomy nor confront the practice itself. Rather than finding out why women defend the practice, they try to convince them to change their minds, by phrasing the issue as one of health. They do so despite the United Nations own research on "traditional practices affecting the health of women and children," which indicates that women who oppose clitoridectomy within those cultures where it is practiced rarely cite health as a reason.[15]

By approaching the issue as one of health, doctrinalists seem to have avoided taking any overtly "political" stance on the issue of clitoridectomy. For them, international human rights law, by guaranteeing a right to health, demands an end to the practice. Approaching clitoridectomy as a health issue raises another concern. If the practice could be done without negative health consequences, international law might actually become complicit in the practice, obligating states to ensure that it is performed under better health conditions. This possibility is one the doctrinalists do not address.[16]

The Institutionalist Approach

The institutionalist approach to women's human rights concentrates on the institutions that have been created by international law to enforce human rights.[17] Those who take this approach do not generally advocate particular rights, and they are not concerned with which international instruments guarantee which rights. They believe that if positive law or doctrine guaranteeing women's rights is to be meaningful, institutions must transform that law or doctrine into action, through pragmatic, meaningful enforcement mechanisms. To the extent that transformation has not occurred, they largely hold responsible the (primarily male) actors that deploy human rights discourse through international institutions. Institutionalists do not attack the international institutional framework per se. Instead, they argue either that mainstream institutions—those institutions that see themselves as enforcing all human rights, not differentiating between women and men—need to rearrange their priorities to include issues of women, or that specialized women's institutions—meant specifically to enforce women's rights and generally comprised of women—must be given power equal to mainstream ones.

Because of their reliance on existing institutional structures to assimilate women's rights, I also consider these advocates liberal feminists. Their approaches, however, could be understood as more radical than those of the doctrinalists, as the institutionalists are critical of the present (male) deployment of the system. The difficulties the institutionalists point to are more directly attributed to a male dominated structure than those identified by the doctrinalists. These advocates provide useful insights into the power plays within the institutional framework that keep men in control and women's rights at the periphery.

Although institutionalists do not generally focus on particular human rights violations, we can imagine a way that they might approach clitoridectomy. They would likely start by taking for granted that the practice is in violation of international human rights law (although a brief discussion with a doctrinalist might be required to convince them.) Their task would then be to see international institutions enforce the rights the doctrinalists derive.

As they make proposals for greater enforcement of women's rights, institutionalists—unlike doctrinalists—are not concerned with the possibility that women might disagree about particular rights. Rather, they focus on what they see as male/female disagreements, which manifest themselves in the bureaucratic structures of international institutions, both mainstream and specialized. In this context, institutionalists often act as if international institutional actors are largely free from the cultures from which they hail (except that male actors are obvious products of patriarchy.) The Exotic Other Female never enters into the sterile institutional framework because within that framework there is nothing to be other to but the male actors who have power to deploy and control international institutions.

Applying their analysis to clitoridectomy, institutionalists would argue that international institutions could in theory, and partly within their present structure, address the issue. For the institutional framework to be effective in combatting the practice, however, they would contend that either mainstream institutions must expand their (presently male) focus, or specialized women's institutions must be granted power equal to the mainstream ones. Institutionalists would generally pursue the second possibility, implying that were the specialized institutions given sufficient power, clitoridectomy could be brought to an end. Hence, although the Commission on Human Rights, through its Sub-commission on the Protection of Minorities, has investigated clitoridectomy as a practice affecting women's health, institutionalists might argue that the issue could be addressed more effectively and directly by a specialized institution, such as the Commission on the Status of Women. But, they would point out, the Commission on the Status of Women could only even potentially do so if it were granted investigatory powers equal to the Commission on Human Rights.

Within the institutionalists' discussions and proposals, however, lies the very real possibility that even if women's institutions were given the power needed to pursue their agendas, women comprising those institutions might reject that power. Margaret Galey, for example, has discussed a meeting of the Commission on the Status of Women where some members were reluctant to accept responsibility for investigating individual cases, a power she sees as essential to enforcing women's rights, because they "recognized that this would involve investigation of allegations, a politically sensitive matter, and a considerable expense, which the Commission's membership was unlikely to support."[18] Although the Commission eventually passed the resolution, its members have continued to debate whether to increase their capacity to receive communications.[19] They have also rejected possibilities for greater power in other areas.[20]

The reality that women, even within specialized women's institutions, might disagree about "what they want," poses a very real, although largely unacknowledged, obstacle to actualizing the solutions these advocates propose. Hence, while those who pursue women's rights institutionally offer a powerful analysis of the workings and priorities of the international institutional framework, as well as of the often gendered nature of presumably neutral bureaucratic structures, they are prevented from fully exploring the changes they seek by only focussing on, and in turn reinforcing, male/female differences.

External Critiques

Other women's human rights advocates begin by situating themselves outside the human rights system, looking in at the discourse. From their (initial) external perches, they raise questions about whether human rights discourse can really assimilate women's issues/demands/rights.

In this section, I identify and discuss three external critiques, each of which suggests a different level of belief in the ability of international rights discourse and the human rights framework to address issues of women. Unlike the doctrinalists and institutionalists, who believe that the human rights framework can assimilate women's rights, the external critics believe structural changes—whether in human rights theory, doctrine, institutions or language—are needed to accommodate women's concerns.

For the most part, I consider those who take these approaches to be radical feminists because they critique the human rights system for the ways it perpetuates women's subordination.[21] To a certain extent, they also approach women's human rights as if all women were essentially the same.

The radical feminist positions of these critics do not, I believe, make them incapable of accepting that women disagree, even about clitoridectomy. Rather, they focus so much on the subordination of women by men that they tend to generalize the extent to which all women have an interest in overcoming men's power, the assumption here being that "genital mutilation" (as they call the practice) is a clear exercise of male power. This near exclusive focus on subordination, I maintain, is largely responsible for the failure of radical feminists to engage the Exotic Other Female. Were the external critics to confront the fact that females disagree about clitoridectomy, they would likely assign "false consciousness" to those whom they consider do not recognize their own oppression.

Integration

The integrationist approach to international human rights challenges human rights advocates to accept a coherent or integrated theory of *human* rights—one that represents the rights of both women and men—and to realize "human rights which are genuinely human."[22] Those who take this approach often refer to the rights of "half of humanity."[23] For them it is because women are human, not just women, that their human rights should be protected. That they are not protected is not directly due to women's differences from men (or from each other) but to the failure of the human rights system to pay attention to women's (human) situation.

Although this approach might sound similar to the doctrinalist approach, since it suggests an underlying belief in a human rights framework that can incorporate women's rights, it differs in an important respect. While the doctrinalists assume that the framework already assimilates women, the integrationists argue that the human rights system must change its focus to accommodate women's rights. And even though the integrationists do not stress women's differences from men—hoping that both male and female can be dealt with under the human rubric—they do have some sense of a gender struggle. The problem with human rights practice, they argue, is that it has focussed on men's rights.

Integrationists begin their critique of the international human rights system by noting rampant violations of what they assume to be women's human rights. One example of such violations is "genital mutilations of women which still kill, maim, and blight the physical and psychological health of millions of women and little children every year."[24] They then argue that the international human rights system is disingenuous because it does not declare clitoridectomy a human rights violation and aim to end the practice.

To the extent that those who take this approach confront the issue of cultural relativism, they see the relativist claim as false and inconsistent, made by those who simply want to exclude practices such as clitoridectomy from human rights analysis. Riane Eisler, for example, abruptly dismisses the argument that "the enactments and enforcement of laws prohibiting genital mutilation would be improper interference with ethnic traditions, constituting merely one more form of 'Western cultural imperialism'"[25] with the following response: "All institutionalized behavior, including cannibalism and slavery, are cultural traditions. And surely no human rights advocate . . . would today dare to justify cannibalism or slavery . . . on cultural or traditional grounds."[26] Implicit in this rejection of the claim is that clitoridectomy is analogous to cannibalism and slavery. Referring to the practice as mutilation makes this analogy more likely; no one would *choose* to be eaten, enslaved, or mutilated.

Integrationists believe that the difficulty in bringing women's rights into the human rights arena lies not with international human rights discourse per se, but rather with its presently exclusive male focus. That focus, which is not only not endemic to human rights theory but in opposition to it, must be changed if the practice of clitoridectomy is to be brought to an end.

Integrationists provide important insights into the often inconsistent claims that keep women's rights at the periphery of international human rights law and discourse. The refusal of the integrationists to see human rights theory as preventing the protection of women's rights allows them to pursue possibilities for using international rights as a site for struggling for the improvement of women's condition. The question they do not explore, however, is what it means to improve women's condition. For them, ending "genital mutilation" is only a matter of changing the focus of the international human rights system. These advocates do not confront the possibility that "culture" might really be an obstacle to achieving change. In particular, they do not consider that resistance to ending the practice, and even to labeling it "mutilation," might come from (some) women themselves. For integrationists, the Exotic Other Female is not to be engaged.

Human rights critics who take this approach do not have as much faith as the integrationists in the ability of human rights theory to merely expand its focus to accommodate women's rights. For them, international human rights theory is seriously flawed because it is centered on a "male" definition of human rights. Hence, to accommodate women's rights, the theory would require reconceptualizing and redefining. Specifically, women would have to define their own rights.

This approach differs from the integrationist approach, then, in a subtle way. Avoiding the possibility that women might need any special rights, the integrationists aim to normalize or universalize women's rights, making them an essential part of human rights (hence the discussion of the *human* rights of women.) Those who call for reconceptualization, on the other hand, embrace women's differences from men, through their call upon women to define their own rights.[27]

If they were to talk about "genital mutilation," reconceptualists might argue that the human rights system has not begun to deal with the issue because women have not defined the rights necessary to end the practice. Without such definition, human rights law regarding women, with its present focus on discrimination, is bound to respond insufficiently to the issue.

For these advocates, once women define their rights, it will become clear that human rights must be reconceptualized. Essential to this reconceptualization is the entry of human rights law into the traditional private sphere. The reconceptualist position assumes a distinction between public and private realms and takes for granted that international human rights, as presently theorized, excludes from its purview the private sphere.[28] From that perspective, clitoridectomy—because it is a "private" (not officially state conducted) practice—cannot be seen as a violation of international human rights until the human rights field has been reconceptualized to include the private.

By calling for women to define their rights, the reconceptualist position, unlike that of the integrationists, in principle opens itself up to the possibility of listening to a multiplicity of women's voices and even to engaging the Exotic Other Female. Yet, one of the central assumptions of this position seems to be that women will agree about what are or should be their rights. The goal of the reconceptualist is, if not to shift from the male vision of human rights, at least to supplement that vision with a female one. Male and female are, for these purposes, static notions.

The reconceptualist position is not, however, unaware of claims of cultural relativism. Noreen Burrows, for example, sees cultural differences as posing difficulties to the process of achieving recognition of women's rights: "Given the diversity in the forms of interpersonal relations and cultural variations which exist, say in the structure of the family, it may prove difficult to specify with sufficient precision those rights which the international community would recognize as being the rights of women."[29] Even as Burrows expresses this concern, however, she never suggests that women themselves might disagree about which rights they have; rather, her concern is that the "international community" might have trouble accepting or properly interpreting the rights because of its apparent sympathy with cultural variations. That women might be a part of that conflictual international community is not an issue she addresses.

Linguistic Critique

Whether through integration or reconceptualization, those who pose the first two external critiques assume that the international human rights framework can be made to accommodate women's concerns. The problems integrationists and reconceptualists identify with human rights theory turn in large part on the view that it has addressed itself, perhaps exclusively, to the concerns of men. They disagree primarily about whether that focus is endemic to the theory. Another external critique poses what I call a linguistic challenge to human rights discourse. Those who aim this critique at international rights discourse generally explicitly situate themselves outside it, identifying with a particular cause or discipline (for example, feminism or biology) to examine the biases reflected in the discourse. For them, human rights discourse is not just male focussed, controlled or deployed; it is "male."

Here I focus on only one strand of this critique, which poses what it considers to be the feminist critique of rights. Although the critique borrows from communitarianism and early Marxism, and resonates with many of the critiques of rights by critical legal theorists, it does so with a strong cultural feminist perspective. That is, it assumes that there are certain essential values that are female and that cannot be realized through traditional rights discourse.

For these critics, "the concept of 'rights' is masculinist and patriarchal, a concept that came into its own with the rise of capitalism."[30] Adding an essentialist feminist twist to other critiques of rights, they suggest that "in our assertion of rights we [feminists] play a masculinist game."[31] Moreover:

> "[r]ights" language seems to assume ... that society is a collection of atomic particles in which any given individual's happiness ... is viewed as mutually disinterested from another's, that communities or love relationships are not ethically relevant in deciding what action ought to be taken. Rights language is fundamentally adversarial and negative. ... Feminists seek a framework that emphasizes positive values such as helping, cooperating and acting out of love, friendship or relatedness, as well as fairness.[32]

Other problems these advocates identify with rights discourse are that it "fails to resolve moral disputes cohesively" and that it is "static and does not challenge the social structures."[33]

Even after setting forth this harsh critique, these advocates (as with many rights critics) return to rights language. They claim to do so, however, "in a nonabsolutist fashion ... affirm[ing] other moral criteria than rights—such as duty, loyalty, friendship, responsibility, goodness, and justice—as the basis of moral action."[34] In the end, then, they accept rights language by adding to their use of it what they consider to be essential women's values.

Although these advocates raise a number of important issues about the lack of neutrality of language and the role(s) that language plays in social struggles, their critique eventually relies on a deeply entrenched male/female dichotomy. Even though all the other advocates, save the doctrinalists, also rely to some extent on this dichotomy, this one is most based on essential, and thereby presumably unchangeable, differences between men and women. Along with their notion that men and women fundamentally differ comes a strong sense that all women are the same. Hence, in their assumption and even promotion of an essential woman's culture, the linguistic critics come the closest of any women's rights advocates to erasing the experiences/beliefs/desires of the Exotic Other Female. Their theory cannot accommodate any recognition of disagreements among women; it would disrupt their totalizing scheme.

All the authors who challenge human rights discourse from the outside—never assuming that it was meant to protect or assimilate their feminist demands—eventually defend the discourse in some form. Their greatest strength, I believe, is their self-conscious approach and insightful understanding of the nuances of language and of power. With all the potential obstacles to achieving women's human rights these advocates identify, however, they fail to consider seriously the possibility that women are not all the same and that legitimate differences might exist among them, particularly regarding issues such as clitoridectomy. The extent to which that failure problematizes their position differs with the various approaches.

Conclusion: Beyond Imagination

At first glance, it would appear that approaching the practice of clitoridectomy as a violation of human rights would prohibit any discussion of cultural relativism. It seems that universal and international human rights implicitly represent a denial of the validity of any cultural difference that might stand in opposition to the declared universal norm. If this were the case, one might expect the debate about clitoridectomy in the international rights context to differ significantly from the debate among feminists described at the beginning of this essay.

It turns out, though, that as with the debate about clitoridectomy in other contexts, some women's rights advocates are sensitive to the desire of the Exotic Other Female to maintain and participate in the practice of her culture, while other women's rights advocates refuse to engage the Other's "desires," presumably because they are mere products of false consciousness. Hence, the possibility or impossibility of taking account of "real" cultural differences and beliefs informs much of how women's rights advocates approach clitoridectomy.

Another puzzle has emerged. Just as it seems that a universal human rights approach would prohibit discussion of cultural relativism, it also would seem that those advocates most committed to formal international legal doctrine would be less sensitive to discussion of cultural difference than those advocates who appear to have a sophisticated understanding of the nuances of legal doctrine. I maintain, however, that at least in the context of women's human rights advocacy, the opposite happens. The more doctrinally oriented the advocate is, the more open she is to recognizing differences among women. And the more she moves outside the formal legal structures, the more she assumes an essential woman's voice.

This puzzle is due in part, I believe, to the differing attitudes that women's rights advocates display toward rights. While the doctrinalists stake their universal claims in liberal positive rights agreed to by sovereigns, those who apply an external critique often rely on some inherent moral basis, generally rights, for their claims. Positive law seems to free up the doctrinalists, allowing them to choose any doctrinally derived right they believe to be effective in persuading the Exotic Other Female. Those who claim moral rights do not experience the same type of liberty; a right is a right regardless of whether those they entitle want to claim it.

The puzzle is also related to the different feminist postures assumed by the advocates. While the most formalist advocates tend to be liberal (tolerant) feminists, those most external to the formal structures tend to be radical (in this case often essentialist) feminists. To the extent that liberal feminists are concerned with increasing women's choices and radical feminists are concerned with increasing women's power,[35] it makes sense that the liberals would be more open to a variety of women's views and desires. The radicals, by concentrating on women's power (versus men's power), are invested in making women one cohesive group.

As advocates move from the more liberal to the more radical positions, they become progressively more concerned about changing the power dynamics, and they move further outside the formal legal structures to try to achieve that change. Hence, institutionalists play the perfect middle-ground, assuming the institutional structures can eventually assimilate their feminist demands but nevertheless recognizing that the male domination of the structure makes the assimilation difficult. The further they move outside doctrine, the more advocates work within a dichotomous male/female framework. That dichotomy seems to keep women's differences, or different women, at bay.

Whether they work inside or outside the doctrinal and institutional frameworks, most women's rights advocates recognize at some level that women have been marginalized, consciously or not, from those frameworks. But they do not generally recognize that their own pursuit of women's rights is also marginalizing. Just as human rights advocates might keep women at the periphery, if not exclude them altogether, women's rights advocates keep the Exotic Other Female at the margins. The Exotic Other Female, however, apparently present or not, affects women's rights advocacy. Whether or not advocates openly acknowledge or engage her needs and desires, she is always just below the surface or around the corner, even as a potential disruption to their critiques and proposals. Perhaps it is to avoid her disruptive power, that she is kept at bay.

I do not mean to suggest in this essay that the "male" side of the male/female split is unproblematic. I believe that it is largely because so many of the women's rights advocates readily accept a stereotypical and essentialist view of men that they are unable to problematize the female side. Being caught in the male/female dichotomy prevents further exploration of either "male" or "female."

Doctrinalists seem to have avoided this trap by assuming that women can assimilate to the (gender-neutral) human rights doctrine. They are able to take account of the existence of the Exotic Other Female through their attempts at persuading her (which requires using doctrine strategically). But through their concentrated effort at bringing all females into the realm of human rights doctrine, they fail to recognize the very biases reflected in that doctrine, as well as in human rights institutions and discourse, that might keep women outside its scope.

It appears, then, that even though each approach provides some valuable insights into the workings of the international human rights framework, none actively engages the Exotic Other Female. Either the advocates maternalistically try to change her mind or they seem to ignore or not believe her desires, often dissipating her by attributing to her false consciousness. Either way, advocates' imagined constructs of her guide their strategies for gaining recognition of women's rights.

Gayatri Spivak has said that "[b]etween patriarchy and imperialism, subject-constitution and object-formation, the figure of the woman disappears, not into pristine nothingness, but into a violent shuttling which is the displaced figuration of the 'Third World Woman' caught between tradition and modernization."[36] The failure of advocates to engage the Exotic Other Female does not erase her; she is not absent. The task ahead for women's human rights advocates is to acknowledge the presence of the Exotic Other Female, even in her sometimes apparent absence, and to use some of those insights already provided by their varied approaches to begin to move from imagination to engagement.

Notes

1. Although this procedure is today most commonly performed in parts of Africa that are predominantly Muslim, it is neither exclusively performed in those areas nor done in all countries of the region. History of the practice in the Sudan indicates that the operation antedates both the arrival of Islam and of Christianity. Janice Boddy, *Body Politics: Continuing the Anticircumcision Crusade,* 5 MED. ANTHROPOLOGY Q. 15, 15 (1991). While Muslim clerics generally insist that clitoridectomy in any of its various forms is not an Islamic religious custom, "most rural Sudanese believe some form of pharaonic circumcision is to be required on religious grounds." *Id.*

2. For (varied) descriptions of the practice, see Halima Warzazi, *Report of the Working Group on Traditional Practices Affecting the Health of Women and Children,* U.N. ESCOR, Commission on Human Rights, 42d Sess., Prov. Agenda item 19, U.N. Doc. E/CN.4/1986/42 (1986) [hereinafter *U.N. Report on Traditional Practices*]; OLAYINKA KOSO-THOMAS, THE CIRCUMCISION OF WOMEN: A STRATEGY FOR ERADICATION 16–17 (1987); Alison Slack, *Female Circumcision: A Critical Appraisal,* 10 HUM. RTS. Q. 437, 440–42 (1988). The different types of practice often account for variations in the language used to describe it. Other language differences stem from a wide range of, and often opposing, views about the practice.

   Although I generally use the term clitoridectomy, I realize that I am failing to accurately portray many of the procedures, both those that are more akin to male circumcision in that they excise only a small portion of the clitoris and those that remove and operate on much more than the clitoris, such as infibulation. The former is often performed in Egypt while the latter is most common in the Sudan. For a more thorough description of practices in those countries, see Daniel Gordon, *Female Circumcision and Genital Operations in Egypt and the Sudan: A Dilemma for Medical Anthropology,* 5 MED. ANTHROPOLOGY Q. 3 (1991).

3. *See generally* NAWAL EL SAADAWI, THE HIDDEN FACE OF EVE: WOMEN IN THE ARAB WORLD (Sherif Hetata ed. & trans., 1980); NAWAL EL SAADAWI, WOMAN AT POINT ZERO (Sherif Hetata trans., 1983).

4. *See* Rhoda E. Howard, *Health Costs of Social Degradation and Female Self-Mutilation in North America, in* HUMAN RIGHTS IN THE TWENTY-FIRST CENTURY: A GLOBAL CHALLENGE 503 (Kathleen E. Mahoney and Paul Mahoney eds., 1993); *see also* Ruth Rosen, *Perspective on Women's Health: Draw the Line at the Knife,* L.A. TIMES, Nov. 17, 1991, at M5 (describing breast implant surgery as "barbaric" and similar to other "mutilations" that are considered violations of human rights, such as foot-binding, dowry deaths, and clitoridectomies).

5. GAYATRI C. SPIVAK, *French Feminism in an International Frame, in* IN OTHER WORLDS: ESSAYS IN CULTURAL POLITICS 134, 151 (1987).

6. I have set forth and defined these approaches in detail in Karen Engle, *International Human Rights and Feminism: When Discourses Meet,* 13 MICH. J. INT'L L. 517 (1992).

7. For a provocative discussion of a similar question in the context of sati in India, see Gayatri C. Spivak, *Can the Subaltern Speak? Speculations on Widow-Sacrifice,* 7/8 WEDGE 120 (1985).

8. In describing this approach to clitoridectomy, I rely primarily on articles by Kay Boulware-Miller and Alison Slack. *See* Kay Boulware-Miller, *Female Circumcision: Challenges to the Practice as a Human Rights Violation,* 8 HARV. WOMEN'S L.J. 155 (1985); Slack, *supra* note 2.

9. *See* Boulware-Miller, *supra* note 8, at 165–69.

10. *See id.* at 169–72.

11. *See id.* at 172–76; Slack, *supra* note 2, at 485–86.

12. Slack, *supra* note 2, at 439.

13. Boulware-Miller, *supra* note 8, at 173; *see also* Slack, *supra* note 2, at 486.

14. Boulware-Miller, *supra* note 8, at 166–67, 171–72. Health arguments have been the most common means of attempting to eradicate clitoridectomy, both by intergovernmental and nongovernmental actors. *See, e.g.,* Halima Warzazi, *Study on Traditional Practices Affecting the Health of Women and Children,* U.N. ESCOR, Commission on Human Rights, 43d Sess., Prov. Agenda item 4, U.N. Doc. E/CN.4/Sub.2/1991/6 (1991); *U.N. Report on Traditional Practices, supra* note 2; KOSO-THOMAS, *supra* note 2. Even those who have taken a more radical approach to clitoridectomy, calling it "genital mutilation" for example, have responded favorably to the health approach. *See, e.g., Progress Report: WIN News Grass Roots Campaign to Eradicate GM [Genital Mutilation],* 18 WOMEN'S INT'L NETWORK NEWS 38–39 (1992).

15. *See U.N. Report on Traditional Practices, supra* note 2, at 15 (discussing reasons women give for opposing the practice as "violation of fundamental human rights," "violation of women's image," "social complications," and "cultural conformism"); *see also id.* at 14 (Of the "sample of persons opposed to female circumcision," only 12.72 per cent gave "illnesses and accidents" as a reason, as opposed to 43.63 per cent who said the practice is pointless and 32.72 per cent who listed "diminution of sensitivity" for the reason.).

16. The possibility is not as remote as it might seem. Gordon reports that in urban parts of the Sudan, there is already an official policy of using the health care system to perform the procedures in order to reduce complications and health risks. Moreover, trained medical personnel with drugs and equipment have been disseminated and used to perform clitoridectomies and other genital operations. *See* Gordon, *supra* note 2, at 12 (citing ASMA EL DAREER, WOMEN, WHY DO YOU WEEP? (1982); FRAN P. HOSKEN, THE HOSKEN REPORT: GENITAL AND SOCIAL MUTILATION OF FEMALES 47, 287 (1982)).

17. I primarily base my description of this approach on Margaret E. Galey, *International Enforcement of Women's Rights,* 6 HUM. RTS. Q. 463 (1984) and Laura Reanda, *Human Rights and Women's Rights: The United Nations Approach,* 3 HUM. RTS. Q. 11 (1981). More recent literature takes very similar approaches. *See, e.g.,* Theodor Meron, *Editorial Comments: Enhancing the Effectiveness of the Prohibition of Discrimination Against Women,* 84 AM. J. INT'L L. 213 (1990); Andrew C. Byrnes, *The "Other" Human Rights Treaty Body: The Work of the Committee on the Elimination of Discrimination Against Women,* 14 YALE J. INT'L L. 1 (1989).

18. Galey, *supra* note 17, at 469.

19. Even as recently as the 1991 meeting of the Commission, members were unable to agree on a resolution that purported to grant greater power to receive or investigate complaints. Indeed, a draft resolution on "Communications concerning the status of women," *Monitoring the Implementation of the Nairobi Forward-Looking Strategies for the Advancement of Women,* U.N. ESCOR, Commission on the Status of Women, 35th Sess., Agenda item 4, U.N. Doc. E/CN.6/1991/L.14 (1991), did not even make it to the floor.

20. In 1988, for example, the Commission chose not to request an increase in the length of its meetings, even though the General Assembly encouraged it to do so. Sandra Colliver, *United Nations Machineries on Women's Rights: How Might They Better Help Women Whose Rights are Being Violated, in* NEW DIRECTIONS IN HUMAN RIGHTS 25, 29 (Ellen L. Lutz et al. eds., 1989).

21. *See* ALISON M. JAGGAR, FEMINIST POLITICS AND HUMAN NATURE 83–85 (1983).

22. Fran P. Hosken, *Toward a Definition of Women's Human Rights,* 3 HUM. RTS. Q. 1, 10 (1981).

228   23. *See, e.g.,* Riane Eisler, *Human Rights: Toward an Integrated Theory of Action,* 9 HUM. RTS. Q. 287, 287, 289 (1987).

24. *Id.* at 295.

25. *Id.*

26. *Id.* at 296.

27. *See, e.g.,* Noreen Burrows, *International Law and Human Rights: The Case of Women's Rights, in* HUMAN RIGHTS: FROM RHETORIC TO REALITY 80, 89–96 (Tom Campbell et al. eds., 1986). In describing this approach, I rely largely on this article by Noreen Burrows and a lecture by Felice Gaer. *See* Felice Gaer, Address at 1988 Harvard Human Rights Program Symposium on Women's Rights and Human Rights: Possibilities and Contradictions (Apr. 16, 1988).

28. This approach to the public/private distinction is also a significant departure from the integrationist approach, which argues that the claim that human rights does not enter the private sphere is as irrational and politically determined as the cultural relativism claim. *See, e.g.,* Eisler, *supra* note 23, at 293.

29. Burrows, *supra* note 27, at 85.

30. Helen B. Holmes & Susan R. Petersen, *Rights Over One's Own Body: A Woman-Affirming Health Care Policy,* 3 HUM. RTS. Q. 71, 73 (1981).

31. *Id.*

32. *Id.*

33. *Id.*

34. *Id.* at 74.

35. *See* Robin L. West, *The Difference in Women's Hedonic Lives: A Phenomenological Critique of Feminist Legal Theory,* 3 WIS. WOMEN'S L.J. 81, 87 (1987).

36. Spivak, *supra* note 7, at 128.

Chapter Twelve

MODERNISM, NATIONALISM, AND THE RHETORIC OF RECONSTRUCTION

Nathaniel Berman

We do not lack systems, but energy—the energy to conform our morals to our ways of feeling.
—M. Barrès, *The Enemy of the Laws* (1893)[1]

Hollow! It's all hollow! A chasm! It's cracking!
Can you hear? There's something—down there
    —that's following us!
Away! Away!
—A. Berg, *Wozzek* (1923)[2]

A PARADOXICAL DOUBLE desire pervades current writings on cultural politics and law. On the one hand, one finds a longing for cultural renewal through contact with raw authenticity, with formerly excluded or repressed sources of cultural vitality; on the other hand, one finds an ambition to transform elite discourse through sophisticated innovations in literary style and legal technique. In this essay, I suggest that critical light can be shed on this double aspiration by situating it in relation to that period of early twentieth century cultural history known as "Modernism." For reasons that should become clear, our own intellectual situation, marked by a revived obsession with cultural politics and law, should be understood more as a reenactment of Modernism rather than as a break with it. By exploring the attractions and dangers of Modernist desire, an inquiry into the Modernist rupture in modernity will help us evaluate the increasingly widespread, unreflective reprise of Modernist theory and practice.

Specifically, I will discuss the relationship between certain broad characteristics of Modernist cultural renewal and the changes wrought in international law by various legal writers between the World Wars. This juxtaposition of forms of law with other forms of culture should not be viewed as a claim of a direct correlation or "influence," but, rather, as indicating an overlapping series of responses to a common cultural situation. The juxtaposition suggests that transformations in legal thought can be productively viewed as participating in, and, indeed, partly creating, deep shifts in Western cultural history. The most important of such shifts in the first decades of our century, I would argue, was the advent of the central Modernist problematic: the paradoxical relationship between "primitivism" and experimentalism—a problematic that gave rise to a range of responses both among and within various cultural domains.

My interest in cultural Modernism should be viewed as part of a challenge to the dominant approaches to legal history, particularly international legal history. In international law, historical work tends to be undertaken with either a jurisprudential or a pragmatic interest. Those who engage in legal history for the purpose of furthering linear progress in either theory or policy tend to gloss over legal history's fundamental breaks and controversies; they also tend to view legal history in isolation from other cultural developments, an isolation that often precludes insight into the deeper meaning of legal change.

My historical study has concentrated on a disparate group of international legal writers—theorists, practitioners, judges—who worked in the aftermath of World War I to recast international law through focusing on the problem of Central European nationalism. In the period preceding the War, four Empires, Germany, Russia, Austria-Hungary, and

Ottoman Turkey, had been understood to provide the primary conditions of the region's political structure. Indeed, as late as 1918, even the Allied Powers viewed the postwar survival of the Dual Monarchy as a European "necessity."[3] This attitude is quite understandable, particularly given our own pre-1989 blindness: an extraordinary act of imagination is required to conceive of a domain of human life absent those structuring elements hitherto perceived as indispensable for coherent thought and action. Nevertheless, one of the central tasks of the post-World War I world—as of our post-Cold War world—would be to figure out the appropriate relationship between national identity and state sovereignty in the complex ethnic and political conditions of Central Europe.

The legal writers on whom I focus sought to create a new and complex way of thinking about postwar Europe that would take into account the subtle issues raised by the passions of peoples. They saw the "old," prewar international law, with its narrow rigor and need for certainties, as a product of an ossified nineteenth century culture, a culture surpassed by the new era's intellectual and political developments; confronted with the nationalist challenge, the "old" law could only attempt in vain either to ignore or to repress what its outmoded concepts could not comprehend.

This legal watershed thus bore a strong affinity with transformations in other areas of high European culture between the 1890s and the 1930s. Like the new international lawyers, cultural Modernists—be they artists, literary writers, psychoanalysts, or nonconformist political theorists of left and right—sought to reinvigorate their respective domains by transcending what they saw as the surface platitudes of nineteenth century bourgeois culture. For the purpose of transforming the current practice of international legal history (and at the consequent risk of oversimplification), I have isolated several basic characteristics of a certain tendency in this movement which I would call "high Modernism."[4] I would describe high Modernism as marked by the following four basic features: 1) the critique of representation; 2) an openness to so-called "primitive" sources of cultural energy; 3) innovative experimentation with the technical means specific to each cultural medium; and 4) the juxtaposition, in a single work, of elements considered irreconcilable under traditional criteria of coherence.

The basic presupposition for high Modernist cultural renewal was the critique of representation—in other words, the abandonment of conformity to given natural or conventional subject matter as the primary goal of cultural creation.[5] Modernists called for "emancipation from dependence on nature,"[6] seeking to displace the privileged criteria by which many had measured Western cultural works since the Renaissance. Modernists demonstrated that these supposedly "natural" criteria were simply those of one possible signifying system, one possible vocabulary of expression. Modernists sought to unleash the signifying imagination, to create new expressive vocabularies whose validity would no longer be measured by traditional criteria. This de-privileging of the object of representation radically brought into question the foundations of culture and politics as they had been understood by some previous versions of "modernity."

Once freed from the constraints of representation, Modernists engaged in two general types of exploration. First, they sought to renew European culture through recourse to what they viewed as "primitive" sources of cultural energy, such as the art of children, peasants, and non-European peoples. The Modernists' "primitives" included the whole catalogue of those whom the high-cultural European male had repressed and fantasized about for millenia. The Modernists now sought them out—or, rather, sought out their own fantasies about them.[7] Secondly, however, the critique of representation led Modernists in a seemingly opposite direction: the radical development of the sophisticated techniques of European high-culture. Released from the constraints of representation, cultural creators would be able to experiment with their media, creating works marked by an unprecedented diversity.[8] Modernist "experimentalism" thus meant specialization, the multiplication of expressive means accomplished through the internal development of the intrinsic resources of each particular medium; "specialization," wrote one Modernist, is the "modern thing."[9]

Intellectual historians have characterized these two dimensions of Modernism in various ways, depending on the aspects of early Twentieth Century culture studied: the "archaic" and the "futuristic,"[10] the "expressive" and the "constructive,"[11] the "primitivist" and the "abstract,"[12] and so forth.[13] Although these two dimensions—whatever form they took and however characterized—seem quite opposed as cultural directions, they were very closely related in Modernist theory and practice; as one commentator notes, "[t]he alliance of primitivism and abstraction is one of the most copiously documented facts of the [Modernist] period."[14]

The "alliance" between these two new dimensions, these two "extremes,"[15] was explicitly stressed by various Modernists. Bartók, for example, wrote that

> it is a noteworthy fact that artistic perfection can only be achieved by
> one of two extremes: on the one hand by peasant folk in the mass,
> completely devoid of the culture of the town-dweller, on the other by
> creative power of an individual genius. The creative impulse of any-
> one who has the misfortune to be born between these two extremes
> leads only to barren, pointless and misshapen works.[16]

Bartók viewed the contemporary musical versions of these "extremes," peasant music and advanced atonal experimentalism, as "apparently opposite tendenc[ies]."[17] Nonetheless, he envisioned their productive juxtaposition in the same work. In works contrasting the "extremes," "the *opposition of the two tendencies reveals more clearly the individual properties of each*, while the effect of the whole becomes all the more powerful."[18] The "alliance" Modernists sought between the two new dimensions of cultural creativity would thus not be some synthesis or balance, but, rather, a disjunctive juxtaposition. The "alliance" would facilitate each of the "extremes" precisely through their polar disparity.

The Modernist understanding of these two new dimensions marked a rupture with "modernity's" previous understanding of the relationship between high culture and its foundational elements. For many Modernists, the subversive "primitive" they now viewed as the vital source of culture had little in common with the notion of stable "first principles." They rejected what they saw as naive, romantic efforts to open high Western culture to influences from its various "others" without challenging Western culture's underlying conception. The Modernists viewed this effort as based on a sentimental view of those "others," a view which imagined one could depict them using traditional methods of representation. For Modernists, the "primitive" was precisely that which resisted traditional representation due to its primal, multiple, or explosive nature.[19]

Paradoxically, Modernists thought that it would be precisely through experimental exploration of the intrinsic resources of cultural media that the "primitive" could be evoked in its authenticity. Conversely, it was only the introduction of the "primitive" into Western culture that would free that culture to engage in sophisticated formal explorations. The experimental and the "primitive" would thus stand in a relationship of reciprocal evocation and facilitation, a reciprocity resting precisely on the radical discontinuity and mutual exclusion of the two dimensions—the "primitive" would not serve as a stable ground for the experimental, nor would the experimental merely provide rational articulation of that which the "primitive" left mute. For the painter Kandinsky, for example, "[t]he freer the abstract form, the purer and more 'primitive' the [spiritual] vibration."[20]

The fourth characteristic of Modernism—the juxtaposition of elements irreconcilable under traditional criteria of coherence—should be seen in relation to the first three. Longing for contact with an explosive, "primitive" reality, Modernists boldly sought unprecedented means of evoking that which could not be traditionally represented. Moreover, freed from traditional representational constraints, Modernists could develop new syntactical combinations whose logic did not conform to the logic of perception.[21] Modernists, therefore, created complex compositions of heterogeneous elements, whose unifying principles only came into being with each individual work.

The paradoxical relationship of radical discontinuity and reciprocal facilitation between the two dimensions of Modernism took various forms. One familiar example is Picasso's painting *Les Demoiselles d'Avignon* (1907), one of the inaugural works of twentieth century art. The painting depicts five female figures, all subjected in various ways to perceptual distortions breaking with the "classical norm for the human figure."[22] One art historian has described the painting in words that capture significant aspects of the Modernist sensibility: the "most immediate quality of *Les Demoiselles* is a barbaric dissonant power," reflecting Picasso's "fascination with the primitive;" the painting shows the depths and range of this fascination "not only in explicit references to Iberian sculpture in the three nudes at the left and to African Negro [SIC] sculpture in the two figures at the right but in the savagery that dominates the painting."[23] This description reflects the way in which such Modernist creations embodied certain characteristic Western fantasies about the "primitive."

Strangely enough, the historical importance of this openness to the "primitive" lay in the way it facilitated Picasso's formal, "purely pictorial" explorations that led to the development of Cubism. Having abandoned the traditional conventions for representing the human figure, *Les Demoiselles d'Avignon* liberated the artist to engage in "painterly" innovations—particularly the abandonment of linear perspective and the use of a single source of light—impossible under a representational regime. It initiated that typically Cubist fragmentation of the depicted object into geometrical facets, a fragmentation in which volume is depicted through contrasting planes, rather than through an illusionistic representation of objects. The juxtaposed facets of the object were thus perceptually

inconsistent, for such "faceting produced a complex structure of planes
at different levels and going in different directions."[24] The Cubists produced richer "purely pictorial" works precisely by abandoning representational accuracy and coherence.[25]

Les Demoiselles and its aftermath thus inaugurated the Modernist pursuit of painterly goals solely through the intrinsic resources of the flat
surface of the canvas, rather than through an appeal to the world of perception. The painting thus marked a peculiarly Modernist conjuncture:
between the European fantasy of the "primitive" as "savage," even
"monstrous," and the creation of a new, eminently sophisticated form of
high European art.[26] Specifically, the painting illustrates the way in
which the disintegration of the traditional "object" of painting, a disintegration occurring under "primitivist" pressure, posed purely artistic
challenges that led to the formal exploration of the high-cultural potential of the medium.

At this point, I would like to present an initial outline of the parallel I
will draw between cultural Modernism and interwar understandings of
the new international law. I would compare the four basic characteristics
of Modernism listed above—the critique of representation, the openness
to the "primitive," the unprecedented exploration of the specific means of
each medium and the juxtaposition of the heterogeneous—with four key
elements of the new international law: 1) the critique of the sovereign
state as the object which defines international law and to which it must
seek to conform its doctrines and institutions; 2) an openness to the hitherto repressed or denied forces of nationalism; 3) the unprecedented
invention of a wide variety of techniques, techniques understood as
specifically "legal"; and 4) the juxtaposition in international legal discourse, doctrines, and institutions of elements incompatible under traditional legal criteria. In the new international law, heterogeneous elements
—reflecting such competing sources of authority as the state, the nation,
the individual, and the international community—would coexist in international legal compositions unified only by the newly heightened legal
medium, rather than by reference to extra-legal sources of legitimacy.
Such complex and sophisticated works would be understood, paradoxically, as putting legal reason in touch with the deepest desires of popular
nationalist energy. Sovereignty, like the representational elements in
Modernist painting, would not be banished but would be pressed into the
service of the new system. Finally, just as the relationship between the
"primitive" and the experimental was understood and expressed in vari-

ous ways by cultural Modernists, so the new international law would be marked by a wide diversity of forms, each a version of international legal Modernism.

Like all Modernists, many interwar lawyers criticized the taken-for-granted objects hitherto thought to define their domain. This legal version of the critique of representation took the form of a rejection of so-called "international legal positivism"—i.e., the notion that established sovereign states were the sole source of international legal authority and that the relationships between sovereigns constituted that law's sole subject matter. Just as other cultural Modernists abandoned representation of stable objects as the goal of art, so international lawyers rejected conformity to the needs of established sovereigns as international law's touchstone.

Many interwar lawyers saw the recognition of the passionate forces of nationalism—unleashed by the central European empires' collapse—as essential to law's renewal, as providing contact with the vital ground of international life lacking in pre-War international law. They did not, however, understand this recognition as the replacement of an inauthentic ground of international law—states—with a rationalist grounding on such "first principles" as the "nation" or the "people." On the contrary, many interwar lawyers' conception of nationalism was strikingly similar to other Modernists' conception of the "primitive."

Just as other Modernists rejected naive, sentimental views of "primitive" culture, so the legal Modernists rejected the liberal nationalist faith of Wilson and his nineteenth century precursors. For liberal nationalists, the nationalist revolt against positivism, against the centrality of traditional, multinational states, was identical with the struggle for the creation of a rational, democratic and peaceful world order. Many interwar writers could no longer accept this unproblematic link between nationalism and liberal democracy. On the contrary, they saw the nationalist revolt that began during World War I as an outgrowth of irrational, explosive passion. The vital, passionate nationalist forces, though they served to clear the debris of ossified legal structures, had to be channeled and given form by newly developed legal concepts, doctrines, and institutions.[27]

In essays like "Le Principe des nationalités," Professor Robert Redslob of Strasbourg was one of those who articulated a Modernist view of the new international law of nationalism. For Redslob, the clash between the revolutionary aspirations of nationalism and the self-preserving will of established states was nothing less than that between "creative freedom

and legality."[28] Nonetheless, these "nearly irreconcilable adversaries,"[29]   *237*
could enter into a relationship of reciprocal facilitation. Thus, on the one
hand, he called for law to renew itself through defering to nationalist passion, through "model[ing] itself on the real movement of nationalities, on
the pathos of an elemental force which arises in the history of peoples."[30]
On the other hand, however, nationalism, the primal "élan of emancipation, the tumultuous flood of history,"[31] can only achieve its truth by giving way to its opposite, i.e., law. In this second moment, law would
become the "ally" of "the thesis of nationalities." Once "[h]aving made a
pact with [law], [nationalism] would submit to its regulative influence.
Henceforth, [nationalism] would no longer abandon itself to impulse, no
longer throw itself into adventures, but would look to the idea of law for
prior justification [*sa justification préalable*]."[32] For Redslob, it is thus not
a question of "balancing" legal reason and nationalist passion, but of a
particular kind of "alliance" between the two. In a quintessentially
Modernist gesture, he both views nationalism as that "elemental force" at
the source of collective life *and* urges it to submit to law's "regulative
influence"; conversely, he urges law both to "model" itself on this
"tumultuous flood" *and* to displace it as its "*justification préalable.*"

The new international law would thus take as its "founding" principle
an inherently explosive element. Redslob insists on the resistance nationalism offers to traditional scientific inquiry: "One must not delude oneself with the hope that one can cast a fully clarifying light on this crater
filled with flames and smoke."[33] Like other cultural Modernists, Redslob
thus notes the intrinsic resistance to traditional representation of the
"primitive" source of his domain's vitality. Accordingly, the goal is not
positivist science, but a Modernist "art,"[34] a new kind of legal reason.

For Redslob, nationalism provides the opportunity for a heightened
competence of the international community to engage in sensitive and
nuanced legal deliberations, as in "the great postwar settlements."[35] After
reviewing the considerations that guided this "comprehensive reconstruction"[36] of Central Europe, Redslob proposed the formulation of a
"Charter delimiting the contest of primordial [nationalist] claims."[37]
This new "Charter" of the international law of nationalism would not be
limited by ultimate principles like sovereignty or nationality, let alone the
traditional rules of positive law; nor would it simply play the humble role
of interest balancing. Rather, it would establish a new domain for an
autonomous international law, the domain of the "*métajuridique.*"[38] This
new domain, opened up for international law by "primordial" nationalist

238   forces, would consist of the free and flexible exploration of the legal medium, without the encumbrances of traditional conceptions. Paradoxically, the "*métajuridique*," a Modernist international law, would be grounded on a principle no more stable than "a crater filled with flames and smoke."

As imagined by my selected international legal writers, "nationalism" thus played a role strikingly similar to the role of the "primitive" in the Modernist imagination generally. The lawyers' construction of this "primitive" source of energy was marked by an ambivalence congruent with that marking other high Modernists' construction of other forms of the "primitive." It was the interwar lawyers' break with both positivism *and* liberal nationalism that marked their radical break with their predecessors; this double break justifies our viewing their work as a form of Modernism in the historically specific sense, the early twentieth century movement for cultural and political renewal.

The Modernist impossibility of relying either on the historically inherited cultural forms ("states") or on any stable "foundation" of those forms (the "people" or "nation") led to a radically heightened role for the legal Modernist. The Modernist lawyers interpreted the Versailles framework as the inauguration of an era of bold legal experimentation, an era of unprecedented legal autonomy. They saw the relationship between the two dimensions of legal renewal—an openness to "primitive" nationalism and an embrace of experimental creativity—in a variety of ways characterized by the Modernist composite of radical discontinuity and reciprocal facilitation.

I turn, therefore, to two forms of the "new international law" which illustrate competing versions of the legal Modernist composite of "primitivism" and experimentalism. In this section, I will discuss Modernist lawyers' interpretations of the two legal techniques most widely applied by the World War I Peace Treaties in response to the destabilization of Europe by separatist nationalism: first, internationally supervised plebiscites, as a method of granting political self-determination to national groups, and, second, international minority protection, in the form of international guarantees for civil rights and cultural autonomy for those national groups not accorded the right to self-determination.

The central theme in the writings of Sarah Wambaugh, the leading interwar plebiscite scholar, is the alliance between modern social scientific "technique" and the passionate aspirations of national groups.[39] This composite constituted a double departure from an international law which formerly left to sovereign discretion how (and, indeed, *whether*) to take into account the wishes of the people. On the one hand, Wambaugh declared that the plebiscite was unavoidable in an age whose characteristic feature was the demand of peoples for control over their own destiny.[40] From this perspective, international law's departure from deference to sovereigns constituted an openness to nationalist desire. On the other hand, she argued that the implementation of these demands could lead to a stable international legal order only through a "scientifically" administered voting procedure. From this perspective, plebiscites constituted an enrichment of law's sophistication through innovative experimentation with its own unique resources. Above all, "science" demanded that the plebiscite territory be effectively "neutralized";[41] thus, the augmentation of international legal authority, though authorized by nationalist desire, mandates the development of precisely those autonomous legal resources most directly contrary to those of passionately "unneutral" nationalism.[42]

Wambaugh's description of the 1935 plebiscite in the Saar territory, a region coveted by France and Germany, provides an example of her conception of this alliance. According to Wambaugh, the Saar plebiscite marked "the highest point yet attained by the technique of the international plebiscite."[43] The great significance of this perfecting of the "technique" was due to the fact that "[t]he duty of the League to administer a free and fair plebiscite ran counter to one of the most ardent national movements in all history"[44]—*viz.*, the German movement, which had fallen under the sway of the Nazis by the time of the plebiscite. The marshalling of the resources of modern "political science"[45] in the face of this "ardent" nationalism assured the world of the "validity" of the "title of the Reich to the Saar."[46] For Wambaugh, the "technique" of the plebiscite thus ran "counter" to "ardent nationalism"—and yet that nationalism served as the opportunity for the "technique's" perfection. Moreover, this alliance between "technique" and "ardency" served to enrich traditional legal forms such as "title." Title would no longer be based on mere historical accident or brute force, but, rather, would acquire "validity" through the perfection of the "technique." For Wambaugh's version of Modernism, international legal doctrines, such as "title," would thus be enriched through technical experimentation made possible by nationalist disruption.

International minority protection was understood as the mirror image of plebiscitary self-determination. The League of Nations' minority pro-

240   tection system did not involve any alteration of sovereign frontiers. Rather, the new and expanded states of Central Europe were required to provide minority groups with civil rights and a certain cultural autonomy. The minority protection system sought to maintain a separate social sphere in which the cultural life of a national minority could flourish—*without* either being assimilated into the general culture of the state in which the minority resided[47] or being allowed direct representation in the international forum.[48] The system did not, for example, allow the national minorities formal legal standing in the World Court or the League Council. Rather, the League embedded its guarantees of minority rights in a complex arbitral, administrative, and judicial system, designed with the most up-to-date institutional techniques. Minority rights would thus be guaranteed by the organized international legal community pressing the sovereigns into the service of the new international legal order. The system thus constituted a departure from deference to traditional sovereign prerogatives, while abstaining from directly replacing the prerogatives of states with the prerogatives of "nations."

Modernist lawyers understood this system in terms of its double departure from a state-centered conception of international life. The World Court declared that the purpose of the minority protection guarantees was to preserve for the national minority the "very essence of its life as a minority" ("l'essence même de sa vie en tant que minorité").[49] Yet, the effect of the recognition of this "essence" was to authorize a heightening of *international* competence, the limitation of sovereign prerogatives by unprecedented international institutions. The nationalist "primitive" was viewed as unrepresentable, incapable of speaking directly in the new legal fora. Paradoxically, the two aspirations of this system were viewed as inextricably related: the specific structure of the new international machinery was required in order to preserve the unrepresentable "essence" of minority cultures.

The contrast between these two solutions to the problem of nationalism should be understood as two versions of the paradoxical Modernist "alliance." For Wambaugh, international law, in response to the "ardent" pressures of nationalist desire, was authorized to suspend the power of state sovereignty to obstruct experimental legal innovation. Once freed from this obstacle, the plebiscitary "technique" was able to perfect its operations, chief among which was the "neutralization" of the plebiscite area. Thus, while subversive nationalist desire served as an authorizing stimulus to legal innovation, that innovation proceeded, indeed was only meaningful if it could proceed, without reference to that "primitive." Conversely, international minority protection installed a complex institutional machinery whose novel procedures attenuated sovereign prerogative in the name of the facilitation of particularistic cultural authenticity. Yet, the exclusion of the national groups from the international forum was viewed as indispensable to the ultimate preservation of their unrepresentable "essence." These two Modernist legal forms thus give inverted accounts of the paradoxical "alliance" between "primitivism" and experimentalism. For one account, "primitive" nationalism serves to authorize the elaboration of its opposite, autonomous legal innovation; for the other account, autonomous legal innovation is designed to facilitate that which it excludes, the nationalist "essence."

These examples suggest some appealing as well as troubling qualities of the Modernist approach. Legal Modernism, in its various forms, continues to supply the model to which most of us look for renewal of our own ossified legal and political forms. We continue to believe in the expansion of the legal framework beyond the sovereign state to novel products of the legal imagination, an expansion we believe will allow formerly repressed national identities to flourish authentically. We continue to view excluded national movements as potential sources of violence and irrationality, while simultaneously supporting their struggles to achieve the paradoxical goal of "independence in Europe." In these and other ways, we continue to nourish the double Modernist program for legal and political renewal.

Nevertheless, the experience of historical Modernism, in both its legal and cultural forms, should make the difficulties of this schema all too clear. Deprived either of a traditional or a rationalist ground for her reason, the Modernist lawyer was subject to certain characteristic difficulties. The two examples of international legal Modernism that I have discussed illustrate two of these problems: first, an uncritical faith in procedural technique on the part of the specialized legal adviser and, second, a set of quandaries concerning the possibility and desirability of the separation of the political and cultural spheres.

The example of the plebiscite in the Saar graphically illustrates the way in which faith in techniques of proceduralization can disarm any critical perspective on the political substance established through those techniques. Faith in the "technique" of the plebiscite, as exemplified by the liberal Wambaugh, was compatible with sanctioning, even celebrating, the result of an election procedurally valid—yet granting the Nazis an important symbolic victory in the early stages of their attack on civilization. In the face of an imagined divide between cultural passion and legal reason, the "purification" of that reason through an emphasis on technical procedures can blind even well-meaning observers to the political consequences.

Conversely, the quandaries involved in all liberal attempts to establish "separate spheres" resurfaced in specifically Modernist form in the minority protection system. The system sought to safely segregate nationalist passion in a legally defined cultural sphere. Such attempts confront the legal reasoner with inherently indeterminate issues of interpretation. No satisfactory measure exists to determine the boundary between "political" autonomy—which was to be denied to national groups —and "cultural" autonomy—in which their aspirations were to be realized. The World Court faced this problem of interpretation repeatedly in its attempts to determine the scope of the Minority Protection Treaties in particular cases.[50]

This problem of indeterminacy is neither a logical difficulty nor simply an ultimate consequence of critical Enlightenment rationality. Rather, it reflects a specific cultural situation: that of the Modernist whose role is both heightened and yet problematized by the critique of representation. The judge is expected to utilize her augmented authority to resolve the characteristic Modernist ambivalence: high culture's relationship to "primitive" forces viewed as both crucial and dangerous. It should come as no surprise that a Court established to regulate such a deep cultural ambivalence would continually come up against the problem of indeterminacy. This problem has given rise in our own time to a series of responses both philosophical and pragmatic. Historical reflection on the formation of our attitudes towards nationalism, however, suggests that we may expect an endless proliferation of such responses unless we reflect critically on this important cultural source of the problem of indeterminacy: once the "founding" principle came to be viewed as inherently resistant to direct representation, as inherently discontinuous with high culture, the sophisticated legal decisionmaker could no longer satisfy traditional criteria of certainty.

The Modernist displacement of traditional cultural forms in the name of a heterogeneous "primitive" immediately raised the question of the coordination of the resulting cultural fragments. For some, the experience of "primitivist" fragmentation led to delight in the free, anarchic play of discontinuous signs; for others, it led to an emphasis on a heightened role

of coordination for the Modernist creator. Cubism has often been seen as
the matrix of both possibilities:[51] Cubist works were marked by an emphasis on highly structured composition precisely in Cubism's most radical
period, the period in which all certainties about perspective, the relationship of figure to ground, etc., were most put into question. Thus, two of
the most prominent successor movements to Cubism were those of the
anarchic Dadaists, on the one hand, and of the earnest Purists, on the
other hand. The latter tendency reached its ultimate expression in the
stress on comprehensive "planning" in Modernist rhetoric—such as the
apotheoses of the "Plan" by the architect Le Corbusier,[52] and the transformation of *"socialisme"* into *"planisme"* by that very Modernist political
theorist and activist, Henri De Man.[53] A brief discussion of the role of the
"Plan" will serve to round out my discussion of Modernism and its
impact on the self-understanding of high-cultural experimenters in various domains.

In international law the impulse toward comprehensive planning culminated in the design, implementation and interpretation of the regimes
for the three internationalized regions of the interwar period: the Saar, a
region claimed by France and Germany, and Danzig and Upper Silesia,
regions claimed by Poland and Germany. Such comprehensive legal constructions combined heterogeneous elements such as traditional forms of
state sovereignty and novel (and divergent) techniques such as plebiscitary self-determination and international minority protection. These
regimes embodied all four of the characteristics of legal Modernism: an
attenuation of the centrality of states as the structuring units of international order, an openness to nationalist desire, an embrace of legal innovation, a juxtaposition of disparate international legal elements to evoke
nationalist "essence." Legal compositions constructed out of such heterogeneous elements constituted a legal equivalent of the artistic technique of *montage*—the "sharp juxtaposition" of "discrete elements"
which "relate in multi-directional ways" to evoke a unified meaning.[54]

The League regime for Upper Silesia was one of the most complex of
these regimes, constructed through the deployment of all of the new
international legal techniques. Georges Kaeckenbeeck, who played a key
role in the workings of that "composite experiment,"[55] repeatedly insisted that the regime remained a specifically *legal* creation—in keeping
with the Modernist stress on the internal development of cultural media.
Kaeckenbeeck emphasized the regime's specifically legal doctrinal and
institutional innovations. In particular, Kaeckenbeeck focused on the

local, yet international, legal institutions set up to administer the regime, the "Arbitral Tribunal" and the "Mixed Commission." These local institutions would play the role of autonomous legal instances coordinating the competing dimensions of international life: the central legal instance of the World Court, the political maneuverings of sovereign states in the League, and the nationalist passions of the populace.

The legal authority that was at once local *and* international was thus the epitome of international legal Modernism. The innovative creation of an autonomous legal instance was made possible by "nationalist passion" and directed toward the creation of a complex, unprecedentedly "detailed," work of international law. Such an instance remained in touch both with its "primitivist" and its experimentalist dimensions by operating on the autonomous, "solid basis of legal principle." In comparison with a local procedure of an autonomous international legal instance, even the World Court could appear as too rooted in traditional notions of the dignity of sovereignty. The local, international institutions boldly asserted creative license to explore the range of specifically legal possibilities, freed from the constraints of an extra-legal positivist or nationalist grounding. International legal Modernism reaches its culmination with this desire for the doctrinal and institutional freedom to coordinate the heterogeneous dimensions of international life.

The dangers of this ultimate Modernist aspiration may be highlighted by comparison with the apotheosis of the "Plan" in other domains. In their Twenties journal *L'Esprit Nouveau,* for example, Le Corbusier and Ozenfant made quite explicit the connection between their solution to the Modernist subversion of pre-established unities and the turn to politically elitist doctrines of coordination.[56] A decade later, under the influence of Sorelian syndicalism,[57] Le Corbusier published *La Ville Radieuse,* a work "Dedicated to AUTHORITY"; the work's opening epigraph illuminated the desire for both this dedication and its Modernist concept of comprehensive planning:

> Plans are not politics.
> Plans are the rational and poetic monument set up in the midst of contingencies.
> Contingencies are the environment: places, peoples, cultures, topgraphies, climates.[58]

Indeed, the desire for a "nonpolitical" Plan to coordinate the heterogeneous contingencies of modern life reflected Le Corbusier's ongoing

advocacy of an "Authority outside the 'established disorder' to assert the   *245*
common good."[59] Unfortunately, as in the case of Henri De Man, Le
Corbusier's Modernist apotheosis of the elite Plan brought him beyond
the authoritarian temptation to an active pursuit of collaboration with
fascism. Following Robert Fishman, I would offer the following hypoth-
esis: when Le Corbusier offered his services to the Vichy government, it
was because he saw in the new regime the specific kind of authority
required to implement his unprecedentedly heterogeneous Plans.[60] The
step from complex Modernist composition to advocacy of authoritarian
social planning and active collaboration was, of course, not inevitable—
nor was it simply coincidental.[61]

The comprehensive compositions of interwar legal Modernism continue to enthrall the international legal imagination: in the post-World
War II period, versions of the Upper Silesia regime have been proposed
for intractable nationalist conflicts from Palestine to Cambodia.[62] We
international lawyers continue to believe in the ability of such comprehensive Plans to deliver on the dual Modernist promise of liberation *and*
order. We must not forget, however, that the ever-present temptation of
this sort of Modernist creativity is that of authoritarianism, a temptation
to which the first administrators of the League of Nations regime for the
Saar succumbed on more than one occasion.[63]

The Modernist break ushers in an ambivalent cultural situation of
emancipatory possibilities and terrifying dangers. The liberal triumphs
of Modernist sensibility, like the music of Bartók, embody nuanced,
ironic juxtapositions of the primal and the sophisticated—the former
demystified, the latter energized. Reactionary Modernists,[64] on the other
hand, lent themselves to the prospect of a demonic nationalist mobiliza-
tion conducted through the most advanced cultural techniques. For their
part, the fascists generally rejected Modernism and Modernists—refusing, with characteristic brutality, much of the help offered by reactionary
Modernists. Nonetheless, the astonishing blindness of some of the "best
minds" of that generation has bequeathed a maddening and unavoidable
challenge to a variety of intellectual disciplines. I would suggest that, for
many of the illustrious interwar intellectuals who succumbed to it, what
Sternhell has ironically called *"le charme secret du fascisme"*[65] stemmed
from a hope that fascism would be capable of providing social implementation of the double Modernist relationship between "primitive,"
authentic energy and sophisticated forms of high culture.

If, as I would claim, legal Modernism continues to shape all of our work, we lawyers, too, must continually reflect upon some of the sources of that blindness—even if it is still rather premature to reach any but the most tentative and partial suggestions on this score. In its legal form, the authoritarian temptation arises from the augmentation of the role of the lawyer that follows the specifically Modernist critique of representation. This temptation is far from diminished by the presence of populist elements, such as the plebiscite, in the toolkit of legal techniques; on the contrary, it arises precisely from the paradoxical Modernist composite of deference to the vital, "primitive" energy of the "people," and insistence on the heightened creativity, authority, and novelty of the high-cultural instance. It is this composite that enabled certain cultural Modernists to articulate our most cherished hopes for liberation and others to ignore the horrific quality of some of our century's distinctive ideologies.

In this essay, I have presented Modernist articulations of three familiar lawyerly roles: specialized adviser, sophisticated judge, comprehensive constitutional designer. In discussing these roles today, we often neglect the cultural assumptions they embody. In the 1990s, we are faced with yet another collapse of the imperial structure of Central Europe, the resurgence of nationalist passion, and a newly heightened confidence among international statesmen in the nobility and efficacy of complex international plans. Despite all our declarations to the contrary, our cultural assumptions remain fundamentally Modernist. Current events make explicating those assumptions, and thereby rendering them accessible to critique, an urgent task. Our post-Modernity is characterized not by our transcendence of Modernism but by our ambivalent, though ineluctable, attachment to it. We can only avoid being deafened by the universal clamor for reconstruction by a vigilant historical critique of its rhetoric.

Notes

1. MAURICE BARRÈS, L'ENNEMI DES LOIS 4 (1910, 1st ed. 1893) (all translations mine unless otherwise noted.) Maurice Barrès's (1862–1923) theoretical and political synthesis of nationalism and socialism foreshadowed much twentieth century ideological activity. *See* ZEEV STERNHELL, MAURICE BARRÈS ET LE NATIONALISME FRANÇAIS (1972).

2. ALBAN BERG, WOZZEK: OPERA IN THREE ACTS AFTER THE DRAMA "WOYZEK" BY GEORG BÜCHNER (London Records,1981; translation modified; 1st ed. 1923). Alban Berg was a composer of the "Second Viennese School" led by Arnold Schoenberg.

3. ALFRED COBBAN, NATION STATES AND NATIONAL SELF-DETERMINATION 53–54 (1969).

4. Following the work of such writers as Peter Burger and Andreas Huyssen, I would distinguish high Modernism from the "avant-garde." *See* PETER BURGER, THEORY OF THE

AVANT GARDE (Michael Shaw trans., 1984); ANDREAS HUYSSEN, AFTER THE GREAT DIVIDE: MODERNISM, MASS CULTURE, POSTMODERNISM (1986).

5. A critique of the centrality of "imitation," "subject matter," the "anecdotal," "representation," etc., abounds in the writings of artists and aestheticians in the first three decades of our century. The painter Léger declared flatly: "I transcribe this question in all its simplicity: 'What does this represent?' ... [I] will try hard, in a very brief essay, to demonstrate this question's total inanity." Fernand Léger, *Les Origines de la peinture et sa valeur représentative* (1913) *in* FONCTIONS DE LA PEINTURE 11 (1965).

6. WASILY KANDINSKY, CONCERNING THE SPIRITUAL IN ART (Francis Golffing et al. trans., 1947) (1912).

7. *See, e.g.,* ROBERT GOLDWATER, PRIMITIVISM IN MODERN ART 250–71 (2d ed. 1986) (analyzing the differences between Modernists' use of "primitive" art and such art taken "in itself").

8. For Kandinsky, for example,

> [l]egitimate and illegitimate combinations of colors, the shock of contrasting colors, the silencing of one color by another, the sounding of one color by another, the checking of fluid color spots by contours of design, the overflowing of these contours, the mingling and sharp separation of surfaces, all these open *great vistas of purely pictorial possibility.*

KANDINSKY, *supra* note 6, at 66 (emphasis added).

9. Léger, *supra* note 5, at 19.

10. CARL SCHORSKE, FIN-DE-SIÈCLE VIENNA: CULTURE AND POLITICS 167 (1981).

11. THEODOR W. ADORNO, AESTHETIC THEORY 363 (C. Lenhardt trans., 1984).

12. *See, e.g.,* J.C. Middleton, *The Rise of Primitivism and its Relevance to the Poetry of Expressionism and Dada, in* THE DISCONTINUOUS TRADITION: STUDIES IN GERMAN LITERATURE IN HONOUR OF ERNEST LUDWIG STAHL 182 (Peter F. Ganz ed., 1971). For Middleton, the Modernists' "primitive" sources included "prelogical or savage art," "naive European art," "alogism in poetry," "infantilism," "resuscitation of folk forms," "exoticism," and "atavism." *Id.* at 184–85.

13. *Cf.* FREDERIC JAMESON, FABLES OF AGGRESSION 14 (1979): "the various modernisms all seek to overcome ... reification ... by the explorations of a new Utopian and libidinal experience of the various sealed realms or psychic compartments to which they are condemned, but which they also reinvent."

14. Middleton, *supra* note 12, at 194.

15. *See* Federico García Lorca, *Teatro para el pueblo* (1934), *quoted in* A. Sinclair, *Elitism and the Cult of the Popular in Spain, in* VISIONS AND BLUEPRINTS: AVANT-GARDE CULTURE AND RADICAL POLITICS IN EARLY TWENTIETH CENTURY EUROPE 221, 230 (Edward Williams & Peter Collier eds., 1988):

> There is one audience we have found not to be fond of us: the middle one, the bourgeoisie, frivolous and given to materialism. Our audience, those who really grasp what the art of the theater is all about, is found at the two extremes: the cultured classes, university educated, or formed by their own artistic or intellectual cultural life, or the people, of the poorest and roughest, uncontaminated, virgin, a fertile ground for all the tremors of grief and the turns and reversals of grace.

Similarly, the Russian Futurists V. Khlebnikov and A. Kruchenykh saw both kinds of departure from traditional verse as crucial for literary renewal. *See* MARJORIE PERLOFF, THE FUTURIST MOMENT: AVANT-GARDE, AVANT GUERRE AND THE LANGUAGE OF RUPTURE 124 (1986).

16. BELA BARTÓK, *The Relation of Folk Music to the Development of the Art Music of our Time* (1921), *in* ESSAYS 320, 322 (Benjamin Suchoff ed., 1976)

17. *Id.* at 323.

18. *Id.* at 324 (emphasis added). *Cf.* WALTER STUCKENSCHMIDT, TWENTIETH CENTURY MUSIC (1969).

19. *See generally* GOLDWATER, *supra* note 7.

20. KANDINSKY, *supra* note 6, at 50.

21. *See, e.g.*, Léger, *supra* note 5; Maurice Raynal, *Conception and Vision* (1912) *reprinted in* EDWARD F. FRY, CUBISM 94 (1966).

22. FRY, *supra* note 21, at 13.

23. ROBERT ROSENBLUM, CUBISM AND TWENTIETH CENTURY ART 12 (1966). It is, of course, highly significant that this inaugural moment of Modernist art occurs through the deformation of the *female* body. *See, e.g.*, JULIA KRISTEVA, LA RÉVOLUTION DU LANGUAGE POÉTIQUE (1974); ALICE JARDINE, GYNESIS: CONFIGURATIONS OF WOMAN AND MODERNITY (1985).

24. DOUGLAS COOPER, THE CUBIST EPOCH 45 (1971).

25. *See* Raynal, *supra* note 21, at 94.

26. "There was also this large painting ... which has since been called 'Les Demoiselles d'Avignon' and which constitutes the point of departure for Cubism.... The painting ... appeared to everyone as something insane or monstrous.... [The right half] is really the point of departure of a new art." DAVID-HENRY KAHNWEILER, MES GALÉRIES ET MES PEINTRES: ENTRETIENS AVEC FRANCIS CRÉMIEUX 55–56 (1961).

27. I would register one important caveat: just as romantic, pre-Modernist attitudes to the "primitive" persisted in art and other cultural domains in the early twentieth century (and, indeed, to our own day), so liberal nationalism persisted in much interwar legal writing. The international legal Modernism I discuss here must be seen as an ideal type. Wilsonian, liberal nationalist commentaries on the Versailles system continued to influence debate even as other legal writings elaborated a new, Modernist conception. Indeed, at times one may discern liberal nationalist and Modernist conceptions in the writings of a single author.

28. ROBERT REDSLOB, LE PRINCIPE DES NATIONALITÉS 93 (1930).

29. *Id.* at 94.

30. *Id.* at 13 (emphasis added).

31. *Id.* at 34–35.

32. *Id.* at 35 (emphasis added).

33. *Id.* at 38.

34. *Id.*

35. *Id.* at 131.

36. *Id.* at 129.

37. *Id.* at 119.

38. *Id.* at 122.

39. *See, e.g.*, Sarah Wambaugh, *La Pratique des plébiscites internationaux*, 18 RECUEIL DES COURS 153, 178 (1927-III) (discussing the alliance between the "scientific attainment of stability" and "stifled nationalist aspirations").

40. *Id.* at 153.

41. "A plebiscite in a country not effectively neutralized is a crime against political science and against the population." *Id.* at 252.

42. In one passage, Wambaugh's insistence on the importance of "neutrals" seemed to extend to the realm of scholarship. She concluded her 1939 preface to her study of the Saar plebiscite with the following: "For the benefit of readers in Germany it should perhaps be noted that the Christian name of the author [Sarah] does not denote Hebraic descent but one from a long line of Calvinists." SARAH WAMBAUGH, THE SAAR PLEBISCITE vii (1940). One would like to assume, of course, that this passage was written in a tone of sarcasm.

43. *Id.* at vi.

44. *Id.*

45. *Id.* at v.

46. *Id.* at vi.

47. *See, e.g.*, C. A. MACARTNEY, NATIONAL STATES AND NATIONAL MINORITIES 277 (1934) (discussing the debates over the "Mello-Franco Thesis," which repudiated the "assimilationist" interpretation of Minorities Treaties).

48. *See The Report of the Committee Instituted by the Council Resolution of March 7, 1929*, LEAGUE OF NATIONS OFFICIAL JOURNAL, SPECIAL SUPPLEMENT NO. 73, 43, 60–61 (1929).

49. Minority Schools in Albania Case, 1935 P.C.I.J. (ser. A/B) No. 64, at 17.

50. The debate between the majority and dissent in the *Minorities School in Albania Case, supra* note 49, is one of the best examples of this quandary.

51. See generally, KENNETH E. SILVER, ESPRIT DE CORPS: THE ART OF THE PARISIAN AVANT-GARDE AND THE FIRST WORLD WAR, 1914–1925 (1989); CHRISTOPHER GREEN, CUBISM AND ITS ENEMIES (1987), for two related, though quite different, views of this matter.

52. *See, e.g.*, LE CORBUSIER, TOWARDS A NEW ARCHITECTURE 45 (Frederick Etchells trans., 1986) (1927). The combination of elements from heterogeneous ideas of social organization—utopian, communist, capitalist, pragmatist—can be seen in the details of Le Corbusier's various planning schemes. *See, e.g.*, CHARLIE JENKS, MODERN MOVEMENTS IN ARCHITECTURE 35 (1973).

    Le Corbusier's relationship to the "primitivism/experimentalism" schema is quite complex. On the one hand, in at least one passage, he articulated this schema in terms similar to those I have been highlighting throughout this essay. In a chapter entitled "Mechanical Spirit and U.S.A. Negroes," Le Corbusier proclaimed that African-American music was the "music of the soul joined to the rhythm of the mechanical." LE CORBUSIER, QUAND LES CATHÉDRALES ÉTAIENT BLANCHES 180 (1937). On the other hand, however, Le Corbusier's theoretical writings generally sought to replace "primitivist" disruption with the search for rational, universal forms. Le Corbusier and his Purist comrade Ozenfant praised the Cubist assault on traditional and natural forms, but rejected Cubist "artitrariness." *See* AMEDEE OZENFANT & CHARLES-EDOUARD JEANNERET [LE CORBUSIER], APRÈS LE CUBISME 14 (1918). C.-E. Jeanneret [Le Corbusier] and A. Ozenfant, *Purism* (1920), *in* MODERN ARTISTS ON ART 58, 65 (Robert L. Herbert ed., 1964). By contrast, Purists would "seek out the invariable constituents of their chosen themes, which could [form] a universal, transmittable language." *Id.* The Purists believed that the "highest delectation of the human mind is the perception of order, and the greatest human satisfaction is the feeling of collaboration in this order." *Id.* at 73. This post-Cubist context helps explain Le Corbusier's glorification of planning. It also explains Le Corbusier's replacement of other Modernists' "primitives" with the "primitives" of the modern world, viz., engineers. *See* LE CORBUSIER, TOWARDS A NEW ARCHITECTURE, *supra* at 14. *See also* REYNER BANHAM, THEORY AND DESIGN IN THE FIRST MACHINE AGE 122–23, 229 (2d ed. 1967).

53. De Man was a leading figure in the Belgian socialist party between the wars. On De Man and his influence in Belgium and France, see ZEEV STERNHELL, NI DROITE, NI GAUCHE: L'IDÉOLOGIE FASCISTE EN FRANCE 156–254 (2d ed. 1987).

250   54. Michael Bell, *Introduction: Modern Movements in Literature, in* THE CONTEXT OF
ENGLISH LITERATURE: 1900–1930 1, 14 (Michael Bell ed., 1980).

55. GEORGES KAECKENBEECK, THE INTERNATIONAL EXPERIMENT OF UPPER SILESIA 25 (1942).
Kaeckenbeeck was the president of one of the international organs that supervised the
Upper Silesia regime, the "Arbitral Tribunal."

56. *See, e.g.,* Le Corbusier & Amedee Ozenfant, *Ce que nous avons fait, ce que nous ferons,* 11
ESPRIT NOUVEAU 1211, 1214 (1921). ("Our desire, then, is for this review to provoke the
indispensable connection of elites. Addressing itself to leaders [*aux conducteurs*], *Esprit
Nouveau* hopes to give them an ever greater understanding of the 'cutting-edge ideas'
[*'idées forces'*].").

57. *See* Robert Fishman, *From the Radiant City to Vichy: Le Corbusier's Plans and Politics,
1928–1942, in* THE OPEN HAND: ESSAYS ON LE CORBUSIER 244 (Russell Walden ed.,
1977). On the relationship between Sorelian syndicalism and fascism, see STERNHELL,
supra note 53, *passim.*

58. LE CORBUSIER, THE RADIANT CITY, title page (Pamela Knight et al. trans., 1967) (1933).

59. Fishman, *supra* note 57 at 251.

60. *Id., passim.*

61. The writings of Henri De Man during the German occupation are one striking illustration of the relationship between the double Modernist critique of prevailing political
forms and the authoritarian temptation. In July 1940, De Man argued that the war had
brought the collapse of an ossified system of capitalist nation-states:

> The war has brought the debacle of the parliamentary regime and of capi-
> talist plutocracy in the so-called democracies. For the working classes and
> for socialism, this collapse of a decrepit world, far from being a disaster, is
> a deliverance. . . . Peace was not able to emerge from the free accord of sov-
> ereign states and rival imperialisms; it will be able to emerge from a
> Europe unified by the force of arms where economic frontiers will have
> been levelled.

Henri De Man, *Manifeste aux membres du parti ouvrier belge, in* LE DOSSIER LEOPOLD
III : ET AUTRES DOCUMENTS SUR LA PÉRIODE DE LA SECONDE GUERRE MONDIALE 183 (Michel
Brélaz ed., 1990). Approximately one year later, he argued that Belgium—whose unity
as a "state" was rendered problematic by the intrinsically multiple nature of the underlying "nation"—both depended for its survival on this new, "unified Europe" and
would facilitate its transcendence of old forms:

> [T]he very existence of Belgium depends entirely on the realization of cer-
> tain conditions on a European scale. . . . [I] see a magnificent task reserved
> to Belgium in a Europe economically unified and ordered for the sake of a
> durable peace, precisely because Belgium constitutes an exception to the
> rule of identity between State, people, and language.

Id. at 212, 216.

62. The first of these postwar Plans, that for Palestine, was an imitative tribute to the
Upper Silesia regime. It succeeded in preventing war for an even shorter period than its
precursor. *See Plan for Partition with Economic Union,* G. A. Res. 181, U.N. GAOR, 2d
Sess. (1947).

63. *See, e.g.,* MICHEL P. FLORINSKY, THE SAAR STRUGGLE 39–44 (1934).

64. I borrow the phrase from JEFFREY HERF, REACTIONARY MODERNISM: TECHNOLOGY,
CULTURE, AND POLITICS IN WEIMAR AND THE THIRD REICH (1984).

65. ZEEV STERNHELL, LA NAISSANCE DE L'IDÉOLOGIE FASCISTE 313 (1989).

◃━◈━◦━◈━▹

CHAPTER THIRTEEN

THE PROPERTIES OF CULTURE AND THE POLITICS OF POSSESSING IDENTITY

NATIVE CLAIMS IN THE CULTURAL APPROPRIATION CONTROVERSY

Rosemary J. Coombe

CANADIANS WITNESSED a remarkable proliferation of controversy on the pages of the *Globe and Mail* in the spring of 1992. This controversy centered around the issue of "cultural appropriation" or "appropriation of voice" in fictional and nonfictional writing. Between March 21, 1992 and April 14, 1992 articles, editorials, and letters to the editor considered the propriety of depicting a culture other than one's own, telling "someone else's story" and whether it was possible to "steal the culture of another." The debate was remarkable because of its emotional intensity, the absurdity of the analogies drawn in support of the respective arguments and the inability of the protagonists to recognize each other's terms of reference. Especially striking were the rhetorical tropes of possessive individualism adopted by all participants in the discussion.

I will use the controversy over cultural appropriation as a point of entry into a wider set of concerns. First, I will examine the philosophical premises about authorship, culture, and property that underly this controversy and define the legal arena in which it is likely to be evaluated. The West has created categories of property—intellectual property, cultural property, and real property—that divide peoples and things according to the same colonizing discourses of possessive individualism that historically disentitled and disenfranchised Native peoples in North America. Exploring the internal logics of intellectual property and cultural property laws, I will question the exhausted concepts of culture and identity upon which they are based, using developments in contemporary cultural anthropology, legal pragmatism, and cultural criticism to put these concepts at issue.

Whose Voice Is It Anyway?

The recent *Globe and Mail* debate began with an innocuous article calling attention to the Canada Council's (the Council) concern with the issue of cultural appropriation.[1] The term was defined to mean "the depiction of minorities or cultures other than one's own, either in fiction or nonfiction."[2] Following a report from its Advisory Committee for Racial Equality in the Arts, the Council deemed cultural appropriation "a serious issue,"[3] and acknowledged that "collaboration with minority groups"[4] was an advisable strategy to avoid perpetuating social stereotypes. Despite the fact that the Council had done nothing to change its existing policies, much less formulate guidelines, rules, or impose any restrictions on funding, the controversy evoked was swift and furious and it quickly polarized upon familiar liberal terrain. I will suggest that these poles—which I will designate as Romantic individualism and Orientalism—operate as dangerous supplements[5] that define an imperialist conceptual terrain that structures our laws of property and may well structure all contemporary political claims for cultural autonomy and public recognition.

In a series of letters to the editor, the tyranny of the state over the individual was evoked, and the transcendent genius of the Romantic author and his unfettered imagination was affirmed. Writers wasted no time evoking the totalitarian state, the memory of the Holocaust, and the Gulag. As Timothy Findley forcefully interjected:

> Put it this way: I imagine—therefore I am. The rest—believe me—is silence. What has happened here? Does no one understand? In 1933

they burned 10,000 booked at the gate of a German university
because these books were written in unacceptable voices. German
Jews, amongst others, had dared to speak for Germany in other than
Aryan voices. Stop. Now. Before we do this again.[6]

Joy Anne Jacoby evoked Russian anti-Semitism to urge the Council "to
rethink the implications of imposing any policy of 'voice appropriation'
lest they find themselves imitating the Russian approach to cultural censorship."[7] Erna Paris titled her intervention in the debate "A Letter to
the Thought Police."[8]

Other critics proclaimed the absolute freedom of the author's imagination. Neil Bissoondath affirmed the autonomy of his ego in a quotation
resplendent with the "I" of Romantic individualism:

> I reject the idea of cultural appropriation completely . . . I reject any-
> thing that limits the imagination. No one has the right to tell me who
> I should or should not write about, and telling me what or how I do
> that amounts to censorship . . . I am a man of East-Indian descent
> and I have written from the viewpoint of women and black men, and
> I will continue to do so no matter who gets upset.[9]

Richard Outram declared that for the past thirty-five years he had been
appropriating the "voices of men, women, dogs, cats, rats, bats, angels,
mermaids, elephants . . . [and] salamanders,"[10] and that he had no intention of consulting with them or seeking their permission:

> In common with every writer worthy of his or her vocation, I refuse
> absolutely to entertain any argument demanding that I do so, or that
> I am to be in any way restricted in my choice of subject matter. I will
> not, in short, submit to such censorship . . .[11]

Russell Smith confidently asserted that "appropriation of voice is what
fiction is,"[12] while Bill Driedger lamented that "if cultural appropriation
had never been permitted, Puccini could never have written La Bohème,
Verdi's Aïda would never have been performed, we would never have
thrilled to Laurence Olivier in Hamlet and we would have been denied
the music of Anna and the King of Siam."[13]

In these constructions of authorship, the writer is represented in
Romantic terms as an autonomous individual who creates fictions with an
imagination free of all constraint. For such an author, everything in the
world must be made available and accessible as an "idea" that can be

transformed into his "expression" which thus becomes his "work." Through his labor, he makes these "ideas" his own; his possession of the "work" is justified by his expressive activity. As long as the author does not copy another's expression, he is free to find his themes, plots, ideas, and characters anywhere he pleases, and to make these his own. (This is also the model of authorship that dominates Anglo-American laws of copyright.) Any attempts to restrict his ability to do so are viewed as censorship and as an unjustifiable restriction on freedom of expression. The dialectic of possessive individualism and liberal democracy is thereby affirmed.

But if the fictitious being of the Romantic author colored one side of the debate, the essentializing voice of Orientalism dominated the other.[14] The article that began the debate was titled "Whose Voice is It Anyway?"[15] The question presupposed that a "voice" was both unified and singular and could be possessed by an individual or a collective imagined as having similar abilities to possess its own expressions. This debate was connected to earlier public discussions in which Native writers insisted that white writers refrain from telling stories involving Indians so as to enable Native peoples to tell "their own stories."[16] Questions of "Who's stealing whose stories and who's speaking with whose voice"[17] had been posed by Native cultural activists as "cases of cultural theft, the theft of voice."[18] Canadians were told that "stories show how a people, a culture, thinks,"[19] and such stories could not be told by others, without endangering the authenticity and authority of cultural works. The Canadian publishing and broadcasting industries had long been accused of stealing the stories of Native peoples and thus destroying their essential meanings in authentic traditions. Native artists asked if "Canadians had run out of stories of their own"[20] and claimed that the telling of Native stories was theft, "as surely as the missionaries stole our religion, the politicians stole our land, and the residential schools stole our language."[21]

Most of those who supported the Canada Council and its Advisory Committee for Racial Equality rested their arguments on a set of assumptions that, I will suggest, are equally problematic, equally Eurocentric, and employ the same tropes of possessive individualism as those of their opponents. Proponents of the Canada Council's suggestion defended their position on the grounds of the integrity of cultural identity. Speaking on behalf of the Canada Council, director Joyce Zemans claimed that cultural appropriation was a serious issue because "we have a need for authenticity. In our society today, there is a recognition that quality has to do with that authenticity of voice."[22] Susan Crean, chair of the Writers Union of Canada, analogized the issue to a legal claim of copyright, in which any unlicensed use of authorial property is theft.[23]

It seems to be assumed in these arguments that Canada is either a country with its own culture or one in which there are multiple discrete cultures, but that one always has a singular culture of one's own, that has a history of its own, and that one possesses an authentic identity that speaks in a univocal voice fully constituted by one's own cultural tradition. As I will argue in more detail, these are extremely contentious propositions that themselves embody contingent concepts integral to Western histories of colonialism and imperialism. Moreover, I will suggest that the concepts of culture, authenticity, and identity that define these arguments are constructed around the same philosophy of possessive individualism that define our legal categories of property.

The challenges that postcolonial struggles[24] pose for Canadian society cannot be met by our traditional reliance upon categories of thought inherited from a colonial era. The conceptual tools of modernity are ill-equipped to deal with the conditions of postmodernity in which we all now live. To make this argument, I will delineate the conceptual logic that developed in the nineteenth century colonial context to categorize art, culture, and authorial identity. This European art/culture system continues to dominate discourses about art, culture, and identity in the Western World, and seem to mark the contemporary limits of the legal imaginary.

The European Art/Culture System

In his influential work *The Predicament of Culture*, historian James Clifford discusses "the fate of tribal artifacts and cultural practices once they are relocated in Western museums, exchange systems, disciplinary archives, and discursive traditions."[25] Clifford delineates an "art-culture system," developed over the nineteenth century in the context of global colonialism and imperialism as a means of categorizing arts and cultural goods. I will suggest that these categories continue to inform our laws of property, and that these categories may no longer be appropriate in a postcolonial context.

Clifford begins his discussion of Western classifications with a critical review of a 1984 exhibit at the Museum of Modern Art in New York (MOMA) titled "Primitivism in 20th Century Art: Affinity of the Tribal and the Modern" which documented the influence of tribal objects in the

256   works of modernist masters such as Picasso, Brancusi and Miró.[26] In the early Twentieth Century, the exhibit suggests, these modernists discover that primitive objects are in fact powerful art and their own work is influenced by the power of these forms. A common quality or essence joins the tribal to the modern in what is described under the universalizing rubric of "affinity." An identity of spirit and a similarity of creativity between the modern and the tribal, the contemporary and the primitive, is recognized and celebrated (a movement that continues to hold persuasive power in the Western World, if the recent television series *Millennium* is any indication).

The humanist appeal of the exhibit, however, rests upon a number of exclusions, evasions, and stereotypes. One could, for example, question the way modernism appropriates otherness, constitutes non-Western arts in its own image and thereby discovers universal ahistorical human capacities by denying particular histories, local contexts, indigenous meanings, and the very political conditions that enabled Western artists and authors to seize these goods for their own ends. Needless to say, the "imperialist contexts that surround the 'discovery' of tribal objects by modernist artists" just as "the planet's peoples came massively under European political economic and evangelical dominion," is not addressed in the MOMA exhibit. Indeed, the emphasis is upon the narrative of European "creative genius recognizing the greatness of tribal works,"[27] thereby bestowing upon these objects the status of "art" in place of their former lowly designation as ethnographic specimens. As Clifford states, "the capacity of art to transcend its cultural and historical context is asserted repeatedly."[28] The category of art, however, is not a universal one, but an historically contingent European category, in which the artistic imagination is universalized in the European image under the name of a putatively "human" Culture.

The "appreciation and interpretation of tribal objects takes place," according to Clifford, "within a modern system of objects which confers value on certain things and withholds it from others."[29] Clifford delineates the "art-culture system" that developed in the nineteenth century as a way of categorizing expressive works of aesthetic value in a context of European imperialism and colonialism and the collection of objects in imperialist forays around the globe.[30] Using a classificatory grid, he demonstrates how two categories have dominated our understanding of expressive works and their proper placement, and two subsidiary categories have encompassed those objects not so easily subsumed by the dominant logic. First, he designates the zone of "authentic masterpieces" created by individual geniuses, the category of "art" properly speaking. Secondly, he identifies the category of "authentic artifacts" created by "cultures" imagined as collectivities. Objects may, therefore, be exhibited in galleries, as examples of a human creative ability that transcends the limitations of time and place to speak to us about the "human" condition; representing the highest point of human achievement they are regarded as testament to the greatness of their individual creators. Alternatively, objects may be exhibited in museums as the authentic works of a distinct collectivity, integral to the harmonious life of an a-historical community and incomprehensible outside of "cultural context"—the defining features of authentic artefacts.

For an object to be accepted as an authentic artefact, it must locate itself in an untouched, pristine state that bespeaks a timeless essence in a particular cultural tradition. That which is recognized as authentic to a culture cannot bear any traces of that culture's contact with other cultures; it must particularly bear no marks of that society's history of colonialism which enabled such works to make their way into Western markets. The tribal life from which such objects magically spring are permitted no histories of their own, relegated to an a-historical perceptual present, perceived as essential traditions that are vanishing, being destroyed, or tainted by the forces of modernization. The capacity of "tribal" peoples to live in history, and to creatively interpret and expressively confront the historical circumstances in which they live, using their cultural traditions to do so, cannot be contemplated, except under marginalized categories like "syncretism" which suggest impurity and decline; "aboriginals apparently must always inhabit a mythic time."[31] Those cultural manifestations that may signal the creative *life* rather than the death of societies are excluded as inauthentic, or, alternatively, denied cultural, social, or political specificity by becoming incorporated into the universalizing discourse of art.

Tribal objects may transcend their original placement—for example, when African objects become elevated and recognized as art, these "artifacts are essentially defined as masterpieces, their makers as great artists, the discourse of connoisseurship reigns ... personal names make their appearance, i.e. art has signature."[32] When non-Western objects fully pass from the status of authentic artefact to the status of art, they also escape the ahistorical location of the "tribal," albeit to enter into a "universal" history, defined by the progression of works of great author/

258 artists (the canon of civilization). They become part of a "human" cultural heritage—Culture capitalized—rather than objects properly belonging to the "cultures" defined by the discipline of anthropology in the nineteenth and early twentieth centuries.

These categories of art, Culture, and culture, and the domains of authentic masterpieces and authentic artefacts to which they relate are mirrored in our legal categories for the valuation and protection of expressive objects. Laws of intellectual property (copyright in particular) and laws of cultural property reflect and secure the logic of the European art/culture system that Clifford outlines. Laws of copyright developed to protect the expressive works of authors and artists—increasingly perceived in Romantic terms of individual genius and transcendent creativity—in the service of promoting universal progress in the arts and sciences. Copyright laws protect works, understood to embody the unique personality of their individual authors, and the expressive component of the original is so venerated that even a reproduction or imitation of it is deemed a form of theft.

Although the history of copyright has been more fully investigated elsewhere,[33] a few points are central to the argument here. The idea of an author's rights to control his expressive creations developed in a context that privileged a Lockean theory of the origin of property in labor in which the expressive creation is seen as the author's "work," albeit mental work, that creates an "Original" arising spontaneously from the vital root of "Genius."[34] Originality in mental labor as opposed to manual labor enabled the author to claim not merely the physical object produced, but the literary or artistic expression itself—the "work" properly defined.

Literary or artistic works were incorporeal entities that sprang from the "fruitful mind" of an author,[35] one of many organic metaphors that proliferated in the Romantic ideology of creativity and resonated with Hegelian theories of personality. The work carries the imprint of the author's personality and always embodies his persona, wherever it surfaces, and whatever the sources of its content or the quality of the ideas it expresses—"even the humblest creative effort is protected because personality always contains something unique. It expresses its singularity . . . that which is one man's alone."[36]

If the expressive, inventive, and possessive individual dominates intellectual property laws, legitimizing personal control over the circulation of texts, laws of cultural property protect the material works (objects of artistic, archaeological, ethnological, or historical interest) of culture.

Culture may be defined here in either of the two ways established in the   *259*
nineteenth century—as the universal heritage of humankind—culture
with a capital C—or in the plural anthropological sense, in which different cultures lay claim to different properties.[37] These two positions on
the nature of the "culture" that can rightfully possess the property at
issue define the poles of an ongoing controversy in legal scholarship.
John Henry Merryman, the most prolific of the legal scholars writing in
this field, defends a position he defines as "cultural internationalism"
which he describes in Enlightenment terms as a commitment to "the
cultural heritage of all mankind" to which each people make their contribution and all people have an interest.[38] This attitude towards cultural
property emerges from the law of war and the need to cease military
activities when cultural objects are endangered, and to treat those
responsible for advances against cultural property as having committed a
crime against humanity. It is enshrined in *The Convention for the
Protection of Cultural Property in the Event of Armed Conflict* enacted in
the Hague on May 14, 1954.[39]

The other position on cultural property that Merryman defines and
denigrates is "cultural nationalism" in which particular peoples have particular interests in particular properties, regardless of their current location and ownership. This attitude towards cultural property is embodied
in *The Convention on the Means of Prohibiting and Preventing the Illicit
Import, Export, and Transfer of Ownership of Cultural Property* of Novem-
ber 14, 1970[40] (hereinafter UNESCO 1970), in which "the parties agree
to oppose the impoverishment of the cultural heritage of a nation
through illicit import, export, and transfer of ownership of cultural property, agree that trade in cultural objects exported contrary to the law of
the nation of origin is illicit and agree to prevent the importation of such
objects and facilitate their return to source nations."[41] As of 1986, fifty-
eight nations had become parties to UNESCO 1970; many of these signatories have policies that prevent all export of cultural property, thus
making any international trafficking of cultural property "illicit."[42]

Merryman derides cultural nationalism as motivated by "Romantic
Byronism"—a curiously Eurocentric term that he indiscriminately applies to all nations with an interest in the preservation and repatriation of
significant cultural objects.[43] For Merryman, such a position can only be
seen as irrational because in the "source nations" who dominate amongst
signatories to UNESCO 1970, the supply of cultural artefacts far exceeds
the internal demand—"they are rich in cultural artefacts beyond any
conceivable use."[44] Because such nations are relatively poor, he believes

that they would be better off exporting such objects to locations where they are valued according to free market principles.

In addition to "Romantic Byronism," Merryman cites the notion of national cultural patrimony and political symbolic uses of cultural property as possible reasons for the popularity of "cultural nationalism," but he lumps such considerations together with "lack of cultural expertise and organization to deal with cultural property as a resource like other resources to be managed and exploited."[45] The possibility that other peoples may entertain other values is considered no more nor less likely than their sheer ignorance and ineptitude in recognizing cultural property as an exportable resource. Merryman seems to find it offensive that source nations have the exclusive voice in determining whether or not cultural objects will be prohibited from export, when dealers, collectors, and museums are deprived of any input into the decision.[46] The interest of dealers, collectors, and museums in such decisions is self-evident; in market terms, they best recognize the value of such objects, and are in the best position to see that value realized on the market.

A more sympathetic and sophisticated case for "cultural nationalism" is made by John Moustakas in a law review note titled "Group Rights in Cultural Property: Justifying Strict Inalienability."[47] Concerned that Greece has been dispossessed of some of its greatest cultural and artistic patrimony, and that the "looting and pillage of cultural heritage continues wholesale"[48] as evidenced by thriving black markets, Moustakas argues that neither international conventions nor national laws have recognized that new concepts of ownership must be created to deal with emerging notions of national cultural identity. Existing laws in both national and international arenas presuppose the alienability of all property, including cultural property, according to market principles. Moustakas argues for recognition of strict market inalienability for those cultural properties integrally related to group cultural identity extending Margaret Jane Radin's test of "property for personhood"[49] to collectivities conceived as persons.

The nexus between a cultural object and a group, culture, or nation should be "the essential measurement for determining whether group rights in cultural property will be effectuated to the fullest extent possible —by holding such objects strictly inalienable from the group."[50] Just as:

> ... property for personhood might describe property so closely bound up with our individual identities that its loss causes pain that cannot be relieved by the object's replacement, ... property for

grouphood expresses something about the entire group's relationship
to certain property ... essential to the preservation of group identity
and self-esteem.[51]

Against those who would argue that such a position is paternalistic, he
argues that the concept of "communal flourishing" provides an important justification for holding such property inalienable.[52] Using the
Parthenon Marbles (the term Elgin Marbles has the effect of ceding
legitimacy to British seizure) as his example, Moustakas argues for recognition that some properties can only properly belong to groups as constitutive of group identity, that such properties cannot be alienated because
future generations are unable to consent to transactions that threaten
their existence as a group, and that commodification and fungibility are
inappropriate ways to treat constitutive elements of grouphood and are
inimical to communal flourishing.

"Cultural nationalism" employs the rhetoric of possessive individualism in its support for the rights of groups to claim certain objects as part
of their essential identities. Anthropologist Richard Handler has written
extensively about the logic of possessive individualism in contemporary
claims to cultural property.[53] Drawing upon C.B. Macpherson's famous
work,[54] Handler argues that possessive individualism—the relationship
that links the individual to property as it was initially formulated in
Locke's labor theory of value—increasingly dominates the language and
logic of political claims to cultural autonomy. Focusing upon the idea of
cultural property as manifested in sixty-odd years of historic preservation
legislation in the province of Quebec, he explicates the tropes used to
defend the protection of a unique cultural heritage. In discussing "le
patrimoine," people in Quebec "envision national culture as property
and the nation as a property-owning 'collective individual.'"[55]

The modern individual is a self-sufficient and self-contained monad
who is complete as a human being:

> Not only is one complete in oneself, one is *completely oneself.* By this
> I mean that we conceive of the individual person as having, as we say,
> "an identity." Identity means "oneness," though it is oneness of a
> special sort ... "sameness in all that constitutes the objective reality
> of a thing."[56]

The second aspect of modern individualism that Handler points to is its
possessive element—in modern culture an individual is defined by the

property he or she possesses and such individuals naturally seek to transform nature into forms of private property. Modernity has extended these qualities to nation states and ethnic groups who are imagined on the world stage and in political arenas as "collective individuals." Like other individuals, these collective individuals are imagined to be territorially and historically bounded, distinctive, internally homogeneous, and complete onto themselves. In this worldview, each nation or group possesses a unique identity and culture that is constituted by its undisputed possession of property. Groups increasingly imagine themselves as individuals prizing their possession of culture and history:

> ... it is our culture and history, which belong to us alone, which make us what we are, which constitute our identity and assure our survival ... within cultural nationalism a group's survival, its identity or objective oneness over time, depends upon the secure possession of a culture ... [and] culture and history become synonymous because the group's history is preserved and embodied in material objects—cultural property.[57]

Material objects, therefore, come to epitomize collective identity—as articulated by a 1976 UNESCO panel in the principle that "cultural property is a basic element of a people's identity,"[58] a rationale used to legitimate the repatriation of objects of overriding importance to group identity. Being is equated with having (and excluding and controlling.)

This collective individual is imagined like a biological organism to be precisely delimited both physically and in terms of a set of traits (its culture, heritage, or "personality") that distinguishes it from all other collective individuals. The nation is said to "have" or "possess" a culture, just as its human constituents are described as "bearers" of the national culture. From the nationalist perspective, the relationship between the nation and culture should be characterized by originality and authenticity. Cultural traits that come to the nation from outside are at best "borrowed" and at worst polluting; by contrast, those aspects of national culture that come from within the nation, that are original to it, are "authentic."[59]

The rhetoric of cultural nationalism clearly bears traces of the same logic that defines copyright. Each nation or group is perceived as an author who originates a culture from resources that come from within and can thus lay claim to exclusive possession of the expressive works that embody its personality. There is, however, a significant difference in the scope of the claims that can be made on behalf of a culture, and those that can be made on behalf of an individual author. Copyright laws enable individual authors not only to claim possession of their original works as discrete objects, but to claim possession and control over any and all reproductions of those works, or any substantial part thereof, in any medium. Cultural property laws, however, enable proprietary claims to be made only to original objects or authentic artefacts. The Western extension of Culture to cultural others was limited to objects of property, not to forms of expression. The full authority of authorship, therefore, was confined to the Western World.

To make this concrete, let us return to the Picasso painting. When a primitive statue, produced in a collectivity for social reasons, makes its way into a Picasso painting, the statue itself may still embody the identity of the culture from which it sprang, but any reproduction of it may be legally recognized as the embodiment of Picasso's authorial personality. The possession of a culture is profoundly limited, whereas the possession of the author extends through time and space as his work is reproduced. If royalties are to flow, they flow not to the statue's culture of origin, but to the estate of the Western author, where the fruits of his original work are realized for fifty years after his death.

In his discussion of "possessive collectivism" Handler agrees with the principle of repatriation as a matter of fair play, but suggests that the cultural identity argument used to support it has the insidious effect of reproducing and extending Western cultural ideologies of possessive individualism on a global scale.[60] The problem with restitutionist arguments, he posits, is that they make use of metaphors "borrowed from the hegemonic culture that the restitutionists are attempting to resist."[61] Arguing from recent developments in anthropology, Handler forcefully asserts that cultures are not bounded, continuous over time, or internally homogenous, that traditions are actively invented and negotiated, and reimagined as social agents negotiate their political lives and relationships.[62] The culture that groups assert as belonging to them and as essentially embodied in particular pieces of property, is, he suggests, not an objective thing that has possessed a continuous meaning and identity over time, but the product of current needs and interpretations.[63] It is, however, as politically dishonest to deny the objective identity of those making culturally nationalist claims as it is to assert an internationalism that privileges the nation-building imperialist enterprises of European

264   countries in the name of "universal human values" or the "common heritage of mankind." Both positions are interested human inventions.

Contemporary Properties of Culture and Identity

The European art/culture system and the legal categories that support and sustain it constitute a limited vision of human expressive possibility and a limited understanding of our various modes of cultural attachment to the phenomena which give meaning to our lives. Ultimately, these categories serve only to culturally impoverish the Western self, while they Orientalize the other. By deeming expressive creations the private properties of authors who can thereby control the circulation of culturally meaningful texts through our intellectual property laws, we deprive ourselves of immense opportunities for creative "worldmaking"[64]—a phenomenon I have explored more fully elsewhere.[65] Denying the social conditions and cultural influences that shape the author's expressive creativity, we invest him with a power that may border on censorship in the name of property. By representing cultures in the image of the undivided possessive individual, we obscure people's historical agency and transformations, their internal differences, the productivity of intercultural contact, and the ability of peoples to culturally express their position in a wider world. The Romantic author and authentic artefacts are both fictions of a world best foregone.

First Nations peoples are faced with many difficulties when attempting to assert representations of identity in contemporary Canadian society. When they specify their unique histories, they are often accused of essentialism, but when they write or paint, their work is often criticized for not being "authentic" or sufficiently "Indian." When First Nations peoples make claims to "their own" images, stories, and cultural themes, however, they do not do so as Romantic authors nor as timeless homogenous cultures insisting upon the maintenance of a vanishing authenticity. They do not lay claim to expressive works as possessive individuals, insisting upon permissions and royalties for the circulation of authorial personas in the public realm. Nor is their assertion of cultural presence made in the name of an ahistorical collective essence, but in the name of living, changing, creative peoples engaged in very concrete contemporary political struggles. The law, however, affords them little space to make their claims. As Amanda Pask explains in a brilliant discussion of the issue, Native peoples face a legal system that divides the world up in a fashion both foreign and hostile to their sense of felt need:

> At every level the claims of aboriginal peoples to cultural rights fall outside the parameters of Western legal discourse. As neither state actors, nor individuals, their claims can be heard neither in the international regimes governing cultural property, nor in the domestic regimes governing intellectual property. This pattern repeats itself internally in each regime: in cultural property law the competing legal values that frame every question are those of national patrimony and the "universal heritage of mankind"; in intellectual property the interests to be balanced are those of "authors" conceived of on an individualistic model and "the public" in their interest in preserving a common public domain. In all cases, aboriginal peoples must articulate their interests within frameworks which obliterate the position from which they speak.[66]

As Pask suggests, the opposition between private, personal interests and universal ones is understood to cover the field of all possible claims, and, as we have seen, when group rights are entertained, they are often conceived in individualistic terms that freeze and essentialize culture in the name of identity.

Even more debilitating for Native claims, perhaps, is the law's rigid demarcation between ideas and expressions, oral traditions and written forms, intangible works and cultural objects, personal property and real property. The law rips asunder what First Nations people view as integrally related, freezing into categories what Native peoples find flowing in relationships that do not separate texts from ongoing creative production, or ongoing creativity from social relationships, or social relationships from people's relationship to an ecological landscape that binds past and future generations in relations of spiritual significance.

The powerful conceptual framework of the European art/culture system seems so deeply embedded in our legal categories of intellectual and cultural property, that they seem immutable, but the claims of non-Western others to objects and representations may well force these Western categories under new forms of scrutiny. As new subjects engaged in postcolonial struggles occupy the categories bestowed upon us by an ignoble past, they may well transform them and eventually perhaps help to crumble the colonial edifice upon which these categories are founded. To understand First Nations claims, we must venture beyond the European categories that constitute the colonial edifice of the law; only by considering Native claims "in context" will we be able to expand "the borders of the legal imagination."[67]

Listening to Native Claims "In Context"

The cultural appropriation debate raises numerous issues and engages many protagonists. I cannot engage all of these arguments here. Rather than attempt to construct a solution to a problem, I will suggest instead that my readers attempt to understand the issues differently. Whereas it may be impossible to delineate formal rules defining, sanctioning, and prohibiting specific acts of "cultural appropriation," it is possible to enact and practice an ethics of appropriation that attends to the specificity of the historical circumstances in which certain claims are made, in which they must be assessed. I will attend to the specific claims about cultural appropriation made by Native peoples and suggest that we consider acts of cultural "borrowing" "in context."

The call to consider claims "in context" has been explored by Martha Minow and Elizabeth Spelman as a characteristic that unites philosophical pragmatists, feminists, and critical race theorists.[68] In making decisions, an emphasis on context requires a sensitivity to the nuances of the particular historical situation in which a claim emerges and the distinctive needs of the persons involved. Against assumptions of liberal legal and political theory that treat principles as universal and the individual self as the proper unit of analysis, the call to context is a call to consider the structures of power in society and the systemic legacies of exclusion involving group-based characteristics of individuals.[69]

Minow and Spelman argue that attention to the contingencies of a situation—the particular cultural and historical background of the persons involved—neither incapacitates us from making moral judgments nor undermines the possibility of criticism across contexts.[70] Instead, a contextualist approach suggests that all human beings are always in social contexts and make judgments contextually and that any form of abstraction to general principles involves a choice of relevant contexts. Exponents of abstraction who stress the need to develop principles that apply across contexts, like the writers of the letters to the editor cited earlier, are themselves situated in ways that limit their understandings, and these limitations must be reflected upon in attempting to understand a context for judgment. Abstract theories, like freedom of expression, authorship, ownership, and censorship, are "rooted in particular contexts and operate within a context with real and particular effects that often benefit some people more than others."[71] Contextualist approaches, moreover, generally do appeal to some more abstract moral or political theory to justify their procedures. Like Cornell West, I point to context here as a means of challenging a political theory that speaks in the name of abstract individual rights with the specific situated experiences of others whose lives bespeak the exclusions effected by those principles.[72]

Native peoples in Canada are making specific claims to stories, imagery, and themes based upon very specific historical trajectories and the specific needs of people engaged in contemporary political struggles in which these stories strategically figure. The claims of First Nations peoples to control the circulation of Native cultural texts cannot be facilely analogized to prohibiting Shakespeare's writing of Hamlet or the Third Reich's prohibition of Jewish writing, under the rubric of freedom of speech, without doing violence to the integrity of Native struggles for political self-determination. Specific historical experiences and contemporary political struggles provide the only relevant contexts for considering claims of cultural appropriation. Only by situating these claims in this context can we understand how supposedly abstract, general, and universal principles (like authorship, art, culture, and identity) may operate to construct systematic structures of domination and exclusion in Canadian society. An evaluation and judgement of Native claims of cultural appropriation without this knowledge of context will only reinforce these larger patterns of injustice.

Notes

1. Stephen Godfrey, *Canada Council Asks Whose Voice Is it Anyway?* GLOBE & MAIL, Mar. 21, 1992, at C1, C15.

2. *Id.* at C1.

3. *Id.*

4. *Id.*

5. The term "dangerous supplement" is borrowed from Jack Balkin, *Deconstructive Practice and Legal Theory*, 96 YALE L. J. 743 (1987), who borrows it from Jacques Derrida.

6. Letter to the Editor, GLOBE & MAIL, Mar. 28, 1992, at D-7, *reprinted in* OUT MAGAZINE: CANADA'S NATIONAL GAY ARTS/ENTERTAINMENT MONTHLY, June 1992.

7. Letter to the Editor, GLOBE & MAIL, Mar. 28, 1992, at D7.

8. THE GLOBE AND MAIL, Mar. 31, 1992, at A16.

9. Godfrey, *supra* note 1, at C15.

10. Letter to the Editor, GLOBE & MAIL, Mar. 28, 1992, at D7.

11. *Id.*

12. Letter to the Editor, GLOBE & MAIL, Apr. 3, 1992, at A3.

13. Letter to the Editor, GLOBE & MAIL, Mar. 28, 1992, at D7.

14. The term "Orientalism" is drawn from Edward Said's pathbreaking work. *See generally* EDWARD SAID, ORIENTALISM. (1978).

15. Godrey, *supra* note 1.

16. Lenore Keeshig Tobias, *Stop Stealing Native Stories*, GLOBE & MAIL, Jan. 26, 1990, at A8.

17. *Id.*

18. *Id.*

19. *Id.*

20. *Id.*

21. *Id.*

22. Godfrey, *supra* note 1, at C1.

23. *Id.* at C15.

24. I have chosen deliberately to use the term postcolonial rather than the term multicultural, and the language of struggle rather than the currently fashionable discourse of cultural diversity, because these alternative terms emphasize rather than obscure the very real histories of colonialism from which all peoples in Canada are still emerging, and the very real relations of power and domination inherited from our diverse colonial pasts that continue to shape social relations of difference in this country. For critical discussions of multiculturalism see Kooglia Moodley, *Canadian Multiculturalism as Ideology*, 6 ETHNIC & RACIAL STUD. 320 (1983), and Chandra Mohanty, *On Race and Voice: Challenges for Liberal Education in the 1990's*, 14 CULTURAL CRITIQUE 179 (1990). For a fine overview of the deployment of the term postcolonial see Patricia Seed, *Colonial and Postcolonial Discourse*, 26 LATIN AM. RES. REV. 181 (1991). For recent criticisms of the term and its range of extension see Arun P. Mukherjee, *Whose Post-Colonialism and Whose Postmodernism?*, 30 WORLD LITERATURE WRITTEN IN ENGLISH 1 (1990); Ella Shohat, *Notes on the 'Post-Colonial,'* 32 SOC. TEXT 99 (1990); Helen Tiffin, *Post-Colonialism, Post-Modernism, and the Rehabilitation of Post-Colonial History*, 23 J. COMMONWEALTH LITERATURE 169 (1988); Ruth Frankenberg & Lata Mani, *Crosscurrents, Crosstalk: Race, 'Postcoloniality' and the Politics of Location*, 17 CULTURAL STUD. (forthcoming). Lynda Hutcheon has written that "Canada [i]s still caught up in the machinations of Empire and colony, imperial metropolis and provincial hinterland"; a context in which the debates about postcolonialism have historically specific relevance, given the experience and ongoing manifestations of British Empire, and the arrival of immigrants from other postcolonial nations. Furthermore, she suggests that

> when Canadian culture is called postcolonial today, the reference is very rarely to the Native culture, which might be the more accurate historical use of the term ... Native and Metis writers are today demanding a voice ... and perhaps, given their articulations of the damage to Indian culture and people done by the colonizers (French and British) and the process of colonization, theirs should be considered the resisting, postcolonial voice of Canada.

See Lynda Hutcheon, *Circling the Downspout of Empire: Post-Colonialism and Postmodernism*, 20 ARIEL 149, 156 (1989) .

25. JAMES CLIFFORD, THE PREDICAMENT OF CULTURE: TWENTIETH CENTURY ETHNOGRAPHY,   *269*
    LITERATURE, AND ART 215 (1988).

26. *Id.* at 189–214.

27. *Id.* at 196.

28. *Id.* at 195.

29. *Id.* at 198.

30. *Id.* at 215–251.

31. *Id.* at 201–202.

32. *Id.* at 205–206.

33. *See* Peter Jaszi, *Toward a Theory of Copyright: The Metamorphoses of 'Authorship,'* 1991
    DUKE L. J. 455; MARK ROSE, AUTHORS AND OWNERS (1993).

34. I am paraphrasing from ROSE, *supra* note 33, at 119) (paraphrasing and quoting EDWARD
    YOUNG, CONJECTURES ON ORIGINAL COMPOSITION (1759)). Young's essay may be found
    in BENJAMIN KAPLAN, AN UNHURRIED VIEW OF COPYRIGHT 27 (1967).

35. WILLIAM ENFIELD, OBSERVATIONS ON LITERARY PROPERTY 21 (1774).

36. Bleistein v. Donaldson Lithographing Co., 188 U.S. 239, 250 (1903) (interpreting the
    nineteenth century artist John Ruskin, a significant figure in the Romantic movement).

37. An overview of the treaties that define the parameters of the international law of cul-
    tural property may be found in Joseph F. Edwards, *Major Global Treaties for the
    Protection and Enjoyment of Art and Cultural Objects,* 22 TOLEDO L. REV. 919 (1991).

38. John Henry Merryman, *Two Ways Of Thinking About Cultural Property,* 80 AM. J. OF
    INT'L L. 831 (1986); John Henry Merryman, *The Public Interest in Cultural Property,* 77
    CAL. L. REV. 339 (1989).

39. 249 U.N.T.S. 240.

40. 823 U.N.T.S. 231, *reprinted in* 10 INT'L LEGAL MATERIALS 289 (1971), *cited in*
    Merryman, *Two Ways of Thinking, supra* note 38, at 833.

41. Merryman, *Two Ways of Thinking, supra* note 38, at 843.

42. *Id.*

43. *Id.* at 833.

44. *Id.* at 832.

45. *Id.* at 832, n.5.

46. *Id.* at 844–845.

47. J. Moustakas, *Group Rights in Cultural Property: Justifying Strict Inalienability,* 74
    CORNELL L. REV. 1179 (1989).

48. *Id.* at 1182.

49. Margaret J. Radin, *Property and Personhood,* 34 STAN. L. REV. 957, 959 (1982).

50. Moustakas, *supra* note 47, at 1184.

51. *Id.* at 1185, note 17 (citing Radin, *supra* note 49, at 959).

52. *Id.* at 185.

53. See Richard Handler, *Who Owns the Past? History, Cultural Property, and the Logic of
    Possessive Individualism, in* THE POLITICS OF CULTURE 63–74 (Brett Williams ed., 1991);
    Richard Handler, *On Having a Culture: Nationalism and the Preservation of Quebec's
    Patrimoine, in* OBJECTS AND OTHERS: ESSAYS ON MUSEUMS AND MATERIAL CULTURE
    192–217 (George W. Stocking ed., 1985).

54. C. B. MACPHERSON, THE POLITICAL THEORY OF POSSESSIVE INDIVIDUALISM: HOBBES TO
    LOCKE (1962).

55. Handler, *On Having a Culture, supra* note 53, at 194.

56. Handler, *Who Owns the Past, supra* note 53, at 64.

57. *Id.* at 66.

58. Cited in Handler, *Who Owns the Past, supra* note 53, at 67.

59. Handler, *On Having a Culture, supra* note 53, at 198.

60. *Id.* at 67.

61. Handler, *Who Owns the Past, supra* note 53, at 68.

62. *Id.* at 68.

63. *Id.* at 69.

64. I borrow this term from NELSON GOODMAN, WAYS OF WORLDMAKING (1978).

65. *See* Rosemary J. Coombe, *Objects of Property and Subjects of Politics: Intellectual Property and Democratic Dialogue,* 69 TEX. L. REV. 1853 (1991); Rosemary J. Coombe, *Publicity Rights and Political Aspiration: Mass Culture, Gender Identity, and Democracy,* 26 NEW ENG. L. REV. 1221 (1992). *See also* David Lange, *At Play in the Fields of the Word: Copyright and the Construction of Authorship in the Post-Literate Millennium,* 55 LAW & CONTEMP. PROBS. 139 (1992).

66. Amanda Pask, *Making Connections: Intellectual Property, Cultural Property, and Sovereignty in the Debates Concerning the Appropriation of Native Cultures in Canada,* 8 INTELL. PROP. J. (forthcoming).

67. I borrow this phrase from Patrick Macklem, *The Borders of the Legal Imagination,* 36 McGILL L. J. 382 (1991).

68. Martha Minow & Elizabeth Spelman, *In Context, in* PRAGMATISM IN LAW AND SOCIETY 247, 247 (M. Brant and W. Weaver eds., 1991).

69. *Id.* at 248–9.

70. *Id.* at 249–255.

71. *Id.* at 258.

72. *See id* at 257 (discussing of West).

PART FIVE

Violence

Introduction to
VIOLENCE

IN THE END we turn to violence. For many, it is the fear of violence that inspires allegiance to the law. Even with all its flaws, law sometimes seems our only bulwark against the tyranny of force. This conception of the relationship between law and violence can have the effect of disabling criticism of law. In the face of the brutal reality of violence, who can criticize law? We are all for law. We are all against violence. Yet, as Robert Cover has taught us, law and violence frequently overlap, often coincide.[1]

The authors in this Part expand upon and challenge Cover's crucial insight by exploring the multiple and often simultaneous and contradictory meanings of law and violence in particular cultural situations. In so doing, they seek to rehabilitate legal criticism from our fear of violence without simply giving in to a corresponding fear of law. Ileana Porras's discussion of terrorism, Kendall Thomas's analysis of gay bashing and Elizabeth Spelman's and Martha Minow's study of the film *Thelma and Louise* explore ways in which terrorists or women or gays or gay bashers can be imagined as both victims and outlaws, as both enforcers of law and lawbreakers.

At the same time, the authors are sensitive to the multiple forms legal violence may take. For example, we might encounter legal violence not only through the apparatus of the state, as in the death penalty or police abuse, but through "private" enforcers, as in the case of gay bashers and domestic abusers. We might even find violence in seemingly progressive law reform when it fails to perceive its own exclusionary practices, as Kimberlé Crenshaw argues about some responses to domestic violence against women of color.

Ileana Porras explores the complex ways cultural images of law and violence are deployed in the context of terrorism. Through an analysis of texts about terrorism, Porras demonstrates how the writers use the presumed opposition between law and violence to construct not only the terrorist, but also the terrorist's victims, the frame for interpreting terrorist violence, and the appropriate ways for responding to it. Like violence itself, the terrorist is often defined in opposition to law. To be against law is to be violent, irrational, immoral, other. To be other is also to be against law, unwilling or unable to accept its constraints and not subject to its limitations. The terrorist, by rejecting law, also rejects its protection; by forswearing law's constraints, the terrorist also forswears law's mercy. As one commentator put it, terrorists engage in "extra-normal" violence to which one must respond with extra-normal (extra-legal) means. Thus, the terrorist—the quintessential outlaw—frees the state from the constraints of law and morality. The state, through legal rules or otherwise, may respond to violence with violence.

Kendall Thomas attempts to negotiate the shifting ground of legality and violence as he asserts a role for law in the protection of gay men and lesbians from violence. Thomas describes a world of violence against gays and lesbians in which the gay bashers are outlaws—terrorists, vigilantes, depraved. In the face of this brutal onslaught, gays and lesbians become innocent victims of outlaw violence. And yet, gays and lesbians can be outlaws too. Many gays and lesbians regularly engage in criminal sodomy; they subvert the laws of church, gender, society; their very being is against the law. Thus, when Thomas focuses on the outlaw status of gay bashers, the victim status of gay men and lesbians seems secure. Yet, when one focuses on the illegal status of homosexual conduct, the victim status of gays seems more uncertain. Both gay bashers and their victims are outlaws. Like terrorists, they may seem unworthy of law's sanction and outside its protective embrace.

But Thomas tells another story, where the "private" violence of gay bashing takes place in a "legal" context. The bashers are not outlaws at all, but rather private enforcers of public morality as legally manifested in criminal sodomy statutes. Gays and lesbians are the outlaws here and, while both gays and lesbians and their abusers break the law, the violence is within the purview of law. It has law's sanction. Thomas challenges this complicity of the state in violence against gays and lesbians as unlawful.

Elizabeth Spelman and Martha Minow have a different take on the notion of "taking the law into one's own hands" in their analysis of the film *Thelma and Louise*. If the gay basher thugs Thomas describes engage in public justice on behalf of the state, Thelma and Louise seem to reverse this story. In the context of the law's relative indifference to male violence against women, they enact their own justice by breaking the law. In so doing, Thelma and Louise become both like gays and lesbians in Thomas's piece   subject to and victims of state sanctioned "terrorism" by men—and like the terrorist outlaws of Porras' piece—affirmatively rejecting legal morality and its constraints. Spellman and Minow parse these shifting images of Thelma and Louise as they explore the ways in which Thelma and Louise seem to construct their outlaw identities through the deployment of violence, and how, at the same time, the murder they commit, like some extra-discursive "fact," seems to write their story for them.

If Spelman and Minow problematize both the victim and the outlaw status of Thelma and Louise, the victim status of women of color in the context of domestic violence is, for Kimberlé Crenshaw, not in dispute. Nor, for that matter, is the status of their abusers open to empathetic reinterpretation. But the physical violence of domestic violence is not the primary focus of Crenshaw's analysis. Rather, turning her gaze on the violence of identity politics in its responses to domestic violence, she demonstrates how the unique needs of women of color are consistently missed by traditional (white) feminist responses and traditional (male) anti-racist responses to domestic violence. Crenshaw argues that focusing remedial responses to domestic violence through the lens of gender without recognizing the impact of race for women of color can be and often is a fatal omission. Similarly, anti-racist responses that view domestic violence through a lens of race without recognizing the impact of gender are similarly flawed. Thus, the violence of domestic abuse is compounded for women of color by the deployment of identity categories that do not seem to fit.

In questioning one of our culture's most basic boundaries—that which separates outlaws and law-abiders—these essays force us to reconsider the seemingly extra-discursive reality of violence as well as the legitimacy and efficacy of law. To some, they will seem to have taken the deconstructive impulses of postmodernism beyond the realm of the tolerable. To others, the essays might even suggest the impossibility of a politics after identity. But we are not so skeptical.

Even as the authors break down the distinctions between law and violence, victim and outlaw, innocent and terrorist, lawful violence and lawlessness, they are deeply concerned with the politics of identity. In fact, they demonstrate that identities are not just invoked or inflected through acts of self-realization or discrimination. Rather, identities are forged, in part through cultural acts and discourses that at times might seem quite independent of identity—even through violence. Each of the essays, for example, explores identities that violence seems to create for certain groups, as well as ways that violence becomes a means for articulating identity.

At the same time, the authors suggest that our legal and cultural means for interpreting and responding to social phenomena like violence are in large part a function of the notions of identity we bring to bear on them. As Crenshaw most dramatically illustrates, our refusal to engage the complexities of identity may result not only in the failure of our legal strategies, but also in a failure to perceive the violence of the legal strategies themselves.

For us, these essays, as well as all the essays in the book, confirm that a multiple, intersectional politics of identity will have an impact on more than just our sense of ourselves. Engagement with the complexity and instability of identity may well lead to the reinterpretation of various forms of cultural and legal production, from sexuality to violence.

Note

1. *See generally* Robert Cover, *Violence and the Word*, 95 YALE L.J. 1601 (1986).

CHAPTER FOURTEEN

>─┼◆>─O─<◆┼─<

BEYOND THE
PRIVACY PRINCIPLE

Kendall Thomas

Trail of Blood:
The Untold Story of *Bowers v. Hardwick*

BY 1986, WHEN the Supreme Court rendered its judgment in *Bowers v. Hardwick*, the concept of the right to privacy had become a central term in the lexicon of Twentieth Century constitutional argument.[1] From our present perspective, it may be difficult to imagine another root concept that would have served as well as this one to articulate and advance the concerns at stake in *Griswold v. Connecticut*[2] and its progeny. With *Hardwick*, however, privacy's term of service seems to have run its course. This, at least, is the lesson I draw from the case and from the terms in which the Supreme Court discussed the constitutional issues it presented.

Let me acknowledge at the outset that the view of *Hardwick* urged here may seem something of a paradox. *Hardwick* seems to be the most private of all privacy cases. After all, one might note, Michael Hardwick

278   was arrested in the privacy of his own bedroom, for conduct that took place there. On this view, *Hardwick* lends itself perfectly to analysis through the lens of privacy, since it appears to present a textbook example of the kind of state practices against which the doctrine was designed to protect. In this perspective, the most likely explanation for the *Hardwick* Court's refusal to apply the doctrine to the private consensual sexual conduct of Michael Hardwick and his partner has more to do with the disposition of the Supreme Court than with any purported defects in the doctrine of constitutional privacy itself.

The first step in response to this claim is to note two crucial and contestable factual predicates on which it may be said to rest. The first assumption is that the relevant focal point for constitutional analysis of the statute challenged in *Hardwick* is, indeed, the time and place of his arrest. The second assumption is that Hardwick was in fact arrested for engaging in the act of homosexual sodomy with which he was formally charged. I want to suggest that both of these assumptions are belied by other, and to my mind, more significant facts of the case. Thus, to the extent that the argument for viewing *Hardwick* in particular through the prism of privacy depends on these empirical premises, it is deeply flawed.

In order to establish this contention, we need to recall certain "public" facts about *Bowers v. Hardwick* that never found their way into the record before the Supreme Court. Taken together, they tell an all too typical story of the gay and lesbian experience under the American legal system. Although we shall have occasion to review that larger history, my immediate theoretical interest is in the local history of the *Hardwick* case itself.[3] When *Hardwick* is viewed in the light of this history, it becomes possible to argue—indeed impossible to deny—that the case presents a number of issues that require a more realistic analysis than the privacy principle can provide.

Michael Hardwick's first encounter with the police power of the state of Georgia took place one morning a block away from the gay bar in Atlanta where he worked. An Atlanta police officer named K.R. Torick stopped Hardwick after seeing him throw a beer bottle into a trashcan outside the bar. As Hardwick recounts the story, the officer "made me get in the car and asked me what I was doing. I told him that I worked there, which immediately identified me as a homosexual, because he knew it was a homosexual bar."[4] Torick then issued Hardwick a ticket for drinking in public. Because of a discrepancy on the ticket between the day and the date he was to appear in court, Hardwick failed to appear. Within two hours of Hardwick's scheduled appearance, Torick went to Hardwick's house with a warrant for his arrest, only to find that he was not at home. When Hardwick returned to his apartment, his roommate told him of the police officer's visit. Hardwick then went to the Fulton County courthouse, where he paid a fifty dollar fine. In Hardwick's words:

> I told the county clerk the cop had already been at my house with a warrant and he said that was impossible. He said it takes forty-eight hours to process a warrant. He wrote me a receipt just in case I had any problems with it further down the road. That was that, and I thought I had taken care of it and everything was finished, and I didn't give it much thought.[5]

Three weeks later, Hardwick arrived home from work to find three men whom he did not know outside his house. In his account of the incident, Hardwick admits that he has no proof that these men were police officers, "but they were very straight, middle thirties, civilian clothes."[6]

> I got out of the car, turned around, and they said "Michael" and I said yes, and they proceeded to beat the hell out of me. Tore all the cartilage out of my nose, kicked me in the face, cracked about six of my ribs. I passed out. I don't know how long I was unconscious. . . . I managed to crawl up the stairs into the house, into the back bedroom. What I didn't realize was that I'd left a trail of blood all the way back.[7]

A few days after this incident, and nearly a month after his first visit, Officer Torick again appeared at Hardwick's home. Torick found Hardwick in his bedroom having sex with another man.

> He said, My name is Officer Torick. Michael Hardwick, you are under arrest. I said, For what? What are you doing in my bedroom? He said, I have a warrant for your arrest. I told him the warrant isn't any good. He said, It doesn't matter, because I was acting under good faith.[8]

Torick handcuffed Hardwick and his partner and took them to jail, where they were booked, fingerprinted, and photographed. As the two men were taken to a holding tank, Hardwick recalls that the arresting officer "made sure everyone in the holding cells and guards and people who were processing us knew I was in there for 'cocksucking' and that I

280 should be able to get what I was looking for. The guards were having a *real* good time with that."[9] Some hours later, Hardwick and his partner were transferred to another part of the building in which he was being held, in the course of which the jail officers made it clear to the other inmates that the men were gay, remarking "Wait until we put [him] into the bullpen. Well, fags shouldn't mind—after all, that's why they are here."[10] Hardwick and his partner remained in jail for the greater part of the day, when friends were permitted to post bail for their release.

Shortly after his release, Hardwick accepted an offer from the Georgia affiliate of the American Civil Liberties Union to undertake his defense in the state courts. Hardwick and his attorneys planned to challenge the constitutionality of the state sodomy law's criminalization of the sexual conduct for which he had been arrested. Before the case came to trial, however, the Fulton County District Attorney declined to seek a grand jury indictment against Hardwick on the sodomy charges. In legal terms, this did not mean that the matter was at an end; the governing statute of limitations rendered Hardwick subject to indictment on the sodomy charges at any time within the next four years. In political terms, it meant that Hardwick (and gays and lesbians throughout the state) continued to be vulnerable to harassment and violence that would likely go unchecked and unchallenged so long as the sodomy statute remained in the Georgia criminal code. Faced with this prospect, Hardwick agreed to take his constitutional claim to the federal courts.

For those who are familiar with the history of sodomy statutes, the story recounted here contains few surprises. *Hardwick* is merely the most visible recent chapter of a larger, unfinished plot.[11] What bears remarking is the degree to which so much of the background biography of *Hardwick* resists translation into the language and logic of sexual privacy. Obviously, I do not want to deny the significance of Hardwick's arrest or discount the importance of the fact that the arrest took place in his bedroom. Nor do I wish to suggest that Officer Torick did not in fact find and arrest Hardwick for engaging in sexual acts prohibited by Georgia criminal law. I mean to make two rather different observations.

The first is that Hardwick's arrest in the privacy of his bedroom was the culmination of a series of events that was set in motion long before, beginning with his public, on-the-street encounter with Officer Torick outside that Atlanta gay bar. A second, related observation is that while Hardwick had certainly engaged in sexual acts punishable by eight to twenty years imprisonment under Georgia law, it is not implausible to think that Hardwick would never have been charged for violating that law had Officer Torick not gone to Hardwick's home to serve the expired warrant. Recall that the first piece of information Hardwick gave Officer Torick outside the bar was about the kind of work he did, not about the kind of sex he practiced. In my view, this aspect of the case provides some basis for a belief that the officer's visit on the day of the arrest had less to do with what Hardwick had done, than with his discovery some weeks before of who and what Hardwick was. Had Michael Hardwick not first been ascribed a homosexual *identity*, it is unlikely that he would ever have been observed or arrested for engaging in prohibited homosexual *acts*.

Two related points of theoretical import are suggested by this sequence of events. First, as a temporal matter, Hardwick's arrest at his home must be situated in a *chronological sequence* whose inaugural moment was the earlier, involuntary revelation of his sexuality during his initial encounter with Officer Torick. Furthermore, an adequate analytical "time chart" of *Hardwick* must also include the bloody beating Hardwick sustained outside his home, as well as the threat of sexualized violence to which he and his partner were deliberately exposed while in police custody. These incidents are not isolable events; they inhabit the same temporal field, whose horizons exceed privacy's chronometry.

Second, as a conceptual matter, when situated in its broader factual context, the formal claim raised and rejected in *Hardwick* must be viewed as a semantic conductor for a complex current of substantive concerns. The criminalization of homosexual sodomy challenged in *Hardwick* belongs to, and must be analyzed as, a *constellation* of diverse practices. My image of homosexual sodomy statutes as the site of a "constellation" of practices is intended to capture the essential inseparability of these laws from the actual methods—public or private, official or unofficial, sanctioned or unsanctioned, act-based or identity-based, instrumental or symbolic—by which the social control of those to whom they are directed is undertaken and achieved. Thus, I am going to take it as a basic premise that the factual background of *Hardwick* undermines the traditional distinction between the formal prohibition of homosexual sodomy and the substantive means by which that prohibition is enforced (or not enforced, as the case may be): form and substance are inextricably linked.

This constellation of prohibitive practices interdicts (homo)social identity *and* (homo)sexual intimacy; enlists the unauthorized, unofficial disciplinary power of private actors *and* the authorized, official police power of state institutions; subjects those designated as "homosexual" to

282   lawless and random aggression and violence *and* lawful and regularized constraint and control; targets the bodies *and* the behavior of those to whom its edicts are directed; enjoins homosexual existence *and* homoerotic acts. Given this complexity, the question becomes whether the factual predicates of the issues presented in *Hardwick* can be cleanly or comprehensively contained within the constitutional category of privacy.

At least three possible answers to this question suggest themselves. One might flatly deny that anything of theoretical consequence flows from what I have said about the public biography of *Hardwick*. This position holds that there is still a close enough conceptual connection between the privacy paradigm and the more public dimensions of *Hardwick* to warrant rejection of an alternative perspective, even if that perspective illuminates aspects of the case that escape the view of privacy. In my view, this position is indefensible. The unmodified privacy framework fails to satisfy a basal requirement that any interpretive model must meet: namely, that the model fit the data it aims to explain.[12] While the resolute refusal to come to grips with *Hardwick*'s public biography may preserve the purity of privacy analysis, the perceived benefits of its preservation entail too great a conceptual cost. We may ignore the mentioned public determinants and dimensions of *Hardwick*, but we cannot erase them altogether: they remain substantive and significant facts of the case.

A second possible response to the claim that *Hardwick* raises issues that cannot be forced into the conceptual grid of the privacy paradigm does not deny the claim's force, but tries instead to deflect it. This response concedes that an adequate constitutional analysis of *Hardwick* cannot justifiably overlook the apparently public features of the case, but rejects the implication that attention to these concerns necessarily entails the abandonment of privacy analysis *tout court*. It begins by noting that the reservations mentioned regarding the value of the privacy model as a framework for analysis of *Hardwick* fail to distinguish between the larger concepts associated with the privacy principle, on the one hand, and the local factual premises that inform its analysis, on the other. With this distinction in mind, one can accept the claim that the factual premises that typically inform privacy thinking overlook the public features of *Hardwick*. At the same time, one can insist that nothing I have said about the contingent factual assumptions of the privacy paradigm warrants repudiation of its core ideas. To put the point another way, one might argue that the basic conceptual framework of privacy analysis is sufficiently elastic to cover these dimensions of *Hardwick*. Our task, then, is simply to reformulate or redescribe the particular public facts of the case in terms that reveal their family resemblance to already acknowledged privacy interests.[13] It is far from clear why this semantic sleight-of-hand is preferable to an open admission that *Hardwick* might be better understood by use of a richer conceptual vocabulary than that which the privacy paradigm is able to offer.

A third response is to contend, as I do, that privacy's narrow temporal and categorical frameworks render it too blunt a tool for the critical task before us.[14] *Hardwick* is not just a story about private homoerotic acts and their interdiction; it is also an account of the harassment, the humiliation, and the violence that await the mere assertion or imputation of homosexual identities and existences in the public sphere. A more extended and unified account of the events that preceded and followed the encounter in Hardwick's bedroom militates toward a broader conception of our analytic object than the privacy principle permits. These events do not simply straddle the boundaries between the public and private; they overrun them altogether. Thus, against the sheer taken-for-grantedness of the view that *Hardwick* is most productively understood within the language and logic of privacy, I would urge that close attention to the public dimensions of *Hardwick* demands analysis in other, more comprehensive terms. We must, in short, force privacy to go public.

The regnant emphasis on abstract, private personhood can never provide more than a partial account of the actual individual against whom homosexual sodomy statutes operate. The constitutional theory we need now must move beyond the axiological premises and perspectives that inform privacy analysis. If the core issue presented by these statutes concerns limitations on the power of the body politic to intervene in the sexual lives of its actual or potential members, it is only fitting that we begin by thinking about the embodied experience of the people who are touched by sodomy laws. It is, after all, the bodies of the individuals that homosexual sodomy laws address that provide the "raw material" on which the police power acts. Reaching a clear understanding of the concrete corporal implications of homosexual sodomy statutes is a crucial task. In order to discharge it, we must be prepared to abandon the assumption that since the laws at issue have to do with sexuality, the language of sexuality ought accordingly to provide the governing terms of analysis. I begin instead from a rather different assumption that the con-

284 ceptual framework that will best enable us to understand the concrete operations of homosexual sodomy law focuses on political power rather than on personal pleasure.

This is a political analysis because it poses and aims to answer one of the most basic questions of our constitutional law: What is the substance of the relationship between the government of the individual and the government of the body politic? Building on an empirical account of the concrete "body politics" of homosexual sodomy law, I want to suggest that the beginnings of an answer to this question may be found in the Cruel and Unusual Punishments Clause of the Eighth Amendment, whose terms allow us to flesh out the rights of "personhood" that privacy analysis so abstractly purports to comprehend. As I read it, the Eighth Amendment is the constitutional marker of a basic political right to be free from state-sanctioned torture and terror. However, the lived experience of gay men and lesbians under the legal regime challenged and upheld in *Bowers v. Hardwick* is one in which government not only passively permits, but actively protects, acts of violence directed toward individuals who are, or are taken to be, homosexual. In my view, this state-legitimized violence represents an unconstitutional abdication of one of the most basic duties of government.

"Choked to Death, Burnt to Ashes": A Political Anatomy of Homophobic Violence

In October 1987, hundreds of people were arrested during the course of a demonstration against the decision in *Bowers v. Hardwick*. Those arrested had participated in a massive act of civil disobedience in which they had literally laid their bodies on the steps outside the Supreme Court building.[15] The protest dramatically underscored the concrete corporal interests that the *Hardwick* Court ignored and evoked the tangible historical experience of gay and lesbian Americans in which the case must be situated.

Stated bluntly, that history is a story of homophobic aggression and ideology. Its central theme is the fear, hatred, stigmatization, and persecution of homosexuals and homosexuality.[16] Over the course of American history, gay men and lesbian women have been discursively marked as "faggots" (after the pieces of kindling used to burn their bodies), "monsters," "fairies," "bull dykes," "perverts," "freaks," and "queers." Their intimate associations have been denominated "abominations," "crimes against nature," and "sins not fit to be named among Christians."[17] This symbolic violence has produced and been produced by congeries of physical violence. Gay men and lesbians in America have been "condemned to death by choking, burning and drowning; ... executed, [castrated], jailed, pilloried, fined, court-martialed, prostituted, fired, framed, blackmailed, disinherited, [lobotomized, shock-treated, psychoanalyzed and] declared insane, driven to insanity, to suicide, murder, and self-hate, witch-hunted, entrapped, stereotyped, mocked, insulted, isolated ... castigated ... despised [and degraded]."[18]

The historical roots of this violence are older than the nation itself. The 1646 Calendar of Dutch Historical Manuscripts reports the trial, conviction, and sentence on Manhattan Island, New Netherland Colony of one Jan Creoli, "a negro, [for] sodomy; second offense; this crime being condemned of God (Gen., c. 19; Levit., c. 18:22, 29) as an abomination, the prisoner is sentenced to be conveyed to the place of public execution, and there choked to death, and then burnt to ashes."[19] On the same date the Calendar records the sentence of "Manuel Congo ... on whom the above abominable crime was committed," whom the Court ordered "to be carried to the place where Creoli is to be executed, tied to a stake, and faggots piled around him, for justice sake, and to be flogged; sentence executed."[20]

The continuity between the seventeenth-century experience and homophobic violence in our own time is startling. A report issued by Community United Against Violence, an organization that monitors incidents of homophobic violence, offers a picture of the violent face of homophobia in contemporary America:

> One man's body was discovered with his face literally beaten off. Another had his jaw smashed into eight pieces by a gang of youths taunting "you'll never suck another cock, faggot!" Another had most of his lower intestine removed after suffering severe stab wounds in the abdomen. Another was stabbed 27 times in the face and upper chest with a screwdriver, which leaves a very jagged scar. Another had both lungs punctured by stab wounds, and yet another had his aorta severed.[21]

Some months before the Supreme Court rendered its judgment in *Hardwick,* the *New York Daily News* printed the story of a homeless gay man in that city who "had his skull crushed by three men who beat him unconscious with two-by-fours while screaming antigay epithets"; the same article recounted an incident in which a motorist "who saw a lesbian standing on a sidewalk in [Manhattan] stopped his car, got out and beat her so badly (while shouting anti-lesbian epithets) that she suffered broken facial bones and permanent nerve damage."[22] Two years after the *Hardwick* decision, the coordinator of a victim assistance program at a New York City hospital reported that "attacks against gay men were the most heinous and brutal I encountered."[23] The hospital routinely treated gay male victims of homophobic violence, whose injuries "frequently involved torture, cutting, mutilation, and beating, and showed the absolute intent to rub out the human being because of his [sexual] orientation."[24]

One would be mistaken to view these stories as aberrant, isolated instances of violence perpetrated by the psychologically imbalanced against individual gay men and women. They are not.[25] All the evidence suggests that there are hundreds, if not thousands of such stories, most of them untold.[26] Violence against gay men and lesbians—on the streets, in the workplace, at home—is a structural feature of life in American society. A study commissioned by the National Institute of Justice (the research arm of the U.S. Department of Justice) concluded that gay men and women "are probably the most frequent victims [of hate violence today]."[27] We may never know the full story of the violence to which gay men and gay women are subjected. In spite of their frequency, it is estimated that a full eighty per-cent of bias violence against gay men and women is never reported to the police.[28] This under-reporting is not surprising, since victims of anti-gay violence have reason to be fearful that the response of state and local officials may be unsympathetic or openly hostile, or that the disclosure of their sexual orientation may lead to further discrimination.[29]

Indeed, government officials and agencies are themselves often complicit in the phenomenon of homophobic violence. Governmental involvement ranges from active instigation to acquiescent indifference. A recent survey of violence against gay men and lesbians cites a 1951 case study of police practices in which a patrolman describes his typical treatment of homosexuals:

> Now in my own cases when I catch a guy like that I just pick him up
> and take him into the woods and beat him until he can't crawl. I have

had seventeen cases like that in the last couple of years. I tell the guy
if I catch him doing that again I will take him out to the woods and I
will shoot him. I tell him that I carry a second gun on me just in case
I find guys like him and that I will plant it in his hand and say that
he tried to kill me and that no jury will convict me.[30]

At October 1986 hearings on homophobic violence convened by the
House of Representatives Committee on the Judiciary, Subcommittee on
Criminal Justice, the district attorney of New York County noted that
"at times, [lesbians and gay men] have been, and in many areas of the
country continue to be, taunted, harassed, and even physically assaulted
by the very people whose job it is to protect them."[31]

Even if we were able to document every instance of homophobic violence in America, our understanding of its effects would still be incom-
plete. To be sure, many men and women in the gay and lesbian
communities have escaped direct physical attack by perpetrators of
homophobic violence. However, the horror and sinister efficacy of homophobic violence are in many ways like those of racist violence. Like people of color, gay men and lesbians always and everywhere have to live
their lives on guard, knowing that they are vulnerable to attack at any
time. As one observer has noted, "being gay means living with the reality that although you may not personally be the victim of outright homophobic attacks every day, at any moment you could be attacked—walking
down the street, going to work, on the job, shopping, or in a restau-
rant."[32] Indeed, much of the efficacy of homophobic violence lies in the
message it conveys to those who are not its immediate victims.

In this respect, homophobic violence bears many of the characteristics
associated with terrorism. As in the case of terrorism, much of the force
of violence against gay men and lesbians lies in its randomness: individuals may know that the assertion or ascription of gay or lesbian identity
marks them as potential targets of homophobic violence, but they cannot
know until too late whether or when they will actually be hit. Like the
terrorist, the perpetrator of homophobic violence strikes without giving
warning.[33] A second characteristic common to terrorism and homophobic violence is its utter impersonality. Like perpetrators of terrorist acts,
those who attack gays and lesbians do not know, and are most often
unknown to, their victims.[34]

Another feature that homophobic violence shares with terrorism is its
"communicative" thrust.[35] Although attacks on gays and lesbians might

288 be random and impersonal, such attacks are far from meaningless. The communicative dimensions of homophobic violence may be seen on a number of levels. Survivors of homophobic violence have reported that their attackers verbally expressed hatred of homosexuality, boasted of heterosexuality, or otherwise taunted them.[36] However, in most instances, perpetrators of violence against gays and lesbians have no need to resort to language to communicate: the expressive force of the violence itself makes verbal communication unnecessary. One of the most salient features of homophobic violence is its excessive brutality. In hearings before the San Francisco Board of Supervisors, a physician at a hospital in that city testified that the "vicious" nature of injuries sustained by the victims of homophobic violence he had treated left no doubt that "the intent is to kill and maim":

> Weapons include knives, guns, brass knuckles, tire irons, baseball bats, broken bottles, metal chains, and metal pipes. Injuries include severe lacerations requiring extensive plastic surgery; head injuries, at times requiring surgery; puncture wounds of the chest, requiring insertion of chest tubes; removal of the spleen for traumatic rupture; multiple fractures of the extremities, jaws, ribs, and facial bones; severe eye injuries, in two cases resulting in permanent loss of vision; as well as severe psychological trauma the level of which would be difficult to measure.[37]

One study of homophobic murders found that in most instances, the victims were not just killed, but were "more apt to be stabbed a dozen or more times, mutilated, *and* strangled, ... [and] [i]n a number of instances, ... stabbed or mutilated even after being fatally shot."[38] The characteristic "overkill and excessive mutilation"[39] of attacks on gay men and lesbians suggest that this is a species of violence whose form conveys its expressive content: the medium is the message.

The terroristic dimensions of homophobic violence compel us to understand it as a mode of power. To put the point in slightly different terms, homophobic violence is a form of "institution," in the sense that John Rawls elaborates that concept.[40] Homophobic violence is a social activity "structured by rules that define roles and positions, powers and opportunities, thereby distributing responsibility for consequences."[41] Viewed systemically, the objective and outcome of violence against lesbians and gays is the social control of human sexuality. Homophobic violence aims to regulate the erotic economy of contemporary American

society,[42] or more specifically, to enforce the institutional and ideological
imperatives of what Adrienne Rich has termed "compulsory heterosexuality."[43] Insofar as homophobic violence functions to prevent and punish
actual or imagined deviations from heterosexual acts and identities, it
carries a determinate political valence and value.

In order to grasp the relations of political power that underlie the phenomenon of homophobic violence, we may draw on Elaine Scarry's
analysis of the practice of torture in *The Body in Pain*.[44] Her remarks
regarding the politically instrumental functions of torture are especially
relevant in this context. Scarry contends that "the display of final product and outcome of torture" is "the fiction of power."[45] She suggests that
a central component of torture inheres in its

> translation of all the objectified elements of pain into the insignia of
> power, the conversion of the enlarged map of human suffering into
> an emblem of the [torturer's] strength. This translation is made possible by, and occurs across, the phenomenon common to both power
> and pain: agency. The electric generator, the whips and canes, the
> torturer's fists, the walls, the doors, the [victim's] sexuality, the torturer's questions, the institution of medicine, the [victim's] screams,
> his wife and children, the telephone, the chair, a trial, a submarine,
> the [victim's] eardrums—all these and many more, everything
> human and inhuman that is either physically or verbally, actually or
> allusively present, has become part of the glutted realm of weaponry,
> weaponry that can refer equally to pain or power. What by the one is
> experienced as a continual contraction is for the other a continual
> expansion, for the torturer's growing sense of self is carried outward
> on the prisoner's swelling pain.[46]

The purpose of torture is quite literally to embody relations of domination and subjugation. It is precisely this feature of the practice that
requires us to view torture as a "political situation."[47]

Scarry's observations about the political character of torture provide a
useful framework for analyzing the political dimensions of homophobic
violence. To extrapolate from Scarry's analysis, the body of the victim of
homophobic violence is an environment for the practice of brutal "biopolitics."[48] The terrorization of gay men and lesbian women through
homophobic violence dramatizes two intersecting political relationships.
The first is the internal relation between perpetrators of homophobic violence and their victims. The second is the external relation in which both

victims and torturers stand to the political regime that variously incites, aids or allows homophobic violence to take place. This latter relation forces the recognition that homophobic violence at one and the same time expresses the power of the perpetrator of that violence and the power of the regime that the perpetrator represents. The person of the torturer (and the torturer's weapon) is the agency through which the strategy of the regime finds its substantive shape and force. If we were to use the conventional language of American constitutional law, we might say then that violence inscribed on the bodies of gay men and lesbians constitutes an extra-legal exercise of police power.

I have argued that homophobic violence is an exercise of political power. I have suggested that the purpose of this violence is to terrorize the population to whom its victims belong. I have also referred to the record of state instigation of, and acquiescence in, the phenomenon of homophobic violence. I have begun to explore the constitutional implications of the connection between governmental instigation of and acquiescence in criminal attacks on gay men and lesbians on the one hand, and criminal statutes against homosexual sodomy on the other. It might be said that the coincidence of the law of homosexual sodomy and the lawlessness of homophobic violence by itself presents a question with which a constitutional analysis of these statutes must reckon.

However, I hope by now to have said enough to clear the ground for a somewhat stronger claim. I contend that the involvement of the state in the phenomenon of homophobic violence is in fact no coincidence at all. A close examination of the political terror directed against gay men and lesbians suggests that the relationship between homosexual sodomy law and homophobic violence is not merely coincident, but coordinate: the criminalization of homosexual sodomy and criminal attacks on gay men and lesbians work in tandem. My task, of course, is to specify the terms of their coordinal interaction. How should we think about the role the state plays in permitting, promoting or participating in homophobic violence?

I have already begun to indicate the direction such an analysis might take. Given the brute physical fact that homophobic violence aims to deform, and often utterly destroy, its targets, I believe that the Eighth Amendment prohibition against "cruel and unusual punishments" provides the most appropriate constitutional and conceptual foundation for specifying the nature of the relationship between homophobic violence and the laws against homosexual sodomy, and for stating the grounds on which a judicial invalidation of those laws might be justified.

Notes

1. The pre-*Hardwick* literature is voluminous. Participants in the debate include Hyman Gross, *The Concept of Privacy*, 42 N.Y.U. L. REV. 34 (1967); Paul Freund, *Privacy: One Concept or Many*, in PRIVACY: NOMOS XIII 182 (1972); Richard B. Parker, *A Definition of Privacy*, 27 RUTGERS L. REV. 275 (1974); Louis Henkin, *Privacy and Autonomy*, 74 COLUM. L. REV. 1410 (1974); Judith Jarvis Thomson, *The Right to Privacy*, 4 PHIL. & PUB. AFF. 295 (1975); Thomas Scanlon, *Thomson on Privacy*, 4 PHIL. & PUB. AFF. 315 (1975); Gary L. Bostwick, Comment, *A Taxonomy of Privacy: Repose, Sanctuary, and Intimate Decision*, 64 CAL. L. REV. 1447 (1976); Jeffrey H. Reiman, *Privacy, Intimacy and Personhood*, 6 PHIL. & PUB. AFF. 26 (1976); Charles Fried, *Correspondence*, 6 PHIL. & PUB. AFF. 288 (1977); Tom Gerety, *Redefining Privacy*, 12 HARV. C.R.–C. L. L. REV. 233 (1977); June Eichbaum, *Towards an Autonomy-Based Theory of Constitutional Privacy: Beyond the Ideology of Familial Privacy*, 14 HARV. C.R.–C. L. L. REV. 361 (1979). The classical theoretical formulation of the case for legal recognition of a right to privacy may of course be found in Samuel D. Warren & Louis D. Brandeis, *The Right to Privacy*, 4 HARV. L. REV. 193 (1890).

2. 381 U.S. 479 (1965) (striking down Connecticut's prohibition against birth control as a violation of a constitutionally protected right of privacy).

3. I shall forego an elaborate methodological defense of my "on the ground" account of the background facts of *Hardwick*, or of my reliance on Michael Hardwick's personal narrative of the case. For a theoretical discussion of the value of constitutional analysis "from the bottom" see my *Rouge et Noir Re-read: A Popular History of* Herndon v. Georgia, 65 S. CAL. L. REV. 2599 (1992).

4. PETER IRONS, THE COURAGE OF THEIR CONVICTIONS 394 (1988).

5. *Id.*

6. *Id.* at 395.

7. *Id.*

8. *Id.* at 395-96.

9. *Id.* at 396.

10. LAURENCE II. TRIBE, AMERICAN CONSTITUTIONAL LAW 1424 n. 32 (2d ed. 1988).

11. *See, e.g.*, Project, *The Consenting Adult Homosexual and the Law: An Empirical Study of Enforcement and Administration in Los Angeles County*, 13 UCLA L. REV. 643 (1966); Anne B. Goldstein, *History, Homosexuality, and Political Values: Searching for the Hidden Determinants of* Bowers v. Hardwick, 97 YALE L. J. 1073 (1988).

12. For a similar argument, see Richard B. Parker, *A Definition of Privacy*, 27 RUTGERS L. REV. 275, 276 (1974).

13. We might, on good precedential authority, view Hardwick's initial encounter with Officer Torick as one in which Hardwick may be said to have had an "expectation of privacy." Katz v. United States, 389 U.S. 347, 361 (1967) (Harlan, J., concurring).

14. For two very different discussions of the relation between the choice of temporal framework and the terms of legal analysis, see BRUCE ACKERMAN, RECONSTRUCTING AMERICAN LAW 47–71 (1984); Mark Kelman, *Interpretive Construction in the Substantive Criminal Law*, 33 STAN. L. REV. 591, 593–94 (1981).

15. *See* Scott Tucker, *Gender, Fucking and Utopia*, 27 SOC. TEXT 3, 21–22 (1990).

292   16. For explications of the concept of homophobia, see JONATHAN DOLLIMORE, SEXUAL DISSIDENCE 233–34 (1991); WAYNE DYNES, HOMOLEXIS: A HISTORICAL AND CULTURAL LEXICON OF HOMOSEXUALITY 67 (1985).

17. *See* JONATHAN KATZ, GAY AMERICAN HISTORY: LESBIANS AND GAY MEN IN THE U.S.A. 11, 22–23, 44, 127–28 (1976).

18. *Id.* at 11.

19. *Id.* at 22–23.

20. *Id.* at 23.

21. DAVID F. GREENBERG, THE CONSTRUCTION OF HOMOSEXUALITY 467 (1988) (quoting Ron Wickliffe, *Queerbashers Meet Resistance in the Streets of San Francisco,* WIN, Aug. 31, 1981).

22. Bob Herbert, *War Against Gays: Stories from the Battlefield,* N.Y. DAILY NEWS, Jan. 30, 1986, at 42.

23. Violence Project, National Gay and Lesbian Task Force, Anti-Gay Violence, Victimization and Defamation in 1988, at 8 (1988).

24. *Id.*

25. A survey of anti-gay violence and harassment in eight major cities revealed some remarkable figures. 86.2% of the gay men and women surveyed stated that they had been attacked verbally; 44.2% reported that they had been threatened with violence; 27.3% had had objects thrown at them; 34.9% had been chased or followed; 13.9% had been spit at; 19.2% had been punched, hit, kicked, or beaten; 9.3% had been assaulted with a weapon; 18.5% had been the victims of property vandalism or arson; 30.9% reported sexual harassment, many by members of their own families or by the police. National Gay Task Force, Anti-Gay/Lesbian Victimization 24 (June 1984).

26. For a summary of this evidence, see GARY O. COMSTOCK, VIOLENCE AGAINST LESBIANS AND GAY MEN 31–90 (1991); HATE CRIMES: CONFRONTING VIOLENCE AGAINST LESBIANS AND GAY MEN (Gregory M. Herek & Kevin T. Berrill eds., 1992) [hereinafter HATE CRIMES].

27. PETER FINN & TAYLOR MCNEIL, THE RESPONSE OF THE CRIMINAL JUSTICE SYSTEM TO BIAS CRIME: AN EXPLORATORY REVIEW 2 (1987). Because of media reports regarding the conclusion reached in this study relating to the incidence of homophobic violence, this report was suppressed by the Department of Justice. *See* Kevin T. Berrill & Gregory M. Herek, *Primary and Secondary Victimization in Anti-Gay Hate Crimes: Official Response and Public Policy, in* HATE CRIMES, *supra* note 26, at 292.

28. *See Anti-Gay Violence: Hearings Before the Subcomm. on Criminal Justice of the House Comm. on the Judiciary,* 99th Cong., 2d Sess. 2, 35 (1986) (testimony of Kevin Berrill, Director, Violence Project, National Gay and Lesbian Task Force).

29. Richard Mohr has argued that this condition demands passage of state and federal legislation forbidding certain forms of discrimination on the basis of sexual orientation. *See* Richard Mohr, *Invisible Minorities, Civic Rights, Democracy: Three Arguments for Gay Rights,* 17 PHIL. F. 1, 2, 5 (1985).

30. Comstock, *supra* note 26, at 153. A recent summary of several studies of homophobic harassment and violence reports that some 20% of the lesbians and gay men surveyed reported victimization at the hands of the police. *See* Kevin T. Berrill, *Anti-Gay Violence and Victimization in the United States: An Overview, in* HATE CRIMES, *supra* note 26, at 31–32 (summarizing studies conducted between 1977 and 1991).

31. *Anti-Gay Violence: Hearings Before the Subcomm. on Criminal Justice of the House Comm. on the Judiciary,* 99th Cong., 2d Sess. 2, 108 (1986) (statement of Robert M. Morgenthau).

32. Mary Fridley, *Homophobia and the Rise of Neo-Fascism in the United States,* 3 PRAC. 35, 40 (1985).

33. For a discussion of randomness as a value in the general economy of terrorism, see Jan Narveson, *Terrorism and Morality, in* VIOLENCE, TERRORISM, AND JUSTICE 116, 119 (R.G. Frey & Christopher W. Morris eds., 1991).

34. *See* COMSTOCK, *supra* note 26, at 57–58.

35. For a discussion of the "communicative purposes" of terrorism, see R.D. Crelinsten, *Terrorism as Political Communication, in* CONTEMPORARY RESEARCH ON TERRORISM 3, 6-14 (Paul Wilkinson & Alasdair M. Stewart eds., 1987).

36. *See* COMSTOCK, *supra* note 26, at 67–69.

37. *Id.* at 46.

38. *Id.* at 47 (quoting Brian Miller & Laud Humphreys, *Lifestyles and Violence: Homosexual Victims of Assault and Murder,* 3 QUALITATIVE SOC. 169, 179 (1980)). Miller and Humphreys further found that although stabbing was the chief cause of death in only 18% of all homicides during the period they studied, in murders involving gay or lesbian victims, stabbing was the main cause of death in 54% of the cases. *See id.*

39. *Id.*

40. *See* JOHN RAWLS, A THEORY OF JUSTICE 55 (1971) (defining "institution" as "a public system of rules which defines officers and positions with their rights and duties, powers and immunities and the like").

41. I take this language from Claudia Card, *Rape as a Terrorist Institution, in* VIOLENCE, TERRORISM, AND JUSTICE, *supra* note 33, at 297–98.

42. In this respect, the experience of gay men and lesbians is like that of countless African-Americans tortured and murdered by Euro-American lynching parties. Studies of the practice have noted the perverted eroticism at its core. The archetypal lynching was often justified by charges that the (usually black male) victim had raped a white woman. "The fear of rape was more than a hypocritical excuse for lynching; rather, the two phenomena were intimately intertwined. The 'southern rape complex' functioned as a means of both sexual and racial suppression." Jacquelyn Dowd Hall, *"The Mind That Burns in Each Body": Women, Rape and Racial Violence,* in POWERS OF DESIRE: THE POLITICS OF SEXUALITY 177, 335 (Ann Snitow et al. eds., 1983). Hall quotes from the testimony of a member of a 1934 lynch mob: "After taking the nigger to the woods … they cut off his penis. He was made to eat it. Then they cut off his testicles and made him eat them and say he liked it." *Id.* at 329 (quoting HOWARD KESTER, THE LYNCHING OF CLAUDE NEAL (1934)).

43. *See* Adrienne Rich, *Compulsory Heterosexualtiy and Lesbian Existence, in* POWERS OF DESIRE: THE POLITICS OF SEXUALITY, *supra* note 42, at 177, 178–81; *see also* Gary Kinsman, *Men Loving Men: The Challenge of Gay Liberation, in* BEYOND PATRIARCHY 103, 104–05 (Michael Kaufman ed., 1987) (development of heterosexuality as an institutional norm serves as an important means of social regulation).

44. ELAINE SCARRY, THE BODY IN PAIN (1985).

45. *Id.* at 57.

46. *Id.* at 56.

47. A stunning literary evocation of torture as a corporealized "graphics" of political power may be found in Franz Kafka's 1919 short story, *In the Penal Colony.* Kafka describes an elaborate death machine that simultaneously enacts and inscribes its "sentence." The colony punishes the individual who has disobeyed one of its commandments by mechanically writing the law on the flesh of the transgressor's body until he dies. *See* FRANZ KAFKA, THE METAMORPHOSIS, THE PENAL COLONY, AND OTHER STORIES 191 (Willa Muir & Edwin Muir trans., 1948).

48. I take this term from Michel Foucault. MICHEL FOUCAULT, THE HISTORY OF SEXUALITY 140–41 (Robert Hurley trans., 1980)

CHAPTER FIFTEEN

> ⊷·∘·⊷ <

ON TERRORISM

REFLECTIONS ON VIOLENCE AND THE OUTLAW

Ileana M. Porras

SCARCELY A WEEK goes by without at least one terrorist-related incident making the headlines. The subject of terrorism has, meanwhile, engendered a vast and growing expert literature. Much of this vast body of literature is pragmatic in nature, in the sense that the authors are concerned with developing policy proposals. They present and analyze the problem of terrorism and then promote what they think is the appropriate response to terrorists, a response that often involves changing the legal framework. The bulk of what I call "terrorism literature" is produced in the "West." For the most part, it is written from the perspective that terrorism is a threat to Western liberal democracies. For purposes of this essay, I have limited my inquiry to such literature and to terrorism as a Western phenomenon.

This essay explores the repetition of rhetorical structures in terrorism literature and their reproduction in media reports of terrorist incidents. The choice of focus is dictated by the belief that terrorism is not just an objective "something" out there to be located with a telescope and examined with a microscope, but that it is also, less obviously, a creation or by-product of Western liberal democracies; that it is intimately linked with the self-image or self-understanding of Western liberal democracies.

The claim that terrorism is a creation or by-product of Western liberal democracies should not be mistaken for the simple claim that "terrorism does not exist" or that "it's all politics, and one man's terrorist is another's freedom fighter." Rather, it is a claim about the origin of the concept of terrorism—not an origin that can be pinpointed in time but a continuing process of origination. It is a claim about the complex function that terrorism has come to perform *vis-à-vis* Western democracies. It is a claim about the way terrorism has come to be the thing against which liberal Western democracies define themselves; about the way terrorism has come to be the repository of everything that cannot be allowed to fit inside the self-image of democracy; and about the way the terrorist has become the "other" that threatens and desires the annihilation of the democratic "self" and an external force against which democracies therefore must strenuously defend. Exploring the rhetorical structures of terrorism literature and media reports provides insight into the meaning and function of terrorism for liberal Western democracies and a means of evaluating our response to terrorism.

In reflecting on terrorism, I seek also to pursue a second inquiry: the question of why critical scholars writing about international law are drawn to themes of violence and the outsider. One obvious response would be that we are simply pursuing the trajectory first traced out by Freud of examining that which is suppressed. One commonly asserted justificatory purpose for international law is the control or suppression of violence, religious passion, the irrational and the exotic/erotic. But imperfectly suppressed, these are constantly threatening to re-enter (and extinguish) the realm of international law. From this perspective, international law might be understood to be engaged in a perpetual struggle for predominance, only just managing to hold at bay its desiring (and desired) exiles. To focus on violence and the outsider is thus a critical strategy that places international law on the couch, in the hopes of healing it by making it acknowledge and come to terms with its violent and passionate fantasies.

At a more prosaic level, another reason for the focus by critical international law scholars on violence might be that we, like everybody else, find ourselves drawn to the subject of violence by the commonly held belief (and the surprisingly seductive notion) that real law is that law

296   which helps our societies maintain or establish order by restraining the chaotic passions otherwise manifested as violence. Thus at the national level we might ultimately believe that real law is criminal law while at the international level we could conclude that real international law is international law about violence. Such a response is not as uninteresting as it might at first seem. The interest of such a response lies in its connection to, even perhaps its derivation from, our deeply held conviction that violence, at least, is real: that violence matters; that the "real" occurs, is discernible, identifiable, recognizable at the moment that violence erupts. Violence, we say, is not just talk. Violence traverses the body leaving traces of its passage. If anything is real, it is the pain of violence. If anything is real, it is the viscerality of death. Violence makes us serious. We righteously condemn those who display a frivolous attitude toward violence (toward real violence on real bodies). Real violence elicits a real reaction (anger) and a real response (law and its correlative: legitimate violence). Forbidden violence thus unleashes approved violence. In the face of violence we have to act. We cannot simply stand by and watch dispassionately. "People are getting killed out there!" If critical scholars are drawn to write about violence in international law, then, it could be because we seek to understand how this connection between violence and the real relates to the development of international law and the consciousness of international law scholars.

In my work, I approach international law as a cultural production—our cultural production—and recognize within it and through it our fascination, our obsession with violence and the outsider. In looking at popular and expert literature about terrorism, I have found that international law plays an important role in forging an intimate and seemingly indissoluble connection between our cultural experience of violence and our images of the outsider (or outlaw). This essay seeks to explore both the construction and the cultural power of this connection between violence and the outlaw and to suggest some of the ways this connection might relate to our own cultural narratives about national identity and democracy.

Reading Terrorism

In looking at both popular and expert literature on terrorism, I have been struck by the way a double project emerges. In both of these literatures, the terrorist is rhetorically transformed from an ordinary deviant into a frightening foreign/barbaric/beast at the same time that extra-normal means are called for to fight terrorism. For example, those wanting the government to take extra-ordinary measures against abortion clinic demonstrators are likely to adopt the terminology of terrorism,[1] and those wanting the government to take extra-ordinary measures against environmental activists do the same.[2] To label a person, group or activity "terrorist" serves not just as a shorthand description, nor even simply as a statement of moral indignation, but primarily as a call to action, a demand for elimination.

Some of the most frequently used mechanisms to transform the terrorist into a creature quite distinct from us are nicely illustrated by Gideon Rafael in the following passage:

> [T]errorism is the crassest antithesis to democracy. It is the attempt to subjugate and pervert the will of the people and its elected leadership by a minute bunch of reckless people resorting to terrifying threats and unbridled violence. They say they kill for the cause. What is that cause? Liberty from oppression? Freedom from want? Justice for a people? If that would be their cause, how could they plot the extermination of another people, terrorize their own kinsmen and stuff their war chests with oil money from Saudi Arabia, to finance the assault against the regimes of these countries? Their cause is killing. Their vocation is violence.
>
> They are not the avant-garde of a popular upsurge, but a fiendish fringe which worships violence and despises humanity.
>
> They are part of an international demolition squad disguised as freedom fighters, presented by perverted publicity as glamorous guerrillas, idolized by a disoriented community of alienated adolescents. They are the outlet for uncontrolled savage passions.[3]

First comes the claim that terrorism is the "antithesis of democracy"; both can therefore not concurrently exist. By necessity one threatens or extinguishes the other. Since democracy is good, terrorism must be evil. Terrorism, we are told, "subjugates and perverts"; these are images of domination and perversion. Terrorists are "reckless" and resort to "unbridled violence." They are out of control. They "plot the extermination of another people"; they are heartless, cruel and extreme and seek the total destruction of their "other," that is, "us." They "terrorize their own kinsmen"; they do not even recognize family ties, the most basic human allegiance. "A fiendish fringe which worships violence and despises humanity," they are devils or devil worshipers and outside the human family. "[T]he outlet for uncontrolled savage passions," they are everything that civilization was created to suppress. They threaten us with falling back into our primitive and savage past.

Although we, the readers, might be tempted by such an outpouring of invective to ask the author what prompted him to say these things, to ask him what evidence he has in support of the appropriateness of his language and his images, we are unlikely actually to challenge him. Even if we think that he really is going a bit far, exaggerating for the sake of dramatic effect, we will hesitate to contradict him. One problem for the critic of name calling as a form of argument is that the literature on terrorism is so full of hyperbole, of hintings and suggestions, of drama and emotion, that to criticize this instance is to take on the whole genre.

An Interlude for the Normative Bind

> The term ["terrorism"] is somewhat "Humpty Dumpty"—anything we choose it to be.[4]

Although it has become popular in the terrorism literature to refer to "terrorism" as being Humpty Dumpty, this seems to be inaccurate. Humpty Dumpty said that a word would mean whatever he wanted it to mean. With "terrorism," on the contrary, everyone means the same thing. What changes is not the meaning of the word but rather the groups and activities that each person would include or exclude from the list. Everyone uses the word "terrorism" to mean a kind of violence of which he or she doesn't approve and about which he or she wants something to be done. The sense of the word always stays the same; it is the referents that change.

How the word terrorism came to be understood universally as pejorative is an interesting question that I will not attempt to answer here. But it is important to examine the implications of the word's inevitably pejorative sense. To say anything about terrorism or terrorists, it turns out, is to be caught in a normative bind: one must either be for or against terrorism. In terrorism discourse, if I am not explicitly against terrorism then I am necessarily for it. There is no middle ground, no ambivalent position available. Not to condemn terrorism is to condone it,[5] and to condone terrorism is to be morally as bad as a terrorist.[6] Indeed to publicly sympathize with terrorism may itself become a terrorist offence.[7]

Thus I find that there is really only one legitimate position that I may hold *vis-à-vis* terrorism and terrorists. I must think terrorism a great evil. This is so even though, or especially because, "[t]he term has no precise and completely accepted definition ... [because] the United Nations [ ] has been unable to agree on a definition of the term"[8] and "[n]o one definition of terrorism has gained universal acceptance."[9]

The normative bind is not easily escaped. I might seek to avoid the problem by saying, for example, that: "Euskadi ta Askatasuna (ETA),[10] in Spain, is a resistance movement whose political purpose is the establishment of a Basque homeland." Although I have not used the word terrorism, I cannot escape it. I am immediately faced with two problems. The first is that, because the words terrorism/terrorist are commonly used to refer to ETA, it will be assumed that my choice of referring to ETA as a "resistance movement" is a pro-ETA statement condoning ETA's activities (although I intended no such thing.) The second is that since ETA is officially/legally declared a terrorist organization, I could be making myself liable to prosecution as a terrorist sympathizer, even if I, in good faith, would not include ETA in my list of terrorists, and yet in fact condemn their acts. The power of the terms terrorism and terrorist thus reach out well beyond their immediately apparent borders. In other words, even though it seems each of us is free to establish the content or reference of the terms terrorism/terrorist, their pejorative sense constrains us at all times, imposing meanings not necessarily intended.

After the Interlude:
Techniques for Transforming
the Terrorist into an Other

Transformation Through Violence

> The U.S. contends that [Mahmud Abouhalima] is the epitome of the modern terrorist, a self-made commando pursuing a homemade agenda to disrupt Western civilization.[11]

Terrorism literature and media reports are replete with statements about the threat that terrorists and terrorism pose to civilization and democracy. The question of how exactly this threat is posed, however, is rarely explored. But the seriousness of the threat is often asserted by reference to violence.

A recurring problem that arises for authors on terrorism is the need to distinguish terrorist violence from other kinds of violence. The terrorist should not be said to be using run of the mill kinds of violence, the everyday kind of violence that affects the citizens of our democracies in a matter of fact way; the violence that we have come to live with. If the violence of terrorism is not distinguishable, then the average terrorist may not seem much worse (if not any better) than the average rapist, murderer, robber or vandal.

An emphasis on the almost metaphysical "innocence" of the terrorist victim is one powerful mechanism that makes terrorist violence different. Indeed terrorism and terrorist violence is often defined in relation to the "innocence" of its victims.[12] Victims of common criminals may be innocent (although we are often quick to blame the victim: the rape victim was asking for it—she was too seductive; the murder victim probably deserved it—he was a bad lot; and the robbery victim was careless—he didn't take sufficient precautionary measures). The terrorist victim is on the contrary doubly innocent. S/he is inherently innocent (not to blame as a victim) but also s/he is innocent because s/he is in some sense sacrificed and sacrificial victim. Sacrificed by the terrorists because s/he stood for the things they despise. Sacrificed in that if our governments had taken strong action against terrorists, as they should have, s/he would not have been a victim. While rhetorically crime often confers guilt on its victims, terrorism always confers innocence. Emphasizing the tragic innocence of terrorist victims serves to distinguish the outrageous and intolerable violence of terrorism from the mundane violence of the everyday. Highlighting the special innocence of terrorist victims also serves to heighten the urgency of the call to action, since the government, through its inaction, is implicated in the innocent victim's death or suffering.

Transformation Through Links to Traditional Enemies, Foreign Ideologies and Pre-Rational Beliefs

Until recently, before the much vaunted end of the cold war, a popular mechanism used to transform the terrorist into a frightening enemy "other" was through the implication that he was directly related to the Soviet Union, to communism or to both. The connection between the Soviet Union, communism and terrorism was sometimes made explicitly and dramatically and sometimes subtly suggested. All terrorist trails at the time of the cold war, it seems, led to Moscow. The force of the "otherness"-creating power of "communism" cannot be overestimated. The saying "[b]etter dead than red," though it has lost some of its currency, does capture the very real fear that communism even today evokes in many Western minds. In some Western liberal democracies, the effect of labelling someone a "communist" may still be almost as harmful as labelling him a "terrorist." Both, for instance, are excludable under the U.S. Immigration and Nationality Act.[13]

The linking of terrorism to communism by Western democracies during the cold war served several ideological purposes. First, the threat posed by each "ism" individually was greatly enhanced by its association with the other. Thus a terrorist seemed more threatening if he was also a communist. His political objective was made both more coherent and more credible by such an association: more coherent because it could then be understood as part of a carefully worked out, powerful and effective political philosophy, and more credible because of the material and logistic support that became presumptively available. At the same time, the demonization of communism was enhanced. As the credibility of the Soviet threat was waning, as the picture of a unidimensional evil Soviet was being displaced by an almost human representation, full of ambivalence, the connection still drawn between terrorism and communism helped reclaim some of the lost territory. The invocation of horrific images of terrorist atrocities, of the total moral degeneracy of the terrorist, powerfully reinvested the Soviets and communism with evil. It helped discredit the still-communist Michael Gorbachev's claim of wanting good relations with the United States and other Western liberal democracies. From the point of view of objectifying the terrorist, the foremost advantage of using the technique of imaginatively linking terrorism and communism was that it provided a ready made and easily assimilable way of both characterizing and explaining terrorism. To the question "why do terrorists do what they do?" a sufficient answer became "because they are communists." The heuristic use of communism eliminated the need to analyze the phenomenon further.

The assertion of the close relationship between religious fanaticism and terrorism has also become an important method of establishing the difference between them and us. Fanaticism is not something we ever attribute to ourselves. We are patriotic. They are fanatical. To be a fanatic is to be pre-rational. To be a fanatic is to be incapable of heroism. To go on a suicide mission if you are a religious fanatic is to be crazy and deluded, not heroic. Crazy and deluded people are frightening. They are

302   capable of anything. We have to do something about them. It is those
kind of people who would be capable of dropping a nuclear bomb. Like
communism, religious fanaticism serves the heuristic function of explaining terrorism.

The terrorist is always "enemy." The trick is to locate him in the category of the most terrifying traditional enemy, that one which the public
is accustomed to think of as the barbarous and primitive outsider. The
enemy of legend and history books, the bloodthirsty invader of our collective imagination and individual nightmares. The moslem moorish
turkish invader of europe dark mysterious turban wearing merciless
scimitar wielding head cutting harem keeping mosque going minaret
prayer chanting magician christian hating jerusalem prophanator holy
war maker of the past has made a remarkable comeback.

Images of "Islamic fundamentalists" as terrorist fanatics who have
infiltrated our country in order to organize secret conspiracies of destruction and terror have come to replace communists in the public imagination of the United States. So closely have the ideas of terrorism and
Islamic fundamentalism come to be connected that the U.S. State
Department, in its *Patterns of Global Terrorism 1992*, issues the following
disclaimer:

> Adverse mention in this report of individual members of any politi-
> cal, social, ethnic, religious, or national group is not meant to imply
> that all members of that group are terrorists. Indeed, terrorists rep-
> resent a small minority of dedicated, often fanatical, individuals in
> most such groups. It is that small group—and their actions—that is
> the subject of this report.[14]

Although the disclaimer does not specify what group or groups it is concerned about, it is not difficult to conclude that the reference is to Islamic
fundamentalists and perhaps to Muslims more broadly. Meritorious
though it is, this disclaimer is belied by the images in the text itself. The
report, which purports to provide a global picture of international terrorism in 1992, includes eight photographs, three on the cover and five
within the text.[15] Of the eight photographs, six depict persons or incidents related to Islamic fundamentalism. Of these six, three depict men
wearing turbans and robes.

The image of terrorists as Arabic fanatics is ubiquitous in the media.
So ubiquitous is this image that the *New Yorker*, in its July 26, 1993
issue, depicts on its cover four children playing at the beach. In multi-

cultural harmony, three children—one African-American, one Hispanic, one Caucasian—build an elaborate sand castle (reminiscent of New York) from which two towers loom prominently. The children gape in horror as a fourth child, wearing Arab headdress and dark glasses, leaps onto the towers. The illustration carries the caption "Castles in the Sand" in the credits.[16] There is no mention of terrorism in the magazine. The illustration needs, it seems, no explanation. It stands alone.

The focus on terrorists wearing turbans or Arab headdress in the popular press is evocative. For example, the American public has been presented with image after image of the blind Sheik Omar Abdel Rahman.[17] Although Rahman has to date not been accused of any violent act, only of inciting others to violence or of condoning such violence, he has become the familiar face of terrorism:

> The striking thing about Sheik Omar Abdel Rahman as he was led by guards into federal court in Manhattan last week was not that he seemed a strange and exotic figure in his clerical robes, dark glasses and red and white turban. Rather it was that he was entirely familiar—the one of the fifteen defendants accused in a terrorist conspiracy on American soil who was immediately recognizable.[18]

It is his turbaned and robed blindness that is immediately familiar. He is more recognizable than the other fourteen accused co-conspirators because he is bedecked with the attributes of his frightening otherness, the turban and the robe of the Islamic Jihad. The turban and the robe of the cruel Ottoman. The turban and the robe of that other fanatic, nemesis of the west, the Ayatollah Khomeini. Sheik Rahman is frequently described as blind, self-exiled and smiling. These are the further attributes of his fanaticism. The blindness of terrorist violence is visibly conveyed. Sheik Rahman's exile is rendered suspicious. He was not forced out, but chose to leave, we are told. He is thus not a refugee but a fugitive. The Sheik's capacity to continue smiling, in the face of the horrors of which he is accused, suggests that he is "crazy" and/or morally degenerate and, therefore, dangerous.

The Terrorist as Nomad
and the Fear of Porous Borders

In describing and displaying these fanatical terrorists we slip not quite consciously into familiar images that reinforce our sense of endangerment.

304   Thus, shortly after the World Trade Center bombing, Mohammed A.
Salameh, "an illegal immigrant from Jordan,"[19] was described in *Time*
magazine as "a slight, dark-skinned man about 5 ft. 8 in. tall, with close
cropped dark hair and beard, dressed in sneakers *and a light gray sweat suit
that billowed around him.*"[20] It is hard to imagine what kind of sweat suit is
being described, until we realize that the author has created an image of
Salameh wearing traditional Arab robes, billowing in the wind. It is an
image not of Salameh but from *Lawrence of Arabia*. Commenting on
Salameh's frequent changes of residence, and induced by the same familiar exotic, an FBI investigator is quoted as saying: "One search is leading
to another. *But these are nomadic people*. While it may lie in the culture,
they bounce from place to place. All different people sleep there, stay a
short time, then leave."[21] The reference to nomads seems strangely
appropriate. His constant moving is attributed not to his status as an illegal immigrant, trying to keep one step ahead of the authorities, but to a
cultural predisposition for shiftiness. Salameh (like all Arabs) is imagined
as a nomad. He moves in and out. Borders are permeable to nomads. Like
terrorists, nomads are migratory. They have no fixed abode. Familiar as
dangerous and destructive of stability and rationality, these nomadic people threaten us with their potentiality for disruption.[22]

Western distrust of nomads has a long history. International law has,
in fact, from its inception been wary of nomads; it has not known what to
do about them. In discussing the European nations' appropriation of the
New World, Emmerich de Vattel in 1758 posed the question "[whether]
a nation may lawfully occupy any part of the vast territory in which are
to be found *wandering tribes* whose small number cannot populate the
whole country."[23] He responds that "[the wandering tribes'] uncertain
occupancy of these vast regions cannot be held as a real and lawful taking
of possession: and when the Nations of Europe, which are too confined
at home, come upon lands which the savages have no special need of and
are making no present and continuous use of, they may lawfully take possession of them and establish colonies in them."[24] And, we might add,
delineate proper boundaries. Henry Wheaton, writing in 1836, states that
"[t]he peculiar subjects of international law are Nations, and those political societies of men called States. . . . *A State is also distinguishable from
an unsettled horde of wandering savages* not yet formed into civil society."[25]
Referring to the European nations' colonization of the African continent,
J.B. de Martens Ferrao, in 1890, states: "Natural rights are born with

man.... But international rights cannot be recognized in those [savage] tribes, for want of the capacity for government. Being nomads or nearly such, they have no international character."[26]

Given the difficulties international law has traditionally had with nomads, it is not surprising that Palestinians function so satisfyingly and convincingly as terrorists. Sharing in the nomadic quality the West ascribes to all Arabs, they are in addition "stateless" and therefore outside of the state system of international law, not recognizable by international law. Stateless and nomadic, they are imagined as highly mobile and invisible, their mobility and invisibility in turn making them effective terrorists.[27]

Terrorists are usually imagined as coming in from the outside. They are foreign or foreign bred, they use foreign tactics, or their ideology is foreign. Terrorists, like nomads, make us worry about our boundaries. They make visible our vulnerability to incursion. Sheik Omar Abdel Rahman is said to have "slipped into the United States in 1990."[28] "Borders are porous; potential terrorists can slip in easily."[29] "[T]he porousness of American borders appear[s] to pose extremely high obstacles to an effective anti-terrorism effort.... As in Europe, the [terrorist] groups in the United States appear to be made up mostly of recent immigrants and a few naturalized American citizens bent on making the country suffer."[30] "It is a tale that highlights the startling ease with which undocumented immigrants are able to enter New York."[31] The solution is that we have to police our borders better, make our frontiers less porous and keep "them" out.[32] Not surprisingly, shortly after the World Trade Center bombing, a number of bills seeking to amend the U.S. Immigration and Nationality Act were introduced in Congress. One's stated purpose was to strengthen border security and defend against acts of international terrorism.[33]

The Terrorist as Outlaw

Terrorists, we are told repeatedly, do not respect the law. "Terrorists do not play by the rules."[34] Now, this is hardly a surprising proposition. Yet, it seems that the authors are claiming more, or something different than: "Like criminals, terrorists do not respect the law." There is something special about the quality of the terrorists' not respecting the law that we are expected to grasp. The complaint is that the terrorist respects no law—not the criminal law, not moral law, not the law of peace and not

306   the law of war. The terrorist is understood to be flouting all of these sets of law simultaneously. Such a complaint is surprising if only because it seems a logical impossibility. In our usual parlance, for instance, war and peace are mutually exclusive. We are either in a regime of peace (in which case we are held to the law of peace) or in a regime of war (in which case we are held to the law of war). Further, it seems that terrorists should either be thought of as acting within the scope of the criminal law (in which case they might be accused of violating criminal law) or they should be thought of as acting within the scope of war and peace (in which case they might be accused of violating either the law of war or the law of peace). The choice between these two conceptions is important because it is critical to a determination of the status of the terrorist.

Surprisingly, the complaint is often stated predominantly in the form that terrorists do not respect the laws of war:

> He has no moral restraints in the choice of his objectives, as he has none in his methods of warfare. . . . He respects no code of law which was ever established for war or peace.[35]

> War, even civil war, is predictable in many ways. It occurs in the light of day and there is no mystery about the identity of the participants. Even in civil war there are certain rules, whereas the characteristic features of terrorism are anonymity and the violation of established norms.[36]

The recognition of the potential existence of a state of war requires recognition of at least two opposing factions (in international law: two states), each capable of adopting a stance of war against the other. By placing terrorists within the realm of "war or peace," charging them with violating the accepted norms of "war and peace," the authors appear to elevate them to the status of an enemy state army, precisely the status that "terrorists" would claim for themselves. Two logical problems then arise. First, as mentioned above, terrorists—often equated with nomads —are generally understood to be stateless. Borders cannot contain them, and without borders there is no state. Second, if terrorists are to be held accountable to the law of war, they must also be entitled to be treated in accordance with the laws of war, such as international rules for the treatment of prisoners of war. This is precisely what a number of terrorist groups have claimed, and they have consistently been denied them because they are terrorists. Only legitimate combatants are entitled to be treated in accordance with the laws of war and terrorists, it is emphatically repeated, are not legitimate combatants. Only by holding firmly to such a position can it be maintained unambiguously and authoritatively that unlike war, for which there is a long tradition of "just war" theories, terrorism can never be justified. The paradoxical result is that terrorists are charged with being violators of the laws of war and yet are treated as being outside of the scope of the law of war, since they can never be recognized as legitimate combatants. One practical result is that, rather than treating captured terrorists as prisoners of war or as war criminals, terrorists are usually treated as if they were common criminals (albeit of a very bad and dangerous kind).

Another effect of claiming that terrorists are not legitimate combatants, that they are engaged not in war but in terrorism, is that it liberates the state from having itself to abide by the laws of war in its "war against terrorism." The strange claim that terrorists don't abide by the law of war gives additional ammunition to the equally strange assertion that they don't deserve to be given the benefit of law. Not only need the state not concern itself with the law of war in its dealing with terrorists, it is morally relieved from its duty to treat terrorists in accordance with normal rights and entitlements recognized by municipal law or international law. By placing himself voluntarily outside of the law, the terrorist loses his claim on the law.

The starting point of terrorism literature is that terrorism is an impermissible and abhorrent kind of violence, a violence qualitatively different from, and worse than, normal everyday violence or the perhaps equally familiar violence of war. Because the devastating effects of war can hardly be denied, the distinction cannot be based on a comparison of the body counts of war and the body counts of terrorism. As we have seen, one way in which terrorism authors seek to distinguish the two is by focusing on rules. War, they insist, is played by the rules. Terrorism, on the other hand, is played by no rules, not even the rules of war. The problem is that terrorism, by definition, can never be played by the rules of war. If it could, it wouldn't be terrorism, but war. At least, the authors seem to imply, there are rules to war (even though they may sometimes be violated) whereas there are no rules to terrorism at all. War is ennobled by its amenability to rules. While we are familiar with the concept of a law of war we cannot imagine a law of terrorism. What would we mean by a violation of the law of terrorism? Terrorism is by its very nature (and/or by definition) incapable of rules. It is not amenable to rules. It is precisely the absence of rules. This is its disruptive potential. This is its destructive potential. The existence of terrorism is a challenge to law. "Practically, [terrorism's] effect is to destroy the law itself—the only thing which stands between humanity and a state of permanent terror."[37] In combatting terrorism the state is defending law, saving humanity from lapsing back into a state of disorder, into its primitive pre-law past. As we reflect on terrorism, we realize that what is terrifying about terrorists is not that they are law violators but that they have situated themselves in that impossible place, located somewhere outside of law.

Yet while the terrorist is imagined as having chosen self-exile, outside the realm of law, he is also paradoxically the perfect subject of international law. Numerous international conventions and resolutions have been adopted condemning specific acts of terrorism.[38] Like the pirate of yore, the terrorist is imagined to be the enemy of all (civilized) mankind and therefore subject to capture by any state and subject to every state's jurisdiction.[39]

> Terrorists deserve no quarter. Terrorists should have no place to hide. We must stamp out terrorist activity.... These people are not worth the time of day.... They're not even people, doing what they're doing.[40]

According to this reading, the terrorist has chosen to become "other," to act as "other." The state is therefore justified in treating him as other. The terrorist is to blame. Counter-terrorism measures are the result of his own actions. The state is blameless. Indeed at the very moment when the state is applying repressive anti-terrorism measures, the state is imagined to be the innocent victim of terrorism. "Increased surveillance and repression may become an irresistible temptation to governments trying to protect their own citizens against violence by a small minority."[41]

Ironically then, the rhetorical transformation of terrorists into frightening alien outlaws suggests a justification for repression by the state, and an excuse for some authoritarian regimes. In fact, repressive measures short of military dictatorship are virtually recommended by the literature on terrorism, not only because the terrorist has put himself voluntarily outside the protection of the law, but because the failure to use all possible means to combat terrorism is to put society at risk of falling either into chaos or military dictatorship.

The effects of the process of transformation of the terrorist into a terrifying other, to whom all sorts of violence can legitimately be done, can be gauged in part by looking at examples of national anti-terrorist legislations, other legal counter-terrorism measures and publicly accepted (or implicitly endorsed) extra-legal counter-terrorism measures. Such an examination is beyond the scope of this essay. It should however be noted that the very application of such measures to combat terrorism assists the transformational process, both in the public mind and in the mind of those charged with carrying out the measures. The whole process is in other words self-fulfilling prophecy. When violence is applied by the state, the terrorist's other nature is reaffirmed and confirmed. The terrorist never seems so alien/different as at the moment the violence is applied and that violence is "legitimate." To be legitimately subject to state violence is to be the opposite of a citizen worthy of the state's protection.

Terrorism and International Law: A Conclusion

In thinking, writing or reacting to terrorism and terrorists, we seem to be drawn to the idea that terrorists are somehow always external to us, somehow always other. They are different. Their difference is manifested as violence. We think of them as boundary violators. They cross international boundaries. They are uncontainable. They violate the accepted boundary between normal and extra-normal violence. They violate the boundary between appropriate and inappropriate victims. They cross the boundary between acceptable challenge to the system and the unacceptable desire to annihilate it. They cross the boundary between civilization and the barbarous primitive.

It is perhaps because we imagine the terrorist as so unremittingly other, so suspiciously foreign, that it seems appropriate that terrorism be treated as a matter for international law. It is almost impossible to treat terrorism as if it were a purely domestic matter. We cannot domesticate terrorism precisely because we need to expel it—to put it back outside where it belongs. The closer we come to admitting that terrorism is an internal domestic problem, the harder it becomes to make a clean break. No longer can we expel what we should never have let in; rather, we will

have to extirpate from ourselves that which we wish to remove, in order
to be rid of it.

From the perspective of Western liberal democracies, it is more acceptable to imagine the terrorist as being fundamentally other, fundamentally alien. Not only does the otherness of the terrorist serve to
explain his violence, but it is his otherness manifested as violence that
calls forth the violence of the state. The state is not doing violence to
itself when it combats terrorism. Instead, it is doing violence to a foreign
body that is seeking to destroy it from within. When it combats terrorism, the state is doing what the state is supposed to do—protecting itself
and its citizens from invasion or destruction by forces from without. We
are more comfortable with an image of removing a cancerous growth
than with an image of self-mutilation.

Placing terrorism as a subject of international law serves a further
function. From its earliest manifestations, international law has been self-
consciously a universalizing project. In the early days, both peoples and
states were understood as being subject to an unchanging and unchangeable law of nature. By extension, all states and peoples were therefore
assumed to hold to broadly identical standards and norms. International
law, or the law of nations, was viewed as nothing but the codification of
the law of nature as it governed inter-sovereign relations. From that perspective, it was self-evident that all states and peoples could be held to
the same standards of conduct since the law of nature was both universal
and knowable. Sovereign consent was relevant only to what might be
thought of as second level rules.

Although international law no longer relies exclusively on a universal
law of nature to explain or justify its general applicability, it is still very
much concerned with setting universal standards through, in particular,
the mechanism of consensus. By framing terrorism as an international
rather than a domestic concern, Western liberal democracies gain the
advantage of establishing universal opprobrium. If terrorism is recognized as an international offense, then in naming a particular violence terroristic, the labelling state can claim to be making a universal rather than
a particularistic claim. The terrorist is thus not only other to the state but
to the international collectivity. Indeed, the labelling state can then imagine the terrorist to be outside of all legitimate boundaries—not just outlaw, but international outlaw. By extension, the labelling state can also
label nonconforming states (which support the activity labelled as terrorism) as deviant and illegitimate. Since there is consensus, the norm is

universal and failure to conform to a universal norm is a violation of the violator's own norm. The violating state is thus outlaw unto itself.

In this as in other respects terrorism seems to turn our categories topsy turvy. Terrorists whom we imagine as nomadic boundary crossers do not simply violate these boundaries; they seem to define them. The boundaries, that is, appear to be drawn in relation to terrorism. For example, we determine where war ends and terrorism begins by rhetorically constructing terrorism as the extreme margin against which war might seem comfortably familiar. Once we have recognized the role of the terrorist in defining our boundaries, the boundaries themselves are brought into question. Why this line and not some other? How do we distinguish between us and them? Our boundaries shift in the wake of these nomads. We cannot hold on to them. Like the terrorists themselves, our boundaries seem unstable and transient. From this perspective, one might understand international law's obsession with violence as a symptom/manifestation of our need for firmer boundaries, sharper distinctions. Hence, as the terrorist other we have made or imagined destabilizes our sense of the discernable distance between self and other, we place the terrorist nomad firmly outside, in a place we cannot really envision, and patrol our boundaries to make them real.

Notes

1. Following the murder of Doctor David Gunn outside an abortion clinic in Pensacola, Florida, pro-choice advocacy groups characterized the killing as "domestic terrorism" and called on the President "to have the FBI investigate the recent spate of violence against abortion providers and to order federal marshals to guard women and doctors at clinics targeted by protestors." *U.S. Reaction to Murder: A Series of Hues, Cries for Protection at Clinics*, SALT LAKE TRIB., Mar. 12, 1993, at A1. These same groups are "seeking legislation to make it a federal crime to block access to an abortion clinic." *Id.*

2. Ranchers who graze their livestock on public lands in AZ, CA and NV are increasingly being targeted by "eco-terrorist" vandalism and threats, Rep. James Hansen (R-UT) told a House panel 5/12.... He was speaking in support of his bill that would make it a felony to kill or harass livestock on public lands, increasing possible penalties to five years in prison and a $250,000 fine. (Jeff Barker, ARIZ. REPUBLIC, May 13, 1992).

   Ranchers: "Eco-Terrorists" Strike Public Land Grazers, GREENWIRE, May 14, 1992, *available in* LEXIS, News Library, Wires File.

3. Gideon Rafael, *Chairman's Opening Remarks before Third Session of Jerusalem Conference on International Terrorism* (July 3, 1979), *in* INTERNATIONAL TERRORISM: CHALLENGE AND RESPONSE 111–12 (Benjamin Netanyahu ed., 1980) [hereinafter IT: C&R].

Ileana M. Porras

312

4. William R. Farrell, The U.S. Government's Response to Terrorism: In Search of an Effective Strategy 6 (1982).

5. "These ecoterrorists are a tiny, fringe group. They in no way represent America's broad environmental movement. . . . [B]y failing to denounce loudly and openly the ecoterrorists, mainstream environmentalists risk bringing their entire movement into disrepute." *Eco-Terrorism: The Dangerous Fringe of the Environmental Movement,* The Heritage Foundation Reports (The Heritage Foundation), April 12, 1990, *available in* LEXIS, News Library, Newsletters File.

6. "Terrorism [is] a moral evil, infecting not only those who commit such crimes, but those who, out of malice, ignorance, or simple refusal to think, countenance them." Benjamin Netanyahu, *Preface* to IT: C&R, *supra* note 3, at 1–2.

7. *See, e.g., Ley Organica 9/1984, de 26 de Diciembre, Contra la Actuacion de Bandas Armadas y Elementos Terroristas, reprinted in* Codigo Penal, § 8, Madrid (1989) (criminalizing collaboration with, incitement to participate in, concealment of or public support of groups associated with terrorist activities). *See also* 28 STRAFGESETZ-BUCH [StGB] § 130a, *translated in* The American Series of Foreign Penal Codes (1987) (criminalizing dissemination, public display, or otherwise rendering accessible a writing which contained support of "terrorist associations").

8. Farrell, *supra* note 4, at 6–7.

9. U.S. Dep't of State, Patterns of Global Terrorism 1992, at v (1993) [hereinafter State Dep't Report].

10. "Euskadi ta Askatasuna" translates as "Freedom for the Basque Homeland."

11. Richard Behar, *The Secret Life of Mahmud the Red,* Time, Oct. 4, 1993, at 56.

12. One author defined terrorism as "the premeditated, deliberate, systematic murder, mayhem and threatening *of the innocent* to create fear and intimidation in order to gain a political or tactical advantage, usually to influence an audience." James M. Poland, Understanding Terrorism: Groups, Strategies and Responses 11 (1988) (emphasis added).

13. *See* Immigration and Nationality Act, 8 U.S.C.A. § 1182(a)(3)(B), (D) (Supp. IV 1992) (regarding excludable aliens).

14. State Dep't Report, *supra* note 9, at v.

15. *Id.* at cover, 3, 11, 14, 15, 16.

16. David Mazzucchelli, *Castles in the Sand,* the New Yorker, July 26, 1993, at cover.

17. A striking example is in the week of March 15, 1993, *Time, Newsweek* and *People* all carried photographs of the blind Sheik juxtaposed with that of David Koresh, leader of the Branch Davidian "sect" besieged in Waco, Texas. At that time, the "blind Sheik" had not been directly connected to the World Trade Center bombing.

18. Richard Bernstein, *American Law Tackles Terrorism,* N.Y. Times, Aug. 29, 1993, Sec. 4, at 1.

19. George J. Church, *A Case of Dumb Luck,* Time, Mar. 15, 1993, at 26.

20. *Id.* at 28 (emphasis added).

21. Ralph Blumenthal, *Suspect in Trade Center Bombing Now Seen As Part of Conspiracy,* N.Y. Times, Mar. 9, 1993, at A1 (emphasis added).

22. *See* Gilles Deleuze & Felix Guattari, Thousand Plateaus: Capitalism and Schizophrenia 351–423 (Brian Massuni trans., 1987) (1980).

23. 3 Emmerich de Vattel, The Law of Nations or the Principles of Natural Law, § 209, 85 (Charles G. Fenwick trans., 1916) (1758) (emphasis added).

24. *Id.*

25. HENRY WHEATON, ELEMENTS OF INTERNATIONAL LAW, §§ 16–17 (Richard H. Dana ed., 8th ed., 1866) (1836) (emphasis added).

26. JOHN WESTLAKE, CHAPTERS ON THE PRINCIPLES OF INTERNATIONAL LAW, 145–46 (1982) (1894) (quoting J.B. DE MARTENS FERRAO, L'AFRIQUE: LA QUESTION SOULEVEE DERNIERE-MENT ENTRE L'ANGLETERRE ET LE PORTUGAL CONSIDEREE DU POINT DE VUE DU DROIT INTERNATIONAL 6 (1890)).

27. "Whatever they do, we can expect terrorists to remain mobile, able to strike targets throughout the world." Robert L. Rabe, *Crisis Management of Terrorist Incidents, in* LEGAL AND OTHER ASPECTS OF TERRORISM 80 (E. Nobles Lowe & Harry D. Shargel eds., 1979).

28. Alison Mitchell, *Bombing Suspect Flown to U.S. After Egypt Puts Him on Plane,* N.Y. TIMES, Mar. 25, 1993, at A1, B7.

29. George J. Church, *The Terror Within,* TIME, July 5, 1993, at 22, 27.

30. Bernstein, *supra* note 18, Sec. 4, at 1.

31. Ralph Blumenthal, *Fitting the Pieces of Terrorism,* N.Y. TIMES, Apr. 26, 1993, at B1.

32. Germany's elite, and now controversial, counter-terrorist police squad, GSG-9, whose name in German, "Grenzshutzgruppe," means "border protection group." Stephen Kinzer, *Police Scandal is Giving Germans an Inside Look at War Against Terrorists,* N.Y. TIMES, Aug. 13, 1993, at A1.

33. S. 1351, 103d Cong., 1st Sess., §§701–04, 803, 805 (1993).

34. Rabe, *supra* note 27, at 49.

35. Benjamin Netanyahu, *Chairman's Opening Remarks, in* IT: C&R, *supra* note 3, at 5.

36. WALTER LAQUEUR, THE AGE OF TERRORISM 3 (1987).

37. Hugh Frazer, *The Tyranny of Terrorism, in* IT: C&R, *supra* note 3, at 23.

38. *See, e.g.,* Convention to Prevent and Punish the Acts of Terrorism Taking the Form of Crimes Against Persons and Related Extortion That Are of International Significance, Feb. 2, 1971, Organization of American States, art. 1, 27 U.S.T. 3949, T.I.A.S. No. 8413 (adopting general standards for punishment and prevention of terrorist acts); G.A. Res. 40/61 U.N. GAOR, 40th Sess., Supp. No. 53 (1985).

39.   International law, historically, took extreme measures to combat piracy: The judicial power of every State extends to the punishment of certain offenses against the law of nations, among which is piracy.... Pirates being the common enemies of all mankind, and all nations having an equal interest in their apprehension and punishment, they may be lawfully captured on the high seas by the armed vessel of any particular State, and brought within its territorial jurisdiction, for trial in its tribunals.

WHEATON, *supra,* note 25, §§ 122, 124, at 192–93.

40. Bernard Gwertzman, *U.S. Backs Raid, Regrets Deaths,* N.Y. TIMES, Nov. 25, 1985, at A1 (citing George Schultz).

41. Rabe, *supra* note 27, at 83.

CHAPTER SIXTEEN

>-+>-o-<+-<

OUTLAW WOMEN

AN ESSAY ON *THELMA & LOUISE*

Elizabeth V. Spelman and Martha Minow

IN THE FILM *Adam's Rib*,[1] Katharine Hepburn plays an attorney defending a woman charged with attempting to murder her adulterous husband. In her closing argument, Hepburn urges the jury to imagine how they would sympathize with a man charged with attempting to murder his adulterous wife. As Hepburn describes each of the individuals—the defendant, the victim, the third parties—she reverses their genders and the film conjures up images of the male characters as female and the female as male. It does not really work. At least for many viewers, the attempt seems awkward and unbelievable. But can anyone elicit sympathy for women outlaws without invoking analogies to men admired or excused for breaking the law?

The noble "outlaw" is an oddly revered character, loosely associated in United States folklore with the West and with romantic ideas about personal development and freedom. The paradigmatic noble outlaw is a male whose lawbreaking can be understood as in some sense virtuous. It is therefore more unlikely that he will belong to any racial or ethnic

314

group which has to fight the perception that its lawbreaking activities can only be the expression of "criminal proclivities." In short, the James Brothers couldn't have been Mexican-American or African-American and still have become American heroes. Nor could they have been the James Sisters—certainly not if we imagine such women's "outlaw" behavior to involve rejecting the sexism they find in society, leaving their husbands, or defying social constraints. Unlike their male counterparts, whose "deviant" outlaw behavior heightens their manhood, such women risk appearing to be not just deviant citizens but deviant women.

There are, then, powerful constraints on the capacity of many United States observers to sympathize with lawbreakers who are not males of a certain description. But the recent movie *Thelma & Louise*[2] attempts to make such understanding possible. Granted, *Thelma & Louise* is not a work of politics, law, or philosophy. It is a movie, and it offers no sustained argument. Nor does it pretend to document reality. Unlike many movies, *Thelma & Louise* provoked wide-spread and intense public debates. The film gives us an occasion to explore not only what it means in our society for women to be outlaws, but also: (1) how different kinds of viewers might perceive and judge outlaw women; (2) how class and race, along with gender, may influence viewer understandings of outlaw figures; and (3) what the world and moral reasoning might look like from the perspectives of the women characters cast as film outlaws.

These are themes about which Mary Joe Frug would have provocative and fabulous things to say. As Mary Joe's work shows,[3] she found her distinctive and irreplaceable voice inside the law as she thought and wrote about the women most terrorized by others and ruled out by law.

The Story and Its Viewers

Thelma & Louise combines the genres of buddy films and on-the-road stories; it is an outlaw film with the twist that the outlaws are two women. They are outlaws on their own; unlike male outlaws' "molls," they break the law without men. Susan Sarandon and Geena Davis play Louise, a waitress, and Thelma, a housewife, who leave a boyfriend and a husband for a weekend of fishing. But instead of fun, they meet crisis. Picked up at a dance-bar by a man who makes aggressive and ultimately violent sexual advances, Thelma is saved when Louise brandishes a gun. But when Harlan, the assaulter, is unrepentant, Louise shoots and kills him.

316   At that moment, Louise and Thelma become outlaws, and they hit the road. As state police and FBI agents search for them, Thelma and Louise head for Mexico, trying to deal with the men they left and the men they encounter. On their way, they encounter a truck driver who ogles them, and a hitch-hiker who seduces Thelma and then steals Louise's money. Thelma sticks up a convenience store to make up for leaving the hitch-hiker alone to steal Louise's money. A police officer stops them for speeding, but Thelma and Louise lock him in the trunk of his squad car. They make telephone contact with the detective who is tracking them and who seems to know about a prior experience with sexual assault Louise endured in Texas.

Reaching ever more spectacular southwestern vistas on their route to Mexico, Thelma and Louise speculate about their crimes, their pasts, their friendship, and their lives. They also undertake a kind of fantasy revenge against the trucker who has harassed them on the road. A chase scene complete with hordes of police and FBI agents includes moments of escape and moments that make capture seem inevitable. But at the close, the two women choose to drive off into the Grand Canyon rather than face death through a shoot out, or worse, capture and a criminal trial. The film does not leave the viewer with this suicide scene, however. Instead, it quickly returns to earlier images of hope, excitement and pleasure on the faces of the two women.[4]

This is at least one version of the film's plot-line and structure. Yet, as Mary Joe Frug taught in her article, "Re-Reading Contracts,"[5] we can all understand a text better if we see how different readers read it differently. The mass media played up these differences, often framing them as male versus female reactions. For example, the *Boston Globe* ran under the heading, "The Great Debate over *Thelma and Louise*," two opposing columns, one by a woman defending the film and one by a man attacking it.[6] The man, John Robinson, wrote: "Male bashing, once the sport of hairy women in denim jackets and combat boots, has flushed like toxic waste into the culture mainstream with the vengeance fantasy 'Thelma and Louise.'"[7] Reading the movie against a backdrop of feminist cultural and political activities, he found that "'Thelma and Louise' is the last straw."[8] He objected to the absence of enough sympathetic male characters who are strong but not obnoxious.[9] He acknowledged that more tyrants and abusers are found among men than among women,[10] yet he asserted, "'Thelma and Louise' would have the world believe that a good man is an exception, and a that bad woman is an oxymoron."[11] He also objected to the entrance into mainstream culture of the kinds of feminist messages that previously had been reserved for more elite artistic expression.[12]

The contrasting column by a woman, reviewer Diane White, argued that "there wasn't enough man-bashing in 'Thelma and Louise.'"[13] White wrote, "I wish they'd nailed that little weasel who ran off with all their money. And Thelma's toad-like yupster husband deserved more than just an emotional shock."[14] Reversing the familiar comment that feminists take things too seriously and lack a sense of humor, White continued, "It's only a movie, and a comedy at that."[15] Yet she herself reported on the strong positive reaction of women in her audience: "They cheered when Louise plugged the roadhouse cowboy who was trying to rape Thelma. And when the two characters blew up the rig of a leering, tongue-waggling trucker, they cheered even louder."[16] She concluded that "[f]or some women 'Thelma and Louise' is a cathartic movie, a bit of wish fulfillment. . . . I know what it's like to be so brutalized and humiliated by a man that you'd like to murder him. But I didn't. Why? Because life isn't a movie. Besides, unlike Louise, I didn't have a gun handy."[17]

These reviews draw the differences in viewers strictly on gender lines, which may be somewhat simplistic. People who share genders may nonetheless respond differently to the film, perhaps because of differences of class, race, or other aspects of personal identity and experience. Similarly, conflicting viewer responses to the recent public drama enacted when Professor Anita Hill accused Supreme Court nominee Clarence Thomas of sexual harassment reflected not only gender, but also racial, class, and other differences in point of view. Nonetheless, an asserted gender difference or gender gap marked a striking dimension of the public debates over both the film and the nomination. It seemed to matter to many observers that more women than men would understand why a victim of sexual harassment would not complain, quit her job, or refuse to follow the harassing boss to an improved career opportunity; it seemed to matter to many observers that many women viewers could identify with and feel empowered by Thelma and Louise, while male viewers might feel threatened by their actions.[18]

Yet the risk in typing viewers according to sociological characteristics is to replicate the pigeonholes that the movie itself critiques. One reviewer optimistically argued that the movie grants empowerment to two women in the midst of the worst trouble of their lives, and "we all gain a realization not only of the different needs of the sexes, but also of how deeply society pigeonholes men and women, and what it takes to

318 even attempt to get out."[19] "We all gain" is the hopeful statement that any viewer, regardless of status identity, can identify with the characters in the movie. The gendered reaction to the film portrayed or manufactured by some reviews neglects this possibility of identification across differences. Actress Geena Davis, who plays Thelma, argued "'Men who feel threatened by this movie are identifying with the wrong characters. It's not a movie to set the record straight. This is a movie about people claiming responsibility for their own lives. This is a film about freedom. Anyone should be able to identify with it.'"[20] Similarly, screen-play author Callie Khouri maintained that the movie is not hostile toward men: "'I think it is hostile toward idiots.'"[21]

Yet even these comments imply that the only differences that matter are gender differences. We think it's more complicated than that. A closer look at "outlaw" status may help.

The Canon of the Gun: On Outlaw Pedigrees

Are Thelma and Louise noble outlaws, or is some other description of their law-breaking more apt? Insofar as "outlaw" suggests someone who self-consciously and consistently breaks the law, Thelma and Louise qualify as outlaws: they knowingly break a number of laws; they come to take pleasure in breaking them, especially as they become more skilled and capable of a kind of fastidiousness in doing so. Escaping the long arm of the law becomes central to their lives and indeed to their deaths. Law's centrality does not mean its utility; Thelma and Louise never feel that they can try to use the law to accomplish their ends such as they emerge.

North American history and literature are filled with examples of daring figures who are presented as having to break the law in order to bring about a kind of justice the law or its agents cannot effect. One late Twentieth Century version of this type, not surprisingly, rode the subway instead of a horse: in a much publicized case, New York City dweller Bernhard Goetz, fed up with being harassed on public transportation, shot at four young men trying to exact money from him on the subway.[22] One of the young men was seriously injured.[23] According to the jury in *People v. Goetz*, the only illegal thing Goetz did was carry an unlicensed handgun.[24]

Whether or not the facts in the case were sufficient to establish that Goetz acted in self-defense,[25] Goetz became a hero, at least in some communities. Goetz's status as a hero reveals the public's admiration for one who dares to do something not permitted by law, and especially for one who enacts common fantasies of unlawful but just revenge.

Flouting the law may be necessary, but it is by no means a sufficient condition for being considered a *noble* outlaw. Those who hailed Goetz as a hero did not admire the young would-be robbers for *their* lawbreaking. Goetz could not have been treated as a noble lawbreaker—a hero—unless those on whom he exacted revenge were seen as ignoble lawbreakers, indeed as criminal scum.

Goetz was frequently referred to as the "Subway Vigilante." "Vigilante" is one of many terms for lawbreakers. Vigilante, outlaw, avenger, bandit, fugitive, criminal, deviant, scofflaw, and thug all have different if not fully determinate meanings, and each suggests a variety of evaluations. When the adjective "noble" is added, the elevated status of public appeal transforms the lawbreaker into a hero.

But as reflections on the *Goetz* case suggest, the gratitude and admiration we feel toward lawbreakers depends on the observer's sense of the justice or fairness of the vision that motivates or is used to defend the lawbreaking activities. This, in turn, depends largely on whether the observer believes the victims of such actions deserve what happens to them. The observer's conclusions are likely to rest not only on what the purported noble outlaws believe but on who they are. Suppose Goetz had been a Black man, and the young men he shot at, white?[26] Or suppose that Goetz, the white man, had shot at other whites—say, fraternity boys out on a little spree?[27]

Viewers of *Thelma & Louise* who are ready to regard the two women as noble outlaws have to be able to think about both the women and those affected by their actions in fairly specific ways. Thelma and Louise have to be seen as acting, preferably self-consciously, in accordance with a just principle or concern. The would-be rapist, Harlan, and others directly affected by the women's actions have to be seen as in some sense deserving what they got, whether or not the law prohibits their being treated that way.

There is, then, much that complicates the answer to the question of whether Thelma and Louise are noble outlaws. It does seem fairly clear that some viewers who love the film greatly admire the outlaw qualities of Thelma and Louise, while many viewers upset by the film are worried that it glorifies an ignoble kind of lawlessness. As Callie Khouri has suggested, perhaps both reactions mistake the film for a political treatise.[28] But even if the film is not such a treatise, it is naive or disingenuous to think about

320   it and the reaction to it in isolation from a volatile political climate in which those clamoring for "law and order" rarely join protests against the everyday forms of the abuse of women on exhibition in the film.

The law has done little to protect women from the violence of rape and other forms of sexual abuse. In such a context, Thelma's and Louise's resistance to Harlan's sense of entitlement, and to his assumption of immunity, invite sympathetic viewers to see the women as heroines. It is, of course, one thing to fight back as Thelma does, and another to shoot Harlan dead as Louise does. But sympathetic viewers' high regard for Thelma's acts of self-defense—acts sanctioned by law—could flow easily into enthusiastic admiration for Louise's murder of Harlan. The movie itself offers an explanation for that murder, but not thereby a justification.[29] Such admiration arises, when it does, despite the fact—or maybe in part because of it—that the canonical list of noble outlaws (such as Robin Hood, Jesse James, and Bernhard Goetz) includes very few women. Such admiration arises, when it does, despite the fact that everyday violence against women has not been among the canonical evils to which outlaw behavior has been regarded as an appropriate response. Young black men who seem threatening to a white man on the subway are one thing; an inebriated white fellow who has earned his right to sleep with a flirtatious, sexy and inebriated lady acquaintance is another. In short, the history of noble outlaws makes it difficult for women to qualify for inclusion, especially if what motivates them is something as apparently banal as everyday violence against "cock-teasing" women.

If, as women, Thelma and Louise are unlikely candidates for outlaw status, the fact that they are working-class women makes the possibility of their becoming outlaws more probable. Their class status may also make their outlaw behavior more palatable to the middle-class audiences to whom the film is directed than if the heroines were solidly middle or upper-middle class.

Compare *Thelma & Louise* with the earlier film classic exhibiting feminist consciousness. In *Adam's Rib*, a female lawyer successfully defends a working-class woman charged with attempting to murder her husband.[30] It would have been quite a different movie altogether if the lawyer had had to defend herself against the charge that she had tried to murder her lawyer husband. The film then would not have provided the cozy, though necessarily tacit, lesson that middle or upper-middle class professional heterosexual couples work out their gender problems in the much more "civilized" way of talk, compared with working-class couples, who are depicted as violent.[31]

Thelma and Louise are working-class women; Harlan, the hitchhiker, and the truck driver are portrayed in ways which seem to signal to viewers that they are working-class.[32] The middle-class viewers who are tempted to describe themselves as identifying with Thelma or Louise might ask themselves how far the identification really goes. After all, the neat thing about admiring outlaws from a class you perceive as lower than your own is that you can have your cake and eat it too: a middle-class woman's partial identification with a working-class female outlaw could enable her to imagine taking unlawful revenge against a man while not having to endure the thought that she is really an outlaw type, or confront the strong possibility that there really are no legal resources on which she could draw. A middle-class woman's admiration for a working-class woman who breaks the law may be easy, as long as the middle-class woman remains confident that she will not be seen and treated as a working-class woman.

This is not to suggest that middle-class women have an easy time using the law to defend themselves against rape and other forms of sexual violence and abuse. But it is to suggest that in the United States in the 1990s, there are sharp differences, partly summarized by class, between women with access to the law and to the chance of pushing it to its limits in order to defend themselves, and someone like Louise who knows the terror of seeing no source of support within the system, no possible legal leeway, and no hope of positive publicity that would mitigate the effects of her avenging act.

One of the privileges of class dominance is to be able to admire what one sees as a courageous act without having to worry about the likely consequences of that act for the agent. In this connection, the film poses a very serious question: are feminists who enthusiastically embrace the film's depiction of direct and violent confrontation with violent and abusive men prepared to give concrete support to women who are confrontative in just those ways? What if those confrontative women are unlikely to have access to the legal and extra-legal resources that might somewhat cushion the blow of such confrontation?

What seems a plausible form of liberation has a great deal to do with the predicted consequences that acts of such liberation are likely to entail. The lack of rebellion by some slaves and Holocaust victims does not

322   inspire blame (although their rebellion would have been courageous, laudable, and inspiring) because rebellion could have cost them or their co-sufferers their lives. *Thelma & Louise* contains—even if it does not explicitly articulate—a very closely related caution: perhaps we ought to be careful about facile praise for people for acting in ways which are audacious, courageous, and inspiring, when we are more likely to be protected from the consequences of such acts than they are. We who differ from them may experience, partially, their world. But, partial vicariousness can be very cruel. It is partial if the viewers hope the characters have an experience which we would like to have too, although the characters have to bear the consequences of it in a way that we would not. And it is partial if the viewer neglects the moral dilemmas and distress experienced by the character herself.[33]

If class difference may make it safe for many viewers to like Thelma and Louise, one might ask whether Harlan and the truck driver seem to deserve what they get because they are presented as working-class men. The notions of appropriate revenge which surface even in our fantasies— perhaps especially in our fantasies—are likely to be class coded. In *Adam's Rib*, the female lawyer gets back at her husband by outdoing him in court,[34] but the working-class female defendant gets her revenge by shooting at her husband. While admiration of outlaws depends on a view of their victims as, in some sense, and perhaps with some regret, expendable, the possibilities of expendability are likely to be closely tied to some of the more invidious aspects of class distinctions. It is worth asking whether the working-class status of Harlan and the truck driver makes it easier for middle-class women to think of them as unregenerate creeps who fully and unquestionably deserve everything Thelma and Louise dish out to them. No doubt their being working-class men makes it easier for middle-class men to deny that they are like these guys and thus to insist that they surely do not deserve to be treated like Harlan and the truck driver.

There is a sense in which Thelma and Louise have questionable status as outlaws: unlike many of their kind, they stumble into this always hazardous and sometimes noble career. These two women who plot a secret get-away weekend from the men in their lives are not portrayed as potential heroines whose visions of justice or creative needs or deep yearnings for freedom require standing outside the law. They are not portrayed, at least early on, as having a criminal or outlaw "mentality" (hence Thelma's husband Darryl's incredulousness while watching a security videotape of Thelma holding up the convenience store). On the contrary,

Thelma and Louise initially have nothing more in mind than a brief bout of naughtiness. It is a measure of their relative lack of freedom and power that what begins as their naughtiness spirals so quickly and so inexorably into their becoming, to their initial horror, continuing surprise, and emerging delight, fugitives from the law. Unlike many noble outlaws, it is not at all as if their visions of the shortcomings of the law and of the society that produces it lead them to put themselves outside it. On the contrary, for Thelma at least, learning that "law is some tricky shit"[35] comes as a result of her becoming an outlaw.

The Outlaws Look At Law and Morality

Thelma and Louise had no lawyers to consult or to guide them through the law's response to their actions. Nonetheless, like many outlaws and many who seem marginal to the law's operations, Thelma and Louise had complex understandings of the legal system and how it would treat them. Although the law put them beyond its ken and beyond its protection, Thelma and Louise engaged in a continual discussion about blame and guilt, and about responsibility and obedience. In their own actions and judgments, they confronted and addressed punishment and proportionality of punishment to offense. Placing at the center these outlaws' views of law and morality displaces societal images of the outlaw as amoral. Their own moral judgments afford a critical perspective on law and conventional morality.

To Thelma and Louise, "law is some tricky shit."[36] Louise knows and Thelma comes to realize that the official legal system will not take seriously a charge of rape or attempted rape by a woman who publicly danced, drank, and flirted with a man who picked her up at a raucous bar. Thelma asks, "shouldn't we go to the cops?" and Louise replies, "who's going to believe" us? Louise starts crying, "we don't live in that kind of world."[37]

Detectives and police officers are to be avoided and diverted; they will not understand women who fight back against violent men. Louise does engage in repeated phone conversations with one detective who claims to understand, but she does not trust him either. She knows that he is trying to keep her on the phone long enough to trace the phone call's source.

Even Thelma, portrayed for the first half of the film as naive and gullible,[38] knows that it could only be the tricky law or its officers which prompted her husband Darryl[39] to be sweet to her on the phone; his very sweetness tells her that police are there with him, so she hangs up the phone. Curiously, Darryl believed the FBI agent who urged him to sweet-talk his wife because "[w]omen love that shit."[40] Maybe they do, maybe they don't, but this advice could only stem from total disinterest in the particularities of the actual relationship between this man and this woman. If its own agents don't care about those actual details, it is no wonder that the law itself seems remote and uncomprehending to the two women it outlaws.

Between themselves,[41] however, the two women constantly discuss issues of moral boundaries, duties, and responsibilities.[42] Shortly after Louise shoots Harlan, she starts to blame Thelma: "If you weren't so concerned about having fun. . . ." But she stops short as Thelma interjects: "So this is all my fault, is it?"[43] Louise and Thelma both hear and reject the echo of societal conversations blaming women who get raped because "they asked for it." Yet both women wrestle with the question of fault and responsibility. Much later, after more time on the road, Thelma says, "I know this whole thing was my fault." But this time Louise says, "This wasn't your fault." And Thelma with appreciation and forgiveness on her own part replies, "I'm glad I came with you."[44] Not only does she affirm their friendship, she also affirms their journey, their jeopardy, and their sacrifice.

Days later, still on the road, Louise says "I think I fucked up. I think I got us in a situation where we both could get killed."[45] Thelma then reveals how much she has been replaying the options, and re-evaluating who is to blame and who is responsible. She observes that if they had sought to prosecute the rapist, no one would have believed them, "probably nothing would have happened to him . . . [and] my life would have been ruined a whole lot worse than it is now. I'm not sorry that son of a bitch is dead."[46] But she is sorry about something—that it was Louise who killed him rather than herself. Given a world without a comprehending legal system, working outside the law is essential. And the best remedies are by the self.[47]

Less intense, but no less expressive of normative concerns, is Louise's warning to Thelma as she starts to throw an empty liquor bottle out of the convertible: "Thelma, don't you litter."[48] Her tone is stern and commanding. Perhaps it reflects a sense of pride in the fantastic scenery, or simply a concern with obeying the rules. The comment certainly occasions laughter from an audience watching the outlaws flee from the law. But more than incongruity is at work here. The comment is true to

Louise's continuing respect for norms, her knowledge of the price of disobedience, and perhaps her sense of right and wrong.

But are they engaged in moral argument or judgment when they commit their own acts of violence? Their concern for one another is at the
center of the violence they encounter and the violence they commit. In
the disturbing scene when Thelma is sexually assaulted by Harlan, who
picked her up at the Silver Bullet bar, the violence escalates when
Thelma tries to halt Harlan's aggression by telling him that Louise will
wonder where she is. Harlan responds, "Fuck Louise."[49] Thelma slaps
him. He whacks her and roughly pins her against a car and starts to rape
her. Louise shows up and pulls out the gun. Harlan tells her, "Calm
down, we're just having a little fun." Louise says, "Looks like you have a
real fucked up idea about fun. . . . In the future, when a woman is crying
like that, she isn't havin' any fun."[50] Harlan says quietly, "Bitch. I should
have gone ahead and fucked her," to which Louise demands, "What did
you say?" Harlan turns defiantly and answers, "I said suck my cock."
Louise shoots him dead and then, after telling Thelma to get in the car,
whispers, "You watch your mouth, buddy."[51]

Louise did not shoot when Harlan was attacking Thelma; pointing the
gun was enough to interrupt him. She shoots when he demonstrates he
is undeterred and unrepentant, and verbally repeating the sexual assault.
She shoots in judgment; she has judged that he will not stop this behavior and that even if Thelma gets away, other women will be victimized.

Although she clearly makes a judgment here, Louise becomes at this
moment an outlaw, not a judge or jury. Indeed, in strictly legal terms,
this judgment makes her conduct intentional and thus, in the eyes of the
law, more culpable than one committed instinctively or in the heat of
passion. Moreover, since Harlan was unarmed and because he stopped
his assault at least temporarily at the sight of the gun, it would be difficult
to fit this scene into the legal framework of self-defense. That framework
uses the archetype of intense hand-to-hand combat between two men.[52]
It does not justify or excuse the use of a gun against a verbal assault. Yet,
precisely because it is so deliberate, Louise's act of violence does serve as
a judgment, a sentence for the audience to reckon with as well as a
moment that changes her own life. She becomes a judge of the proper
response to the crime when she later chastises Thelma for laughing at the
thought of the look on Harlan's face when he was shot. Thelma says,
between laughs, "he sure wasn't expecting that." Louise says sharply,
"It's not funny." Thelma sobers up: "I know."[53]

Thelma herself becomes an outlaw when she robs a convenience store after failing to guard Louise's life savings from a hitchhiker.[54] Louise is horrified by Thelma's crime. Thelma argues back: "It's not like I killed anybody."[55] Intended or not as a comparison with Louise's crime, Thelma's statement raises the moral question: which act is more serious, which deliberate violation of the law is more excusable or justifiable—the shooting of an unrepentant rapist or the burglary of a store for cash and liquor?[56] Louise mulls over this implicit question. Later, she tells Thelma her conclusion: there is "no such thing as justifiable robbery."[57]

Louise and Thelma engage in what they perceive to be justifiable action when they teach a lesson to the truck driver who several times leers, ogles, and harasses them with sexual remarks and gestures when they pass him on the road. It is a fantasy revenge scene, but it is as remarkable for the women's restraint as it is for their revenge. They operate with calculated judgment and a sense of proportionality rather than the boundless fury that revenge so often unleashes. They first lure him off the road with the suggestion that they accept his overtures. The camera shows him take off his wedding ring, spray some breath freshener in his mouth, and hop out of the enormous oil rig, ready for action. But to his initial surprise and disbelief, he encounters not a sexual opportunity but a lecture and an invitation to apologize. "We think you have really bad manners. Where do you get off" behaving so obnoxiously?[58] Thelma and Louise try to instruct him: what if some man did this to your mother or your sister or your wife? They invite him to grow, to learn. He does not get it. They ask why he ogles women by flapping his tongue repeatedly; they try to communicate how disgusting that is from their point of view. He still does not get it, and indelicately responds: "You women are crazy. I ain't apologizing for shit."[59] They ask him to say he's sorry. "Fuck that" is his answer.[60] And then the fantasy of revenge takes off.

They shoot the tires on his truck; it marvelously sinks into the ground. "God damn, you bitch" is his comment.[61] Thelma tells Louise, "I don't think he's gonna apologize."[62] They shoot the truck again, and it explodes, beautifully, dramatically, clouds billowing against the desert's expanse. Riding toward him in their car, they grab his hat as a souvenir, encircle him with the car and ride off. The difficulties he will encounter getting help and explaining what happened are suggested by the camera shots of his isolation with the burning truck; the women's satisfaction with their act is contagious. But the revenge *was* restrained. He was unharmed physically, though humiliated and left powerless. The punishment thus fit the crime, giving the perpetrator some of his own medicine. It is as if Thelma and Louise are saying, now you know how women feel when you humiliate them and leave them helpless.[63]

Does the movie make its own moral judgment about Thelma and Louise? It gives them no way out, underscoring how there is no place in this world for women who resist with violence. It offers them only the dignity and transcendence of chosen, joint, sisterly suicide.[64] Yet the film itself is forgiving and even adoring of Thelma and Louise. Pursued by a horde of police cars and helicopters, they leap in the car into the Grand Canyon, and immediately the film cuts back to prior, vibrant images of the women, replacing their death with their lives. The closing moments then are snippets of the high points of the film; the audience is left with their smiles, their excitement about their week-end away, their hair waving in the wind and the open space of the T-bird.[65] Different viewers, of course, may have different reactions.

Conclusion: At the Brink of the Canyon

As we suggested in our introduction, there is a sense in which *Thelma & Louise* picks up where *Adam's Rib* left off. There are important differences in structure and outcome between the two films. The Katherine Hepburn figure won her case—suggesting that the jury in the film found the sex-change fantasy of her closing argument believable, even if as viewers we cannot imagine how it could have been convincing. The avenging wife, played by Judy Holliday, broke the law. Perhaps she nevertheless was not an outlaw. Surely she was not the film's heroine. That status clearly belongs to the female lawyer, who, at apparent risk and deliberate challenge to her relationship with her prosecutor husband (Spencer Tracy), initiated contact with the accused, then cleverly used every legal and extra-legal device she could to get her client acquitted.

In contrast, no lawyer appears in *Thelma & Louise*. Thelma and Louise neither seek nor are sought out by legal counsel. This helps delineate their status as outlaws in two distinct and important senses. They do not turn to the law to effect the justice they envision. Nor are they under the protection of the law, inasmuch as they neither consult nor even imagine anyone who knows its tricky ways to be their witness or their defender. *Thelma & Louise* underscores yet a third sense in which the story of these two women is an outlaw story. Suppose they had, like Judy Holliday's

328 character, the defendant in *Adam's Rib*, come to have the law used in their defense. Most of what we learned about them on the road would be irrelevant or at best damaging in a courtroom. It is of no interest to the law or its agents what the accused think about the law and its failure to fit with their lives. The law has its own rules about what are the relevant and irrelevant facts about people's lives. The price of being protected by the law in court is to surrender control over the telling of your story. Its rich, complicated and confusing textures are not digestible by the legal record. People's real stories are outside the law. Had Thelma and Louise turned themselves over to the law—whether to the sheriff or to an attorney—they would have become subject to constraints much like those from which they found themselves fleeing, constraints which among other things make their versions of themselves and of the world irrelevant.

Screen author Callie Khouri thus might be said to have a view of the law well articulated by Mary Joe Frug: we have as much to learn about the law from those who find themselves (in both senses of that phrase) outside it as from those who enforce it, wield it, or study it.[66] Mary Joe's legal scholarship began to create a way of making room within the law for outlaw stories. She no doubt would have loved being in the T-bird convertible with Thelma and Louise, half in and half out of its protective metallic body, of narrative constraints, of law-abiding society.

Notes

1. ADAM'S RIB (Loews, Inc. 1939).

2. THELMA & LOUISE (Metro-Goldwyn-Mayer Pathe 1991).

3. Mary Joe Frug, *A Postmodern Feminist Legal Manifesto*, 105 HARV. L. REV. 1045 (1992), reprinted in this volume at 7.

4. Nonetheless, some viewers perceive the ending of the movie as a statement that the world holds no place for women who rebel. *See, e.g.*, Claire Reinelt, *Letters to the Editor*, BOSTON GLOBE, June 21, 1991, at 14 (Thelma and Louise "would rather die of their own choice than be subjected to male authority.... There was no other alternative for them, and that is a sad commentary on the fate of women who refuse to play by men's rules.").

5. Mary Joe Frug, *Re-Reading Contracts: A Feminist Analysis of a Contracts Casebook*, 34 AM. U. L. REV. 1065 (1985). The article identifies eight fictional readers who "resemble students and colleagues"—the Feminist, the Woman-Centered Reader, the Reader with a Chip on the Shoulder, the Innocent Gentleman, the Reader Who is Undressed for Success, the Individualist, the Civil Libertarian, and the Undeserving Male or Female Reader. We rely here on public comments about the movie *Thelma & Louise* to illustrate different kinds of viewers.

6. Diane White, *The Great Debate over "Thelma and Louise,"* BOSTON GLOBE, June 14, 1991, at 29; John Robinson, *The Great Debate over "Thelma and Louise,"* BOSTON GLOBE, June 14, 1991, at 29.

7. Robinson, *supra* note 6, at 29.

8. *Id.* at 36.

9. *Id.*

10. "Men know that for every Pam Smart there are legions of wife abusers. For every Inquisition-minded Queen Isabella there are a dozen Stalins and Hitlers. For every Witch of Wall Street there are armies of Donald Trumps and Henry Kravises and Ivan Boeskys." *Id.*

11. *Id.*

12. *Id.*

13. White, *supra* note 6, at 29.

14. *Id.*

15. *Id.*

16. *Id.*

17. *Id.* at 36. Elsewhere, Terrence Rafferty expressed a different reaction: "In the end, 'Thelma & Louise' seems less a feminist parable than an airy, lyrical joke about a couple of women who go off in search of a little personal space and discover that they have to keep going and going and going to find a space that's big enough." Terrence Rafferty, *The Current Cinema: Outlaw Princesses*, NEW YORKER, June 3, 1991, at 87.

18. *Compare* Larry Rohter, *The Third Woman of "Thelma and Louise,"* N.Y. TIMES, June 5, 1991, at C21 (Callie Khouri, who wrote the screenplay, describes "the controversial scene in which Louise kills Thelma's assailant" as "'a very cathartic scene for women'") *with* Peter Keough, *Who's Bashing Who?*, BOSTON PHOENIX, May 24, 1991, at 6 ("Audiences are used to seeing men pull triggers on malefactors, but the sight of a woman offing a man in defense of a member of her own sex touches off some fundamental anxieties.").

19. Kenneth Turan, *Smooth Ride for "Thelma & Louise,"* L.A. TIMES, May 24, 1991, at F1.

20. Keough, *supra* note 18, at 6 (quoting Geena Davis).

21. Rohter, *supra* note 18, at C21 (quoting Callie Khouri, Interview with Callie Khouri, in Los Angeles, Cal. (June 1991)).

22. People v. Goetz, 497 N.E.2d 41, 43 (N.Y. 1986).

23. *Id.* at 44.

24. People v. Goetz. 520 N.Y.S.2d 919 (N.Y. Sup. Ct. 1987), *aff'd*, 529 N.Y.S.2d 782 (N.Y. App. Div.), *aff'd*, 532 N.E.2d 1273 (N.Y. 1988). Goetz was convicted of one count of criminal possession of a weapon in the third degree. *Id.*

25. *See* Martha G. Duncan, *"A Strange Liking": Our Admiration for Criminals*, 19 U. ILL. L. REV. 1 (1991).

26. PATRICIA J. WILLIAMS, THE ALCHEMY OF RACE AND RIGHTS (1991).

27. Are young black men in New York ever described as being "out on a little spree," and allowed the impunity of "boys will be boys"?

28. Rohter, *supra* note 18, at C21.

29. *See infra* notes 49–51 and accompanying text (separating Louise's pointing the gun from her shooting).

30. ADAM'S RIB, *supra* note 1.

31. *Id.* Prosecutor Spencer Tracy elicits that defendant Judy Holliday had on occasion hit her husband just as he hit her. *Id.*

32. THELMA & LOUISE, *supra* note 2. What about Thelma's husband, Darryl? Some may describe him as yuppified; he's a car salesman/manager.

33. See *infra* notes 41–48 and accompanying text for Thelma's and Louise's discussions about moral responsibility.

34. ADAM'S RIB, *supra* note 1. But Spencer Tracy says she has crossed the bounds and shows no respect for law *inside* this very civilized courtroom fight. Still, they are *in it* together enough to have words instead of guns (until Spencer fakes an entrance with a gun—that turns out to be licorice). *Id.*

35. THELMA & LOUISE, *supra* note 2.

36. *Id.*

37. *Id.* Louise also knows something from a prior, veiled and terrible experience in Texas. She asks Thelma to find a route on the map to Mexico without going through Texas; Thelma says, "We're running for our lives. . . . Can't you make an exception?" Louise finally answers, "You shoot off a guy's head with his pants down and Texas is not the place you want to get caught." *Id.*

38. In many ways, the film is about Thelma's coming of consciousness as a woman, as an adult, and as a critic of male dominance. She says toward the end of the film, "I feel awake. . . . Wide-awake. I don't remember ever feeling this awake. . . . Everything looks different. You feel like that, too—like you got something to look forward to?" *Id.* This is when they are quite desperately racing from the police and hoping to reach Mexico. Still later, and somewhat lighter, she says that she feels a little crazy; Louise responds, "You've always been crazy. This is the just first chance you've ever really had to express yourself." *Id.*

39. Manager of a car dealership, Darryl has a license plate on his car that reads: "THE 1." *Id.*

40. *Id.*

41. It's not the case, though, that they can discuss anything with each other. Thelma says to Louise, "It happened to you, didn't it[?] . . . You was raped." Louise stops the car. "I'm warning you—just drop it. . . . I'm not talking about it." *Id.*

42. It is not a verbal comment, but Louise throws up soon after she shoots Harlan—not a typical reaction in movie depictions of shootings, yet one that says something about sensibilities and visceral judgment.

43. THELMA & LOUISE, *supra* note 2.

44. *Id.*

45. *Id.*

46. *Id.*

47. Perhaps Thelma is thinking that it is better for the victim herself to fight back rather than to be aided by a friend, and that it is better to keep a friend out of it and better to find one's own strength to fight back.

48. THELMA & LOUISE, *supra* note 2.

49. *Id.*

50. *Id.*

51. *Id.*

52. Consider the efforts to fit the conduct of battered women who kill their batterers in their sleep into the self-defense framework.

53. THELMA & LOUISE, *supra* note 2.

54. Thelma and J.D. engage in mutual seduction. This underscoring of the film's morality does not reject sexuality and sensuality, but does reject violent and nonconsensual sex.

55. THELMA & LOUISE, *supra* note 2.

56. Watching a video of the robbery, Thelma's husband, the FBI agents, and a police detective each intone the divinity: "Jesus Christ," "Good God," and "My Lord," as if only the highest judge could understand what had happened. *Id.*

57. *Id.* Detective Slocum actually implies a kind of excuse for the robbery when he interrogates J.D., the hitchhiker, about his role in what happened. Slocum inquires of J.D. whether he thinks that Thelma would have committed armed robbery if he "hadn't taken all their money.... [T]here's two girls out there ... they had a chance ... and now they're in some serious trouble.... I'm gonna hold you personally responsible." *Id.*

58. *Id.*

59. *Id.*

60. *Id.*

61. *Id.*

62. *Id.*

63. Proportionality also characterizes their treatment of a lone police officer who stops them for speeding. Knowing that a radio check would alert the officer to the FBI search for them, Thelma points the gun at him, shoots airholes in the trunk, directs the officer into it, and throws the trunk keys a few yards away. No greater violence is used than is needed to let the outlaws get away, and solicitation for the officer's needs is shown. The officer begs for mercy because he has a wife and children, and Thelma treats this as an occasion for a moral lesson. "You're lucky. You be sweet to 'em. Especially your wife. My husband wasn't sweet with me, look how I turned out." *Id.*

In a strange follow-up scene, a Rastafarian bicyclist comes across the apparently abandoned squad car and hears the officer banging from inside the truck and asking for help. The bicyclist responds by blowing reefer smoke through the airholes in the trunk. *Id.*

64. Yigael Yadin, Masada: Herod's Fortress and the Zealot's Last Stand 11–12 (Moshe Pearlman ed., 1966).

65. Displayed like snapshots are pictures of the two women waving at the camera and smiling in the wind. The last song on the soundtrack uses the lyric: "you're a part of me, I'm a part of you"—perhaps playing on the viewers' capacities to identify with the characters. Thelma & Louise, *supra* note 2.

66. Frug, *supra* note 5.

CHAPTER SEVENTEEN

MAPPING THE MARGINS

INTERSECTIONALITY, IDENTITY POLITICS, AND VIOLENCE AGAINST WOMEN OF COLOR

Kimberlé Crenshaw

OVER THE LAST two decades, women have organized against the almost routine violence that shapes their lives.[1] Drawing from the strength of shared experience, women have recognized that the political demands of millions speak more powerfully than the pleas of a few isolated voices. This politicization in turn has transformed the way we understand violence against women. For example, battering and rape, once seen as private (family matters) and aberrational (errant sexual aggression), are now largely recognized as part of a broad-scale system of domination that affects women as a class.[2] This process of recognizing as social and systemic what was formerly perceived as isolated and individual has also characterized the identity politics of African-Americans, other people of color, and gays and lesbians, among others. For all these groups, identity-based politics has been a source of strength, community, and intellectual development.

The embrace of identity politics, however, has been in tension with dominant conceptions of social justice. Race, gender, and other identity categories are most often treated in mainstream liberal discourse as vestiges of bias or domination—that is, as intrinsically negative frameworks in which social power works to exclude or marginalize those who are different. According to this understanding, our liberatory objective should be to empty such categories of any social significance. Yet implicit in certain strands of feminist and racial liberation movements, for example, is the view that the social power, in delineating difference, need not be the power of domination; it can instead be the source of social empowerment and reconstruction.

The problem with identity politics is not that it fails to transcend difference, as some critics charge, but rather the opposite—that it frequently conflates or ignores intragroup differences. In the context of violence against women, this elision of difference in identity politics is problematic, fundamentally because the violence that many women experience is often shaped by other dimensions of their identities, such as race and class. Moreover, ignoring difference *within* groups contributes to tension *among* groups, another problem of identity politics that bears on efforts to politicize violence against women. Feminist efforts to politicize experiences of women and antiracist efforts to politicize experiences of people of color have frequently proceeded as though the issues and experiences they each detail occur on mutually exclusive terrains. Although racism and sexism readily intersect in the lives of real people, they seldom do in feminist and antiracist practices. And so, when the practices expound identity as woman or person of color as an either/or proposition, they relegate the identity of women of color to a location that resists telling.

My objective in this essay is to advance the telling of that location by exploring the race and gender dimensions of violence against women of color.[3] Contemporary feminist and antiracist discourses have failed to consider intersectional identities such as women of color. Focusing on male violence against women through battering, I consider how the experiences of women of color are frequently the product of intersecting patterns of racism and sexism,[4] and how these experiences tend not to be represented within the discourses of either feminism or antiracism. Because of their intersectional identity as both women *and* of color within discourses that are shaped to respond to one *or* the other, women of color are marginalized within both.

In an earlier article, I used the concept of intersectionality to denote the various ways in which race and gender interact to shape the multiple dimensions of black women's employment experiences.[5] My objective there was to illustrate that many of the experiences black women face are not subsumed within the traditional boundaries of race or gender discrimination as these boundaries are currently understood, and that the intersection of racism and sexism factors into black women's lives in ways that cannot be captured wholly by looking at the race or gender dimensions of those experiences separately. I build on those observations here by exploring the various ways in which race and gender intersect in shaping structural, political, and representational aspects of violence against women of color.

I should say at the outset that intersectionality is not being offered here as some new, totalizing theory of identity. Nor do I mean to suggest that violence against women of color can be explained only through the specific frameworks of race and gender considered here. Indeed, factors I address only in part or not at all, such as class or sexuality, are often as critical in shaping the experiences of women of color. My focus on the intersections of race and gender only highlights the need to account for multiple grounds of identity when considering how the social world is constructed.[6]

I have divided the issues presented in this article into two categories. In the first section, I discuss structural intersectionality, the ways in which the location of women of color at the intersection of race and gender makes our actual experience of domestic violence and remedial reform qualitatively different than that of white women. I shift the focus in the next section to political intersectionality, where I analyze how both feminist and antiracist politics have, paradoxically, often helped to marginalize the issue of violence against women of color.

Structural Intersectionality

I observed the dynamics of structural intersectionality during a brief field study of battered women's shelters located in minority communities in Los Angeles.[7] In most cases, the physical assault that leads women to these shelters is merely the most immediate manifestation of the subordination they experience. Many women who seek protection are unemployed or underemployed, and a good number of them are poor. Shelters serving these women cannot afford to address only the violence inflicted

by the batterer; they must also confront the other multilayered and routinized forms of domination that often converge in these women's lives,
hindering their ability to create alternatives to the abusive relationships
that brought them to shelters in the first place. Many women of color, for
example, are burdened by poverty, child care responsibilities, and the
lack of job skills. These burdens, largely the consequence of gender and
class oppression, are then compounded by the racially discriminatory
employment and housing practices women of color often face,[8] as well as
by the disproportionately high unemployment among people of color
that makes battered women of color less able to depend on the support of
friends and relatives for temporary shelter.

Where systems of race, gender, and class domination converge, as they
do in the experiences of battered women of color, intervention strategies
based solely on the experiences of women who do not share the same
class or race backgrounds will be of limited help to women who because
of race and class face different obstacles. Such was the case in 1990 when
Congress amended the marriage fraud provisions of the Immigration and
Nationality Act to protect immigrant women who were battered or
exposed to extreme cruelty by the United States citizens or permanent
residents these women immigrated to the United States to marry. Under
the marriage fraud provisions of the Act, a person who immigrated to the
United States to marry a United States citizen or permanent resident had
to remain "properly" married for two years before even applying for permanent resident status,[9] at which time applications for the immigrant's
permanent status were required of both spouses.[10] Predictably, under
these circumstances, many immigrant women were reluctant to leave
even the most abusive of partners for fear of being deported.[11] When
faced with the choice between protection from their batterers and protection against deportation, many immigrant women chose the latter.
Reports of the tragic consequences of this double subordination put pressure on Congress to include in the Immigration Act of 1990 a provision
amending the marriage fraud rules to allow for an explicit waiver for
hardship caused by domestic violence.[12] Yet many immigrant women,
particularly immigrant women of color, have remained vulnerable to battering because they are unable to meet the conditions established for a
waiver. The evidence required to support a waiver "can include, but is
not limited to, reports and affidavits from police, medical personnel, psy-
chologists, school officials, and social service agencies."[13] For many
immigrant women, limited access to these resources can make it difficult

to obtain the evidence needed for a waiver. And cultural barriers often further discourage immigrant women from reporting or escaping battering situations. Tina Shum, a family counselor at a social service agency, points out that "[t]his law sounds so easy to apply, but there are cultural complications in the Asian community that make even these requirements difficult. . . . Just to find the opportunity and courage to call us is an accomplishment for many."[14] The typical immigrant spouse, she suggests, may live "[i]n an extended family where several generations live together, there may be no privacy on the telephone, no opportunity to leave the house and no understanding of public phones."[15] As a consequence, many immigrant women are wholly dependent on their husbands as their link to the world outside their homes.[16]

Immigrant women are also vulnerable to spousal violence because so many of them depend on their husbands for information regarding their legal status. Many women who are now permanent residents continue to suffer abuse under threats of deportation by their husbands. Even if the threats are unfounded, women who have no independent access to information will still be intimidated by such threats. And even though the domestic violence waiver focuses on immigrant women whose husbands are United States citizens or permanent residents, there are countless women married to undocumented workers (or who are themselves undocumented) who suffer in silence for fear that the security of their entire families will be jeopardized should they seek help or otherwise call attention to themselves.[17]

Language barriers present another structural problem that often limits opportunities of non-English-speaking women to take advantage of existing support services. Such barriers not only limit access to information about shelters, but also limit access to the security shelters provide. Some shelters turn non–English-speaking women away for lack of bilingual personnel and resources.[18]

These examples illustrate how patterns of subordination intersect in women's experience of domestic violence. Intersectional subordination need not be intentionally produced; in fact, it is frequently the consequence of the imposition of one burden that interacts with preexisting vulnerabilities to create yet another dimension of disempowerment. In the case of the marriage fraud provisions of the Immigration and Nationality Act, the imposition of a policy specifically designed to burden one class—immigrant spouses seeking permanent resident status— exacerbated the disempowerment of those already subordinated by other structures of domination. By failing to take into account the vulnerability of immigrant spouses to domestic violence, Congress positioned these women to absorb the simultaneous impact of its anti-immigration policy and their spouses' abuse.

The enactment of the domestic violence waiver of the marriage fraud provisions similarly illustrates how modest attempts to respond to certain problems can be ineffective when the intersectional location of women of color is not considered in fashioning the remedy. Cultural identity and class affect the likelihood that a battered spouse could take advantage of the waiver. Although the waiver is formally available to all women, the terms of the waiver make it inaccessible to some. Immigrant women who are socially, culturally, or economically privileged are more likely to be able to marshall the resources needed to satisfy the waiver requirements. Those immigrant women least able to take advantage of the waiver— women who are socially or economically the most marginal—are most likely to be women of color.

Political Intersectionality

The concept of political intersectionality highlights the fact that women of color are situated within at least two subordinated groups that frequently pursue conflicting political agendas. The need to split one's political energies between two sometimes opposing groups is a dimension of intersectional disempowerment that men of color and white women seldom confront. Indeed, their specific raced *and* gendered experiences, although intersectional, often define as well as confine the interests of the entire group. For example, racism as experienced by people of color who are of a particular gender—male—tends to determine the parameters of antiracist strategies, just as sexism as experienced by women who are of a particular race—white—tends to ground the women's movement. The problem is not simply that both discourses fail women of color by not acknowledging the "additional" issue of race or of patriarchy but that the discourses are often inadequate even to the discrete tasks of articulating the full dimensions of racism and sexism. Because women of color experience racism in ways not always the same as those experienced by men of color and sexism in ways not always parallel to experiences of white women, antiracism and feminism are limited, even on their own terms.

Among the most troubling political consequences of the failure of antiracist and feminist discourses to address the intersections of race and gender is the fact that, to the extent they can forward the interests of "people of color" and "women," respectively, one analysis often implicitly denies the validity of the other. The failure of feminism to interrogate race means that the resistance strategies of feminism will often replicate and reinforce the subordination of people of color, and the failure of antiracism to interrogate patriarchy means that antiracism will frequently reproduce the subordination of women. These mutual elisions present a particularly difficult political dilemma for women of color. Adopting either analysis constitutes a denial of a fundamental dimension of our subordination and precludes the development of a political discourse that more fully empowers women of color.

That the political interests of women of color are obscured and sometimes jeopardized by political strategies that ignore or suppress intersectional issues is illustrated by my experiences in gathering information for this essay. I attempted to review Los Angeles Police Department statistics reflecting the rate of domestic violence interventions by precinct because such statistics can provide a rough picture of arrests by racial group, given the degree of racial segregation in Los Angeles.[19] L.A.P.D., however, would not release the statistics. A representative explained that one reason the statistics were not released was that domestic violence activists both within and outside the Department feared that statistics reflecting the extent of domestic violence in minority communities might be selectively interpreted and publicized so as to undermine long-term efforts to force the Department to address domestic violence as a serious problem. I was told that activists were worried that the statistics might permit opponents to dismiss domestic violence as a minority problem and, therefore, not deserving of aggressive action.

The informant also claimed that representatives from various minority communities opposed the release of these statistics. They were concerned, apparently, that the data would unfairly represent Black and Brown communities as unusually violent, potentially reinforcing stereotypes that might be used in attempts to justify oppressive police tactics and other discriminatory practices. These misgivings are based on the familiar and not unfounded premise that certain minority groups—especially Black men—have already been stereotyped as uncontrollably violent. Some worry that attempts to make domestic violence an object of political action may only serve to confirm such stereotypes and undermine efforts to combat negative beliefs about the Black community.

This account sharply illustrates how women of color can be erased by the strategic silences of antiracism and feminism. The political priorities of both were defined in ways that suppressed information that could have facilitated attempts to confront the problem of domestic violence in communities of color.

Domestic Violence and Antiracist Politics

Within communities of color, efforts to stem the politicization of domestic violence are often grounded in attempts to maintain the integrity of the community. The articulation of this perspective takes different forms. Some critics allege that feminism has no place within communities of color, that the issues are internally divisive, and that they represent the migration of white women's concerns into a context in which they are not only irrelevant but also harmful. At its most extreme, this rhetoric denies that gender violence is a problem in the community and characterizes any effort to politicize gender subordination as itself a community problem. This is the position taken by Shahrazad Ali in her controversial book, *The Blackman's Guide to Understanding the Blackwoman.*[20] In this stridently antifeminist tract, Ali draws a positive correlation between domestic violence and the liberation of African-Americans. Ali blames the deteriorating conditions within the Black community on the insubordination of Black women and on the failure of Black men to control them.[21] Ali goes so far as to advise Black men to physically chastise Black women when they are "disrespectful."[22] While she cautions that Black men must use moderation in disciplining "their" women, she argues that they must sometimes resort to physical force to reestablish the authority over Black women that racism has disrupted.

Ali's premise is that patriarchy is beneficial for the Black community, and that it must be strengthened through coercive means if necessary.[23] Yet the violence that accompanies this will to control is devastating, not only for the Black women who are victimized, but also for the entire Black community. The recourse to violence to resolve conflicts establishes a dangerous pattern for children raised in such environments and contributes to many other pressing problems.[24] It has been estimated that nearly forty percent of all homeless women and children have fled violence in the home,[25] and an estimated sixty-three percent of young men between the ages of eleven and twenty who are imprisoned for homicide

340   have killed their mothers' batterers.[26] And yet, while gang violence, homicide, and other forms of Black-on-Black crime have increasingly been discussed within African-American politics, patriarchal ideas about gender and power preclude the recognition of domestic violence as yet another compelling incidence of Black-on-Black crime.

Efforts such as Ali's to justify violence against women in the name of Black liberation are indeed extreme.[27] The more common problem is that the political or cultural interests of the community are interpreted in a way that precludes full public recognition of the problem of domestic violence. While it would be misleading to suggest that white Americans have come to terms with the degree of violence in their own homes, it is nonetheless the case that race adds yet another dimension to why the problem of domestic violence is suppressed within nonwhite communities. People of color often must weigh their interests in avoiding issues that might reinforce distorted public perceptions against the need to acknowledge and address intracommunity problems. Yet the cost of suppression is seldom recognized, in part because the failure to discuss the issue shapes perceptions of how serious the problem is in the first place.

The controversy over Alice Walker's novel *The Color Purple* can be understood as an intracommunity debate about the political costs of exposing gender violence within the Black community.[28] Some critics chastised Walker for portraying Black men as violent brutes.[29] One critic lambasted Walker's portrayal of Celie, the emotionally and physically abused protagonist who finally triumphs in the end. Walker, the critic contended, had created in Celie a Black woman whom she couldn't imagine existing in any Black community she knew or could conceive of.[30]

The claim that Celie was somehow an unauthentic character might be read as a consequence of silencing discussion of intracommunity violence. Celie may be unlike any Black woman we know because the real terror experienced daily by minority women is routinely concealed in a misguided (though perhaps understandable) attempt to forestall racial stereotyping. Of course, it is true that representations of Black violence—whether statistical or fictional—are often written into a larger script that consistently portrays Black and other minority communities as pathologically violent. The problem, however, is not so much the portrayal of violence itself as it is the absence of other narratives and images portraying a fuller range of Black experience. Suppression of some of these issues in the name of antiracism imposes real costs. Where information about violence in minority communities is not available, domestic violence is unlikely to be addressed as a serious issue.

The political imperatives of a narrowly focused antiracist strategy support other practices that isolate women of color. For example, activists who have attempted to provide support services to Asian and African-American women report intense resistance from those communities.[31] At other times, cultural and social factors contribute to suppression. Nilda Rimonte, director of Everywoman's Shelter in Los Angeles, points out that in the Asian community, saving the honor of the family from shame is a priority.[32] Unfortunately, this priority tends to be interpreted as obliging women not to scream rather than obliging men not to hit.

Race and culture contribute to the suppression of domestic violence in other ways as well. Women of color are often reluctant to call the police, a hesitancy likely due to a general unwillingness among people of color to subject their private lives to the scrutiny and control of a police force that is frequently hostile. There is also a more generalized community ethic against public intervention, the product of a desire to create a private world free from the diverse assaults on the public lives of racially subordinated people. The home is not simply a man's castle in the patriarchal sense, but may also function as a safe haven from the indignities of life in a racist society. However, but for this "safe haven" in many cases, women of color victimized by violence might otherwise seek help.

There is also a general tendency within antiracist discourse to regard the problem of violence against women of color as just another manifestation of racism. In this sense, the relevance of gender domination within the community is reconfigured as a consequence of discrimination against men. Of course, it is probably true that racism contributes to the cycle of violence, given the stress that men of color experience in dominant society. It is therefore more than reasonable to explore the links between racism and domestic violence. But the chain of violence is more complex and extends beyond this single link. Racism is linked to patriarchy to the extent that racism denies men of color the power and privilege that dominant men enjoy. When violence is understood as an acting-out of being denied male power in other spheres, it seems counterproductive to embrace constructs that implicitly link the solution to domestic violence to the acquisition of greater male power. The more promising political imperative is to challenge the legitimacy of such power expectations by exposing their dysfunctional and debilitating effect on families and communities of color. Moreover, while understanding links between racism and domestic violence is an important component of any effective intervention strategy, it is also clear that women of color need not await the ultimate triumph over racism before they can expect to live violence-free lives.

Race and the Domestic Violence Lobby

Not only do race-based priorities function to obscure the problem of violence suffered by women of color; feminist concerns often suppress minority experiences as well. Strategies for increasing awareness of domestic violence within the white community tend to begin by citing the commonly shared assumption that battering is a minority problem. The strategy then focuses on demolishing this strawman, stressing that spousal abuse also occurs in the white community. Countless first-person stories begin with a statement like, "I was not supposed to be a battered wife." That battering occurs in families of all races and all classes seems to be an ever-present theme of anti-abuse campaigns.[33] First-person anecdotes and studies, for example, consistently assert that battering cuts across racial, ethnic, economic, educational, and religious lines.[34] Such disclaimers seem relevant only in the presence of an initial, widely held belief that domestic violence occurs primarily in minority or poor families. Indeed some authorities explicitly renounce the "stereotypical myths" about battered women.[35] A few commentators have even transformed the message that battering is not *exclusively* a problem of the poor or minority communities into a claim that it *equally* affects all races and classes.[36] Yet these comments seem less concerned with exploring domestic abuse within "stereotyped" communities than with removing the stereotype as an obstacle to exposing battering within white middle and upper-class communities.

Efforts to politicize the issue of violence against women challenge beliefs that violence occurs only in homes of "others." While it is unlikely that advocates and others who adopt this rhetorical strategy intend to exclude or ignore the needs of poor and colored women, the underlying premise of this seemingly univeralistic appeal is to keep the sensibilities of dominant social groups focused on the experiences of those groups. Indeed, as subtly suggested by the opening comments of Senator David Boren (D-Okla.) in support of the Violence Against Women Act of 1991, the displacement of the "other" as the presumed victim of domestic violence works primarily as a political appeal to rally white elites. Boren said,

> Violent crimes against women are not limited to the streets of the
> inner cities, but also occur in homes in the urban and rural areas
> across the country.
>   Violence against women affects not only those who are actually
> beaten and brutalized, but indirectly affects all women. Today, our
> wives, mothers, daughters, sisters, and colleagues are held captive by
> fear generated from these violent crimes—held captive not for what
> they do or who they are, but solely because of gender.[37]

Rather than focusing on and illuminating how violence is disregarded when the home is "othered," the strategy implicit in Senator Boren's remarks functions instead to politicize the problem only in the dominant community. This strategy permits white women victims to come into focus, but does little to disrupt the patterns of neglect that permitted the problem to continue as long as it was imagined to be a minority problem. The experience of violence by minority women is ignored, except to the extent it gains white support for domestic violence programs in the white community.

Senator Boren and his colleagues no doubt believe that they have provided legislation and resources that will address the problems of all women victimized by domestic violence. Yet despite their universalizing rhetoric of "all" women, they were able to empathize with female victims of domestic violence only by looking past the plight of "other" women and by recognizing the familiar faces of their own. The strength of the appeal to "protect our women" must be its race and class specificity. After all, it has always been someone's wife, mother, sister, or daughter that has been abused, even when the violence was stereotypically Black, Brown, and poor. The point here is not that the Violence Against Women Act is particularistic on its own terms, but that unless the Senators and other policymakers ask why violence remained insignificant as long as it was understood as a minority problem, it is unlikely that women of color will share equally in the distribution of resources and concern. It is even more unlikely, however, that those in power will be forced to confront this issue. As long as attempts to politicize domestic violence focus on convincing whites that this is not a "minority" problem but *their* problem, any authentic and sensitive attention to the experiences of Black and other minority women probably will continue to be regarded as jeopardizing the movement.

While Senator Boren's statement reflects a self-consciously political presentation of domestic violence, an episode of the CBS news program

344   *48 Hours*[38] shows how similar patterns of "othering" nonwhite women
are apparent in journalistic accounts of domestic violence as well. The
program presented seven women who were victims of abuse. Six were
interviewed at some length along with their family members, friends,
supporters, and even detractors. The viewer got to know something
about each of these women. These victims were humanized. Yet the sev-
enth woman, the only non-white one, never came into focus. She was literally unrecognizable throughout the segment, first introduced by
photographs showing her face badly beaten and later shown with her face
electronically altered in the videotape of a hearing at which she was
forced to testify. Other images associated with this woman included shots
of a bloodstained room and blood-soaked pillows. Her boyfriend was pictured handcuffed while the camera zoomed in for a close-up of his blood-
ied sneakers. Of all the presentations in the episode, hers was the most
graphic and impersonal. The overall point of the segment "featuring"
this woman was that battering might not escalate into homicide if battered women would only cooperate with prosecutors. In focusing on its
own agenda and failing to explore why this woman refused to cooperate,
the program diminished this woman, communicating, however subtly,
that she was responsible for her own victimization.

Unlike the other women, all of whom, again, were white, this Black
woman had no name, no family, no context. The viewer sees her only as
victimized and uncooperative. She cries when shown pictures. She
pleads not to be forced to view the bloodstained room and her disfigured
face. The program does not help the viewer to understand her predicament. The possible reasons she did not want to testify—fear, love, or
possibly both—are never suggested.[39] Most unfortunately, she, unlike
the other six, is given no epilogue. While the fates of the other women
are revealed at the end of the episode, we discover nothing about the
Black woman. She, like the "others" she represents, is simply left to herself and soon forgotten.

I offer this description to suggest that "other" women are silenced as
much by being relegated to the margin of experience as by total exclusion. Tokenistic, objectifying, voyeuristic inclusion is at least as disempowering as complete exclusion. The effort to politicize violence against
women will do little to address Black and other minority women if their
images are retained simply to magnify the problem rather than to
humanize their experiences. Similarly, the antiracist agenda will not be
advanced significantly by forcibly suppressing the reality of battering in

minority communities. As the *48 Hours* episode makes clear, the images   *345*
and stereotypes we fear are readily available and are frequently deployed
in ways that do not generate sensitive understanding of the nature of
domestic violence in minority communities.

Race and Domestic Violence Support Services

Women working in the field of domestic violence have sometimes reproduced the subordination and marginalization of women of color by
adopting policies, priorities, or strategies of empowerment that either
elide or wholly disregard the particular intersectional needs of women of
color. While gender, race, and class intersect to create the particular context in which women of color experience violence, certain choices made
by "allies" can reproduce intersectional subordination within the very
resistance strategies designed to respond to the problem.

This problem is starkly illustrated by the inaccessibility of domestic violence support services to many non-English-speaking women. In a letter
written to the deputy commissioner of the New York State Department of
Social Services, Diana Campos, Director of Human Services for
Programas de Ocupaciones y Desarrollo Económico Real, Inc. (PODER),
detailed the case of a Latina in crisis who was repeatedly denied accomo-
dation at a shelter because she could not prove that she was English-
proficient. The woman had fled her home with her teenaged son, believing
her husband's threats to kill them both. She called the domestic violence
hotline administered by PODER seeking shelter for herself and her son.
Because most shelters would not accommodate the woman with her son,
they were forced to live on the streets for two days. The hotline counselor
was finally able to find an agency that would take both the mother and the
son, but when the counselor told the intake coordinator at the shelter that
the woman spoke limited English, the coordinator told her that they could
not take anyone who was not English-proficient. When the woman in crisis called back and was told of the shelter's "rule," she replied that she
could understand English if spoken to her slowly. As Campos explains,
Mildred, the hotline counselor, told Wendy, the intake coordinator

> that the woman said that she could communicate a little in English.
> Wendy told Mildred that they could not provide services to this
> woman because they have house rules that the woman must agree to
> follow. Mildred asked her, "What if the woman agrees to follow your

rules? Will you still not take her?" Wendy responded that all of the
women at the shelter are required to attend [a] support group and
they would not be able to have her in the group if she could not communicate. Mildred mentioned the severity of this woman's case. She
told Wendy that the woman had been wandering the streets at night
while her husband is home, and she had been mugged twice. She also
reiterated the fact that this woman was in danger of being killed by
either her husband or a mugger. Mildred expressed that the woman's
safety was a priority at this point, and that once in a safe place,
receiving counseling in a support group could be dealt with.[40]

The intake coordinator restated the shelter's policy of taking only
English-speaking women, and stated further that the woman would have
to call the shelter herself for screening. If the woman could communicate
with them in English, she might be accepted. When the woman called
the PODER hotline later that day, she was in such a state of fear that the
hotline counselor who had been working with her had difficulty understanding her in Spanish.[41] Campos directly intervened at this point, calling the executive director of the shelter. A counselor called back from the
shelter. As Campos reports,

> Marie [the counselor] told me that they did not want to take the
> woman in the shelter because they felt that the woman would feel iso-
> lated. I explained that the son agreed to translate for his mother dur-
> ing the intake process. Furthermore, that we would assist them in
> locating a Spanish-speaking battered women's advocate to assist in
> counseling her. Marie stated that utilizing the son was not an accept-
> able means of communication for them, *since it further victimized the
> victim*. In addition, she stated that they had similar experiences with
> women who were non-English-speaking, and that the women eventu-
> ally just left because they were not able to communicate with anyone.
> I expressed my extreme concern for her safety and reiterated that we
> would assist them in providing her with the necessary services until
> we could get her placed someplace where they had bilingual staff.[42]

After several more calls, the shelter finally agreed to take the woman.
The woman called once more during the negotiation; however, after a
plan was in place, the woman never called back. Said Campos, "After so
many calls, we are now left to wonder if she is alive and well, and if she
will ever have enough faith in our ability to help her to call us again the
next time she is in crisis."[43]

Despite this woman's desperate need, she was unable to receive the protection afforded English-speaking women, due to the shelter's rigid commitment to exclusionary policies. Perhaps even more troubling than the shelter's lack of bilingual resources was its refusal to allow a friend or relative to translate for the woman. This story illustrates the absurdity of a feminist approach that would make the ability to attend a support group without a translator a more significant consideration in the distribution of resources than the risk of physical harm on the street. The point is not that the shelter's image of empowerment is empty, but rather that it was imposed without regard to the disempowering consequences for women who didn't match the kind of client the shelter's administrators imagined. And thus they failed to accomplish the basic priority of the shelter movement—to get the woman out of danger.

Here the woman in crisis was made to bear the burden of the shelter's refusal to anticipate and provide for the needs of non-English-speaking women. Said Campos, "It is unfair to impose more stress on victims by placing them in the position of having to demonstrate their proficiency in English in order to receive services that are readily available to other battered women."[44] The problem is not easily dismissed as one of well-intentioned ignorance. The specific issue of monolingualism and the monistic view of women's experience that set the stage for this tragedy were not new issues in New York. Indeed, several women of color reported that they had repeatedly struggled with the New York State Coalition Against Domestic Violence over language exclusion and other practices that marginalized the interests of women of color.[45] Yet despite repeated lobbying, the Coalition did not act to incorporate the specific needs of nonwhite women into their central organizing vision.

Some critics have linked the Coalition's failure to address these issues to the narrow vision of coalition that animated its interaction with women of color in the first place. The very location of the Coalition's headquarters in Woodstock, New York—an area where few people of color live—seemed to guarantee that women of color would play a limited role in formulating policy. Moreover, efforts to include women of color came, it seems, as something of an afterthought. Many were invited to participate only after the Coalition was awarded a grant by the state to recruit women of color. However, as one "recruit" said, "they were not really prepared to deal with us or our issues. They thought that they could simply incorporate us into their organization without rethinking any of their beliefs or priorities and that we would be happy."[46] Even the

348   most formal gestures of inclusion were not to be taken for granted. On one occasion when several women of color attended a meeting to discuss a special task force on women of color, the group debated all day over including the issue on the agenda.[47]

The relationship between the white women and the women of color on the Board was a rocky one from beginning to end. Other conflicts developed over differing definitions of feminism. For example, the Board decided to hire a Latina staffperson to manage outreach programs to the Latino community, but the white members of the hiring committee rejected candidates favored by Latina committee members who did not have recognized feminist credentials. As Campos pointed out, by measuring Latinas against their own biographies, the white members of the Board failed to recognize the different circumstances under which feminist consciousness develops and manifests itself within minority communities. Many of the women who interviewed for the position were established activists and leaders within their own community, a fact in itself suggesting that these women were probably familiar with the specific gender dynamics in their communities and were accordingly better qualified to handle outreach than other candidates with more conventional feminist credentials.[48]

The Coalition ended a few months later when the women of color walked out.[49] Many of these women returned to community-based organizations, preferring to struggle over women's issues within their communities rather than struggle over race and class issues with white middle-class women. Yet as illustrated by the case of the Latina who could find no shelter, the dominance of a particular perspective and set of priorities within the shelter community continues to marginalize the needs of women of color.

The struggle over which differences matter and which do not is neither an abstract nor an insignificant debate among women. Indeed, these conflicts are about more than difference as such; they raise critical issues of power. The problem is not simply that women who dominate the antiviolence movement are different from women of color but that they frequently have power to determine, either through material or rhetorical resources, whether the intersectional differences of women of color will be incorporated at all into the basic formulation of policy. Thus, the struggle over incorporating these differences is not a petty or superficial conflict about who gets to sit at the head of the table. In the context of violence, it is sometimes a deadly serious matter of who will survive—and who will not.[50]

Notes

1. Feminist academics and activists have played a central role in forwarding an ideological and institutional challenge to the practices that condone and perpetuate violence against women. *See generally* SUSAN BROWNMILLER, AGAINST OUR WILL: MEN, WOMEN AND RAPE (1975); LORENNE M.G. CLARK & DEBRA J. LEWIS, RAPE: THE PRICE OF COERCIVE SEXUALITY (1977); R. EMERSON DOBASH & RUSSELL DOBASH, VIOLENCE AGAINST WIVES: A CASE AGAINST THE PATRIARCHY (1979); NANCY GAGER & CATHLEEN SCHURR, SEXUAL ASSAULT: CONFRONTING RAPE IN AMERICA (1976); DIANA E.H. RUSSELL, THE POLITICS OF RAPE: THE VICTIM S PERSPECTIVE (1974); ELIZABETH ANNE STANKO, INTIMATE INTRUSIONS: WOMEN'S EXPERIENCE OF MALE VIOLENCE (1985); LENORE E. WALKER, TERRIFYING LOVE: WHY BATTERED WOMEN KILL AND HOW SOCIETY RESPONDS (1989); LENORE E. WALKER, THE BATTERED WOMAN SYNDROME (1984); LENORE E. WALKER, THE BATTERED WOMAN (1979).

2. *See, e.g.,* SUSAN SCHECHTER, WOMEN AND MALE VIOLENCE: THE VISIONS AND STRUGGLES OF THE BATTERED WOMEN S MOVEMENT (1982) (arguing that battering is a means of maintaining women's subordinate position); BROWNMILLER, *supra* note 1 (arguing that rape is a patriarchal practice that subordinates women to men); Elizabeth Schneider, *The Violence of Privacy,* 23 CONN. L. REV. 973, 974 (1991) (discussing how "concepts of privacy permit, encourage and reinforce violence against women"); Susan Estrich, *Rape,* 95 YALE L.J. 1087 (1986) (analyzing rape law as one illustration of sexism in criminal law); *see also* CATHARINE A. MACKINNON, SEXUAL HARASSMENT OF WORKING WOMEN: A CASE OF SEX DISCRIMINATION 143–213 (1979) (arguing that sexual harassment should be redefined as sexual discrimination actionable under Title VII, rather than viewed as misplaced sexuality in the workplace).

3. This article arises out of and is inspired by two emerging scholarly discourses. The first is critical race theory. For a cross-section of what is now a substantial body of literature, see PATRICIA J. WILLIAMS, THE ALCHEMY OF RACE AND RIGHTS (1991); Robin D. Barnes, *Race Consciousness: The Thematic Content of Racial Distinctiveness in Critical Race Scholarship,* 103 HARV. L. REV. 1864 (1990); John O. Calmore, *Critical Race Theory, Archie Shepp, and Fire Music: Securing an Authentic Intellectual Life in a Multicultural World,* 65 S. CAL. L. REV. 2129 (1992); Anthony E. Cook, *Beyond Critical Legal Studies: The Reconstructive Theology of Dr. Martin Luther King,* 103 HARV. L. REV. 985 (1990); Kimberlé Williams Crenshaw, *Race, Reform and Retrenchment: Transformation and Legitimation in Antidiscrimination Law,* 101 HARV. L. REV. 1331 (1988); Richard Delgado, *When a Story is Just a Story: Does Voice Really Matter?,* 76 VA. L. REV. 95 (1990); Neil Gotanda, *A Critique of "Our Constitution is Colorblind,"* 44 STAN. L. REV. 1 (1991); Mari J. Matsuda, *Public Response to Racist Speech: Considering the Victim's Story,* 87 MICH. L. REV. 2320 (1989); Charles R. Lawrence III, *The Id, the Ego, and Equal Protection: Reckoning with Unconscious Racism,* 39 STAN. L. REV. 317 (1987); Gerald Torres, *Critical Race Theory: The Decline of the Universalist Ideal and the Hope of Plural Justice—Some Observations and Questions of an Emerging Phenomenon,* 75 MINN. L. REV. 993 (1991). For a useful overview of critical race theory, see Calmore, *supra,* at 2160–2168.

   A second, less formally linked body of legal scholarship investigates the connections between race and gender. *See, e.g.,* Regina Austin, *Sapphire Bound!,* 1989 WISC. L. REV. 539; Crenshaw, *supra*; Angela P. Harris, *Race and Essentialism in Feminist Legal Theory,* 42 STAN. L. REV. 581 (1990); Marlee Kline, *Race, Racism and Feminist Legal Theory,* 12 HARV. WOMEN'S L.J. 115 (1989); Dorothy E. Roberts, *Punishing Drug Addicts Who Have Babies: Women of Color, Equality and the Right of Privacy,* 104 HARV. L. REV. 1419 (1991); Cathy Scarborough, *Conceptualizing Black Women's Employment Experiences,* 98

YALE L.J. 1457 (1989); Peggie R. Smith, *Separate Identities: Black Women, Work and Title VII*, 14 HARV. WOMEN'S L.J. 21 (1991); Judy Scales-Trent, *Black Women and the Constitution: Finding Our Place, Asserting Our Rights*, 24 HARV. C.R-C.L. L. REV. 9 (1989); Judith A. Winston, *Mirror, Mirror on the Wall: Title VII, Section 1981, and the Intersection of Race and Gender in the Civil Rights Act of 1990*, 79 CAL. L. REV. 775 (1991).

4. Although this article deals with violent assault perpetrated by men against women, women are also subject to violent assault by women. Violence among lesbians is a hidden but significant problem. One expert reported that in a study of ninety lesbian couples, roughly 46% of lesbians have been physically abused by their partners. Jane Garcia, *The Cost of Escaping Domestic Violence: Fear of Treatment in a Largely Homophobic Society May Keep Lesbian Abuse Victims from Calling for Help*, L.A. TIMES, May 6, 1991, at 2; *see also* NAMING THE VIOLENCE: SPEAKING OUT ABOUT LESBIAN BATTERING (Kerry Lobel ed., 1986); Ruthann Robson, *Lavender Bruises: Intralesbian Violence, Law and Lesbian Legal Theory*, 20 GOLDEN GATE U. L. REV. 567 (1990). There are clear parallels between violence against women in the lesbian community and violence against women in communities of color. Lesbian violence is often shrouded in secrecy for similar reasons that have suppressed the exposure of heterosexual violence in communities of color—fear of embarassing other members of the community, which is already stereotyped as deviant, and fear of being ostracized from the community. Despite these similarities, there are nonetheless distinctions between male abuse of women and female abuse of women that in the context of patriarchy, racism and homophobia, warrants more focused analysis than is possible here.

5. Kimberlé Crenshaw, *Demarginalizing the Intersection of Race and Sex*, 1989 U. CHI. LEGAL F. 139.

6. Professor Mari Matsuda calls this inquiry "asking the other question." Mari J. Matsuda, *Beside My Sister, Facing the Enemy: Legal Theory Out of Coalition*, 43 STAN. L. REV. 1183 (1991). For example, we should look at an issue or condition traditionally regarded as a gender issue and ask, "Where's the racism in this?"

7. During my research in Los Angeles, California, I visited Jenessee Battered Women's Shelter, the only shelter in the Western states primarily serving Black women, and Everywoman's Shelter, which primarily serves Asian women. I also visited Estelle Chueng at the Asian Pacific Law Foundation and I spoke with a representative of La Casa, a shelter in the predominantly Latino community of East L.A.

8. Together they make securing even the most basic necessities beyond the reach of many. Indeed one shelter provider reported that nearly eighty-five percent of her clients returned to the battering relationships, largely because of difficulties in finding employment and housing.

9. 8 U.S.C. § 1186a (1988). The Marriage Fraud Amendments provide that an alien spouse "shall be considered, at the time of obtaining the status of an alien lawfully admitted for permanent residence, to have obtained such status on a conditional basis subject to the provisions of this section." § 1186a(a)(1). An alien spouse with permanent resident status under this conditional basis may have her status terminated if the Attorney General finds that the marriage was "improper," § 1186a(b)(1), or if she fails to file a petition or fails to appear at the personal interview. § 1186a(c)(2)(A).

10. The Marriage Fraud Amendments provided that for the conditional resident status to be removed, "the alien spouse and the petitioning spouse (if not deceased) *jointly* must submit to the Attorney General...a petition which requests the removal of such conditional basis and which states, under penalty of perjury, the facts and information." § 1186a(b)(1)(A) (emphasis added). The Amendments provided for a waiver, at the Attorney General's discretion, if the alien spouse was able to demonstrate that deportation would result in extreme hardship, or that the qualifying marriage was terminated for good cause. § 1186a(c)(4). However, the terms of this hardship waiver have not ade-

quately protected battered spouses. For example, the requirement that the marriage be
terminated for good cause may be difficult to satisfy in states with no-fault divorces.
Eileen P. Lynsky, *Immigration Marriage Fraud Amendments of 1986: Till Congress Do Us
Part*, 41 U. MIAMI L. REV. 1087, 1095 n.47 (1987) (citing Jerome B. Ingber & R. Leo
Prischet, *The Marriage Fraud Amendments, in* THE NEW SIMPSON-RODINO IMMIGRATION
LAW OF 1986, 564–65 (Stanley Mailman ed., 1986)).

11. Immigration activists have pointed out that "[t]he 1986 Immigration Reform Act and
the Immigration Marriage Fraud Amendment have combined to give the spouse apply-
ing for permanent residence a powerful tool to control his partner." Jorge Banales,
Abuse Among Immigrants; As Their Numbers Grow So Does the Need for Services, WASH.
POST, Oct. 16, 1990, at E5. Dean Ito Taylor, executive director of Nihonmachi Legal
Outreach in San Francisco, explained that the Marriage Fraud Amendments "bound
these immigrant women to their abusers." Deanna Hodgin, *"Mail-Order" Brides Marry
Pain to Get Green Cards*, WASH. TIMES, Apr. 16, 1991, at E1. In one egregious instance
described by Beckie Masaki, executive director of the Asian Women's Shelter in San
Francisco, the closer the Chinese bride came to getting her permanent residency in the
United States, the more harshly her Asian-American husband beat her. Her husband,
kicking her in the neck and face, warned her that she needed him, and if she did not do
as he told her, he would call immigration officials. *Id.*

12. Immigration Act of 1990, Pub. L. No. 101–649, 104 Stat. 4978. The Act, introduced by
Representative Louise Slaughter (D-N.Y.), provides that a battered spouse who has
conditional permanent resident status can be granted a waiver for failure to meet the
requirements if she can show that "the marriage was entered into in good faith and that
after the marriage the alien spouse was battered by or was subjected to extreme mental
cruelty by the U.S. citizen or permanent resident spouse" H.R. REP. No. 723(I), 101st
Cong., 2d Sess. 78 (1990), *reprinted in* 1990 U.S.C.C.A.N. 6710, 6758; *see also* 8 C.F.R.
§ 216.5(3) (1992) (regulations for application for waiver based on claim of having been
battered or subjected to extreme mental cruelty).

13. H.R. REP. NO. 723(I), *supra* note 12, at 79, *reprinted in* 1990 U.S.C.C.A.N. 6710, 6759.

14. Hodgin, *supra* note 11.

15. *Id.*

16. MILDRED DALEY PAGELOW, WOMAN-BATTERING: VICTIMS AND THEIR EXPERIENCES 96
(1981). The seventy minority women in the study "had a double disadvantage in this
society that serves to tie them more strongly to their spouses." *Id.*

17. Incidents of sexual abuse of undocumented women abound. Marta Rivera, director of
the Hostos College Center for Women's and Immigrant's Rights, tells of how a 19-year-
old Dominican woman had "arrived shaken...after her boss raped her in the women's
restroom at work." The woman told Rivera that "70 to 80 percent of the workers [in a
Brooklyn garment factory] were undocumented, and they all accepted sex as part of the
job.... She said a 13-year-old girl had been raped there a short while before her, and
the family sent her back to the Dominican Republic." Vivienne Walt, *Immigrant Abuse:
Nowhere to Hide; Women Fear Deportation, Experts Say*, NEWSDAY, Dec. 2, 1990, at 8.

18. PAGELOW, *supra* note 16, at 96–97.

19. Most crime statistics are classified by sex or race but none are classified by sex *and* race.
Because we know that most rape victims are women, the racial breakdown reveals, at
best, rape rates for Black women. Yet, even given this head start, rates for other nonwhite women are difficult to collect. While there are some statistics for Latinas, statistics for Asian and Native American women are virtually non-existent. *Cf.* G. Chezia
Carraway, *Violence Against Women of Color*, 43 STAN. L. REV. 1301 (1991).

20. SHAHRAZAD ALI, THE BLACKMAN S GUIDE TO UNDERSTANDING THE BLACKWOMAN (1989).

21. Shahrazad Ali suggests that the "[Blackwoman] certainly does not believe that her dis-
repect for the Blackman is destructive, *nor* that her opposition to him has deteriorated

the Black nation." ALI, *supra* note 20, at viii. Blaming the problems of the community on the failure of the Black woman to accept her "real definition," Ali explains that "[n]o nation can rise when the natural order of the behavior of the male and the female have been altered against their wishes by force. No species can survive if the female of the genus disturbs the balance of her nature by acting other than herself." *Id.* at 76.

22. Ali advises the Blackman to hit the Blackwoman in the mouth, "[b]ecause it is from that hole, in the lower part of her face, that all her rebellion culminates into words. Her unbridled tongue is a main reason she cannot get along with the Blackman. She often needs a reminder." *Id.* at 169. Ali warns that "if [the Blackwoman] ignores the authority and superiority of the Blackman, there is a penalty. When she crosses this line and becomes viciously insulting it is time for the Blackman to soundly slap her in the mouth." *Id.*

23. In this regard, Ali's arguments bear much in common with those of neoconservatives who attribute many of the social ills plaguing Black America to the breakdown of patriarchal family values. *See, e.g.,* William Raspberry, *If We Are to Rescue American Families, We Have to Save the Boys,* CHI. TRIB., July 19, 1989, at C15; George F. Will, *Voting Rights Won't Fix It,* WASH. POST, Jan. 23, 1986, at A23; George F. Will, *"White Racism" Doesn't Make Blacks Mere Victims of Fate,* MILWAUKEE J., Feb. 21, 1986, at 9. Ali's argument shares remarkable similarities to the controversial "Moynihan Report" on the Black family, so called because its principal author was now-Senator Daniel P. Moynihan (D-N.Y.). In the infamous chapter entitled "The Tangle of Pathology," Moynihan argued that

> the Negro community has been forced into a matriarchal structure which, because it is so out of line with the rest of American society, seriously retards the progress of the group as a whole, and imposes a crushing burden on the Negro male and, in consequence, on a great many Negro women as well.

OFFICE OF POLICY PLANNING AND RESEARCH, U.S. DEPARTMENT OF LABOR, THE NEGRO FAMILY: THE CASE FOR NATIONAL ACTION 29 (1965), *reprinted in* LEE RAINWATER & WILLIAM L. YANCEY, THE MOYNIHAN REPORT AND THE POLITICS OF CONTROVERSY 75 (1967).

24. A pressing problem is the way domestic violence reproduces itself in subsequent generations. It is estimated that boys who witness violence against women are ten times more likely to batter female partners as adults. *Women and Violence: Hearings Before the Senate Comm. on the Judiciary on Legislation to Reduce the Growing Problem of Violent Crime Against Women,* 101st Cong., 2d Sess., pt. 2, at 89 (1991) [hereinafter *Hearings on Violent Crime Against Women*] (testimony of Charlotte Fedders). Other associated problems for boys who witness violence against women include higher rates of suicide, violent assault, sexual assault, and alcohol and drug use. *Id.*, pt. 2, at 131 (statement of Sarah M. Buel, Assistant District Attorney, Massachusetts, and Supervisor, Harvard Law School Battered Women's Advocacy Project).

25. *Id.* at 142 (statement of Susan Kelly-Dreiss) (discussing several studies in Pennsylvania linking homelessness to domestic violence).

26. *Id.* at 143 (statement of Susan Kelly-Dreiss).

27. Another historical example includes Eldridge Cleaver, who argued that he raped white women as an assault upon the white community. Cleaver "practiced" on black women first. ELDRIDGE CLEAVER, SOUL ON ICE 14–15 (1968).

28. ALICE WALKER, THE COLOR PURPLE (1982).

29. *See, e.g.,* Gerald Early, *Her Picture in the Papers: Remembering Some Black Women,* ANTAEUS, Spring 1988, at 9; Daryl Pinckney, *Black Victims, Black Villains,* N.Y. REVIEW OF BOOKS, Jan. 29, 1987, at 17; Jacqueline Trescott, *Passions Over Purple; Anger and Unease Over Film's Depiction of Black Men,* WASH. POST, Feb. 5, 1986, at C1.

30. Trudier Harris, *On the Color Purple, Stereotypes, and Silence*, 18 BLACK AM. LIT. F. 155, 155 (1984).

31. The source of the resistance reveals an interesting difference between the Asian-American and African-American communities. In the African-American community, the resistance is usually grounded in efforts to avoid confirming negative stereotypes of African-Americans as violent; the concern of members in some Asian-American communities is to avoid tarnishing the model minority myth. Interview with Nilda Rimonte, Director of the Everywoman Shelter, in Los Angeles, California (Apr. 19, 1991).

32. Nilda Rimonte, *Cultural Sanction of Violence Against Women in the Pacific-Asian Community*, 43 STAN. L. REV. 1183 (1991); *see also* Nilda Rimonte, *Domestic Violence Against Pacific Asians*, *in* MAKING WAVES: AN ANTHOLOGY OF WRITINGS BY AND ABOUT ASIAN AMERICAN WOMEN 327, 328 (Asian Women United of California ed., 1989).

33. *See, e.g., Hearings on Violent Crime Against Women, supra* note 24, pt. 1, at 101 (testimony of Roni Young, Director of Domestic Violence Unit, Office of the State's Attorney for Baltimore City, Baltimore, Maryland) ("The victims do not fit a mold by any means."); *Id.,* pt. 2, at 89 (testimony of Charlotte Fedders) ("Domestic violence occurs in all economic, cultural, racial, and religious groups. There is not a typical woman to be abused."); *id.* at 139 (statement of Susan Kelly-Dreiss, Executive Director, Pennsylvania Coalition Against Domestic Violence) ("Victims come from a wide spectrum of life experiences and backgrounds. Women can be beaten in any neighborhood and in any town.").

34. *See, e.g.,* LENORE F. WALKER, TERRIFYING LOVE: WHY BATTERED WOMEN KILL AND HOW SOCIETY RESPONDS 101–02 (1989) ("Battered women come from all types of economic, cultural, religious, and racial backgrounds.... They are women like you. Like me. Like those whom you know and love."); MURRAY A. STRAUS, RICHARD J. GELLES & SUZANNE K. STEINMETZ, BEHIND CLOSED DOORS: VIOLENCE IN THE AMERICAN FAMILY 31 (1980) ("Wife-beating is found in every class, at every income level."); Natalie Loder Clark, *Crime Begins At Home: Let's Stop Punishing Victims and Perpetuating Violence,* 28 WM. & MARY L. REV. 263, 282 n.74 (1987) ("The problem of domestic violence cuts across all social lines and affects 'families regardless of their economic class, race, national origin, or educational background.' Commentators have indicated that domestic violence is prevalent among upper middle-class families.") (citations omitted).

35. For example, Susan Kelly-Dreiss states:

    > The public holds many myths about battered women—they are poor, they are women of color, they are uneducated, they are on welfare, they deserve to be beaten and they even like it. However, contrary to common misperceptions, domestic violence is not confined to any one socioeconomic, ethnic, religious, racial or age group.

    Hearings on Violent Crime Against Women, supra note 24, pt. 2, at 139 (testimony of Susan Kelly-Dreiss, Executive Director, Pa. Coalition Against Domestic Violence).

36. However, no reliable statistics support such a claim. In fact, some statistics suggest that there is a greater frequency of violence among the working classes and the poor. *See* STRAUS, GELLES & STEINMETZ, *supra* note 34, at 31. Yet these statistics are also unreliable because, to follow Waits's observation, violence in middle and upper-class homes remains hidden from the view of statisticians and governmental officials alike. *See* note 35, *supra.* I would suggest that assertions that the problem is the same across race and class are driven less by actual knowledge about the prevalence of domestic violence in different communities than by advocates' recognition that the image of domestic violence as an issue involving primarily the poor and minorities complicates efforts to mobilize against it.

37. 137 Cong. Rec. S611 (daily ed. Jan. 14, 1991) (statement of Sen. Boren).

354   38. *48 Hours: Till Death Do Us Part* (CBS television broadcast, Feb. 6, 1991).

39. *See* Christine A. Littleton, *Women's Experience and the Problem of Transition: Perspectives on Male Battering of Women*, 1989 U. Chi. Legal F. 23.

40. Letter of Diana M. Campos, Director of Human Services, PODER, to Joseph Semidei, Deputy Commissioner, New York State Department of Social Services (Mar. 26, 1992) [hereinafter *PODER Letter*].

41. The woman had been slipping back into her home during the day when her husband was at work. She remained in a heightened state of anxiety because he was returning shortly and she would be forced to go back out into the streets for yet another night.

42. *PODER Letter, supra* note 40 (emphasis added).

43. *Id.*

44. *Id.*

45. Roundtable Discussion on Racism and the Domestic Violence Movement (April 2, 1992.

46. *Id.*

47. *Id.*

48. *Id.*

49. Ironically, the specific dispute that led to the walk-out concerned the housing of the Spanish-language domestic violence hotline. The hotline was initially housed at the Coalition's headquarters, but languished after a succession of coordinators left the organization. Latinas on the Coalition board argued that the hotline should be housed at one of the community service agencies, while the board insisted on maintaining control of it. The hotline is now housed at PODER. *Id.*

50. Said Campos, "It would be a shame that in New York state a battered woman's life or death were dependent upon her English language skills." *PODER Letter, supra* note 40.

INDEX

Note: The concerns and interests that prompted this book—understandings about the multiplicity and indeterminacy of categories of identity and thought, and about the interconnections, juxtapositions, and elisions of meaning that emerge from this situation of complexity and fluidity—also animate and inform this index. In using the index, patience and care may be required. With luck, though, this exercise will prove an invaluable tool in plumbing the intricacies of the text.

PERMISSIONS

NOTES ON CONTRIBUTORS

Regina Austin is Professor of Law at the University of Pennsylvania Law School.

Nathaniel Berman is Associate Professor of Law at Northeastern University School of Law.

Rosemary J. Coombe is Associate Professor, Faculty of Law, at the University of Toronto and the author of *Cultural Appropriations: Intellectual Property Laws and Postmodern Politics*, forthcoming from Routledge.

Kimberlé Crenshaw is Professor of Law at UCLA Law School.

Dan Danielsen is an Associate at Foley, Hoag & Eliot and Lecturer of Law at Harvard Law School and at Northeastern University School of Law.

Karen Engle is Associate Professor of Law at the University of Utah College of Law.

Jerry Frug is Professor of Law at Harvard Law School and the author of *Local Government Law*.

The late **Mary Joe Frug** was Professor of Law at New England School of Law and the author of *Women and the Law* and *Postmodern Legal Feminism*.

Janet E. Halley is Associate Professor of Law at Stanford Law School.

David Kennedy is Professor of Law at Harvard Law School and the author of *International Legal Structures*.

Duncan Kennedy is Professor of Law at Harvard Law School and the author of *Sexy Dressing, Etc.*

Kathryn Milun is Assistant Professor of Anthropology at Rice

University.

Martha Minow is Professor of Law at Harvard Law School and the author of *Making All The Difference.*

Gary Peller is Professor of Law at Georgetown University Law Center.

Ileana M. Porras is Associate Professor of Law at the University of Utah College of Law.

Elizabeth V. Spelman is Professor of Philosophy at Smith College and the author of *Inessential Woman.*

Kendall Thomas is Professor of Law at Columbia University School of Law.

Gerald Torres is Counsel to the Attorney General of the United States and a Professor of Law at the University of Texas School of Law.

Patricia J. Williams is Professor of Law at the Columbia University School of Law and the author of *The Alchemy of Race and Rights.*